MW00605004

AutoCAD
Programming
in C/C++

AutoCAD Programming in C/C++

Owen Ransen

JOHN WILEY & SONS
Chichester • New York • Weinheim • Brisbane • Singapore • Toronto

Copyright © 1997 by John Wiley & Sons Ltd,
Baffins Lane, Chichester,
West Sussex PO19 1UD, England

National   01243 779777
International (+44) 1243 779777

e-mail (for orders and customer service enquiries): cs-books@wiley.co.uk

Visit our Home Page on http://www.wiley.co.uk
or
http://www.wiley.com

All rights reserved. No part of this publication may be reproduced, stored in a retrieval system, or transmitted, in any form or by any means, electronic, mechanical, photocopying, recording, scanning or otherwise, except under the terms of the Copyright, Designs and Patents Act 1988 or under the terms of a licence issued by the Copyright Licensing Agency, 90 Tottenham Court Road, London, UK W1P 9 HE, without the permission in writing of the publisher, with the exception of any material supplied specifically for the purpose of being entered and executed on a computer system for exclusive use by the purchaser of the publication.

Neither the authors nor John Wiley & Sons Ltd accept any responsibility or loss or damage occasioned to any person or property through using the material, instructions, methods or ideras contained herin, or acting or refraining from acting as a result of such use. The authors and Publisher expressly disclaim all implied warranties, including merchantability or fitness for any particular purpose. There will be no duty on the authors or Publisher to correct any errors or defects in the software.

Designations used by companies to distinguish their products are often claimed as trademarks. In all instances where John Wiley & Sons is aware of a claim, the product names appear in initial capital or all capital letters. Readers, however, should contact the appropriate companies for more complete information regarding trademarks and registration.

Other Wiley Editorial Offices

John Wiley & Sons, Inc., 605 Third Avenue,
New York, NY 10158-0012, USA

Weinheim • Brisbane • Singapore • Toronto

British Library Cataloguing in Publication Data

A catalogue record for this book is available from the British Library

ISBN   0 471 96336 4

Produced from camera-ready copy supplied by the author
Printed and bound in Great Britain by Bookcraft (Bath) Ltd
This book is printed on acid-free paper responsibly manufactured from sustainable forestation, for which at least two trees are planted for each one used for paper production.

Contents

13 PRACTICAL SUGGESTIONS FOR PROGRAMMING AUTOCAD   231

14 INTRODUCTION TO ARX   244

15 FIRST STEPS WITH ARX   253

Preface

Who should read this book?

This book is designed for a wide range of people:

- C and C++ programmers who want to enter into the AutoCAD world
- AutoLISP programmers who want to move up to C and C++ and the ADS and ARX programming environments
- AutoCAD users who want to start to do more than simple customisation of the interface
- students and teachers of programming and engineering who want to use AutoCAD as their base environment for Computer Aided Design programming courses and research (taking advantage of Autodesk's educational discounts)
- "hobbyists" who simply want to create their own custom applications.
- programmers who need to port their existing programs to AutoCAD.

What do I need to start programming AutoCAD in C and C++?

Here is a generalised list of what you need to start programming in C and/or C++ with AutoCAD.

1. An IBM-PC or compatible with *at least* 8 Mbytes of memory.
2. AutoCAD installed on your computer, versions 11, 12, 13 or 14. AutoCAD LT is *not* programmable, and therefore *not* suitable. For ARX programming you will need AutoCAD 13 or 14.
3. A C/C++ compiler and the relevant libraries.

4. A basic knowledge of computers, AutoCAD, and C. A knowledge of C++ is not required for ADS programming, though it is for the ARX programming (introduced in Chapters 14 to 17). A knowledge of AutoLISP will help too but is by no means necessary.

5. Operating systems: DOS, Windows 3.1, Windows-95 or Windows NT:in fact any operating system where AutoCAD will run. Most of the code in this book should also run under any UNIX system supported by AutoCAD, but I make no guarantees.

See Appendix A for more details.

A note on the text

It is best to follow some conventions about the text format when writing a book about programming; here are the ones used in this book.

- Listings, variable names and function names use this font: `{ a part of a listing}`, `A_Variable`, `A_Function()`.
- C/C++ *functions* are distinguished from C/C++ *variables* by ending the name with parentheses, for example: `Xyz_C_Func()`. This is a useful and common practice in the C and C++ books and manuals, as you can see immediately whether the object is a function or not.
- AutoLISP functions are always in parentheses, just as they would appear in an AutoLISP program. Here is an example: `(ssget)`.
- Unless otherwise specified,when I refer to "Release 12", "Release 14" and so on, I am referring to releases of AutoCAD.

Listings are placed at the end of each chapter. The names of the listings follow the format LST_ch_n.C, or LST_ch_n.H, or LST_ch_n.CPP, where "ch" is be the number of the chapter, and "n" is the number of the listing within that chapter. So LST__7_3.C is the third listing in Chapter 7.

Source code availability

If you bought the book with the disk included then all the source files in the listings of this book are included on the disk. There are also some directories with "template" programs and project and make files for specific compilers and environments.

If you have access to Internet you may want to download the *latest* version of the code from one of the following WEB sites:

```
http://www.wiley.com/compbooks/
http://www.buildingweb.com/progacad
```

In both cases, disk or Internet, you should read the file README.TXT before copying over the files into you own computer.

Acknowledgements

Thanks to:
- Autodesk S.p.A. Italia, Milano, Italy, and Autodesk Development B.V., Neuchatel Switzerland, especially Markus Kraus who helped out with ARX programming examples and supplied the LST_17_1.CPP example.
- Giorgio Martini of Fratelli Martini Spa, Modena, Italy, who gave permission to use images created with the MOONLITE and MOONREND AutoCAD applications. Giorgio was also the person who made MOONLITE useable by demanding a decent user interface, including DCL dialog boxes, see Chapter 12. MOONLITE and MOONREND were written exclusively for Martini S.p.A by the author.
- David Whynot for the use of his CAD WEB site as a place for the listings of this book (see above).
- The unknowing collaborators in the comp.cad.autocad newsgroup. I used their questions, and sometimes their answers, to make this book more comprehensive.
- Last, but not least, Oreste, the resident dog of Bar Colombina, who got me to relax and forget the book for a few minutes every day by dragging me outside to chase imaginary cats.

Contacting the author

Suggestions and criticisms are always welcome. I can be contacted by email or fax:

EMAIL: rans001@pn.itnet.it
FAX: +39 331 404 318

Programming AutoCAD

1.1 Introduction

This chapter is a general overview of programming and customising AutoCAD. The reasons for using AutoCAD are covered, and I make a comparison between the LISP C and C++ programming languages for AutoCAD. For practical details on what you need to program AutoCAD in C and C++ (compilers, environments and so on) see Appendix A.

1.2 Why use AutoCAD?

AutoCAD (from Autodesk Corporation) is the world's best selling PC Computer Aided Design software package, available in hundreds of countries and languages. It is currently available for DOS, UNIX, Windows 3.1, Windows NT and of course Windows-95. AutoCAD is used by architects, mechanical engineers, electrical engineers, electronic engineers, scientists in physical and chemical fields and even dentists! How can a single CAD package be suitable for such a wide range of professionals? The answer is its programmability.

The "programming" (or "customisation") of AutoCAD can be roughly divided into three types or levels:

- Simple: Anyone with a word processor can change the layout and commands of the menus of AutoCAD to suit his or her own work habits.
- Medium: A few lines of the programming language AutoLISP are enough to program useful "CAD utilities" which replace tedious and repetitive keystrokes and mouse motions. Sometimes these tiny programs are called "MACRO".
- Complex: A whole CAD system specialising in the layout of microwave circuits (for example), can be written in "C" or "C++" which uses the basic AutoCAD functions but adapts them to a higher level application.

The above is rather an over-simplification, because it is perfectly possible to program a large project using AutoLISP and a small one using C++. As a general rule though AutoLISP routines are short and simple and do not perform time consuming floating point calculations, while C and C++ are be used for larger programs which may have to do a lot of calculation and/or database access.

Graphics and CAD programming is easy in AutoCAD because you can try out your ideas "by hand" as it were, directly at your PC, and when you are convinced that the idea or procedure can be automated you write the program to do it.

All the special functions needed to do useful things in 2D graphics, 3D graphics and user interaction are already available in AutoCAD, there is no need to write them yourself. You can concentrate more on *what* you want to do, not *how* you do it. If you need to ask the user to draw a line, there is a function to do it; if you need the user to pick a point in 3D space there is a function to do it; if you need to do a high quality three dimensional rendering of an object there is a function to do it.

So the answer to the question "Why use AutoCAD?" is "AutoCAD is popular, flexible, extensible and contains most of the graphics functions you need".

1.3 AutoLISP, C or C++?

There are three programming languages for use with AutoCAD, AutoLISP, C and C++; all have advantages and disadvantages.

AutoLISP was the first real programming language for AutoCAD. The advantages of AutoLISP are as follows.

- AutoLISP comes *free* with AutoCAD.
- AutoLISP is "interactive", so the "production cycle" of a program can be very short. That is, ideas can be tried out very quickly, with no need to recompile after every program change.
- There are many books and magazines with examples, hints, and tips on programming in AutoLISP.
- AutoLISP is ideal for very short utilities, using only few lines of code.
- AutoLISP is very portable, a program running on an IBM-PC (or compatible) will run on a UNIX workstation or Apple Mac computer without modification, and no recompilation is necessary
- AutoLISP is very safe; it is very difficult to write a program that will corrupt memory and/or cause a disastrous crash.

The disadvantages of AutoLISP are:

- AutoLISP is a specialised subset of LISP, the artificial intelligence language, and it not generally well known outside of two specific communities, the Artificial Intelligence community and the AutoCAD community.
- AutoLISP is slow in execution; complex or repetitive programs make take minutes, hours or even days to execute.
- Autodesk (the producers of AutoCAD) are discouraging the use AutoLISP for new large programs.

From AutoCAD Release 11 it was possible to program AutoCAD in C using the AutoCAD Development System, ADS. The advantages of using C in the ADS environment are as follows.

- C is a well known general programming language, and almost all compilers support the ANSI (American National Standards Institute) standard for C.
- A C program runs much faster than an equivalent AutoLISP program.
- C compilers are generally available for all computing environments.
- C with AutoCAD is "future proof", Autodesk will support it for a long time to come. Some evidence for this is that dictionaries (a feature of the Release 13 ARX C++ programming environment) are accessible using ADS C functions.
- Old C programs can be adapted to run in the AutoCAD environment.
- It is difficult to crash AutoCAD when using the pure ADS environment. See below for a definition of pure ADS as opposed to rxADS.
- Applications can be ported to other CAD systems which support C programming (Microstation from Bentley Brothers springs to mind) relatively easily.

The disadvantages of C and ADS are as follows.

- C is not free, you have to buy (or have access to) a compiler.
- C is not interactive, the production cycle is longer than in AutoLISP; you need to recompile the program after editing it and before reloading it into AutoCAD.
- C is not inherently "object oriented".
- The interface to the AutoCAD database is slower than with ARX and C++.

It is perfectly possible to program ADS in C++ *without* ARX; all your sources are in C++ but you call the normal C functions of ADS. So-called "wrapper" functions are used to make ADS seem more like a C++ environment. Some hints on how to program in ADS mixing C *and* C++ are given in Appendix A Section A.3.

From AutoCAD Release 13 AutoCAD Runtime eXtension (ARX) environment made its appearance. The advantages of C++ with ARX are as follows.

- C++ is object oriented, as is ARX. You can derive your own *customised* objects and entities from AutoCAD defined standard ones.
- C++ is becoming a new standard language for large programs and projects.
- A C++ program runs much faster than an equivalent AutoLISP or C program.
- C++ compilers are generally available for all computer environments.
- C++ with AutoCAD is "future proof"; Autodesk will support it for a long time to come.
- C++ has an even more direct access to the AutoCAD database than C.

The disadvantages of C++ with ARX are as follows.
- C++ is not free, you have to buy (or have access to) a compiler.
- C++ development is not very interactive; the production cycle is longer than in AutoLISP, as with C you have to edit, then compile, then reload the program. Modern debuggers are helping change this cycle though, by allowing more interaction with the program at run-time.
- C++ generally uses more memory than C.
- C++ is more complex than C.
- The AutoCAD C++ environment, called ARX is more "dangerous" than either AutoLISP or ADS; you can crash AutoCAD itself, with all the consequent loss of data for the user.
- If you use ARX to its full potential (deriving your own custom objects and entities from AutoCAD ones) then your application will be locked quite securely in the AutoCAD environment.

It is conceivable to program ARX in C, but you have to have such a good knowledge of C++ (to interface to the ARX libraries) that it is probably not a "natural" thing to do. It is also possible to program partly in AutoLISP and partly in C or C++. This is a good way for AutoLISP programmers to pass over slowly to C and C++; see Chapter 20 Section 20.2.

Summarising: AutoLISP is good for tiny utilities, but medium or large projects need to be written in C and/or C++ to be fast and future-proof.

1.4 Pure ADS, ARX and rxADS

1.4.1 Pure ADS

ADS is an acronym of AutoCAD Development System and is the C programming interface to AutoCAD. It first appeared with AutoCAD 11. To you, the programmer, it is a set of .H include files and .LIB libraries. The libraries contain functions to access the drawing database and to perform actions such as drawing or deleting entities.

When talking about "pure" ADS, programmers mean ADS which runs "outside" of AutoCAD, the program is not part of the memory space of AutoCAD. This means that while the communication with AutoCAD is slower,

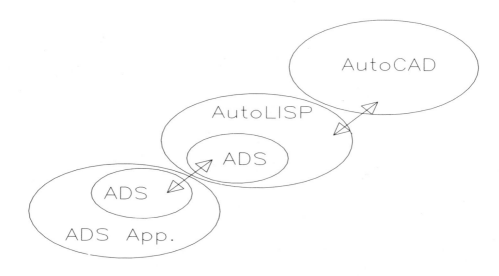

Figure 1.1 How pure ADS communicates with AutoCAD

it is more difficult for a pure ADS program to crash AutoCAD.

Pure ADS communicates with AutoCAD via AutoLISP, see Figure 1.1, though this is practically transparent to the programmer and user. An enormous advantage of this approach to Autodesk was that not a single line of the AutoCAD program code had to be changed when ADS was introduced.

1.4.2 ARX

ARX is an acronym of AutoCAD Runtime eXtension, and is the C++ interface to AutoCAD. As with ADS, it is a set of .H include files and libraries. ARX was itself written in C++ and the structure of the interface to AutoCAD reflects the idea of communicating with AutoCAD "objects" and "entities". You can "derive" your own versions of these objects and entities to create your own custom objects.

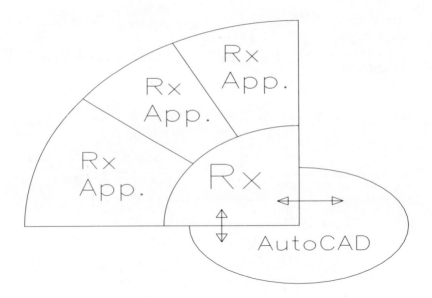

Figure 1.2 How ARX is integrated into AutoCAD

ARX functions are created as Dynamic Link Libraries (DLLs), which AutoCAD loads to have access to the functions you have written. These DLLs have the extension .ARX, unlike most DLLs which have the extension .DLL.

Unlike pure ADS, ARX shares the memory space with AutoCAD, see Figure 1.2, and because of this it is easier to crash both your own application and AutoCAD itself if you do not program carefully.

1.4.3 rxADS

A new version of ADS is called rxADS, which is for the most part source compatible with ADS. It has the advantage of the very high speed of ARX communication and the disadvantage of sharing the same memory space as AutoCAD, with the same possibilities of disastrous crashes if you do not program carefully.

Most of the functions of ADS and rxADS are common, but some are reserved for pure ADS use only and some are reserved for rxADS use only. rxADS was introduced in Release 13, but it preserves Release 12 functionality.

1.4.4 Mixed ADS and ARX programming

You need to know both ADS and ARX programming environments if you want to program in ARX. This is because ADS must be used for user input-output, programmable dialog boxes. Dynamic Data Exchange (DDE) with other programs is easier with ADS.

Getting started in C for AutoCAD

2

2.1 Introduction

In this chapter I will explain how your C program communicates with AutoCAD using ADS libraries. The example program will be used as a starting point for all the other ADS and C examples. Before you try to get this program going make sure that you can compile and run the sample programs supplied with Autodesk for your own compiler and platform; see Appendix A.

The communication is very simple; we will send string commands to AutoCAD just as if we had typed them at the command line, followed by parameters to specify coordinates and distances.

The examples here are in "pure ADS", which means that even if your program crashes, your AutoCAD will not crash with it!

2.2 Communicating with AutoCAD

LST__2_1.C shows a simple ADS program which draws polygons and squares; see Figure 2.1 Let us go over the program step by step.

There are four header files, STDIO.H, STRING.H and MATH.H are normal C include files; ADSLIB.H is the include file which defines functions and constants used for communicating with AutoCAD using ADS library. It can be found under your \ACAD\ADS (or equivalent) directory.

Next there is the declaration of functions used in LST__2_1.C. These are called "function prototypes", and they help the compiler detect errors when you call the functions themselves later in the program. It is always a good idea to use function prototypes to help you write correct programs which can be checked by the compiler. Some modern compilers will complain if function prototypes are not present for every function called. The body of each function is specified later in the file.

These functions are declared static, which in other words means that they are not visible to *other* C files, only in LST__2_1.C. They will be used only here, inside LST__2_1.C. Some compilers are able to use this information to produce smaller executable files, and it also stops the functions being visible in totally unrelated .C files. Large ADS applications often have many user commands, and keeping as many functions as local as possible (using the static keyword) keeps the compilation and linking cycle shorter.

What follows is a define ELEMENTS to extract the number of elements in an array. This will be used later in the program.

The struct func_entry associates a string with a function. The string is the command which the user will type at the AutoCAD command line to call the function. The actual table is called func_table and it consists of two entries, one for the command "polys" and one for the command "squares". It is here that you can add new commands as you try out examples from this book and your own experiments.

The C: at the begin of each string means that the function is callable simply by typing the string at the command line. So C: = "this is a user command". AutoLISP programmers will recognise this convention.

In AutoCAD ADS functions which are callable from outside the ADS application are called "external functions". They can be callable either by the user (if defined with the C: prefix) or by another application.

Next comes the main() which starts with an ads_init() (ignoring argc and argv), which starts up communication with AutoCAD. Note that almost all functions defined in ADSLIB start with ads_ . The for loop runs for ever, accepting messages from AutoCAD, and acting on them.

This seems strange, you may think, is it not the application which should be telling AutoCAD what to do? Well, what happens (after all the initialisation is over) is that the user types in a command at the AutoCAD command line (or calls one via a menu or dialog box), for example "POLYS", AutoCAD sees that it is not one of its own commands so it looks to see if it is a command of an application program. This is where we come in.

The function ads_link() at the start of the for loop really contains the rest of the world! That is, most of the time, when our program is not doing anything, and AutoCAD pure and simple is running, you can think of AutoCAD running inside ads_link(). Only when ads_link() returns control to our program, with a status value, can we actually do anything.

That status value that ads_link() returns tells us what AutoCAD is requesting our program to do. In this example you can see from the switch statement that there are only really three things to do, according to stat :

- RQXLOAD : Define the our functions which are known to AutoCAD and/or available to the user by calling funcload(), described below. This value will appear when AutoCAD starts up and each time a new drawing is loaded. funcload() is where you should do initialisations required with every drawing load. Most of the programs in this book are simple and do not required initialization every drawing load.

- RQSUBR : Execute one of our functions. This value will appear, for example, when a user types in one of the new commands we are implementing in this ADS program.
- RQXUNLD : Our application is being unloaded (with the AutoLISP (xunload filename) function), or AutoCAD is ending, we must "tidy up" if we need to. Any open files should be closed, any allocated memory should be freed and so on. Any selection sets (see Chapter 6) should be released.

By the way RQXLOAD and the other constants are all defined in the H files in the ADS directory of AutoCAD. By including <ADSLIB.H> you have access to all the defines and function prototypes required to talk to AutoCAD. Remember that to be able to use the angle brackets < > instead of the full directory

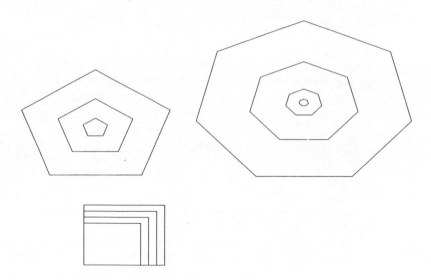

Figure 2.1 Example output from test application

containing ADSLIB.H you should be in your compiler's H file search path. This is often specified using the DOS SET command in your AUTOEXEC.BAT file, or in the OPTIONS menu of your compiler. Alternatively you can use the full pathname in quotes, which will depend on where you installed AutoCAD, e.g.

```
#include "D:\R13\COM\ADS\ADSLIB.H"
```

Obviously the first thing AutoCAD will ask us to do is RQXLOAD (which tells our program to define the functions we are "adding" to AutoCAD), so we call funcload() and set scode to the result of the attempt to load our functions.

Looking at the definition of funcload() you can see that it is a simple for loop repeatedly calling ads_defun() (similar to (defun) of AutoLISP). ads_defun() associates the index of the function we are loading with the name of the function we are loading. When AutoCAD calls our functions it will use that index to identify the function. In our simple example "C:polys" will be associated with the index 0, and "C:squares" will be associated with the index 1. If there were 10 functions the last would have the index 9.

Note that in funcload() we use ads_printf() not printf(). This is for two reasons, the first is that if we are running under Windows then the standard C printf will not print anything; the second reason is that if we are running under Extended DOS printf() will probably print over the graphics screen, if at all. ads_printf() on the other hand prints on the text window of AutoCAD and/or the command line of the graphics window.

ads_defun() returns a value to indicate if the function has been registered with AutoCAD successfully or not. If there is an error at any point funcload() abandons the loading of functions and returns RTERROR. If all goes well it returns RTNORM. An error may occur if you invent a command which has the same name as a command already present in AutoCAD.

Going back to the main(), scode is set according to the success or failure of the function load.

Assuming that you load all your functions OK, the next time ads_link() returns it will probably be with the RQSUBR status. This means AutoCAD is calling one of your functions, which means in turn that the user has typed in one of your commands. In the program you can see that we call dofun(), which in turn calls ads_getfuncode() to see which function has been requested. In our example the function code is called Func_Code, and should be either 0 or 1, since we have only defined two functions. A check is performed on Func_Code to see that it is within range (and here we use the ELEMENTS define mentioned above).

Here we come to the all important part, where the function you have written is actually called. The line which does it is:

```
Ret_Val = (*func_table[Func_Code].func)() ;
```

If Func_Code is 0 then the line above is equivalent to

```
Ret_Val = polys_func () ;
```

If Func_Code is 1 then the line becomes

```
Ret_Val = squares_func () ;
```

So we actually call one of the functions in the `func_table`, using `Func_Code` to select which one to call.

The remainder of `dofun()` simply returns the `Ret_Val`, which signals to AutoCAD whether our function completed correctly or not.

All of this seems very complicated, but happily you can forget about it once it is working. You will be more concerned with `polys_func()` and `squares_func()` and other functions you will write. How they are called and how they return values to AutoCAD is all handled by the procedure described above. Another happy point is that from now on you can add functions as you wish, without having to change a single line of the code which communicates with AutoCAD. For simple examples almost all the code between the first line of `main()` and the last line of `dofun()` will remain unchanged.

One last point before we go on to the meat of the program. I have used sleight of hand to describe this communication with AutoCAD. Actually the communication is with AutoLISP, not AutoCAD. The reasons why I have omitted references to AutoLISP are :

1. it makes not one iota of difference to the structure of the program.
2. it complicates the explanation
3. AutoLISP is simply another link in the chain between your application, AutoCAD and the user.

2.3 Drawing nested polygons

Now we come to the really useful part of LST__2_1.C, a function which draws nested polygons, `polys_func()`.

To see the function in action compile and link the file to create LST__2_1.EXP (for Extended DOS versions), run AutoCAD as normal, load the file by typing

```
(xload "/MYDIR/ADS/LST__2_1")
```

at the AutoCAD command line (do not forget the parentheses) and then type

```
POLYS
```

You will be asked how many sides you want, how many polygons you want, the center of the polygon, and the radius of the outer polygon. To the last two questions you can reply either by typing in numbers (e.g. 3,1 and 4 for a polygon centred at 3,1 radius 4) or by using the mouse to point to the center point and then moving it away to indicate distance.

A note on forward and back slashes: When you type (xload "progname") you can use either a single forward slash / to separate directories, or you can use two back slashes \\. The former is a UNIX and LISP standard, the latter is a

DOS and C programming standard. You could have loaded the above program by typing:

```
(xload "\\MYDIR\\ADS\\LST__2_1")
```

If at any time you hit Control-C (under DOS) or ESCAPE (under Windows) instead of replying to the question the command "polys" is abandoned, just like normal commands of AutoCAD.

Now let us look at the code to see how this all works.

The first thing you notice is the definition of a constant TWOPI of type ads_real. This is an ADS compatible real number. It is this which helps the portability of the same ADS program between compilers. Usually ads_real is defined to be a double length floating point number.

Then we come to the actual definition of the function polys_func(). It is a function that returns an integer which indicates if the function worked OK.

The call to ads_retvoid() tells AutoCAD that this function returns nothing to AutoLISP. If you did not include this call you would get a NIL printed on the command line after you called "polys", not a serious problem, but irritating to the user. For more information on returning values to AutoLISP see Chapter 20, Section 20.2. AutoLISP programmers might like to know that ads_retvoid() can be thought of as the C equivalent of the (princ) function.

Next come four functions which ask the user for input. ads_getint() is used to ask the user how many sides the polygons should have. Its return value is put in Res, and is an integer which indicates the success or failure of the function. The user sees the prompt

"How many sides?"

and replies with an integer number, which the function returns in its second parameter N_Sides. As is usual with AutoCAD the user can abort an operation by hitting Control-C (in DOS) or ESCAPE (in Windows). If the user hits aborts the command instead of replying with an integer then ads_getint() returns RTCAN to Res. If on the other hand all went well then RTNORM is returned.

Those of you moving from AutoCAD under DOS to AutoCAD under Windows should remember that control-C in Windows programs almost always means "copy the clip-board". Where you once used control-C to abandon a command you should now use the ESCAPE key. Whether the application itself runs under DOS or Windows versions, ads_getxxx() functions always return RTCAN if the user abandons the command.

So we check that RTNORM has been returned, and if it *has not* we abandon the function by RTNORM. This second use of RTNORM is to let AutoCAD know that the function ended OK, there were no errors, it is just that the user hit control-C or ESCAPE.

Next we use ads_getint() again to ask the user how many nested polygons to draw.

Then we ask for the center of the polygons by calling ads_getpoint(). In ADS a 3D coordinate is called an ads_point and is defined as

```
typedef ads_point ads_real[3] ;
```

So a 3D point is simply a list of 3 real numbers.

ads_getpoint() has three parameters, we will start with the second, which is the prompt issued to the user. The last parameter is the place to put the result, i.e. the point selected by the user (either by mouse or by typing), in our example Center.

The first parameter of ads_getpoint() is either NULL or a valid ads_point. If it is an ads_point then a rubber-band line is drawn from that point to the cross-hairs of the mouse. If the first parameter is NULL no rubber band line is drawn and the user sees only the cross-hairs of the mouse. The rubber band line can be used to help orient the user if a point has to be selected *relative* to another point.

Next the user is asked for the radius of the outer polygon by a call to ads_getdist(). This too has the rubber-banding option for mouse input, and in fact we use it by having Center as the start of the rubber band line. As the mouse is moved by the user one end of the line is attached to Center and the other to the mouse cross-hairs. When the user finally clicks the mouse the result is returned in Radius.

Both ads_getpoint() and ads_getdist() return RTCAN if the user aborts the command.

The nested for loops actually draw the polygon sides by repeatedly calling the standard AutoCAD command "_LINE". We can skip the maths and go on to the line command:

```
Res = ads_command (RTSTR, "_LINE",...
```

Commands and data for commands are sent to AutoCAD via ads_command(). A list of pairs are sent ending in a single value RTNONE which marks the end of the list.

The first pair we send specifies that we are sending a string (RTSTR) and that it is "_LINE".

Writers of international software note: from AutoCAD Version 12 onwards, to aid international compatibility all copies of AutoCAD will recognise commands in the local language (for example "LINEA" in Italian) as well as the English command preceded by an underscore (i.e. "_LINE"). So if you want your application to run all over the world use the "_ENGLISHWORD" convention. See also Chapter 13, Section 13.4

The next two pairs are

```
RT3DPOINT, Start,
RT3DPOINT, End,
```

which specify that we are sending an `ads_point` called `Start` and an `ads_point` called `End`. Next we send the empty string (to exit from the _LINE command) and `RTNONE` to say that the list is finished.

So, summarising, we draw a single line from `Start` to `End`.

`ads_command()` returns a value which will be `RTNORM` if AutoCAD understood the command, or `RTERROR` if it did not. For simplicity this is not used in this example, but until you become expert it would be better to check the return value of every `ads_command()` call.

So there you are. Compile and test this program, then fill in the missing code of `squares_func()`, left as "an exercise for the reader"!

2.4 Loading ADS programs

You will find as you start to program in ADS that it is tedious to load the programs by hand every time you exit and enter AutoCAD. It is possible to load programs automatically by using the file ACAD.ADS.

2.4.1 Loading ADS programs manually

First of all let us look in more detail at loading programs manually. The AutoLISP function `(xload)` is used for this and has the format

```
(xload Progname Errfunc)
```

`Progname` is usually a string containing the name of the program without extension. `Errfunc` is an optional parameter and you can leave it out altogether. If a function *is* specified then it is an AutoLISP function which will be called if `(xload)` fails. AutoLISP programmers may want to write an error handling function, but the errors are usually very obvious, "File does not exist", "File not of the correct type" and so on.

An example is

```
(xload "testprog")
```

If you do not specify a search path as in the above example, `(xload)` searches for the program in the directories specified by the AutoCAD library path as follows:

1 the current directory
2 the directory that contains the current drawing file
3 the directories specified by the Support Path environment variable (DOS) or the support path (Windows)

4 the directory that contains the AutoCAD program files, for example
   ACAD.EXE.

If you use (xload) with a full path name, for example
"D:/CPROGS/TESTPROG", (xload) does not search the other directories.
rxADS programs can also be loaded as described above, but using (arxload)
instead of (xload).

Another way of manually loading applications is to use the _APPLOAD
command, which calls a file dialog menu, so that you can search all over your
disk if you have forgotten where the compiled program is. For ADS programs
you must look for files with the EXP or .EXE extension. This command also
allows you to build up a list of frequently used applications in a dialog box,
which you can select and load as and when you want. You can type
"APPLOAD" at the command line or find it in the menu. In AutoCAD Release
13 for Windows appload is under the "TOOLS-->Applications..." menu entry.

2.4.2 Loading ADS programs automatically

To load an ADS program automatically every time you start up AutoCAD you
need to create a small file called ACAD.ADS in your working directory. There
will already be a file of this name in your main AutoCAD directory. The file
consists of a list of ADS programs to load at start up time. AutoCAD searches
for ACAD.ADS using the standard library search path described above. If you
are writing several (unrelated) ADS programs it is best to have separate
directories for each application, and in each separate directory to put a single
ACAD.ADS file.

For example this is an ACAD.ADS file for a program called PCBLAY:

```
PCBLAY
D:\MYFUNX\HELPER
```

This file would be put in the application directory (C:\PCBLAY for example),
and forces AutoCAD to load two ADS applications when run from that
directory, PCBLAY and HELPER. (ARX programs use a similar file called
ACAD.RX, see Chapter 15, Section 15.3)

2.5 Code fragments and the example program

The examples in the rest of this book will not contain the start-up code shown in
LST__2_1.C. You should take LST__2_1.C as a template, to which you can add
the other examples in the book. You can add them in the same file (if they are
short) or in a separate file(s) if they are longer. The point is that the first part of

LST__2_1.C changes very little. To add in new functions callable by the user you need to do three things:

1. add in the function prototype of the function after `squares_func()`
2. add an entry to `func_table`
3. write the new function after the definition of `squares_func()`

Many of the C ADS examples in this book are put inside a function called `test_func()`, so, following the above sequence, you should add

```
static int test_func (void) ;
```

in the list of function prototypes, and add

```
{"C:test", test_func},
```

in the `func_table`, and finally write the new function, `test_func`, after `squares_func`:

```
static int test_func (void)
{
    ... new test code in...
    ... here please ...
} ;
```

I have explained the sequence rather laboriously here, but it should help you start programming sooner if you follow it step by step.

Many of the listings are structured with `test_func()` calling other "helper" functions in the same listing, for example LST__5_1.C contains two helper functions (`Print_Rb_List()` and `Print_Rb_Data()`), and illustrates their use by calling them in `test_func()`. `test_func()` is also used to illustrate ADS functions. The idea is that after you have experimented and understood the helper functions they should be put in a separate source file. This source file can be used to create a library of useful functions. As you go step by step through the book you will build up a set of functions useful to you in ADS and ARX programming.

If you are new to C programming you can leave the helper functions in the same file as the `test_func()`. When you have gained more experience and know how to link several files together, or how to make a library, you can put the helper functions in a separate file.

When constructing your separate source file of helper functions remember to make an include file for these helper functions. This H file should also include any constants required and function prototypes for the helper functions. Most modern compilers will give a warning if a function prototype is not found for every function called. Do *not* ignore these warnings. In the above example. In the LST__5_1.C example mentioned above the *prototypes* are at the beginning of the C file, while the *definitions* of the functions come after `test_func()`. To make the functions `Print_Rb_List()` and `Print_Rb_Data()` checkable by the compiler the two prototypes should be placed in a general include file.

Many of the calls to ADS functions in the listings are preceded by (void). For example:

```
(void)ads_relrb (rb) ;
```

This means "I know the function returns a value, and I am deliberately ignoring it". This is not good practice, but checking the return value of all ADS functions called would use three lines where one is enough to illustrate the call. This problem is dealt with in Chapter 13.

Unless otherwise specified you should always run the test application in a single viewport. The handling of multiple viewports is not a subject with which to start learning AutoCAD programming.

One last point, to see which ADS files are currently loaded in AutoCAD just type (ads), complete with brackets, at the AutoCAD command line. If there are none then AutoCAD will print "nil". The same goes for ARX applications, just type (arx).

2.6 Listings

```
///////////////////////////////////////////////////////////
//    LST__2_1.C
//
//       Illustrating initialisation and communication between
//       an ADS C program and AutoCAD.


#include   <stdio.h>      // Standard C include file
#include   <string.h>     // Standard C include file
#include   <math.h>       // Standard C include file
#include   <ADSLIB.H>     // Interface to ADS library


// Declare functions used in this file
static int funcload    (void) ;
static int dofun       (void) ;

/*
 * The following functions will be made callable by the ACAD user
 * Add you own functions here as you try examples from the book
 */
static int polys_func (void) ;
```

```
static int squares_func (void) ;

// Definition to get an array's element count (at compile time).

#define ELEMENTS(array) (sizeof(array)/sizeof((array)[0]))

/*
 *  All the functions that we'll define will be listed in a
 *  single table, together with the internal function that we
 *  call to handle each. All functions return an integer
 *  (RTNORM or RTERROR for good or bad status).
 *  First, define the structure of the table:
 *          a string giving the AutoCAD name of the function,
 *          and a pointer to a function returning type int.
 */

struct func_entry {
    char *func_name;     // Name of func as seen by AutoCAD user
    int (*func)(void);   // func takes no parameters, returns int
};

/*
 * Here we define the array of function names and handlers.
 * Add your functions here as you try out examples fom the book
 */
static struct func_entry func_table[] = {
            {"C:polys",   polys_func},    // User types "polys"
            {"C:squares", squares_func}   // User types "squares"
};


void main (int argc, char* argv[])
{
    short scode = RSRSLT;   // Normal result code (default)
    int stat;

    ads_init (argc,argv);   // Open comms with AutoLISP

    // For-ever loop
    for ( ;; ) {             // Request/Result loop

        if ((stat = ads_link(scode)) < 0) {
            printf ("\nERROR,stat=%d",stat) ;
            exit(1); // < 0 means error
        }

        scode = RSRSLT ;        // Reset result code

        switch (stat) {
```

```
        case RQXLOAD:      // Load & define functions
            scode = funcload() == RTNORM ? RSRSLT : RSERR;
            break;

        case RQSUBR:       // Handle external function req
            scode = dofun() == RTNORM ? RSRSLT : RSERR;
            break;

        // See text to find out what to do with the
        // following when your program gets more
        // complicated. Ignore them in this simple program
        case RQXUNLD :
        case RQEND :
        case RQQUIT :
            break ;

        default:
            break;
        }
    }
}

static int funcload (void)
/*
PURPOSE: To tell ACAD the names of functions in the app.
NOTES: 1) .func_name is what you have to type in at keyboard
       2) This is called after EVERY DRAWING LOAD.
*/
{
  int i;

  for (i = 0; i < ELEMENTS(func_table); i++) {
      if (!ads_defun (func_table[i].func_name, (short)i)) {
          ads_printf ("\n***funcload failure***\n") ;
          return (RTERROR);
      }
  }

  return (RTNORM) ;
}

static int dofun (void)
/*
 * PURPOSE: executes external func (called upon an RQSUBR
 * request). Return value from the function executed will be
 * RTNORM or RTERROR.
 */
{
```

```c
    int Func_Code ;        // Which function to call
    int Ret_Val ;          // Return value of called function

    // Get the function code and check that it's in range.
    if ((Func_Code = ads_getfuncode()) < 0 ||
         Func_Code >= ELEMENTS(func_table)) {
        ads_fail ("Received nonexistent function code.");
        return (RTERROR) ;
    }

    /*
     * This is where we actually call the function we have
     * added to AutoCAD, returning the result of the
     * function. In this example code func will either
     * be "polys" or "squares"
     */
    Ret_Val = (*func_table[Func_Code].func)();
    return (Ret_Val) ;
}

/*
You add code from hereon as you try examples from the book.
*/

const ads_real TWO_PI = 6.28 ;

static int polys_func (void)
/*
PURPOSE: To create a series of nested polygons
*/
{
    int        Res,a ;
    int        N_Sides,N_Polys,r ;
    ads_point  Center,Start,End ;
    ads_real   Radius,Angle ;

    ads_retvoid() ; // Tell AutoLISP no return value

    /*
     * Get all the data required to draw the polygons...
     */
    Res = ads_getint ("\nHow many sides?",&N_Sides) ;
    if (Res != RTNORM) {
        return (RTNORM) ;
    }

    Res = ads_getint ("\nHow many polygons?",&N_Polys) ;
    if (Res != RTNORM) {
        return (RTNORM) ;
```

```c
        }

        Res = ads_getpoint (NULL,"\nCenter?",Center) ;
        if (Res != RTNORM) {
            return (RTNORM) ;
        }

        Res = ads_getdist (Center,"\nRadius?",&Radius) ;
        if ((Res != RTNORM) || (Radius <= 0))  {
            return (RTNORM) ;
        }

        // The polygon is flat in the Z=0 plane
        Start[Z] = 0.0 ;
        End[Z]   = 0.0 ;

        // Draw a sequence of polygons of varying sizes
        for (r = 0 ; r < N_Polys ; r ++) {
            Radius = Radius / (r + 1 ) ;
            // Draw a polygon as a sequence of lines
            for (a = 0 ; a < N_Sides ; a++) {
                Angle    = a * TWO_PI / N_Sides ;
                Start[X] = Center[X] + Radius*sin(Angle) ;
                Start[Y] = Center[Y] + Radius*cos(Angle) ;
                Angle    = ((a+1)% N_Sides) * TWO_PI / N_Sides ;
                End  [X] = Center[X] + Radius*sin(Angle) ;
                End  [Y] = Center[Y] + Radius*cos(Angle) ;
                Res = ads_command (RTSTR,"_LINE",
                                   RT3DPOINT,Start,
                                   RT3DPOINT,End,
                                   RTSTR,"", // Leave line command
                                   RTNONE) ; // End of varlen list
            }
        }
    return (RTNORM) ;
}

static int squares_func (void)
/*
PURPOSE: To create a series of nested squares
*/
{
    ads_retvoid() ; // Tell AutoLISP no return value

    // Ask for a point to start the first square,
    // use ads_getpoint()

    // Ask for size of the square, use ads_getdist()
```

```
    // Draw squares of decreasing sizes by repeatedly
    // calling "_LINE" 4 times

    return (RTNORM) ;
}

//                 -- End of LST__2_1.C --
```

Getting AutoCAD to do the work

3

3.1 Introduction

This chapter deals in detail with sending commands to AutoCAD to do things that you can also do directly from the command line of AutoCAD. This means that *any* sequence of commands typed in at the command line can be automated in an AutoCAD ADS program. It also means that you can try out sequences by hand before starting to program them.

This chapter also covers basic ADS type definitions, how to suppress the echoing of commands to speed up execution, and how to allow the user to abort commands.

3.2 Telling AutoCAD what to do: the ads_command() function

3.2.1 ads_command() with no user input

The function `ads_command()` is used to send commands to AutoCAD; as we saw in Chapter 2. `ads_command()` is a variadic function, which means that it can take a variable number of parameters, just like printf and `ads_printf()`, the ADS equivalent of printf. Unlike `printf()`, however, `ads_command()` needs a terminating parameter to signal the end of the parameter list, while printf knows the number of parameters in the list by scanning the format string. In LST__2_1.C we used it to draw a line; here is an example of using it to draw a circle:

```
ads_point Center ;
ads_real  Radius ;
```

```
...code which sets Center and Radius...
Res = ads_command (RTSTR, "_CIRCLE",   // Send string "_CIRCLE"
                   RT3DPOINT, Center,  // Specify the center
                   RTREAL, Radius,     // Specify the radius
                   RTNONE) ;           // Mark end of the list
```

Center is an `ads_point` and that `Radius` is an `ads_real`. These are types defined in the ADS include files and are explained in the following section. RTNONE is the symbol used to mark the end of the list, and it must always be present in an `ads_command()` list. Values are sent in pairs, a type specifier and a value.

It is also possible to send the same command entirely as strings, for example:

```
Res = ads_command (RTSTR,  "_CIRCLE",   // Send string "_CIRCLE"
                   RTSTR, "0.5,0.5,0.0", // Specify the center
                   RTSTR, "1.2"         // Specify the radius
                   RTNONE) ;            // Mark end of list
```

This works exactly the same as the previous example, but sends strings instead of points and reals.

WARNING: A common error when using `ads_command()` is to pass a string when you mean to pass a point or a real. The following code fragment is *wrong*:

```
ads_point A_Point ;
...initialise the point somehow...
ads_command (RTSTR,"_LINE",
             RT3DPOINT,"3.3,5.6,0.0", // WRONG!!!
             RT3DPOINT,A_Point,       // OK.
             RTSTR,"",                // OK.
             RTNONE) ;
```

Anything in quotes is a string, and strings need the RTSTR code.

A command can be split up, for example, into two separate `ads_command()` calls. For example:

```
Res = ads_command (RTSTR,  "_CIRCLE", // Send string "_CIRCLE"
                   RTSTR, "0.5,0.5,0.0", // Specify the center
                   RTNONE) ; // Mark end of the varlen list
Radius = Special_Function() ;
Res = ads_command (RTREAL, Radius // Specify the radius
                   RTNONE) ;      // Mark end of the varlen list
```

Note in the above that though there is only one AutoCAD command, there are two lists, and both lists end with RTNONE.

Res in the above case will usually be RTNORM, meaning that the function succeeded. For more details on the return values of `ads_command()` see Table 4.2 in Chapter 4.

WARNING: You should not use `ads_command()` to call "_OPEN" or "_NEW" commands.

3.2.2 `ads_command()`, pausing for user input

Sometimes you need to get hold of user input, for example the program must specify the center of a circle and the user the radius, or the program must specify the radius and the user the position. In these cases a special symbol is used in the `ads_command()` parameter list, called RTPAUSE (or sometimes simply PAUSE). It is defined in the ADS include files as follows:

```
#define RTPAUSE "\\"    // Pause in command argument list
```

As an example here is a program fragment which allows the user to specify the radius of a circle to be drawn, and the position is specified by the program.

```
Res = ads_command (RTSTR, "_CIRCLE", // Send the string "_CIRCLE"
                   RTSTR, "0.5,0.5,0.0", // Specify the center
                   RTSTR, RTPAUSE    // User specifies radius
                   RTNONE) ; // Mark end or variadic list
```

As you can see the RTPAUSE symbol is the second half of the RTSTR pair. In the case where the command pauses for input it is possible that the user hits ESCAPE (in Windows) or control-C (in DOS and UNIX) to abandon the command. If this happens then `ads_command()` will return RTCAN. For this reason, when using `ads_command()` with user input you should *always* check the return value. RTCAN may also be returned by other ADS functions which require user input. If you do not respect this rule the user might start getting angry because he cannot abandon the command, and then you are likely to get GIGO, Garbage In Garbage Out.

So you can mix input from the program with input from the user in any way you want.

Comparing these calls with the ones in Chapter 2 to draw lines. note that the end of the _LINE command is marked with a RTSTR,"" pair. This is because _LINE is a command that continues drawing until the user ends it explicitly with ENTER. This is not required for the _CIRCLE command because it ends automatically after the radius has been specified.

You should always be sure of the sequence of key strokes or tablet/mouse inputs for each command before using `ads_command()`. There is an error in the following code fragment:

```
ads_command (RTSTR, "_CIRCLE",
             RT3DPOINT. Center,
             RTREAL, 22.0
```

```
            RTSTR,"",       // Equivalent to ENTER on keyboard
            RTNONE) ;
```

The error is that _CIRCLE does not need an extra ENTER at the end of the command. What will happen is that AutoCAD will take the extra ENTER as a "repeat last command" instruction, and will try to draw another _CIRCLE. From here onwards the program becomes completely out of step with AutoCAD and you are likely to have a page full of error messages, as AutoCAD asks for REALs and the program gives it POINTs, and so on.

LST__3_1.C gives you some examples of the ideas in this section.

3.2.3 `ads_command()` and wild-cards

Remember that many AutoCAD commands accept "wild-cards". Just as you can list the files which begin with Z in a (DOS) directory by typing DIR Z* you can also freeze all the layers which begin with A using the following commmand sequence:

```
ads_command (RTSTR,"_LAYER",      // Start LAYER command
             RTSTR,"_FREEZE",     // FREEZE sub command
             RTSTR,"A*",          // all layers beginning with A
             RTSTR,"",            // End LAYER command
             RTNONE) ;            // End list to ads_command.
```

Extending this idea a little, you can see that if your program uses several layers for different purposes it may be convenient to give them names which all start with the same characters. For example "TAPP_GROUND", "TAPP_CEILING", "TAPP_WORKSURF" and so on. In this way you can operate on all of them by using the `wild-card` "TAPP_*" .

3.2.4 Using `ads_command()` to execute SHELL

It is possible to execute a single SHELL command using ads_command(). SHELL commands are used to temporarily call system commands, for example COPY or DEL. Here is an example of how you can copy some files using this technique:

```
ads_command (RTSTR,"_SHELL",            // The shell command
             RTSTR,"COPY *.BAT *.BAK", // The DOS command
             RTNONE) ;                  // End list to
ads_command.
```

A user can type SHELL and then ENTER and he goes into the DOS shell where he can do as many things as he wants before typing EXIT to return to

AutoCAD. This does not work with `ads_command()`. If you want to send several DOS commands in sequence then you have to use several calls to `ads_command()`, each having the format shown in the example above.

3.3 ADS types and type specifiers

3.3.1 Basic ADS C types

The ADS header files define several "ADS types" which you must always use when compiling for ADS. The header file that most ADS applications include is called "ADSLIB.H", this in turn includes many other files, one of which is "ADSDEF.H". This last file contains the definition of ADS types. Here is a summary of some of the basic types:

```
typedef double ads_real ;
typedef ads_real ads_point[3];
#define     X   0
#define     Y   1
#define     Z   2
typedef ads_real * ads_pointp;
typedef ads_real ads_matrix[4][4];
```

An ads_real is a double, an ads_point is an array of 3 doubles, X, Y, Z are defined to be indices into an ads_point (which you should always use instead of 0,1,2),and an ads_matrix is an array of 4 by 4 doubles. Sometimes you need a pointer to a point, and so `ads_pointp` has also been defined.

These types are always used when communicating with ADS functions. If by chance you *do* pass a float instead of an ads_real to an ADS function your compiler should convert it. However, if you pass an array of two floats instead of an `ads_point` (i.e. instead of an array of three doubles) your compiler may not notice the difference, but your program will not work.

When working in three dimensions it is usual to use 4 by 4 matrices to specify transformations (scalings, rotations, moves and so on). The `ads_matrix` is used for this purpose.

3.3.2 Linking in non-ADS files

Problems can arise when you have, an old C program which you want to adapt to AutoCAD. It would be tempting to be lazy and use, for example, "double" instead of "ads_real", but dangerous for the future portability. The old C program probably uses normal C types such as `double`, `float`, etc.

One solution is to say "I am adapting this program to run with AutoCAD and I will never use any of the source files with any other environment". In this case you can redefine all your doubles as `ads_reals`, all your three dimensional points as `ads_points` and so on. This is the simplest solution, but it means that if, by chance, you have to port the program to some other environment you will have to go back to normal C types again.

Another solution is illustrated in LST__3_1.C and LST__3_2.C. Here the idea is to completely separate the AutoCAD independent calculation from the AutoCAD interface. Remember that the LST__3_1.C needs to be added to the end of LST__2_1.C, the file which interfaces to AutoCAD, and changes made to LST__2_1.C as explained in section 2.5. So LST__3_1.C is an ADS source, while LST__3_2.C should be fairly portable.

The portability is achieved in LST__3_2.H, which redefines POINT and REAL according to whether you are compiling for ADS or another system. When you compile for ADS you should set the compiler options so that ADS is defined. On the command line of most compilers this is achieved with "/D IN_ADS=1" for example. Compilers with an Integrated Development Environment (IDE) often let you specify a define in a menu. Whichever method you use, make sure that IN_ADS is defined when you are compiling LST__3_2.C to create an ADS application.

So when you compile the program for ADS, POINTs are defined as `ads_points`, and when you are compiling for normal C, POINTs are defined as `double[3]`. The source code can be used for both ADS and DOS and UNIX without any fear of future incompatibilities. For those of you new to C and C++ this is called "conditional compilation". We will see another example of its use in Chapter 9.

LST__3_2.C contains a simple single function to calculate the gravitational attraction between two planets. It's inputs are two three-dimensional points and two real numbers. It returns the force calculated. LST__3_1.C prints the result of the calculation.

When you are trying to share source files among two or more environments you should try to use the technique explained above; it will reduce the amount of typing you have to do!

3.3.3 Type defining codes

When you send values to AutoCAD with `ads_command()` you sent them as pairs, a type specifier code and a value. The type specifiers are defined in "ADSCODES.H", and here is a selection:

```
#define RTNONE     5000 /* No result, or end of command list */
#define RTREAL     5001 /* Real number, ads_real */
#define RTPOINT    5002 /* 2D point X and Y only, Z=0 */
#define RTANG      5004 /* Angle, ads_real */
```

```
#define RTSTR     5005 /* String, 0 terminated string */
#define RT3DPOINT 5009 /* 3D point - X, Y, and Z */
```

The only ones we have not so far met are RTPOINT and RTANG. RTPOINT is used when you are sure you are only using two-dimensional points, and in fact could be used instead of RT3DPOINT in all the examples and code fragments we have met so far. RTANG would be used to specify the angle in degrees of rotation of an object in a "_ROTATE" command. Here is a code fragment that uses both:

```
ads_point Position ;
ads_real Angle ;
....
ads_command (RTSTR, "_ROTATE",
             RTSTR, "_L",        // Specify last object inserted
             RTSTR, "",          // End selection of objects
             RTPOINT, Position,  // Specify 2d position, Z ignored
             RTANG, Angle,       // Specify rot angle (degrees)
             RTNONE) ;           // End of the variable length
list
```

Note the RTSTR, "" pair used to end the selection of objects. For the above example to work you must have at least one object inserted in the drawing, or else selecting the LAST object will not work.

3.3 Command echoing

You will have noted that as you send commands to AutoCAD with the ads_command() function the commands are echoed in the text window. This is fine for debugging and useful when you are pausing for user input, but can slow things down a lot if you have to send a lot of commands. It is also distracting for the user.

This command echoing can be switched off simply by setting the AutoCAD variable "CMDECHO". For more information on AutoCAD variables see Appendix C.

The ADS function used to set AutoCAD variables is ads_setvar(). Here is a short function that makes setting integer variables of AutoCAD tidier.

For the moment we will ignore the details, but you can see that the inputs to the function are a variable name (such as "CMDECHO" or "BLIPMODE") and a short. (Whole number variables in AutoCAD are shorts, and they range in size from -32,768 to +32,767.) rb is a result buffer, which will be explained in more detail in Chapter 5, but basically it is a structure containing a type identifier (in this case RTSHORT) and a union containing the value. ads_setvar() returns a value to say if all went well, and a message is printed if it did not. The message would be printed if for example you mis-spelled the name of the variable.

If the above function is called like this:

```
Set_Int_Var ("CMDECHO", 0) ;  // Turn off command echo
```

then the commands of ads_command() will not be visible to the user until you
call it with 1 instead of 0. This is illustrated in the listing LST__3_1.C.

When debugging you may want to leave CMDECHO = 1 so that you can see
what is going on. For speed and tidiness, once the program runs well, it is best
to set CMDECHO = 0.

3.4 Listings

```
/////////////////////////////////////////////////////////////
// LST__3_1.C
//      Illustrates drawing circles and calling functions
//      in other files
//

#include "lst__3_2.h" // Interface to lst__3_2.C

void Set_Int_Var (const char* Varname, const short Int_Val) ;

static int test_func (void)
/*
 * Function to illustrate various ways of using ads_command()
 * by drawing circles.
 */
{
    int      Res ;
    ads_point Center,Center2 ;
    ads_real  Radius,Radius2,Force ;

    ads_retvoid () ; // No return value to AutoLISP

    Set_Int_Var ("CMDECHO",0) ; // Echo following commands

    // Simply draw a circle at a given position
    Center[X] = 100.0 ;
    Center[Y] = 200.0 ;
    Center[Z] = 000.0 ; // Not yet doing 3D!
    Radius    = 300.0 ;
    Res = ads_command (RTSTR,"_CIRCLE",
                       RT3DPOINT,Center,
                       RTREAL,Radius,
                       RTNONE) ;
    if (Res != RTNORM) {
```

```
        ads_printf ("\nCould not draw circle1") ;
    }


    // Simply draw a circle in two ads_command calls
    Center[X] = 150.0 ;
    Center[Y] = 160.0 ;
    Center[Z] = 000.0 ; // Not yet doing 3D!
    Radius    = 100.0 ;
    Res = ads_command (RTSTR,"_CIRCLE",
                       RT3DPOINT,Center,
                       RTNONE) ;
    if (Res != RTNORM) {
        ads_printf ("\nCould not draw circle2a") ;
    }


    Radius    = 1.0 ;
    Res = ads_command (RTREAL,Radius,
                       RTNONE) ;
    if (Res != RTNORM) {
        ads_printf ("\nCould not draw circle2b") ;
    }


    Set_Int_Var ("CMDECHO",1) ; // Echo following commands

    // Draw a circle at a fixed position, with radius
    // specified by the user
    Res = ads_command (RTSTR,"_CIRCLE",
                       RT3DPOINT,Center,
                       RTSTR,PAUSE,      // Radius from user
                       RTNONE) ;
    if (Res != RTNORM) {
        ads_printf ("\nCould not draw circle3") ;
    }


    // Draw a circle with fixed radius,
    // position specified by the user
    Res = ads_command (RTSTR,"_CIRCLE",
                       RTSTR,PAUSE,     // Center from user
                       RTREAL,Radius,
                       RTNONE) ;
    if (Res != RTNORM) {
        ads_printf ("\nCould not draw circle4") ;
    }


    // Example of calling a function in another file
    Center2[X] = 90.0 ;
    Center2[Y] = 99.0 ;
    Center2[Z] = 00.0 ;
    Radius2    =  3.0 ;
```

```
    Force = Gravitational_Force (Center,Center2,
                                 Radius,Radius2) ;
    ads_printf ("\nGravitational force = %f Newtons",Force) ;

    return (RTNORM) ;
}

void Set_Int_Var (const char* Varname, const short Int_Val)
/*
PURPOSE: To set one of the integer (short,16 bit) ACAD vars.
*/
{
    struct resbuf rb ;

    rb.restype     = RTSHORT ;
    rb.resval.rint = Int_Val ;
    if (ads_setvar (Varname,&rb) != RTNORM) {
        ads_print ("\nWARNING,SIV(%s,%d),"
                   " could not setvar", Varname,Int_Val) ;
    }
}

//                      -- End of LST__3_1.C -- .

//////////////////////////////////////////////////////////
// LST__3_2.C
//      An example of calling non ads types functions from
//      an ADS source file (see also LST__3_1.C)


#include <math.h>
#include "list_3_2.h"

REAL Gravitational_Force (POINT Center1,
                          POINT Center2,
                          REAL  Radius1,
                          REAL  Radius2)
/*
Return the gravitational force between two planets using
Force = G * M1 * M2 / R^^2. Assume that both planets have
the same density
*/
{
    float Mass1,Mass2,Force,Dist_2rd ;
    int c ;
    const float Density = 1.0E4 ;

    // Find distance between the planets
    Dist_2rd = 0.0 ;
```

```
    for (c = 0 ; c < 3 ; c++) {
        Dist_2rd += ((Center1[c] - Center2[c])*
                    (Center1[c] - Center2[c])) ;
    }

    // Find the masses of the planets
    Mass1 = Density * PI * 0.75 * Radius1*Radius1*Radius1 ;
    Mass2 = Density * PI * 0.75 * Radius2*Radius2*Radius2 ;

    Force = (G_CONST * Mass1 * Mass2) / Dist_2rd ;

    return (Force) ;
}

//                  -- End of LST__3_2.C


// LST__3_2.H
//    An interface to LST__3_2.C

#ifdef IN_ADS  // define (or not) as a compiler option
    #include <adslib.h>  // definitions of ads_point etc
    #define POINT ads_point
    #define REAL  ads_real
#else
    #define POINT double[3]
    #define REAL  double
#endif

#define   PI       3.14159
#define   G_CONST  6.67E-11



// Function prototype
REAL Gravitational_Force (POINT Center1,
                          POINT Center2,
                          REAL  Radius1,
                          REAL  Radius2) ;
```

User input

4

4.1 Introduction

In this chapter I deal with obtaining information from the user in one of the following ways:

- AutoCAD command line; the user manually types in coordinates, angles and so on.
- using the mouse, the user selects a point or distance or angle on the graphics screen.
- filename input using a standard AutoCAD dialog box.

I also explain keyword input and the ads_alert() function.

For user selection of entities see Chapter 6, and for information on creating *custom* dialog boxes see Chapter 12.

4.2 User input with the `ads_getxxx()` functions

LST__4_1.C shows some examples of the most common ads user input functions. The function Tidy_End() is explained in Section 4.7. These are known in general as the ads_getxxx() functions. All the functions print a prompt which you specify and can be NULL if you want the standard AutoCAD prompt for that input. I do not look at the return values in this listing, so all the ads_getxxx() calls are cast to void.

ads_getint() and ads_getreal() requires that the user types in a number, and the result is returned in the second and last parameter.

ads_getdist(), ads_getangle(), ads_getorient(), ads_getpoint() and ads_getcorner() all allow the input to come from the mouse or tablet as well as the keyboard. This is a great boon to the user who can simply choose the position or angle with the mouse.

`ads_dist()`,   `ads_getangle()`,   `ads_getorient()`   and `ads_getpoint()` all allow you to specify a base point; in the current example this base point (the first parameter of the call) is set to NULL. If instead you pass an `ads_point`, and the user is using a mouse, this point is used as the first

Table 4.1: Flags for `ads_initget()`	
Symbol	Meaning
RSG_NONULL	Disallow NULL input, force correct input or abort
RSG_NOZERO	Disallow zero (0) input
RSG_NONEG	Disallow negative input
RSG_NOLIM	Allow points to be specified outside of drawing limits
RSG_DASH	Rubber-band lines are drawn as dashed lines
RSG_2D	ads_getdist looks only at X and Y coordinates
RSG_OTHER	Allow whatever the user types

point of a "rubber-band" line which will illustrate the distance or angle being selected. As the user moves the mouse, so the end point of the line moves.

`ads_getcorner()` actually gets a point forming the second diagonal point of a rectangle. The first diagonal point is the first parameter of the call and is *not* optional. As the user moves the mouse he sees a "rubber-band" rectangle being drawn.

`ads_getstring()` prompts the user to type in a string. If the first parameter is 1 then spaces are allowed in the string, and the string is terminated with ENTER. If the first parameter is 0 then either ENTER or a space will terminate the input. This is made clear in LST__4_1.C where a sentence and a word are requested from the user.

When passing points or strings to `ads_getxxx()` functions you do not need to use the & (address of) operator, because these are arrays, and C passes them as addresses anyway. When you want to use `ads_getint()`, `ads_getreal()` or `ads_getdist()` you need to pass the address of the variable where you want the result to be stored; hence in LST__4_1.C we pass `&Integer`, `&Real`, `&Dist`.

4.3 Using `ads_initget()` to control user input

Sometimes you want to limit what the user is allowed to type in or point at; for example the user response to a certain `ads_getint()` has to be positive and non-zero. ADS supplies a function called `ads_initget()` for that purpose.

You should call `ads_initget()` just before calling the `ads_getxxx()` function, and the settings made by `ads_initget()` last for one `ads_getxxx()` call only. The following code fragment illustrates the idea:

```
ads_initget (RSG_NOZERO | RSG_NONEG,NULL) ;
ads_getint ("Give me a non-zero positive integer:", &Value) ;
```

If the user types in "-1" as a response to the prompt he will be prompted again to input a non-zero positive integer. This will go on until he either complies or aborts the command with Control-C or ESCAPE. `ads_initget()` takes an integer argument which is the OR of some flags defined in the ADS include file. In the above example we have OR-ed the NOZERO flag with the NONEG flag. (This OR-ing of bit flags is a common technique in AutoCAD, especially for integer variables which store modes of working, see Chapter 5.)

The last parameter of `ads_initget()` is a `char*`; it can be a list of keywords that you want the following `ads_getxxx()` to accept. In these simple examples we always set it to NULL.

The behaviour of all the afore-mentioned `ads_getxxx()` functions can be modified by `ads_initget()`. The flags are shown in Table 4.1.

Table 4.1 is self explanatory. Obviously RSG_NOZERO has no meaning when using `ads_getpoint()`, and RSG_NOLIM has no meaning when using `ads_getint()`, and so on.

LST__4_2.C gives some examples of using `ads_initget()` and some `ads_getxxx()` functions which specify base points. When you use base points the user only has to specify a single point, thus saving time. For example the call to `ads_getdist()` uses `Base_Point` instead of NULL, and the rubber band line (which will be dashed because of the RSG_DASH) will start at the coordinates of `Base_Point`, the point moving around as the user moves the mouse.

4.4 Allowing default responses to `ads_getxxx()`, RSG_NONULL

AutoCAD often prompts the user for a value, with a default value specified. If the user simply hits the ENTER or SPACE key then the default value is used. You can do the same simply by *not* OR-ing in RSG_NONULL to the `ads_initget()` parameter. If you do want to force the user to input a valid value then you should OR-in RSG_NONULL.

As an example see the first two calls to `ads_getint()` in LST__4_2.C. The first does not allow null input; the user must either type in a valid input or abort the command. If he aborts (`Res == RTCAN`) the test_func returns immediately.

If he does input a valid integer we move on to the next `ads_getint()`, for which RSG_NONULL has not been set. The prompt is constructed with sprintf(), and it includes the standard AutoCAD method of specifying a default value (the value is placed in angle brackets, for example <9.5>). If the user simply hits

ENTER (i.e. a NULL input) then `Integer` is not changed, and the default value is accepted. Alternatively he can type in a new integer.

This explanation has been for integer inputs, but it applies to all types of `ads_getxxx()` functions.

4.5 `ads_getxxx()` return values, gracefully accepting rejection, RTCAN

Every `ads_getxxx()` function returns a value; in the examples in this book it is normally stored in a variable called `Res`. Table 4.2 shows the values that `Res` can take.

LST__4_2.C shows how to react when the user abandons the input. If the user hits control-C or ESCAPE in response to the request for input all of the `ads_getxxx()` functions return RTCAN. To be consistent with the AutoCAD way of working you should read RTCAN as "I want to abandon the command". In the examples here we simply return from the function, giving control back to

Table 4.2:	Return values from `ads_getxxx()` functions	
Symbol	Value	Meaning
RTNORM	5100	User input a correct value
RTNONE	5000	The user hit ENTER (or SPACE in some circumstances)
RTERROR	-5001	The function call failed
RTCAN	-5002	The user hit control-C (DOS and R12 Windows) or ESCAPE (R13 Windows)
RTREJ	-5003	AutoCAD rejected the request as invalid. It could mean a non-existent text style, or maybe non-existent layer, specified for an entity, among other things
RTKWORD	-5005	A keyword was entered. See Section 4.6

AutoCAD.

If the user hits ENTER or SPACE and you have not used RSG_NONULL (see previous section) then the `ads_getxxx()` function will return RTNONE.

The next section describes how to handle the RTKWORD return value.

4.6 Keyword input to help selection

In complicated drawings and applications it is sometimes a good idea to let the user specify a point or value or distance with a keyword, rather than typing in coordinates at the keyboard or searching on the graphics screen with the mouse.

The technique is used in AutoCAD where you can type "L" to specify the Last entity in the database rather than picking it with the mouse. Another example is object snapping, where you can type "END" to specify the END point of a selected line rather than explicitly entering the coordinates.

LST__4_3.C is an example of how to use specify and use your own keywords for your ADS application. The idea is that you have written a helicopter designing program. The user often wants to locate, or draw to, or change the UCS (User Coordinate System, see Chapter 9) origin to two special points in the helicopter, the center of gravity and the center of the rotor blades assembly. To help in this you define two keywords ("Cg" and "Rotcen") which can be used to find these points when using the `ads_getpoint()` function:

```
ads_initget (RSG_NONULL,"Cg Rotcen") ; // Define keywords (chars)
```

So the user can either select an arbitrary point with the mouse, or type in coordinates at the command line, or type in one of two keywords. If the user types in one of the keywords then it is up to your program to find the point specified. Note that each keyword has a single upper-case character. This is a shortcut for the user, instead of typing in "Rotcen" he could simply type in "R", and instead of "Cg" he could type in simply "C". The capital letter indicates the shortcut character does not need to be at the start of the string.

LST__4_3.C starts with two dummy definitions; they would be more complicated if it was a real helicopter designing program. One is a function to find the center of gravity of the helicopter, the other is the center of the rotor. In practice both of these would be variable, though they are fixed in this example.

The definition of test_func starts with an `ads_initget()` which specifies that NULL input is not accepted and that two keywords can be accepted, "CG" or "ROTCEN".

Then we call `ads_getpoint()` and examine the return value, which will be one of those shown in Table 4.2. The function only explicitly looks for two return values RTCAN (see previous section) and RTKWORD. If Res is neither of these then we assume that an arbitrary point has been input. If Res is RTKWORD, however, then the user typed a string, probably either "CG" or "ROTCEN". `ads_getinput()` is used to retrieve the keyword typed and we set Point to the appropriate value by comparing Key_Word with "CG" and "ROTCEN".

Another example of where keywords would be useful is a GIS (Geographical Information System) program which automatically designs roads in mountainous areas. You would like to make a function that takes two points from the user and designs the shortest and safest road between these points. The user can select the points with the mouse, or simply by naming two cities or by selecting one point and naming a single city. In this case the keyword list which you pass to `ads_initget()` is a list of cities, for example:

```
ads_initget (RSG_NONULL, "Palermo Florence Milan Naples
pOntito");
```

Note that the Palermo shortcut character is P, while the Pontito shortcut character is O.

There is also a function which obtains just keywords, `ads_getkword();` see Appendix B.

4.7 Two ready-made dialog boxes

Chapter 12 covers custom dialog boxes programmed in the DCL (Dialog Control

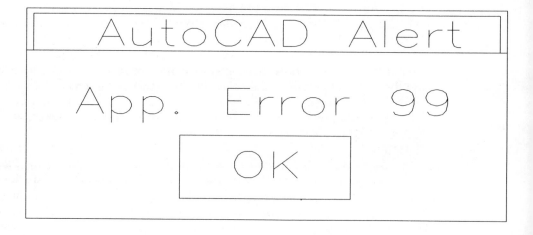

Figure 4.1 The `ads alert()` dialog box

Language), but there are three ready made dialog boxes which you can use without any knowledge of DCL.

4.7.1 The **ads_alert()** function

This function displays a dialog box containing a message and an OK button. Usually the message is a warning or reports an error. The function does not return until the user reacts by clicking on OK with the mouse. Here is an example of its use:

```
(void)ads_alert ("App. Error 99") ;
```

The message can have multiple lines by including the "\n" new line character, but the maximum number of characters permitted is 133, including the 0 terminator and new line characters. The detailed appearance of the dialog box will depend on the platform (Windows, DOS, or UNIX) and the graphics board driver you are using. LST__4_4.C gives an example of a call to ads_alert().

4.7.2 The file selection dialog box

If you need to ask the user for a filename then it is easiest to use the function ads_getfiled(), which is a flexible dialog box creator, see Figure 4.2. LST__4_4.C gives an example of its use. The prototype for the function is

```
int ads_getfiled (const char* Title,
                        const char* Default_Path_And_Name,
                        const char* Default_Ext,
                        int flags,
                        struct resbuf* result);
```

Title is what appears at the top of the dialog box, for example "Load Configuration File".
Default_Path_And_Name specifies two fields of the dialog box, the path or initial directory of the dialog box, and the default name show in the File edit box. If you pass NULL then the initial directory is set to the current directory and no default name appears in the File edit box. For example to set the initial directory to "D:\SOURCES" and the default filename to "MACHINE" Default_Path_And_Name would be the C-string "D:\\SOURCES\\MACHINE". Note that the double backslashes are required in C-strings to produce a single back slash.
Default_Ext is self-explanatory, except that if you pass NULL then it defaults to "*".
Flags is an bitwise OR-ed combination of four values, as shown in the Table 4.3.
In LST__4_4.C we see again the use of "result buffers". For the moment we can say they are structures used to pass information back and forth between your program and AutoCAD. ads_newrb() creates a new buffer called rb for use in ads_getfiled(), and releases the memory at the end of the function.

Moving on to the call to `ads_getfiled()`, the title of the dialog box is "Open Config File", the initial directory is "C:\SOURCES", there is no default filename, the `NEWFILE` flag has been specified, the default extension is "CFG", and the result is put into rb.

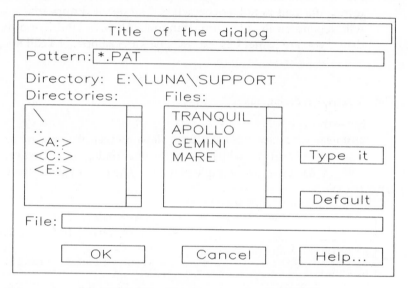

Figure 4.2 The `ads_getfiled()` dialog box

So the user now sees a file dialog box, much like the "OPEN FILE" dialog box of AutoCAD. He can search the hard disk(s) and directories for a place to open this *new* file. If he wants, he can click on the Type It button and type in the name at the command line.

`ads_getfiled()` returns with either `RTNORM` or `RTERROR`. The latter occurs if the user has aborted the dialog box by clicking on "CANCEL" or hitting ESCAPE. Otherwise Res == `RTNORM` and we have to examine the result buffer to see what has been selected. If the type of the result buffer is `RTSTR` then we can find the file name in `rb->resval.rstring`. If the type of the result buffer is `RTSHORT` then the user has hit the Type It button, and your program should do an `ads_getstring()` to read what the user will type.

4.8 Other text output

You can write to various parts of the AutoCAD screen using `ads_grtext()` which will write to the screen menu (the vertical menu to the right of the screen if enabled), to the mode area of the status bar and the coordinates area of the status bar. See Appendix B under the `ads_grtext()` heading.

Setting the MODEMACRO system variable you can give the user additional information about the "mode" your application is in. It is a string which is printed on the status line (usually at the bottom of the Windows screen and at the top of the DOS screen). This code fragment gives an example:

```
Set_String_Var ("MODEMACRO", "Calculating...") ;
... calculate...
Set_String_Var ("MODEMACRO", "Finished.") ;
... tidy things up...
Set_String_Var ("MODEMACRO","") ; // "Layer 0" string returns
```

In DOS systems the MODEMACRO string can overwrite the LAYER string at the extreme left of the status bar. You should reset the MODEMACRO as shown in the last line above to make LAYER to re-appear.

4.9 Long loops and aborting commands, `ads_usrbrk()`

Table 4.3 `ads_getfiled()` flag values		
SYMBOL	Value	Meaning
NEWFILE	1	Request to create a new file, shows alert if file already exists
NOTYPEIT	2	Disable "TYPE IT" button
ARBEXT	4	User can enter an arbitrary filename extension
LIBSRCH	8	Perform a library search of filename entered, see Section 2.4.1.

One of the reasons for leaving AutoLISP behind and programming in a compiled language is speed of calculation. Calculations which were unthinkable in AutoLISP are very possible in C or C++. However there is always the possibility that the calculation may take several minutes (physical simulations require a notorious amount of computing power). A way of letting the user abort a long calculation is needed. This is where `ads_usrbrk()` comes in. It checks to see if the user has hit control-C (in DOS) or ESCAPE (in Windows).

`ads_usrbrk()` returns 1 if the user has tried to abort the current command (i.e. the command that *you* have created, not standard AutoCAD commands and

0 if the user has not (yet) tried to abort the command. Note that this is *not* a substitute for checking the result of `ads_getxxx()` functions.

If you are doing a long calculation or operation, and want the user to be able to abort it you should call `ads_usrbrk()` every now and then. Usually when there is a long calculation there is a loop or some nested loops. You should put the call to `ads_usrbrk()` in one of these. Here is an example, part of an imaginary function which calculates w:

```
for (x = 0 ; x < 20000 ; x++) {
    for (y = 0 ; y < 20000 ; y++) {
        for (z = 0 ; z < 20000 ; z++) {
            if (ads_usrbrk()) {
                    ads_printf ("\nUser aborted calculation") ;
                    return (0.0) ;
            }
            w = w + Heavy_Calculation (x,y,z) ;
        }  // z
    }  // y
}  // x
ads_printf ("\nCalculation completed") ;
return (w)..
```

Here `ads_usrbrk()` is placed in the innermost loop, but it could have been placed at the start of any of the three loops. The difference is only in reaction time; in the innermost loop the function will react faster than in the outermost loop, but it may slow down the calculation *appreciably*.

How you actually handle the user break depends on the application you are writing. If the calculation would have taken many minutes then you should think about saving the partial results (maybe in a file), ready to restart the process at some later date.

Do not make the mistake of thinking that this handling of `ads_usrbrk()` is a "frill"; it is not. The days are gone when people were content to wait for computers, and if a user wants to abandon an operation she should be allowed to whenever she wants.

If the user has hit ESCAPE or Control-C then AutoCAD will store this information in a flag, even though you may have not called `ads_usrbrk()`. You need to clear this flag by calling `ads_usrbrk()` before you start receiving new user input. If you do not do this then the first time you get user input AutoCAD will see an ESCAPE which corresponds to an old input. For this reason I often use the following function in my main ADS file:

```
int Tidy_End (int Ret_Val)
/*
All user called ADS functions must end well, and this is what
this function does.
*/
```

```
{
    (void)ads_usrbrk () ;   // Clear ^C and or ESC flag
    (void)ads_retvoid () ; // Tell AutoLISP we've nothing return.
    return (Ret_Val) ;      // Tell AutoCAD how the command went
}
```

This does three jobs: it clears the user break flag, if the user hit it when you were not looking, and it stops NIL appearing on the command line when the function ends (AutoLISP programmers do this by calling (princ) as the last line of their functions). It also informs AutoCAD how the function went, Ret_Val is usually either RTNORM (meaning all went well) or RTERROR. If your return RTERROR AutoCAD will print an error message saying that the ADS function did not run properly. The call to Tidy_End() should be the last thing you do at the end of each user function that you add, see the last lines of test_func in LST__4_1.C.

We are not interested in the return values of ads_usrbrk() and ads_retvoid(), so we deliberately cast them to void.

The alternative to using a function like Tidy_End() is to write the three lines it contains every time you want to be able to return (tidily) from an ADS function. Tidy_End() "factorises out" those three lines.

4.10 Listings

```
/////////////////////////////////////////////////////////////
// LST__4_1.C
//
//      Illustrating ADS user IO, the ads_getxxx() functions

// Defines for ads_getstring function
#define ACCEPT_SPACES 1
#define NO_SPACES     0
#define MAX_CHARS     133  // See ACAD dox for current value!

// Tidily end your user callable functions
static int Tidy_End (int Ret_Val) ;

static int test_func (void)
/*
 * Function to illustrate how to get user input
 * Note that this version stupidly ignores the return values
 * of the ads_getxxx functions.
 *
 */
{
    int Integer ;
    ads_real Dist,Real,Angle,Orient ;
```

```
    ads_point Point0,Point1 ;
    char Word[MAX_CHARS],Sentence[MAX_CHARS] ;

    (void)ads_getint ("\nInput an integer please:",&Integer) ;

    (void)ads_getreal ("\nInput a real number please:",&Real) ;

    (void)ads_getdist (NULL,"\nInput a distance (use the"
                       " mouse if you want!)",&Dist) ;

    // Get an angle oriented to 0 degrees as specified
    // in ANGBASE variable)
    (void)ads_getangle (NULL,"\nInput an angle (use the"
                        " mouse if you want!)",&Angle) ;

    // Gets an angle (oriented to 0 degrees to the right)
    (void)ads_getorient (NULL,"\nInput an orientation angle"
                         " (mouse ok too)",&Orient) ;

    // Get a point, later be used as the 1st corner of a rect
    (void)ads_getpoint (NULL,"\nInput a point"
                        " (use mouse or keyboard)",Point0) ;

    // Get the other corner of the rectangle, using Point0 as
    // the base
    (void)ads_getcorner (Point0, "\nother corner "
                         "(use mouse or keyboard)",Point1) ;

    // Get a string, accepting spaces as valid characters
    (void)ads_getstring (ACCEPT_SPACES,"\nInput a sentence:",
                         &Sentence) ;

    // Get a string, treating spaces as ENTER
    (void)ads_getstring (NO_SPACES,"\nInput a word:",&Word) ;

    // Show the results
    (void)ads_printf ("\nInteger = %d, Real = %f,"
                      "\nDist= %f, Angle = %f,"
                      "\nOrient = %f, Point0 = %f, %f, %f,"
                      "\n          Point1 = %f, %f, %f"
                      "\nSentence = <%s>, Word=<%s>",
                      Integer, Real, Dist, Angle, Orient,
                      Point0[X],Point0[Y],Point0[Z],
                      Point1[X],Point1[Y],Point1[Z],
                      Sentence, Word) ;

    return (Tidy_End (RTNORM)) ; // Typical use of Tidy_End,
                                 // see text.
}
```

```
int Tidy_End (int Ret_Val)
/*
All user called ADS functions must end well.
You should call this function at the end of each user-callable
function. An example is given above.
*/
{
    (void)ads_usrbrk () ;       // Clear ^C and or ESC flag
    (void)ads_retvoid () ;      // Tell AutoLISP we've nothing to
tell him (no NIL).
    return (Ret_Val) ;          // Tell AutoCAD how the command went
}


//                 -- End of LST__4_1.C


//////////////////////////////////////////////////////////////
// LST__4_2.C
//
//     Function to illustrate how to get user input, including
//     checking for user abort (control-C or ESCAPE) and
//     limiting allowed inputs with ads_initget function

#define MAX_CHARS 133

static int test_func (void)
{
    int Integer,Res ;
    ads_real Dist,Real ;
    ads_point Base_Point ;
    char Prompt[MAX_CHARS] ;

    ads_initget (RSG_NONEG | RSG_NONULL, NULL) ;
    Res = ads_getreal ("\nInput a positive real"
                        " number please:",&Real) ;
    if (Res == RTCAN) {
        ads_printf ("\nUser aborted operation") ;
        return (Tidy_End (RTNORM)) ;
    }

    // Get a point used as a base for ads_getdist which follows
    ads_initget (RSG_NONULL, NULL) ;
    Res = ads_getpoint (NULL,"\nInput a base point"
                        " for distance:",Base_Point) ;
    if (Res == RTCAN) {
        ads_printf ("\nUser abandoned input") ;
        return (Tidy_End(RTNORM)) ;
    }
```

```
        // Now get the user to specify a distance from Base_Point
        // using a dashed rubber band line
        ads_initget (RSG_DASH | RSG_NONULL, NULL) ;
        Res = ads_getdist (Base_Point,"\nInput a distance:",&Dist) ;
        if (Res == RTCAN) {
            ads_printf ("\nUser aborted operation") ;
            return (Tidy_End (RTNORM)) ;
        }

        // Get an integer, forcing the user to reply by using
        // the RSG_NONULL flag.
        // The value input by the user will be used as the default
        // in the second call to ads_getint.
        ads_initget (RSG_NONULL,NULL) ;
        Res = ads_getint ("\nInput an integer please:",&Integer) ;
        if (Res == RTCAN) {
            ads_printf ("\nUser aborted operation") ;
            return (Tidy_End (RTNORM)) ;
        }

        // Prompt for an integer, do not use ads_initget(RSG_NONULL),
        // so null input allowed. Use can type a new value or
        // simply ENTER to accept current value
        sprintf (Prompt,"Default value is <%d>,"
                        " new value please: ",Integer) ;
        Res = ads_getint (Prompt,&Integer) ;
        if (Res == RTCAN) {
            ads_printf ("\nUser aborted operation") ;
            return (Tidy_End (RTNORM)) ;
        }
        ads_printf ("\nThe integer is now %d",Integer) ;

        // Show the results
        (void)ads_printf ("\nInteger = %d, Real = %f,"
                          "\nBase_Point = %f, %f, %f,"
                          "\nDist= %f",
                          Integer, Real,
                          Base_Point[X],Base_Point[Y],Base_Point[Z],
                          Dist) ;

    return (Tidy_End (RTNORM)) ; // Typical use of Tidy_End,
                                 // see text.
}

//              -- End of LST__4_2.C

///////////////////////////////////////////////////////////
// LST__4_3.C
```

```
//    Illustrates POINT input for a helicopter designing
//    ADS program

#include <string.h>  // For string comparison functions

#define MAX_CHARS 133

// The following would really be an AutoCAD database accessing
// function in a real helicopter designing program! It would
// put the center of gravity of the helicopter in x. Here we
// simply initialize it
#define Get_Helicopter_CG(x) x[X]=14.0;x[Y]=12.0;x[Z]=10.0

// Rotor center would probably be a variable in a real program
const ads_point Rotor_Center = {14.0,12.0,11.0} ;

static int test_func (void)
/*
 * Function to illustrate keyword input.
 *
 */
{
    int        Res ;
    ads_point Point ;
    char       Key_Word[MAX_CHARS] ;

    // Define two keywords which the following
    // ads_getxxx function can accept as valid input
    // Notice upper case 'C' and 'R' used as shortcuts
    ads_initget (RSG_NONULL,"Cg Rotcen") ;

    Res = ads_getpoint (NULL,"\nSpecify position,"
                       " or C(g) or R(otcen):",Point) ;
    if (Res == RTCAN) {
        // User hit ESCAPE or Contrl-C
        ads_printf ("\nUser abandoned input") ;
        return (Tidy_End(RTNORM)) ;
    } else if (Res == RTKWORD) {
        // The user has typed in a string instead of
        // specifying a point
        if (ads_getinput (Key_Word) == RTNORM) {
            // The keyword was entered normally
            if (stricmp ("Cg",Key_Word)==0) {
                ads_printf ("\nProg searches for"
                           " Center of Gravity") ;
                Get_Helicopter_CG (Point) ;
            } else if (stricmp ("Rotcen",Key_Word)==0) {
                ads_printf ("\nProg searches for"
                           " ROTator CENter") ;
```

```
                    memcpy (Point,Rotor_Center,sizeof(ads_point)) ;
             } else {
                    ads_printf ("\nBad keyword:%s",Key_Word) ;
                    return (Tidy_End(RTNORM)) ;
             }
         } else {
             ads_printf ("\nUser abandoned input") ;
             return (Tidy_End(RTNORM)) ;
         }
    }

    ads_printf ("\nPoint selected was %f %f %f",
                Point[X],Point[Y],Point[Z]) ;

    return (Tidy_End (RTNORM)) ; // Typical use of Tidy_End,
                                 // see text.
}

//                -- End of LST__4_3.C

///////////////////////////////////////////////////////////////
// LST__4_4.C
//      Illustrates READY MADE DIALOG BOXES

#include <string.h>

// Flags of ads_filed function
#define NEWFILE     0x01
#define NOTYPEIT    0x02
#define ARBEXT      0x04
#define LIBSRCH     0x08

static int test_func (void)
/*
 * Function to illustrate ready made dialog boxes.
 */
{
    int      Res ;
    struct resbuf* rb ;

    (void)ads_alert ("Testing\nMultiple line"
                     "\nalert box function") ;

    // Get memory for a result buffer in which to store the
    // result of the ads_getfiled function. Assume that
    // ads_getfiled will return a string.
    rb = ads_newrb (RTSTR) ;

    Res = ads_getfiled ("Open Config File",  // title
```

```
                         "C:\\SOURCES\\",   // no suggestion
                         "CFG",            // extension
                         NEWFILE,          // flags
                         rb) ;             // where to put result
    if (Res == RTNORM) {
        // See what sort of result buffer has been resturned
        if (rb->restype == RTSTR) {
            ads_printf ("\nThe user selected <%s>",
                         rb->resval.rstring) ;
        } else if (rb->restype == RTSHORT) {
            ads_printf ("\nRequest to type at the"
                         " command line.") ;
        } else {
            ads_printf ("\nStrange return type:%d",
                         rb->restype) ;
        }
    } else {
        ads_printf ("\nUser abandoned dialog box") ;
    }

    (void)ads_relrb (rb) ; // Release Ram malloced by ads_newrb

    return (Tidy_End (RTNORM)) ;
}
//                   -- End of LST__4_4.C
```

Result buffers, variables and symbol tables

5

5.1 Introduction

This chapter deals with result buffers, what they are and how they are used to communicate with ADS functions. AutoCAD variables (we saw one in Chapter 3, "CMDECHO") are introduced, and some of the most common ones described. Finally I will explain symbol tables, where linetypes, block definitions and so on are stored.

For a complete list of AutoCAD system variables see Appendix C.

5.2 Result buffers and data types

For the newcomer to C and/or AutoCAD, result buffers can cause some confusion, so let us go slowly. A result buffer is a C structure defined in ADSDEF.H as follows:

```
union ads_u_val {          // This union accessed as...
    ads_real rreal;        // ...a real using resval.rreal
    ads_real rpoint[3];    // ...a point using resval.rpoint
    short rint;            // ...an int using resval.rint
    char *rstring;         // ...a char pointer using
resval.rstring
    long rlname[2];        // ...as an ads_name using resval.rlname
    long rlong;            // ...as a long, 32bits, using
resval.rlong
    struct ads_binary rbinary;
};
struct resbuf {
```

```
struct resbuf *rbnext; // Allows them to be "linked"
short restype;
union ads_u_val resval;
};
```

(By the way you should *never* copy the above structure definition from this book or from an AutoCAD manual, but always include the H file found on the distribution disks or CD-ROM of AutoCAD. Autodesk may decide to change a definition slightly, and the only way to be sure that you are correctly accessing the ADS functions and data is to use the include files supplied.)

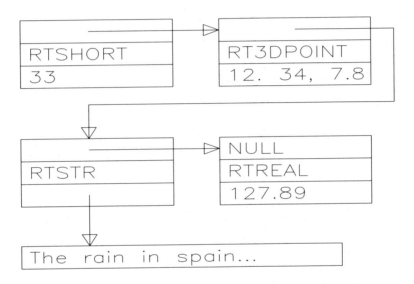

Figure 5.1 An example result buffer list

First lets look at `struct resbuf` which is a simple structure with three fields. The first is a pointer to another resbuf, which permits long sequences of values to be stored in a linked list of result buffers. The end of the chain is marked by *rbnext* being set to NULL. If you program in ADS you will find yourself writing lots of code to scan or create these result buffer linked lists.

The next field is `restype` which indicates what sort of value is stored in the last field (which is a C union) `resval`. Some of these codes we have already met in Chapter 3, used for specifying what sort of data we sent to the `ads_command()` function. Table 5.1 is not exhaustive because often result buffers given to us by AutoCAD contain DXF codes, while the ones we send to AutoCAD use the ones shown in the table. DXF codes always have values less than 2000 so it is easy to distinguish between these and others.

Look at the definition of `ads_u_val`. A union is a way of allowing the same piece of memory to contain different types of data at different times. It was invented to *save space*. In our case the union could hold an `ads_real` or a `short` among other things. `resval` is the code which tells us what this piece of memory (this union) is containing currently. Note that a union *cannot* store different types at the same time, only one type at a time.

It is an *error* to put a real in a union and then read it as an int. For example:

```
struct resbuf x ;
x.restype = RTREAL ; // Not required in this fragment, but safer
x.resval.rreal = 13.0 ;
ads_printf ("\nThe value of the union is %d",x.resval.rint) ;
// The above line is WRONG! The following line is CORRECT
ads_printf ("\nThe value of the union is %f",x.resval.rreal) ;
```

The table shows which parts of the retval are used with the corresponding type specified in restype.

Linked lists of result buffers are used because they can be variable length and can contain mixed data types. The examples where we have used them so far have been as simple *single* buffers but very often ADS functions can take as parameters, or can return, linked lists of result buffers, i.e. *sequences* of result buffers. Why do you need a sequence of result buffers? Well to describe a line for example you need a buffer for the start point, a buffer for the end point, a buffer for the colour, a buffer for the layer, linetype and so on.

A word of warning about the difference between a shorts, ints and longs. Since Release 13 AutoCAD has gone completely into the 32 bit world, and an int is now 32 bits, do not be misled that by the name resval.rint, it contains a 16 bit short. Shorts are always 16 bits, longs are 32 bits.

Figure 5.1 shows a linked list of four result buffers. The end of the list is marked by the NULL in the rbnext field of the last buffer. The first buffer is a short 16 bit integer, the second is three-dimensional point, the third is a string (actually a pointer to a string) and the last is a real number.

How could we scan a list like this in C? The following code fragment is a typical way of doing it:

```
struct resbuf* Current_Rb ; // The 'current' result buffer
Current_Rb = First_Rb ; // Initialise to start of linked list
while (Current_Rb != NULL) {
    // Do something with current result buffer....
    ...examine, change, print, verify, whatever....
    // Get the next result buffer from the current one
    Current_Rb = Current_Rb->rbnext ; // Is NULL at end of list
}
```

Going over the above code with Figure 5.1 in mind the first result buffer is the RTSHORT with value 33. At the start of the while loop `Current_Rb` is this first result buffer. We do something with this result buffer and then go on to look at the next one. The rbnext field of the RTSHORT points to the RT3DPOINT result buffer whose value is 12,34,7.8. Again we do what we need to with this result buffer and go onto the next one. When we get to the RTREAL of value 127.89 the nextrb is NULL, and therefore Current_Rb becomes NULL, test at the start of while statement becomes FALSE, and we exit the loop.

ADS provides a function for dynamically creating result buffer lists, ads_buildlist(), which is described in Chapter 6 Section 6.3.5.

LST__5_1.C is an example of printing out the properties of the last object in the drawing. When you test this function draw a line or a circle before calling "test", do not use an empty drawing, otherwise you will get a viewport data structure, which is not as easy to understand as a line or a circle.

LST__5_1.C. has three functions, the main one is test_func() as usual in these examples, the other two are "helper" functions. It would have been possible to put all three in one function, but the helper functions may be useful to you elsewhere; keeping them independent like this allows code re-use.

As often happens when describing ADS functions with working code, I have to call functions which I have not yet described. In LST__5_1.C there are two. There is ads_entlast(), which sets its "entity name" parameter to the last entity in the drawing (i.e. the last one which has been inserted, be it line or block or circle or whatever). An entity name is of type ads_name. If this function fails we call an alert box and return with RTERROR.

By the way, entity names are only valid for the AutoCAD session in which they have been obtained, they are *not* saved to the drawing file. If you want to permanently identify objects from drawing session to drawing session you will need to use "handles". "Handles" could be turned on and off before Release 13. From Release 13 onwards they are always on. See the ads_handent() function in Appendix B. Now back to LST__5_1.C.

If the ads_entlast() goes well then we obtain the result buffer list of the entity using the second new function ads_entget(), which takes an entity name as a parameter and returns a result buffer list. It allocates memory for the result buffers and fills it with the appropriate date.

Getting and using entity names and so on will be explained in Chapter 6; suffice to say here that in LST__5_1.C if all goes well then rb contains a linked list of result buffers describing the last entity in the drawing. Refer to Figure 6.1 to have an idea of the relationship between entity names and result buffer lists. Result buffer lists "dangle" from entity names, and contain data about the entity.

Next we call Print_Rb_List(), which takes what it assumes to be the head of a linked list and prints out all the data contained in it.

After we have printed out the data we release the memory allocated for the list by calling ads_relrb(). Note that this will free *all* the memory allocated by ads_entget(), including any memory automatically allocated for strings. For example the third result buffer of Figure 5.1 has allocated some space for the string "The rain in Spain...". This string space would be freed by ads_relrb().

`Print_Rb_List()` is simply a while loop which continuously calls `Print_Rb_Data()` until it comes to the end of the list. Remember that the end of the list is marked by `rbnext` being equal to the `NULL` pointer, as in the fourth buffer of Figure 5.1.

`Print_Rb_Data()` is the function that actually prints the contents of each result buffer onto the screen. The first part of the function classifies each result buffer as an integer or a string or a point and so on. The second part then prints the appropriate values. The codes in the first part are DXF codes, as used in the DXF file format, see Chapter 18 and Appendix D.

Ranges of DXF codes correspond to variables of the same type. For example all codes from 0 to 9 inclusive correspond to string values. This structure is reflected in the first part of LST__5_1.H.

Table 5.1: Type codes used in result buffers		
Code	Union field	Meaning
RTNONE		No result value
RTREAL	resval.rreal	Floating point value
RTPOINT	resval.rpoint	Two dimensional point, Z=0.0
RTSHORT	resval.rint	16 bit integer
RTANG	resval.rreal	Angle (floating point value)
RTSTR	resval.rstring	Null terminated string
RTENAME	resval.rlname	Entity name
RTPICKS	resval.rlname	Selection set name
RTORIENT	resval.rreal	Orientation (floating point angular value)
RT3DPOINT	resval.rpoint	Three dimensional point all X Y and Z used
RTLONG	resval.rlong	32 bit integer
RTVOID		No value
RTLB		List begin marker (for nested lists)
RTLE		List end marker (for nested lists)
RTDOTE		AutoLISP dotted pair
RTT		AutoLISP TRUE value
RTNIL		AutoLISP NIL (FALSE) value
RTDXF0		Group 0 code, only for `ads_buildlist()`

Once we have decided basic type of the result buffer by setting `Res_Type`, we go on to print the values found.

If you run this ADS application just after having drawn a circle you will get an output something like this:

```
(-1 -- (12345678 9871234))
(0 -- "CIRCLE")
(5 -- "2F")
(100 -- "AcDbEntity")
(67 -- 9)
(8 -- "0")
(100 -- "AcDbCircle")
(10 -- 23.4 45.6 0.0)
(40 -- 12.6)
(210 -- 0.000 0.000 1.000)
```

The actual list you see may have more or fewer items, less if you are using AutoCAD 12. AutoLISP programmers will be familiar with this representation of an object. Figure 5.2 is a graphical representation of the list above, ignoring a few of the result buffers. I will not completely explain all the data shown here, just the simpler and more immediate parts. For more information on DXF codes see Chapter 18 and Appendix D. It is recommended that you ignore data you do not need when scanning result buffer lists, extracting only what you are interested in. In the above example perhaps your program is interested in the fact that the object is a CIRCLE centred on 23.4, 45.6, 0 with a radius of 12.6. All the rest of the data can be thrown away.

The first line, -1, is the entity name, actually an array of two longs. See the definition of E_NAME in LST__5_1.H. The entity name uniquely defines *that* entity; in struct resbuf it is the resval.rlname field. It is also the data that ads_entlast() puts in its single ads_name parameter.

The next pair of values (0 -- "CIRCLE") gives you the type of entity. 0 is the DXF code for entity type name; see the definition of ENTITY_TYPE_CODE in LST__5_1.H.

The (8 -- "0") tells you that the circle is on layer "0", 8 being the DXF code for the string naming a layer, see the definition of LAYER_NAME_CODE.

The (10 -- 23.4 45.6 0.0) gives the center of the circle. Here you have to be careful for two reasons. The first is that in DXF codes 10 is often described as the X coordinate code, whereas in ADS it serves as XYZ coordinate code, giving you all three values. The second is that the 10 code sometimes means "center of circle" and sometimes means "startpoint of line" and so on. The actual meaning of 10 as a DXF code depends on the context in which it was read. In this case 10 obviously means "center of circle" since we are reading data about a circle!

(40 -- 12.6) means that the radius of the circle is 12.6. As with the 10 DXF code described before, the 40 DXF code can mean different things in different contexts. It most often means "radius" (of circles, arcs, circular dimensions and so on), but it can also mean "starting width" for polylines.

(210 -- 0.000 0.000 1.000) is the definition of the extrusion direction, i.e. the normal of the entity (in this case the circle). Here the circle is flat in the X-Y plane and the extrusion direction is simply the unit Z vector. If the value of this pair is *not* the unit Z vector, then you will have to use a strange and complicated procedure called the arbitrary axis algorithm to extract sensible data from the 10 (center of circle) code described previously.

So LST__5_1.C has shown you how to extract data from an object using ADS result buffers.

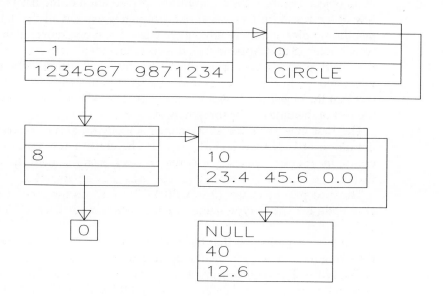

Figure 5.2 The result buffer list of a CIRCLE

5.3 AutoCAD variables

5.3.1 What are AutoCAD variables?

AutoCAD variables are numbers or strings associated with each AutoCAD drawing. They have many purposes:

- setting user interface conditions; for example the integer variable OSMODE sets the object snap mode.
- getting status information from AutoCAD; for example the integer variable ERRNO contains a number identifying the type of the last error which occurred
- defining how AutoLISP and ADS/ARX programs behave; for example CMDECHO described in Chapter 3
- setting the current layer or colour; for example CLAYER is a string variable specifying the current layer.

The values of AutoCAD variables are stored in the drawing (and also in the DXF file of the drawing) and the settings of the variables will be the same when you re-open a drawing as when you closed it.

Some variables are read-only; that is, for information of applications only, and cannot be set directly, they have to be set by calling normal AutoCAD commands. An example is VIEWMODE, which gives information about the current view, but which can only be changed by calling the DVIEW command.

5.3.2 Some commonly used variables

For a complete list of AutoCAD variables see Appendix C. This section describes the most commonly used variables.

ACADVER (string, DXF code 1) the AutoCAD drawing database version number. Currently the defined versions have the following values:
- "AC1006" = R10,
- "AC1009" = R11 and R12,
- "AC1011" = R13.
This is a read-only variable.

BLIPMODE, (integer, DXF code 70) if set to 1 shows causes small crosses ("blips") to be placed on key points when the user creates an entity, for example at the endpoints of a line or the center of a circle. These blips disappear after a regen or redraw.

CECOLOR, (integer, DXF code 62) specifying the current entity color number. If your program sets this variable then all entities drawn afterwards will have this color. 0 = BYBLOCK, 256 = BYLAYER, numbers from 1 to 255 are standard AutoCAD color indices. See the drawings COLORWH.DWG or CHROMA.DWG to see what colors the indices correspond to.

CELTYPE, (string, DXF code 6) the current entity linetype. As with CECOLOR setting this variable affects the linetype of all the entities drawn. It is a string variable containing either "BYBLOCK" or "BYLAYER" or a user-defined linetype.

CLAYER, (string, DXF code 8) the current entity layer. As with CECOLOR setting this variable affects the layer of all the entities drawn. The default AutoCAD layer is "0".

COORDS, (integer, DXF code 70), defines how coordinates in the status bar (at the top of the screen) are displayed, an integer variable with one of three values:
1 static coordinate display, coordinates change only when the user picks a point
2 continuous update, the coordinates change continuously as the user moves the mouse
3 "distance<angle" format, the status bar display shows the current mouse position relative to a given point as a distance and an angle.

DWGNAME, (string, no DXF code) is the current drawing name. It may contain the path if the user opened the drawing with the full path name.

ERRNO, (integer, no DXF code), gives an indication of the last error which occurred with an AutoLISP or C or C++ function. This variable is obviously *not* stored in the drawing file. This is useful for debugging, and you will find symbolic codes for the errors that can occur in OL_ERRNO.H. The listing LST__5_2.C gives an example of its use. ERRNO is cleared to zero at the start of an AutoCAD session and when a new drawing is opened. Your program should inspect ERRNO as soon as it notices that something went wrong with a call to an ADS function. It can be set to zero afterwards.

ORTHOMODE (integer, DXF code 70), if nonzero only orthogonal (90 degree) lines can be drawn. When using ads_command() it is best to set this (perhaps temporarily) to 0 so that your program can draw lines in any direction.

OSMODE (integer, DXF code 70) current object snap modes. Object snap is useful for the user but may cause chaos when you program with the ads_command(). It is best to set this to 0 while you use ads_command() and then to restore it to its previous value when your ADS function has finished.

PICKFIRST (integer, DXF code 70), if non-zero then objects can be picked before calling the command to operate on them. For example you can select a circle with the mouse and then call the MOVE to move it. This is more in line with the Windows way of doing things, that is object followed by command.

TEXTSTYLE, (string, DXF code 7) the current text style name. If you use text in your ADS programs you should always check this variable to make sure that the user has not set a different text style to the one you want.

5.3.3 Getting and setting variable values

LST__5_2.C shows some useful C functions for setting and reading AutoCAD system variables. They use single result buffers; there is clearly no need for a linked list of result buffers when we are dealing with only one value, a single string, a single real, a single integer, or a single point.

The first part of the file is the function prototypes for the seven helper functions defined later. The next part is the function which tests the helper functions. Then comes the definitions of the helper functions themselves. We have already met Set_Int_Var in Chapter 3.

test_func starts by resetting the ERRNO variable, so that when we read it we are sure that it applies to a recent error.

Next test_func sets and gets various AutoCAD system variables, printing out the results of the variable gets. Note that setting the current layer to a non-existent layer will cause an error. You should run the program before and after creating a layer called "RESULTS" to see if and how the error is reported. Anticipating that there will be an error, the program inspects the ERRNO variable and prints an error message if it is non-zero.

The ADS functions used in LST__5_2.C are `ads_setvar()` and `ads_getvar()` which send result buffers to AutoCAD. In the case of ads_setvar RTNORM will be returned if all went well, in the case of `ads_getvar()` you should look at both the return value and the return type to be sure that all went well. `Get_Real_Var()` for example checks that `ads_getvar()` returns RTNORM *and* that the value in the result buffer is an RTREAL. This double check ensures that you have spelt the name of the variable correctly and that it is the type you expected.

If there is an error, the functions print an error message, and where necessary return a default value.

I suggest that you use these "wrapper" functions rather than the `ads_getvar()` and `ads_setvar()` functions directly to reduce code space and source length and to include automatic checking.

5.4 Symbol tables

5.4.1 Data contained in symbol tables

The symbol tables are where AutoCAD stores linetypes, layers, text styles and so on. Each AutoCAD drawing has its own set of tables, and when the drawing is saved these tables are saved with it. The tables present in a drawing are as follows.

- LAYER. Data about the layers in the drawing are stored in this table: if it is frozen, if it is locked, its color, if it is on and so on. LST__5_3.C gives an example of getting information from the layer table. Section 5.4.3 below illustrates how to create layers from within your program

- LTYPE. Contains information about named linetypes
- VIEW. Data about named views, the viewpoint and the target point, the lens length the twist angle, whether grid and snap are activated in this view and so on. A view is a three-dimensional object, not to be confused with VPORT, see below. A VIEW can be created by the DVIEW command. See also Chapter 10.
- STYLE. Contains the text style definitions, with the name of the STYLE, the angular direction of the text, the height, the font, and so on.
- BLOCK. Definitions of blocks used in the drawing. You should note that though BLOCK is a table, in DXF files it has a separate section all to itself. Blocks are dealt with in detail in Chapter 8.
- UCS. This table will contain a list of named User Coordinate Systems, created either by your program or the user to ease drawing in three dimensions. The data present in this section will be the name of the UCS, the origin, and the X and Y vectors
- DIMSTYLE. This table contains details about named dimensioning styles.
- VPORT. Data about the viewports on the AutoCAD screen when the viewports are tiled (i.e. TILEMODE is set to 1 and so "paper space" is not visible). It is a two-dimensional object describing in the Display Coordinate System (DCS) where the viewports are and how big they are.
- APPID. The name given by programmers to the applications used. Applications which want to create extended data (see Chapter 11, Working with extended data) need to "register"; registering causes the application name to appear in this table.

5.4.2 Accessing symbol table data

Often you would like to know if a table already contains a named object, for example a BLOCK which you would like to use. The following function, Table_Object_Exists(), interrogates the table and returns 1 if the object is already defined, or else it returns 0.

```
int Table_Object_Exists (const char* Table, const char* Object)
/*
PURPOSE: To return TRUE if the given object exists in the
tables of the ACAD drawing database.
Table should be one of:
    LAYER,LTYPE,VIEW,STYLE,BLOCK,UCS,VPORT,APPID
*/
{
    struct resbuf* rb ;
    rb = ads_tblsearch (Table,Object,0) ;
    if (rb == NULL) { // means object or table do not exist
```

```
        return (0) ;
    } else {
        (void)ads_relrb (rb) ;
        return (1) ;
    }
}
```

An example of the utility of this function is given in Chapter 8, LST__8_1.C. It is called as follows:

```
Block_Already_Exists = Table_Object_Exists ("BLOCK","NUT03") ;
```

Alternatively, to see if a layer has already been created:

```
Layer_Already_Exists = Table_Object_Exists ("LAYER","BELOW_SEA");
```

Another example is to see if a user coordinate system has been saved:

```
My_Ucs_Saved = Table_Object_Exists ("UCS","MYUCS");
```

Obviously it is no good looking for blocks in the layer table, and vice versa!

ads_tblsearch() returns a result buffer containing data about the object if found, else it returns NULL. Note that the (valid) result buffer is released by a call to ads_relrb(). In the above example we are only interested in whether it exists or not, and do not scan the result buffer list.

The last parameter of ads_tblsearch(), 0 in the above example, affects how another ADS function, ads_tblnext(), will subsequently behave. ads_tblnext() is used for scanning linearly through tables. If the last parameter of ads_tblsearch() is non-zero then ads_tblnext() will carry on scanning after the last entry found by ads_tblsearch. This is used mostly for the VPORT table, which can have several entries with the same name.

LST__5_3.C shows how to get detailed information about a layer using ads_tblsearch(), and also how to use ads_tblnext() to scan linearly through the BLOCK table.

The listing starts by including LST__5_1.H which contains the DXF codes for various entities and their properties. Then test_func is defined, and it starts by using an ads_getstring() to prompt the user for a layer name, which is then used to do a table search using ads_tblsearch().

If ads_tblsearch() returns NULL then the table has not been found and we return from the function. In the case that a valid result buffer is returned we use a while loop to scan over it, printing out the data we find in it. The usual trick of recognising the end of the result buffer by looking for NULL in rbnext is used.

We switch on rb->restype to print out the appropriate value of the buffer. Note that though 8 (LAYER_NAME_CODE) gives the name of the layer that an entity is *on*, in the layer table it is 2 (NAME_CODE) which gives the name of the layer *present*. We print the layer color (negative color means that a layer is OFF), the Flags of the layer, and the linetype of the layer. If the `Flags` contain any set bits, indicating that the layer is frozen or locked, we print out this data.

The second half of the function illustrates the use of `ads_tblnext()`. First we prompt with keyword entry (see Chapter 4) for the name of a table to scan. Then we use `ads_tblnext()` with a reset parameter of 1 to reset the scanning of the table to the beginning. The while loop which follows ends when `ads_tblnext()` returns `NULL`, which means that the end of the table has been reached. Within the while loop, `Lrb`, the head of the result buffer list for the given table entry, is used as a starting point to scan the data of the entry found. As usual we ignore most of the data, because in this example we are just interested in the name of the entry found, which we print. Had the user typed "BLOCK" at the second prompt of this function then a list of the block names would be printed.

You should test this function with complicated drawings with lots of layers and blocks and styles.

Summarising, `ads_tblsearch()` is used when you know the name (string of characters, not `ads_name`) of the entry you are searching for and want to jump straight to it, or when you would like to know if an entry exists. `ads_tblnext()` is used to scan linearly through the table, used when you want to obtain a list of all the entities in a given table.

5.4.3 Creating and modifying layers

Often you would like to be able to draw certain objects on certain layers, and you would like the program to create the layer. Before creating a new layer in a drawing you should check that it does not already exist using `Table_Object_Exists()` described above. Maybe the layer was created by the very same program in an earlier drawing session. For a practical example look at the following code fragment:

```
if (!Table_Object_Exists("LAYER","BLOOD")) {
    // create the missing layer
    if (ads_command (RTSTR,"_LAYER",
                     RTSTR,"_N",       // New...
                     RTSTR,"BLOOD",    // ...new layer name.
                     RTSTR,"_C",       // Colour change...
                     RTSHORT,1,        // ...red is the colour...
                     RTSTR,"BLOOD",    // ...assigned to BLOOD
layer.
                     RTSTR,"", RTNONE) != RTNORM) {
        ads_printf ("\nWARNING: Could not do LAYER command") ;
    }
}
```

Note that in the above fragment a new layer is created, called "BLOOD" and in the same command we assign its color, 1. That is why "BLOOD" occurs twice in the call to ads_command().

If you want to modify a layer and you are using AutoCAD *13* or later you can use the function ads_tblobjname(), to obtain the entity name of the layer, from which dangle the result buffers. Then you can change the entries in the result buffer chain, followed by a call to ads_entmod()

5.5 Listings

```c
////////////////////////////////////////////////////////////
// LST__5_1.C
//      Illustrating the scanning of result buffer lists.

#include "LST__5_1.H" // DXF codes

// Function prototypes
// Print linked list
void Print_Rb_List (struct resbuf* rb) ;
 // Print single buffer
void Print_Rb_Data (struct resbuf* eb) ;

static int test_func (void)
/*
To print out the association list of the last entity in the
AutoCAD database, if one exists
*/
{
    struct resbuf* rb ;
    ads_name en ;

    if (ads_entlast (en) != RTNORM) {
        ads_alert ("\nCannot get last entity"
                    "\nmaybe no entities in drawing?") ;
        return (Tidy_End (RTERROR)) ;
    }

    rb = ads_entget (en) ;   // You will have to free rb at the
end
    if (rb == NULL) {
        ads_alert ("\nError with ads_entget") ;
        return (Tidy_End (RTERROR)) ;
    }

    // Print the linked list of result buffers which
    // describe the last object inserted into the drawing
```

```
        Print_Rb_List (rb) ;

        // Free the ram used for the association list
        if (ads_relrb (rb) != RTNORM) {
            ads_printf ("\nError, could not release rb.") ;
            return (Tidy_End (RTERROR)) ;
        }
        return (Tidy_End (RTNORM)) ;
    }


void Print_Rb_List (struct resbuf* First_Rb)
/*
PURPOSE: To print out the the contents of the result buffer
         list looking along the chain. First_Rb is the first
         result buffer in the linked list
*/
{
    struct resbuf* Res_Buf ; // The 'current' result buffer

    Res_Buf = First_Rb ; // Initialise to start of linked list

    // Print out the linked list
    while (Res_Buf != NULL) {
        // Show contents of current result buffer....
        Print_Rb_Data (Res_Buf) ;

        // Get the next result buffer from the current one
        Res_Buf = Res_Buf->rbnext ; // Is NULL at end of list
    }
}


void Print_Rb_Data (struct resbuf* eb)
/*
PURPOSE: To print out the result buffer (DXF) code and value.
*/
{
    int Res_Type ;

    if (eb == NULL) {
        return ;  // Nothing to print
    }

    ads_printf ("\n") ;
    /*
     * Entity result buffer lists contain DXF codes rather than
     * those shown in Table 5.1. Here we translate (and
     * condense) them into the simpler Table 5.1 versions to
     * allow a simpler switch at the end of this function.
     */
```

```c
    if ((eb->restype >= STRGRP_START) &&
        (eb->restype <= STRGRP_END)) {
        Res_Type = RTSTR ;        // strings
    } else if ((eb->restype >= CRDGRP_START) &&
               (eb->restype <= CRDGRP_END)) {
        Res_Type = RT3DPOINT ;    // Co-ordinates
    } else if ((eb->restype >= RLGRP_START) &&
               (eb->restype <= RLGRP_END)) {
        Res_Type = RTREAL ;       // Reals
    } else if ((eb->restype >= SHOGRP_START) && (eb->restype <=
SHOGRP_END)) {
        Res_Type = RTSHORT ;      // Shorts
    } else if ((eb->restype >= CRD2GRP_START) &&
               (eb->restype <= CRD2GRP_END)) {
        Res_Type = RT3DPOINT ; // Co-ordinates, again
    } else if ((eb->restype >= ESTRGRP_START) &&
               (eb->restype <= ESTRGRP_END)) {
        Res_Type = RTSTR ;      // Extended data strings
    } else if ((eb->restype >= ERLGRP_START) &&
               (eb->restype <= ERLGRP_END)) {
        Res_Type = RTREAL ;     // Extended data reals
    } else if (eb->restype == SUBCLASS) {
        Res_Type = RTSTR ;
    } else if (eb->restype == E_NAME) {
        // E_NAME and RTENAME are NOT #defined the same
        Res_Type = RTENAME ;
    } else if ((eb->restype >= RTREAL) &&
               (eb->restype <= RTT)) {
        // Type from AutoLISP or other ADS functions
        Res_Type = eb->restype ;
    } else {
        Res_Type = RTNONE ;
    }

    /*
     * Now use Res_Type to print the restype spec and the
     * value of the result buffer
     */
    switch (Res_Type) {
        case RTSHORT :
            ads_printf ("(%d - %d)",eb->restype,
                                    eb->resval.rint) ;
            break ;
        case RTLONG :
            ads_printf ("(%d - %d)",eb->restype,
                                    eb->resval.rlong) ;
            break ;
        case RTREAL :
            ads_printf ("(%d - %0.3f)",eb->restype,
```

```
                                          eb->resval.rreal) ;
            break ;
         case RTSTR :
            ads_printf ("(%d - \"%s\")",eb->restype,
                                        eb->resval.rstring) ;
            break ;
         case RT3DPOINT :
            ads_printf ("(%d - %0.3f %0.3f %0.3f)",eb->restype,
                        eb->resval.rpoint[X],
                        eb->resval.rpoint[Y],
                        eb->resval.rpoint[Z]) ;
            break ;
         case RTENAME :
            ads_printf ("(%d - entity:   [%d %d])",eb->restype,
                        eb->resval.rlname[0],
                        eb->resval.rlname[1]) ;
            break ;
         case RTNONE :
            ads_printf ("(%d - unknown type)",eb->restype) ;
            break ;
         case RTPICKS :
            ads_printf ("(%d - pick set: [%d %d])",eb->restype,
                        eb->resval.rlname[0],
                        eb->resval.rlname[1]) ;
            break ;
         default :
            ads_printf ("(%d -- ?)",Res_Type) ;
            break ;
      }
}


//                     -- End of LST__5_1.C --


////////////////////////////////////////////////////
// LST__5_1.H, common DXF codes
// Oddly enough there is no standard AutoCAD
// file for these codes


/*************** DXF GROUP CODES *****************/

// Strings
#define STRGRP_START     0
#define STRGRP_END       9

// Coordinates
#define CRDGRP_START     10
#define CRDGRP_END       19
```

```
// Real values
#define RLGRP_START      38
#define RLGRP_END        59

// Short integer values
#define SHOGRP_START     60
#define SHOGRP_END       79

// New in Release 13,
#define SUBCLASS         100

// More coordinates
#define CRD2GRP_START    210
#define CRD2GRP_END      239

// Extended data strings
#define ESTRGRP_START    1000
#define ESTRGRP_END      1009

// Extended data reals
#define ERLGRP_START     1010
#define ERLGRP_END       1059


#define Y8_COORD_CODE       28
#define Z0_COORD_CODE       30
#define Z8_COORD_CODE       38

#define POINT_COORD_CODE    10
#define INSERT_COORD_CODE   10

#define CRD2GRP_START       210
#define CRD2GRP_END         239

#define THICKNESS           39
#define FIRST_REAL_CODE     THICKNESS
#define LAST_REAL_CODE      59
#define FIRST_INT_CODE      60
#define ATTFLAGS_CODE       70
#define PLINE_FLAGS_CODE    70
#define LAYER_FLAGS_CODE    70
#define FLD_LEN_CODE        73 // Inside ATTRIB resbuf
#define LAST_INT_CODE       79
#define X_EXTRU_CODE        210
#define Y_EXTRU_CODE        220
#define Z_EXTRU_CODE        230
#define COMMENT_CODE        999

// Start and endpoints of a line
```

```
#define LINE_START_CODE       10   // Followed by x coord
#define LINE_END_CODE         11   // Followed by x coord

// Some codes used by blocks
#define BLOCK_FLAGS_CODE      70   // An int containing flags
#define BLOCK_BASE_CODE       10   // Origin of block definition
#define XREF_DEPENDENT        16   // If a block contains an XREF
#define XREF_RESOLVED         32   // If a XREF resolved ok
#define REFERENCED            64   // If a block is ref'd in DWG

#define XSCALE_CODE           41
#define YSCALE_CODE           42
#define ANGLE_CODE            50
#define INS_POINT_CODE        10   // Followed by x of ins pnt
#define NAME2_CODE             3   // Second appearance of name

// Some codes used by circle entities
#define CENTER_CODE           10   // Followed by x of center
#define RADIUS_CODE           40   // Followd by radius of circle

#define COND_OP_CODE          -4   // Conditional op,ads_ssget

// When using ads_buildlist you MUST use RTDXF0 instead of these
#define ENTITY_TYPE_CODE       0   // Then there is LINE, 3DFACE..
#define SES_CODE               0   // Start End String Code
#define FILE_SEP_CODE          0   // File separator
#define SOT_CODE               0   // Start Of Table
#define TEXTVAL_CODE           1
#define NAME_CODE              2
#define BLOCK_NAME_CODE        2
#define SECTION_NAME_CODE      2
#define ENT_HAND_CODE          5   // What follows is hexa string
#define TXT_STYLE_CODE         7   // Inside attributes
#define LAYER_NAME_CODE        8   // What follows is layer name
#define FIRST_XCOORD_CODE     10   // Group code x of 1st coord
#define FIRST_YCOORD_CODE     20   // Group code y of 1st coord
#define FIRST_ZCOORD_CODE     30   // Group code z of 1st coord
#define L_START_CODE          10
#define L_END_CODE            11
#define TXTHI_CODE            40
#define SCALE_X_CODE          41
#define SCALE_Y_CODE          42
#define SCALE_Z_CODE          43
#define BULGE_CODE            42   // Used in PLINE verts for arcs
#define ROTATION_CODE         50
#define COLOUR_CODE           62   // What follows is a color int
#define LTYPE_CODE             6   // What follows is a linetype
```

```
// Attribute flags
#define ATTS_FOLLOW_CODE     66
#define ATT_TAG_CODE          2
#define ATT_VAL_CODE          1
#define ATT_FLAGS_CODE       70   // 4 1 bit flags as follows...
#define ATT_INVIS_FLAG        1
#define ATT_CONST_FLAG        2
#define ATT_VERIFY_FLAG       4 // Prompt and verify
#define ATT_PRESET_FLAG       8 // No prompt and no verify


// PLINE defines
// Flags
#define OPEN_PLINE         0x00
#define CLOSED_PLINE       0x01
#define POLYLINE3D         0x80
#define PFACE_MESH         0x40
#define PGON_MESH          0x10
// Vertices follow entity, required in POLYLINES
#define VERTS_FOLLOW_CODE   66 // Value should always be 1
#define VERTEX_COORD_CODE   10



// LAYER flags
#define FROZEN           1
#define FROZEN_BY_DEF    2
#define LOCKED           4
#define OBJECT_USED     64    // Object is ref'd in the dwg

#define BLOCK_EN_CODE    -2   // Block entity definition
#define E_NAME           -1   // Entity name

// Extended data codes
#define EXTD_SENTINEL    (-3)
#define EXTD_STR         1000
#define EXTD_APP_NAME    1001
#define EXTD_CTL_STR     1002
#define EXTD_LYR_STR     1003
#define EXTD_CHUNK       1004
#define EXTD_HANDLE      1005
#define EXTD_POINT       1010
#define EXTD_POS         1011
#define EXTD_DISP        1012
#define EXTD_DIR         1013
#define EXTD_FLOAT       1040
#define EXTD_DIST        1041
#define EXTD_SCALE       1042
#define EXTD_INT16       1070
#define EXTD_INT32       1071
```

```
// UCS codes for use in ads_trans
#define WCS_TRANS_CODE     0
#define UCS_TRANS_CODE     1
#define DCS_TRANS_CODE     2
#define PCS_TRANS_CODE     3


//      -- End of LST__5_1.H --


/////////////////////////////////////////////////////////
// LST__5_2.C
//      Useful functions for setting and reading AutoCAD
//      system variables.

// Function prototypes
void  Set_Int_Var (const char* Varname, const short Int_Val) ;
short Get_Int_Var (const char* Varname) ;
ads_real Get_Real_Var (const char* Varname) ;
void  Set_Real_Var (const char* Varname, const ads_real Value);
void  Set_String_Var (const char* Varname, const char* Value) ;
void  Get_String_Var (const char* Varname, char* Value) ;
void  Get_Point_Var (const char* Varname, ads_point Value) ;

#define MAX_CHARS 256 // For the string variables

/*****  Examples of using the above functions *********/

static int test_func (void)
/*
To show how to get and set AutoCAD system variables by calling
the helper functions below:
*/
{
    char       Clayer[MAX_CHARS] ;
    ads_point  Ucs_Origin ;
    int        Err_No ;

    // Reset the error number variable for inspection later
    Set_Int_Var ("ERRNO",0) ;

    // Object snap mode
    Set_Int_Var ("OSMODE",0x10) ;
    ads_printf ("\nOSMODE = %d ",Get_Int_Var ("OSMODE")) ;

    // Linetype scale
    Set_Real_Var ("LTSCALE",99.9) ;
    ads_printf ("\nThe current line type scale = %6.3f",
                Get_Real_Var ("LTSCALE")) ;

    // Current layer
```

```
        Set_String_Var ("CLAYER","RESULTS") ; // Will fail if
                                              // RESULTS layer
                                              // does not exist.
        Err_No = Get_Int_Var ("ERRNO") ;
        if (Err_No > 0) {
            ads_printf ("\nAn error was encountered,"
                        " number %d",Err_No) ;
            Set_Int_Var ("ERRNO",0) ;
        }

        Get_String_Var ("CLAYER",Clayer) ;
        ads_printf ("\nThe current layer is <%s> ",Clayer) ;

        // Model space User Coordinate System origin
        Get_Point_Var ("UCSORG",Ucs_Origin) ;
        ads_printf ("\nThe current UCS origin is"
                    " %6.3f, %6.3f %6.3f",
                    Ucs_Origin[X], Ucs_Origin[Y], Ucs_Origin[Z]) ;

        return (Tidy_End (RTNORM)) ;

}

/********  The ACAD system variable helper functions ********/

void Set_Int_Var (const char* Varname, const short Int_Val)
/*
PURPOSE: To set one of the integer (short) ACAD variables.
*/
{
    struct resbuf rb ;

    rb.restype    = RTSHORT ;
    rb.resval.rint = Int_Val ;
    if (ads_setvar (Varname,&rb) != RTNORM) {
        ads_printf ("\nWARNING in SIV(%s,%d), could not setvar",
                    Varname,Int_Val) ;
    }
}


short Get_Int_Var (const char* Varname)
/*
PURPOSE: To get one of the integer (short) ACAD variables.
*/
{
    struct resbuf rb ;

    if (ads_getvar (Varname,&rb) == RTNORM) {
```

```
            if (rb.restype == RTSHORT) {
                return (rb.resval.rint) ;
            }
        }

    ads_printf ("\nWARNING, GIV, could not get %s",Varname) ;

    return (0) ; // Return something sensible at least
}


ads_real Get_Real_Var (const char* Varname)
/*
PURPOSE: To get one of the real ACAD system variables.
*/
{
    struct resbuf rb ;

    if (ads_getvar (Varname,&rb) == RTNORM) {
        if (rb.restype == RTREAL) {
            return (rb.resval.rreal) ;
        }
    }

    ads_printf ("\nWARNING, in GRV, could not get %s",Varname) ;

    return (0.0) ; // Return something sensible
}

void Set_Real_Var (const char* Varname, const ads_real Value)
/*
PURPOSE: To set one of the real ACAD variables.
*/
{
    struct resbuf rb ;

    rb.restype      = RTREAL ;
    rb.resval.rreal = Value ;
    if (ads_setvar (Varname,&rb) != RTNORM) {
        ads_printf ("\nWARNING in SRV(%s,%6.3f), could"
                    " not setvar",Varname,Value) ;
    }
}


void Set_String_Var (const char* Varname, const char* Value)
/*
PURPOSE: To set one of the string ACAD variables.
Note that here the result buffer is a local variable which
```

```
will dissappear when this function ends. The pointer to
the string however has to be destroyed (freed) explicitly
because it was mallocced explicitly.
*/
{
    struct resbuf rb ;
    rb.restype = RTSTR ;
    rb.rbnext  = NULL ;

    rb.resval.rstring = malloc (MAX_CHARS) ;

    if (rb.resval.rstring == NULL) {
        ads_printf ("ERROR,SSV(%s,%s) could not malloc",
                    Varname,Value) ;
        return ;
    }

    if (strlen (Value) >= MAX_CHARS) {
        ads_printf (" WARNING,SSV(%s,%s) Value string"
                    " too long.",Varname,Value) ;
        return ;
    }

    (void)strcpy (rb.resval.rstring,Value) ;

    if (ads_setvar (Varname,&rb) != RTNORM) {
        ads_printf (" WARNING,SSV(%s,%s), could not setvar",
                    Varname,Value) ;
    }

    free (rb.resval.rstring) ;
}

void Get_String_Var (const char* Varname, char* Value)
/*
PURPOSE: To set one of the integer (short) ACAD variables.
NOTE: It is very important the Value has enough space for
      the string to copy
*/
{
    struct resbuf rb ;
    int Ok ;

    Ok = FALSE ;

    if (ads_getvar (Varname,&rb) == RTNORM) {
        if (rb.restype == RTSTR) {
            if (strlen (rb.resval.rstring) < MAX_CHARS) {
                (void)strcpy (Value,rb.resval.rstring) ;
```

```
                    Ok = TRUE ;
                }
                free (rb.resval.rstring) ;
            }
        }

    if (!Ok) {
        ads_printf ("\nWARNING, in GSV, could not get %s.",
                    Varname) ;
        Value[0] = (char)0 ;
    }
}

void Get_Point_Var (const char* Varname, ads_point Value)
/*
PURPOSE: To return a Var which is a 3D point.
*/
{
    struct resbuf rb ;
    int Ok ;

    Ok = FALSE ;

    if (ads_getvar (Varname,&rb) == RTNORM) {
        if ((rb.restype == RT3DPOINT)||(rb.restype == RTPOINT)) {
            ads_point_set (rb.resval.rpoint,Value) ;
            Ok = TRUE ;
        }
    }

    if (!Ok) {
        // Report the error and put something sensible in Value
        int i ;
        ads_printf ("\nWARNING, in GPV, could not get %s",
                    Varname) ;
        for (i = X ; i <= Z ; i++) {
            Value[i] = 0.0 ;
        }
    }
}
//                 -- End of LST__5_2.C --


//////////////////////////////////////////////////////////////
// LST__5_3.C
//      Illustrating how to get layer data and how to scan
//      through the blocks table.
```

```c
#include "LST__5_1.H"

#define MAX_CHARS 255

int test_func (void)
{
    struct  resbuf* Lrb,*rb ;
    short   Flags ;
    char    Layer [MAX_CHARS] ;
    char    Table [MAX_CHARS] ;
    int     Res,Colour ;

    // Get a string, 0 means no spaces allowd
    Res = ads_getstring (0,"\nInput a layername:",Layer) ;
    if (Res != RTNORM) {
        return (Tidy_End(RTNORM)) ;
    }

    // Search in the LAYER table for Layer
    Lrb = ads_tblsearch ("LAYER",Layer,0) ;
    if (Lrb == NULL) {
        // Means the table entry does not exist
        ads_printf ("\nLayer <%s> not found.", Layer) ;
        return (Tidy_End(RTNORM)) ;
    }

    // Scan over the result buffer list which contains
    // data about the layer found in the table
    rb = Lrb ;
    while (rb != NULL) {
        switch (rb->restype) {
            case LAYER_FLAGS_CODE:
                Flags = rb->resval.rint ;
                ads_printf ("\nLayer flags are %x",Flags) ;
                break ;
            case NAME_CODE:
                ads_printf ("\nLayer name is <%s>",
                            rb->resval.rstring) ;
                break ;
            case COLOUR_CODE:
                Colour = rb->resval.rint ;
                if (Colour < 0) {
                    // Negative color means that the
                    // layer is OFF
                    ads_printf ("\nThe layer is OFF,"
                                " and has colour %d",
                                -Colour) ;
                } else {
                    ads_printf ("\nThe layer is ON",
```

```
                                " and has colour %d",
                                Colour) ;
                }
                break ;
            case LTYPE_CODE : // Linetype for this layer
                ads_printf ("\nThe linetype of this"
                            " layer is <%s>",
                            rb->resval.rstring) ;
                break ;
        }
        rb = rb->rbnext ; // Go on to next result buffer
    }

    (void)ads_relrb (Lrb) ; // Release RAM of result buffer

    // Summarise data found in Flags
    if (Flags & LOCKED) {
        ads_printf ("\nThe layer is locked") ;
    }
    if (Flags & FROZEN) {
        ads_printf ("\nThe layer is frozen") ;
    }

    /*
     * Now ask the user to name a table he would like to
     * scan through
     */

    // Define the keywords which are valid as table names
    ads_initget (RSG_NONULL,"LTYPE STYLE UCS VPORT VIEW BLOCK"
                            " DIMSTYLE LAYER APPID") ;
    Res = ads_getstring (NULL,"\nWhich table "
                "(LTYPE STYLE UCS VPORT VIEW BLOCK "
                "DIMSTYLE LAYER APPID) ?", Table) ;
    if (Res == RTCAN) {
        // User hit ESCAPE or Contrl-C
        return (Tidy_End(RTNORM)) ;
    } else if (Res == RTKWORD) {
        // The user has typed in a keyword
        if (ads_getinput (Table) == RTNORM) {
            // The keyword was entered normally and is valid
        } else {
            // Error getting the keyword
            return (Tidy_End(RTNORM)) ;
        }
    }

    // The keyword is in "Table", start the scan of that table
    Lrb = ads_tblnext (Table,1) ; // 1 = rewind to start
```

```
    while (Lrb != NULL) {
        // Search result buffer chain for the name of entry
        for (rb = Lrb ; rb != NULL ; rb = rb->rbnext) {
            if (rb->restype == NAME_CODE) {
                ads_printf ("\nFound an entry for <%s>",
                        rb->resval.rstring) ;
            }
        }

        (void)ads_relrb (Lrb) ; // Free the ram of the resbuf

        Lrb = ads_tblnext (Table,0) ;  // 0 means get next
                                       // entry in table
    }

    // When you get here Lrb is already NULL so no
    // need to release it with ads_relrb.

    return (Tidy_End (RTNORM)) ;
}

//                  -- End of LST__5_3.C --
```

Accessing the AutoCAD
database with ADS

6

6.1 Introduction

This chapter shows you how to access the AutoCAD database, how to obtain entity data, how to prompt the user to select entities and how to create and modify entities. I also explain the use of filters with the `ads_ssget()` function, which are useful for selectively selecting entities of a certain type, color or layer.

As you read this chapter you should keep in mind the representation of the AutoCAD database given in Figure 6.1. This shows a drawing file containing four entities. The details of each entity are stored in the result buffer lists attached to the entity name. Think of result buffer lists as chains of data dangling from entity names.

6.2 Scanning the drawing database, `ads_entnext()` and `ads_entget()`

LST__6_1.C is an example of how to get information on all the entities in the drawing. It scans the database using the ADS function `ads_entnext()` which takes as input the `ads_name` of the "current" entity and returns the `ads_name` of the "next" entity. If the first parameter is NULL then `ads_entnext()` gets the first entity in the database, as you can see in the first call. In Figure 6.1 it could be explained by saying that we scan the list of four entities starting at the far left going to the far right. `ads_entnext()` is the function which moves us from one `ads_name` to the next. As will be explained later `ads_entget()` is the function which gives us the result buffer list we see hanging from each `ads_name`.

A bit of explanation about entity names, which are of type ads_name, they uniquely identify every object currently in the database, and even those which have been deleted in this session. The important words in the previous sentence are "currently" and "this session". An entity will almost always have a different entity name every session, so you should not store these entity names in a file (for example), hoping that when AutoCAD next runs that blue circle will have

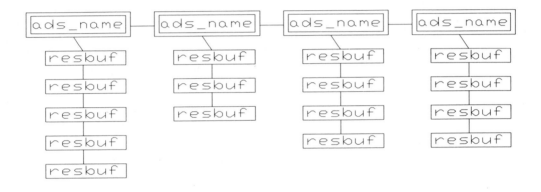

Figure 6.1 A drawing file with four entities

the same ads_name as in the previous session. It appears, though it is nowhere documented, that entity names are sequential; so the latest entity added will have an entity name greater than the previous entity created. ads_name is currently defined as an array of two longs. Back to the program.

If all goes well with obtaining the first entity we go into a while loop which repeatedly calls ads_entnext() with the first parameter being the "current" entity, returning with the "next" entity in the second parameter.

The top of the while loop has a call to ads_entget() (not to be confused with the ads_getxxx() functions explained in Chapter 4). ads_entget() takes as a parameter an ads_name of an entity and returns the result buffer list of that entity. If the ads_name is not valid it returns NULL. This should never happen if you use ADS functions to get hold of the ads_names correctly.

Next we use a function described in Chapter 5, Print_Rb_List(), to print out the result buffer list, release the result buffer list and then pause so that the user can read what was printed.

The ADS function `ads_name_set()` is actually a macro defined in ADS.H, it copies the first ads_name to the second ads_name. Remember that ads_names are arrays of longs so you cannot simply use "a_name = b_name". In LST__6_1.C it is used to put `This` ads_name into `Prev` ads_name. `Prev` is then used in `ads_entnext` to get the next entity in the database, whose ads_name is placed in `This`.

`ads_entnext()` will return `RTNORM` if the next entity was found OK, and `RTERROR` if it was not. Normally `RTERROR` is returned because we have reached the end of the database. We check that this is the case by checking the ERRNO variable if `ads_entnext()` returns `RTERROR`. `Get_Int_Var()` was defined in LST__5_2.C. You should include OL_ERRNO.H if you want to use the symbolic names for error codes as we do here. If the error code is OL_EEOEF (end of entity file) then all is OK.

You should run this application on a drawing with a variety of entities to get an idea of how much and what sort of data is stored for each entity.

You need to understand the important distinction to make between `ads_name` and `struct resbuf`. An `ads_name` identifies uniquely an entity (a line or a block insert or a circle and so on), all entities have different ads_names. No two lines will have the same ads_name. A result buffer on the other hand is data *about* the entity, its layer, coordinates and so on. `ads_entget()` uses an ads_name of an entity to get hold of its internal data.

Strangely enough, when using `ads_entnext()`, the database is returned in reverse order to how it was created. For example if you open a new drawing and draw a line, then a circle, and lastly a polyline, `ads_entnext()` will return these entities in the order: polyline, circle, line. This is not a documented feature, and it may change in future releases.

6.3 `ads_ssget()`

6.3.1 An overview of `ads_ssget()`

The previous example showed how to get hold of *all* the entities in the database, but maybe you want the user to choose some entities which you will then process with your ADS application, or you want to select only entities with certain characteristics. This is called "getting a selection set", i.e. a set of entities selected by the user, and the function to use is `ads_ssget()`.

`ads_ssget()` is very flexible, and as a consequence it has a huge combinational variety of input parameters. Here is the function prototype of `ads_ssget()`:

```
int ads_ssget (const char* str, const void* pt1,
               const ads_point pt2,
               const struct resbuf* filter,
               ads_name ss);
```

The second parameter, pt1, is a void pointer because it will be a general NULL pointer, or an ads_point or result buffer list. Void pointers can point to any type of variable. Which of these three depends on the str parameter. pt2 is used when we want to make a selection by using a window; it is the second corner of the window. The first corner is pt1. The filter parameter will be either NULL or a result buffer list used to filter the selection set. The selection set is returned in ss as an ads_name.

You should free the selection set after use by calling ads_ssfree(). As with failure to release result buffers with ads_relrb(), failing to release selection sets with ads_ssfree() will cause your application to slowly grind to a halt as the memory of the computer is gradually eaten up! You should free the selection set with ads_ssfree() even if it is an empty set with zero items in it.

The str parameter can be one of the following:

- NULL: If all the other parameters (except ads_name) are NULL and there is a valid PICKFIRST set then the name of the selection set placed in ss is that PICKFIRST set. If there is not a valid PICKFIRST set the AutoCAD prompts the user with its normal "Select entities" prompt. For more information on the PICKFIRST variable see Chapter 5 section 5.3.1. See section 6.3.2 for more details and an example.

- "I": Implied selection; a PICKFIRST selection set is returned in ss if it exists, otherwise ads_ssget() returns RTERROR.

- "C": Crossing selection; pt1 and pt2 specify the corners of a crossing window, any entities within or touching the borders of the window will be selected. pt1 in this case will be an to ads_point.

- "CP": Crossing Polygon selection; pt1 will point to a result buffer list of ads_point which define the polygon and pt2 *must* be NULL. Any entities within or crossing the polygon will be included in the selection set. You do not need to close the polygon explicitly, ads_ssget() will do that.

- "F": Fence selection; pt1 is a result buffer list of points defining the fence and pt2 *must* be NULL. A fence is a polyline used to select all the entities it crosses. There is no idea of inside and outside the fence, only entities which the fence touches are selected.

- "L": Last, selects the last entity created. You would do better to use ads_entlast() as described in Chapter 5, section 5.2. The pt1 and pt2 must be NULL.

- "P": Previous selection set. If a previous selection set exists this will be returned in ss.

- "W": Window selection set; pt1 and pt2 are ads_points which specify the corners of the window.

- "WP": Window Polygon selection; pt1 is a list of points that define the polygon, all entities entirely inside the polygon are selected, and pt2 must be NULL. You do not need to close the polygon explicitly, ads_ssget() will do that.

- "X": Filter selection only. See section 6.3.3 for more details and an example of use.

I have found that in practice the `str == NULL` (letting the user select whatever he wants) and `str == "X"` (not asking the user at all but letting `ads_ssget()` perform a filtering operation on the database) modes are most commonly used. Another useful way of using `ads_ssget()` is to allow the user to select what he wants (`str == NULL`), but then filtering the selection by passing the appropriate result buffer list to ent mask.

The other modes are useful to know about as a user (when prompted by AutoCAD to select some objects), but for a programmer they are rather awkward.

6.3.2 Prompting the user for entities

LST__6_2.C shows how to use `ads_ssget()` to prompt the user to select some entities and then to print out data about the entities he has selected.

All the parameters of the call to `ads_ssget()` are `NULL`, apart from `Set`, where the result of the selection is put. The first `NULL` means that the user will see the standard AutoCAD prompt "Select entities:" and will be able to select the entities that he is interested in using any of the normal AutoCAD methods, crossing, window, fence, picking and so on.

If `ads_ssget()` returns `RTNORM` then we know that the user has selected at least one entity.

`ads_sslength (Set, &Len)` tells us how many entities are in the set passed to it. Note that the second parameter Len is a long and its address is passed. In Release 13 16 bit compilers are no longer supported and there is no difference between the number of bits in a long and an int. Your compiler may complain, however, if you pass an int address rather than a long address. (If you are using (for example) the Borland 16 bit compiler and compiling for AutoCAD 12 it is required that you pass a long rather than an int.)

The for loop goes over every `ads_name` in the selection set by calling `ads_ssname (Set, n, E_Name)`, the *nth* `ads_name` in the selection set is placed in E_Name. Then we use `ads_entget()` to get the result buffer of the entity, which is subsequently printed. The function ends by freeing the selection set with `ads_ssfree()`.

You should test this function with a drawing full of different sorts of entities on different layers and with different colors.

6.3.3 Filtering the database to produce a selection set

LST__6_3.C shows how to scan the database using `ads_ssget()` and a filter in the form of a result buffer list.

The function starts with the construction of the result buffer list, two result buffers, one specifying the layer "TECHNE" and the other specifying the entity type "CIRCLE". This list acts as a filter which will select CIRCLEs on the TECHNE layer and nothing else. Note how rbnext of `Layer_Rb` points to `Et_Rb`, and that rbnext of `Et_Rb` is `NULL`, signifying the end of the list. The layer then entity order is not important, it could just as well have been entity layer.

There is no need to free this result buffer list because it was not constructed by ADS or `malloc()`. All the space used is on the local stack of the function `test_func()` and so will be released automatically when the function ends.

Next we call `ads_ssget()` with the "X" parameter, which as explained above does not prompt the user for anything and simply puts all entities which correspond to the filter list into the selection set.

The program prints out how many entities it found corresponding to the filter and then frees the selection set with `ads_ssfree()`.

Obviously this is not a very useful function, but it illustrates how in a real application you could be selecting, for example, entities on the "PLUMBING" layer or "POLYLINE" entities on the "MAPPING" layer and so on. There are comments and hints in the listing itself about how to ignore the layer of the objects which are selected.

To test LST__6_3.C you should create a drawing with various entities on various layers, including CIRCLEs on the TECHNE layer.

6.3.4 Filtering the user's selection set

LST__6_4.C shows how to use `ads_ssget()` to prompt the user for a selection set, discarding, however, any entities which do not fit your filter. It is identical to LST__6_3.C in the construction of the result buffer filter list, but the call to `ads_ssget()` is different. The first parameter is `NULL`, so the user is prompted, and the filter parameter is not `NULL`, so a filter is applied to what the user selects.

This sort of selection is very helpful to the user in crowded drawings where it may be difficult to select only certain entities. It also helps the programmer in that he can be certain that only entities of a certain type can be selected.

On the AutoCAD graphics screen, when the user selects the entities, only those which satisfy the filter list will be highlighted, giving the user immediate feedback about which entities are valid.

Again we get the length of the selection set using `ads_sslength()` and we print how many of the entities selected are acceptable to the filter.

The last part of the program is similar to LST__6_2.C where we for-loop over the selection set printing out details of the entities selected. The function ends by freeing the selection set, as always.

You should use the same sort of drawing to test this function as you did in the previous section.

The PICKFIRST and PICKADD variables control some other aspects of user selection of entities; see Appendix C.

6.3.5 `ads_buildlist()` and filters with boolean operators

The filters that we have seen so far are implicitly "AND" combinations of conditions. In the previous example the filter was "if the entity is on layer TECHNE AND it is a CIRCLE then accept it". If you want to select entities that are CIRCLEs or LINEs you can use conditional filtering. An example is given in LST__6_5.C.

The listing starts with a call to `ads_buildlist()` which is an ADS function used to dynamically create result buffer lists. The function prototype of it is:

```
struct resbuf* ads_buildlist(int rtype, ...);
```

As you can see from the ellipsis (...) it takes a variable length argument list. You give it a pair of values and the function constructs the result buffer for that pair. In LST__6_5.C 5 pairs are passed to it and the end of the list is marked with RTNONE, very similar to the `ads_command()` format. The result buffer list is created and the head of the list is returned to rb.

The list created can be read as follows: (On TECHNE layer AND (Is a line OR is a Circle)). All lines and circle on the TECHNE layer will be selected. The OR combination (bracketing) is started with "<OR" and is ended, closed, with the "OR>".

Here is a complete list of conditional operators you can use in selection set lists:

- "<AND" followed by one or more operands, closed with "AND>".
- "<OR" followed by one of more operands, closed with "OR>".
- "<XOR" followed by two operands, closed with "XOR>".
- "<NOT" followed by one operand, closed with "NOT>".

It is also possible to nest the conditions, for example ((LAYER1 AND CIRCLE) OR (LAYER2 AND LINE)).

The use of `ads_buildlist()` is of course not limited to `ads_ssget()` filter list construction, it should be used when a long result buffer list has to be constructed. An example of the use of `ads_buildlist()` to create a block is given in listing LST__8_2.C in Chapter 8. The list is created dynamically and after use should be freed by a call to `ads_relrb()`.

An awkward thing about `ads_buildlist()` is that it cannot accept ENTITY_NAME_CODE as a type specifier (the first value of each pair). This is because the DXF code for ENTITY_NAME_CODE is 0, and `ads_buildlist()` takes that as meaning "end of the list". For this reason Autodesk have defined RTDXF0, which you should use when you would normally have used a *real* DXF code 0. In LST__6_5.C it is used twice as the name code for "CIRCLE" and "LINE".

Having constructed the list there is a call to `ads_ssget()`, the user is prompted to select some entities. Since list construction is error prone (you may forget to close an "<AND" for example, or you may have forgotten to use RTDXF0 instead of ENTITY_NAME_CODE) if an error occurs the ERRNO is printed. If ERRNO is 0 then probably the user did not select any entities which matched the filter list.

Finally the number of entities selected is printed and both the filter result buffer list and the selection set are freed.

A drawing containing CIRCLEs and LINEs on and off the TECHNE layer should be used to test this function.

Two functions not covered in this Chapter, but which you should know about, are `ads_ssadd()` and `ads_ssdel()`, see Appendix B.

6.4 Creating, modifying and deleting entities

6.4.1 Creating entities with `ads_entmake()`

While it is perfectly possible to create entities by using the `ads_command()` function a more direct way is with `ads_entmake()`. The function prototype is

```
int ads_entmake (const struct resbuf* Ent);
```

The `Ent` is a result buffer list containing a description of an entity; usually this list is created using `ads_buildlist()`.

In LST__6_6.C ten circles are created of different colors in different positions inside a for-loop. At the top of the loop `Center` is changed according to the loop index x, and `ads_buildlist()` is called to create the result buffer list of the circle we want to create. The color of the circle also depends on x. If all goes well we call `ads_entmake()` with the result buffer to add the circle to the database. If *that* succeeds then the result buffer is freed and we go back to the top of the for-loop with another value of x.

There are some restrictions on what `ads_entmake()` can do.

- The first or second buffer in the list *must* contain the entity type, in the example it is the RTDXF0, "CIRCLE" pair. It is usually the first buffer.
- Any text styles, linetypes, shapes or blocks in the list must be present in the drawing before calling `ads_entmake()`. Undefined layers *are* accepted and will be created "on the fly". You *can* also specify frozen layers, the object will appear when the layer is unfrozen.
- `ads_entmake()` cannot create Viewport, Xref, Xdef or Xdep entities.
- `ads_entmake()` cannot specify the entity's handle (DXF groups 5 and 105).
- `ads_entmake()` ignores fields associated with the "object extension dictionary" (An ARX version of extended data, see Chapter 17).

If `ads_entmake()` fails it will return `RTREJ` instead of `RTNORM`. If this happens you should print the ERRNO variable (and Appendix 5 of this book) to see the reason for the rejection, as shown in LST__6_6.C. Apparently correct result buffer lists will fail if you specify a layer which does not exist in the drawing for example.

`ads_entmake()` can be used to create complex entities like polylines and block definitions. Complex entities have what are known as sub-entities within them, for example a polyline's sub-entities are vertices. The creation of blocks using `ads_entmake()` is covered in Chapter 8, section 8.6.

6.4.2 Modifying existing entities with `ads_entmod()`

If there are some entities which already exist in the drawing which you want to change, the diameter of circles on the "PLUMBING" layer for example, then you should use `ads_entmod()`. While `ads_entmake()` can be replaced by a series of `ads_command()` calls (which you may find more natural and obvious though slower in execution) there is no real alternative to `ads_entmod()`.

LST__6_7.C is an example of the use of `ads_entmod()`, allowing the user to select some CIRCLEs and then changing the radius of them. The first part of the function uses `ads_ssget()` to ask the user to select some circles. The `Et_Rb` ensures that only circles are placed in the selection set.

The number of circles found is printed and a for-loop goes over every entity in the selection set. We get the name of the entity, then we get the result buffer describing that entity, the radius buffer in the result buffer list is changed and we hand it back to the AutoCAD database using `ads_entmod()`. If you had printed out the result buffer list (either before or after the change) you would find an entry of the entity name. As explained above, this `ads_name` uniquely identifies that entity, and tells AutoCAD which entity is being modified.

The function `Change_Radius()` is not complicated. It simply goes over the result buffer handed to it, and when it finds the radius entry (DXF code 40, symbolic name in LST__5_1.H RADIUS_CODE) it changes the value to `New_Radius`. Note that we need not check that the entity is a CIRCLE because we have used a CIRCLE-filtered selection set. In other circumstances you may not be able to assume that the entity is a CIRCLE, and if that is so 40 will not correspond to radius but to some other attribute.

6.4.3 Deleting and undeleting entities with `ads_entdel()`

The function to delete entities from the database is `ads_entdel()`, and has the following function prototype:

```
int ads_entdel (const ads_name Ent);
```

If Ent is a valid entity then the entity is removed from the database and the function returns RTNORM. If an error occurs then RTERROR is returned and you should look at the ERRNO variable to see what went wrong.

You can use ads_entdel() to *undelete* an entity, but this only works during the current drawing session, partly because entity names change from drawing session to drawing session. So a second call to ads_entdel() will restore the entity that you deleted with the first call.

This function works only on main entities. Attributes and polyline vertices cannot be deleted independently from their parents entities. (You can use ads_command(), or ads_cmd(), with the commands ATTEDIT or PEDIT to do that.)

You can also use ads_entmod() to create a redefined copy of the original entity.

You cannot pass symbol tables and symbol table entries to ads_entdel().

6.5 Saving and restoring the user's settings

The user often sets the object snap, snap spacing, grid visibility, current layer, current colour and so on. You would like your program to be able to change these variables as it requires, but restoring them to the original settings when it has finished. A pair of functions to do this are given in LST__6_8.C, and the function prototypes are:

```
void Save_User_State (void) ;
void Restore_User_State (void) ;
```

You should call the first before your program starts messing around with AutoCAD variables, and you should call the second when it has finished. The first also sets the CMDECHO variable to zero for you, and the second restores it to 1.

The listings shows fourteen variables which I have found it most useful to save, though you can add and remove whatever variables you want to the list as long as you change the define of N_USER_VARS appropriately.

The simple test() function draws 20 randomly coloured lines, which have the start point in the center of the unit square, and the end point at a random place within the unit square. Before drawing the lines I save the user state, and after drawing them I restore the user state. If I had not done this then the current entity colour, CECOLOR, after the application had run would not have been restored to what it was just before the run.

It is useful to turn the grid and UCS icon off when drawing with ads_command() in three dimensions. This for two reasons:

- it is annoying for the user to see the UCS icon (and maybe the grid) bouncing around the screen as you shift the coordinate system

- drawing the UCS icon and the grid slows down the program, in much the same way as echoing commands does.

One other point about the two functions. Their use should be balanced, but in a very complicated program it is not always possible to know whether the user state has already been saved (or restored) or not. For this reason there is a flag Saved which is used to make sure that the calls are balanced. If you call Save_User_State() twice in a row, only the first will actually do something. The same argument applies to calls to Restore_User_State().

6.6 Listings .

```c
/////////////////////////////////////////////////////////////
// LST__6_1.C
//      Illustrating how to get all the objects in the
//      AutoCAD drawing database.

#include "LST__5_1.H"
#include <OL_ERRNO.H>   // Symbolic names for error codes

int test_func (void)
{
    int             Res,Err_No ;
    struct resbuf*  rb ;
    ads_name        This,Prev ;
    char            Dummy [MAX_CHARS] ;

    // Get the first entity in the database
    Res = ads_entnext (NULL,This) ;
    if (Res != RTNORM) {
        ads_printf ("\nads_entnext failed on first call") ;
        return (Tidy_End(RTNORM)) ;
    }

    while (Res == RTNORM) {
        rb = ads_entget (This) ;
        if (rb == NULL) {
            ads_printf ("\nCannot get entity data,"
                        " ads_entget failed") ;
            return (Tidy_End(RTNORM)) ;
        }
        Print_Rb_List (rb) ;
        Res = ads_relrb (rb) ; // Release memory
        if (Res != RTNORM) {
            ads_printf ("\nCannot free result buffer") ;
            return (Tidy_End(RTNORM)) ;
```

```
        }

        // Force a pause so the user can read the data printed
        (void)ads_getstring (0,"\nENTER to continue",Dummy) ;

        ads_name_set (This,Prev) ;       // This becomes Prev
        Res = ads_entnext (Prev,This) ;  // Put next entity
                              // which follows Prev into This
        // Res will become RTNORM or RTERROR,
        // RTERROR usually means "end of database", check
        // that the expected error has occurred
        if (Res != RTNORM) {
            if ((Err_No = Get_Int_Var("ERRNO")) != OL_EEOEF) {
                // OL_EEOEF means end of entity data, if the
                // error number is not this then something
                // very strange has happened
                ads_printf ("\nVery strange error: %d",Err_No);
            }
        }
    }
    return (Tidy_End(RTNORM)) ;
}
//                -- End of LST__6_1.C --

///////////////////////////////////////////////////////////////
// LST__6_2.C
//      Illustrating how to prompt the user to select some
//      objects and then printing out data about them.

int test_func (void)
{
    struct resbuf* rb ;
    int             Res ;
    long            Len,n ;
    ads_name        Set,E_Name ;
    char            Dummy[MAX_CHARS] ;

    // Let the user choose whatever he wants in whatver
    // way he wants...
    Res = ads_ssget (NULL,NULL,NULL,NULL,Set) ;
    if (Res != RTNORM) {
        return (Tidy_End(RTNORM)) ;
    }

    // Get the number of objects selected. Note that
    // the address of Len is passed (&Len)
    (void)ads_sslength (Set,&Len) ;

    ads_printf ("\nYou have selected %d objects",Len) ;
```

```
        for (n = 0 ; n < Len ; n++) {
            // Get the nth ads_name of the selection set, the
            // result is placed in E_Name.
            Res = ads_ssname (Set,n,E_Name) ;
            if (Res != RTNORM) {
                ads_printf ("\nAn error occurred with ads_ssname");
                (void)ads_ssfree (Set) ; // Free ram of Set
                return (Tidy_End(RTNORM)) ;
            }

            // Print out the data of the nth entity
            rb = ads_entget (E_Name) ;
            if (rb == NULL) {
                ads_printf ("\nAn error has occurred"
                            " with ads_entget") ;
                (void)ads_ssfree (Set) ; // Free ram of Set
                return (Tidy_End(RTNORM)) ;
            }
            Print_Rb_List (rb) ;

            // Pause to let user see what was selected
            (void)ads_getstring (0,"\nHit any key"
                                    " to continue",Dummy) ;
        }
        (void)ads_ssfree (Set) ; // Free ram of the set

        return (Tidy_End(RTNORM)) ;
}
//                  -- End of LST__6_2.C --


//////////////////////////////////////////////////////////
// LST_6_3.C
//        Illustrating how to get all the objects in the
//        database which satisfy the criteria of a filter
//        made of result buffers. If you want to ignore the
//        layer of the objects then modify this code to
//        have a filter consisting of only one result
//        buffer by taking out all references to Layer_Rb
//        and Layer_Str

int test_func (void)
{
    char           Layer_Str[MAX_CHARS],Et_Str[MAX_CHARS] ;
    struct resbuf  Layer_Rb ; // Will become Layer filter
    struct resbuf  Et_Rb ; // Will become Entity type filter
    int            Res ;
    long           Len ;
    ads_name       Set ;
```

```
    // Construct the result buffer which contains
    // the layer name TECHNE
    (void)strcpy (Layer_Str,"TECHNE") ;
    Layer_Rb.restype        = LAYER_NAME_CODE ;
    Layer_Rb.resval.rstring = Layer_Str ;
    Layer_Rb.rbnext         = &Et_Rb ; // Connect to Et_Rb

    // Construct the result buffer which contains
    // the entity type "CIRCLE"
    (void)strcpy (Et_Str,"CIRCLE") ;
    Et_Rb.restype        = ENTITY_TYPE_CODE ;
    Et_Rb.resval.rstring = Et_Str ;
    Et_Rb.rbnext         = NULL ; // Mark end of rb list

    // X means use filter only, no prompt to the user. If you
    // want to ignore the Layer of the circles simply pass in
    // Circle_Rb here instead of Layer_Rb, not forgetting
    // the "&"!!!
    Res = ads_ssget ("X",NULL,NULL,&Layer_Rb,Set) ;

    if (Res != RTNORM) {
        ads_printf ("\nNo TECHNE CIRCLES found in the DWG.") ;
        return (Tidy_End (RTNORM)) ;
    }

    (void)ads_sslength (Set,&Len) ;

    ads_printf ("\n%d TECHNE CIRCLES found in the DWG",Len) ;

    // At this point you know how many entities are in the set
    // and can use a for-loop and ads_ssname function to
    // interrogate or change the entities

    (void)ads_ssfree (Set) ; // Free ram of the set

    return (Tidy_End(RTNORM)) ;
}

//          -- End of LST__6_3.C --

/////////////////////////////////////////////////////////////
// LST__6_4.C
//      Illustrating how to get the user to select some
//      objects, filtering out the ones you are not
//      interested in, all in one fell swoop.

int test_func (void)
{
```

```
char              Layer_Str[MAX_CHARS],Et_Str[MAX_CHARS] ;
struct resbuf     Layer_Rb,Et_Rb ; // Filters
struct resbuf*    rb ;
int               Res ;
long              Len,n ;
ads_name          Set,E_Name ;
char              Dummy[MAX_CHARS] ;

(void)strcpy (Layer_Str,"TECHNE") ;
Layer_Rb.restype        = LAYER_NAME_CODE ;
Layer_Rb.resval.rstring = Layer_Str ;
Layer_Rb.rbnext         = &Et_Rb ;

(void)strcpy (Et_Str,"CIRCLE") ;
Et_Rb.restype        = ENTITY_TYPE_CODE ;
Et_Rb.resval.rstring = Et_Str ;
Et_Rb.rbnext         = NULL ;

Res = ads_ssget (NULL,NULL,NULL,&Layer_Rb,Set) ;

if (Res != RTNORM) {
    return (Tidy_End (RTNORM)) ;
}

(void)ads_sslength (Set,&Len) ;

ads_printf ("\nOf the objects you have selected %d of"
            " them have passed the ssget filter.",Len) ;

for (n = 0 ; n < Len ; n++) {
    // Get the nth ads_name of the selection set, the
    // result is placed in E_Name.
    (void)ads_ssname (Set,n,E_Name) ;

    // Print out the data of the nth entity
    rb = ads_entget (E_Name) ;
    Print_Rb_List (rb) ;

    (void)ads_getstring (0,"\nENTER to continue",Dummy) ;
}

(void)ads_ssfree (Set) ; // Free ram of the set

return (Tidy_End(RTNORM)) ;
}
//                -- End of LST__6_4.C --

/////////////////////////////////////////////////////
// LST__6_5.C
```

```
//         Illustrating construction of boolean filter lists
//         for use in ads_ssget calls.

int test_func (void)
{
    struct resbuf* rb ; // Will be resbuf with boolean filters
    int             Res ;
    long            Len ;
    ads_name        Set ;

    // Create a result buffer list which will be a filter for
    // the call to ads_ssget
    rb = ads_buildlist (LAYER_NAME_CODE,"TECHNE",
                        COND_OP_CODE,"<OR",
                        RTDXF0,"CIRCLE", // Can't use 0 in call
                        RTDXF0,"LINE",   // to ads_buildlist
                        COND_OP_CODE,"OR>",
                        RTNONE) ;
    if (rb == NULL) {
        ads_printf ("\nError with ads_buildlist") ;
        return (Tidy_End(RTNORM)) ;
    }

    Res = ads_ssget (NULL,NULL,NULL,rb,Set) ;

    if (Res != RTNORM) {
        ads_printf ("\nNo matching objects found, Res = %d"
                    " ERRNO=%d",Res,Get_Int_Var("ERRNO")) ;
        return (Tidy_End (RTNORM)) ;
    }

    (void)ads_sslength (Set,&Len) ;

    ads_printf ("\nOf the objects you tried to select %d"
                " of them passed the ssget filter.",Len) ;

    (void)ads_ssfree (Set) ;
    (void)ads_relrb (rb) ; // Because made with ads_buildlist

    return (Tidy_End(RTNORM)) ;
}
//              -- End of LST__6_5.C --

/////////////////////////////////////////////////////////
// LST__6_6.C
//      Illustrating the use of ads_entmake to create
//      entities in the AutoCAD database

int test_func (void)
```

```c
{
    struct resbuf* rb ;
    ads_point       Center;
    int             Res,x ;
    ads_real        Radius ;

    Center[Z] = 0.0 ; // Still in 2d eh?

    for (x = 0 ; x < 10 ; x++) {

        Center[X] = x ;
        Center[Y] = x ;

        // Create a result buffer list which defines a circle
        rb = ads_buildlist (RTDXF0, "CIRCLE",
                            COLOUR_CODE, x,
                            CENTER_CODE, Center,
                            RADIUS_CODE, 1.0,
                            RTNONE) ;

        if (rb == NULL) {
            ads_printf ("\nads_buildlist failed.") ;
            return (Tidy_End(RTNORM)) ;
        }

        // Try to make the circle
        Res = ads_entmake(rb) ;
        if (Res != RTNORM) {
            ads_printf ("\nads_entmake failed,"
                        " Res=%d,ERRNO=%d",Res,
                        Get_Int_Var ("ERRNO"));
        }

        (void)ads_relrb (rb) ;
    }

    return (Tidy_End(RTNORM)) ;
}
//                      -- End of LST__6_6.C

//////////////////////////////////////////////////////////////
// LST__6_7.C
// Illustrating the use of ads_entmod to modify
// entities in the AutoCAD database

// Function prototype
void Change_Radius (struct resbuf* rb, ads_real New_Radius) ;

int test_func (void)
```

```
{
    char            Et_Str[MAX_CHARS] ;
    struct resbuf   Et_Rb ;
    struct resbuf*  rb ;
    int             Res ;
    long            Len,n ;
    ads_name        Set,E_Name ;

    (void)strcpy (Et_Str,"CIRCLE") ;
    Et_Rb.restype        = ENTITY_TYPE_CODE ;
    Et_Rb.resval.rstring = Et_Str ;
    Et_Rb.rbnext         = NULL ;

    // Ask the user to select entites, anything not a CIRLE
    // will automatically filtered out.
    Res = ads_ssget (NULL,NULL,NULL,&Et_Rb,Set) ;

    if (Res != RTNORM) {
        return (Tidy_End (RTNORM)) ;
    }

    (void)ads_sslength (Set,&Len) ;

    ads_printf ("\nFound %d circles.",Len) ;

    for (n = 0 ; n < Len ; n++) {
        // Get the nth ads_name
        (void)ads_ssname (Set,n,E_Name) ;

        // Get the data of the nth entity
        rb = ads_entget (E_Name) ;

        // Change the radius of the (assumed) CIRCLE
        Change_Radius (rb,2.0) ;

        // Update the database with new result buffer
        Res = ads_entmod (rb) ;

        if (Res != RTNORM) {
            ads_printf ("\nERROR,ads_entmod failed,"
                        " ERRNO=%d",Get_Int_Var("ERRNO")) ;
            ads_relrb (rb) ;
            ads_ssfree (Set) ;
            return (Tidy_End (RTNORM)) ;
        }
    }

    (void)ads_ssfree (Set) ; // Free ram of the set
```

```
        return (Tidy_End(RTNORM)) ;
}


void Change_Radius (struct resbuf* rb, ads_real New_Radius)
/*
PURPOSE: Takes a result buffer list assumed to be a CIRCLE
and changes the DXF code 40 to New_Radius. Note that if rb is
NOT a circle then DXF code 40 will not mean circle but
something else.
*/
{
    struct resbuf* Res_Buf ;

    Res_Buf = rb ;

    // Print out it's association list
    while (Res_Buf != NULL) {
        if (Res_Buf->restype == RADIUS_CODE) {
            Res_Buf->resval.rreal = New_Radius ;
            return ; // RADIUS_CODE, 40, found geddout quick
        }
        Res_Buf = Res_Buf->rbnext ;
        // RADIUS_CODE, 40, not yet found
    }
}
//                 -- End of LST__6_7.C --


/////////////////////////////////////////////////////////////
// LST__6_8.C
//      Showing a pair of functions for saving and restoring
//      the state of the AutoCAD variables while your
//      application is running.

void Save_User_State (void) ;
void Restore_User_State (void) ;

int test_func (void)
{
    short p ;
    char Colour[32] ;
    ads_point Pos ;

    Save_User_State () ;

    Pos[Z] = 0 ;

    // Draw 20 lines of random colours and angles
    for (p = 0 ; p < 20 ; p++) {
        Pos[X] = ((ads_real)(rand() & 0xFF)) / 256.0 ;
```

```
        Pos[Y] = ((ads_real)(rand() & 0xFF)) / 256.0 ;
        sprintf (Colour,"%d",(int)(rand() & 0x7) + 1) ;
        Set_String_Var ("CECOLOR",Colour) ;
        (void)ads_command (RTSTR,"_LINE",
                           RTSTR,"0.5,0.5,0",
                           RT3DPOINT,Pos,
                           RTSTR,"",
                           RTNONE) ;
    }

    Restore_User_State () ;

    return (Tidy_End (RTNORM)) ;
}



#define N_USER_VARS 14
#define INT_V  1
#define REAL_V 2
#define STR_V  3

typedef struct {
    char* Name ;
    short Type ;  //  Which of the following two fields to use
    union {
        short    Int ;
        ads_real Real ;
        char     Str[32] ;
    } Val ;
} User_Var_t ;

static User_Var_t User_Vars [N_USER_VARS] = {
    {"BLIPMODE",   INT_V, 0 },   {"SNAPMODE",   INT_V, 0 },
    {"OSMODE",     INT_V, 0 },   {"ORTHOMODE",  INT_V, 0 },
    {"UCSICON",    INT_V, 0 },   {"GRIDMODE",   INT_V, 0 },
    {"COORDS",     INT_V, 0 },   {"PDMODE",     INT_V, 0 },
    {"ANGDIR",     INT_V, 0 },   {"ANGBASE",    REAL_V,0 },
    {"PDSIZE",     REAL_V,0 },   {"CLAYER",     STR_V, 0 },
    {"LIMCHECK",   INT_V, 0 },   {"CECOLOR",    STR_V, 0 }} ;

static int Saved = FALSE ;

void Save_User_State (void)
{
    int v ;

    if (!Saved) {
        Set_Int_Var ("CMDECHO",0) ;
```

```
            for (v = 0 ; v < N_USER_VARS ; v++) {
                switch (User_Vars[v].Type) {
                    case INT_V :
                        User_Vars[v].Val.Int =
                            Get_Int_Var (User_Vars[v].Name) ;
                        break ;
                    case REAL_V :
                        User_Vars[v].Val.Real =
                            Get_Real_Var (User_Vars[v].Name);
                        break ;
                    case STR_V :
                        Get_String_Var (User_Vars[v].Name,
                                        User_Vars[v].Val.Str) ;
                        break ;
                }
            }
            Saved = TRUE ;
        }
}


void Restore_User_State (void)
/*
PURPOSE: To restore the state of ACAD when the user called me.
NOTES:    1) If we have not saved the user state then we restore
            nothing.
*/
{
    int v ;

    if (Saved) {
        for (v = 0 ; v < N_USER_VARS ; v++) {
            switch (User_Vars[v].Type) {
                case INT_V :
                    Set_Int_Var (User_Vars[v].Name,
                                User_Vars[v].Val.Int);
                    break ;
                case REAL_V :
                    Set_Real_Var (User_Vars[v].Name,
                                User_Vars[v].Val.Real);
                    break ;
                case STR_V :
                    Set_String_Var (User_Vars[v].Name,
                                    User_Vars[v].Val.Str);
                    break ;
            }
        }
        Saved = FALSE ;
```

```
        Set_Int_Var ("CMDECHO",1) ;
    }
}

//              -- End of LST__6_8.C --
```

ADS geometric utilities

7

7.1 Introduction

The chapter covers two and three-dimensional utilities provided by ADS and also useful functions for vector and matrix manipulation.

7.2 Finding distance, angle and intersection point

LST__7_1.C is an example of how to use ADS functions to find the relationship between two lines. It is very simple.

The function prompts for two points using `ads_getpoint()`, using the first point as the "base" of the second point, as explained in Chapter 4.

If two points are successfully obtained from the user the distance between the two points is calculated by `ads_distance (Point0, Point1)` and printed.

`ads_command()` is used to draw a line between the two points, and `ads_angle (Point0, Point1)` calculates the angle between the line and the X axis of the UCS. If the line is three-dimensional `ads_angle()` ignores the Z coordinates, in effect projecting the line onto the two-dimensional UCS. The angle is in *radians*. By the way, those of you using Microsoft should be aware that `ads_angle()` does not always work in Release 12.

Two more points are created by copying the original ones and changing the coordinates a little; these points are used to draw a second line.

`ads_inters()` is called to find the intersection point between two lines. The prototype this function is:

```
int ads_inters (const ads_point p1, const ads_point p2,
                const ads_point p3, const ads_point p4,
```

```
int    Teston, ads_point Result);
```

The first line is defined by the first two points, the second line by the second two points. The intersection between the two points is returned in Result. If there is an intersection then `ads_inters()` returns RTNORM. If `Teston == 0` then the lines are considered to be infinite in length and an intersection beyond the limits of the two lines is considered valid. If `Teston == 1` only if the two lines cross is an intersection considered valid. In LST__7_1.C we check for crossing of infinite lines.

If an intersection does occur between the two lines we print the coordinates of the intersection draws a point there. To be sure that the point will be visible we set the two point display mode variables PDMODE and PDSIZE. PDMODE 3 means that all points will be drawn as crosses, X. PDSIZE set to -5.0 means that the size of all points will be 5% of the viewport size.

You should try this function with a new drawing and see how the two lines intersect. To force a failure you could type in arbitrary three-dimensional coordinates for the first two points.

7.3 Matrix and vector utilities

LST__7_2.C is a set of useful geometric utilities such as matrix initialisation and matrix-vector multiplication.

In this book I do not intend to cover matrix mathematics, and this section is a brief practical approach to `ads_matrix` and how it is used.

In ADS, vectors and points have 3 components and transformation matrices have 4 by 4 = 16 components. Here are the details of a matrix-vector multiplication as done by the function `ads_mat_x_vec()`:

```
void ads_mat_x_vec (const ads_matrix mat,  // Matrix
                    const ads_point pin,   // Input
                    ads_point pout) ;      // Output
```

```
a b c d    x       xo
e f g h    y   =   yo
i j k l    z       zo
m n o p    w       wo
```

Letters a to p represent the 16 components of the `ads_matrix` mat, letters x to z represent the 3 components of an ads_vector pin, w is not explicitly used. The output vector is placed in pout, letters xo, yo, zo. The column d, h, l of the matrix specifies translation, and the diagonal a, f, k specify, scaling, m, n, o are usually all 0. The square delimited by a,c,k,i is used for rotations about the X, Y or Z axes.

You should think of *premultiplication* of vectors by matrices when you use these utility functions.

Note the difference between `ads_mat_x_pt` and `ads_mat_vec()`. The first works on points and any translations (*shiftings* of the x,y or z coordinates) in the matrix are present in the output. The second, `ads_mat_vec()`, applies to vectors (directions) and translations are *not* present in the output vector. This difference is the equivalent of w being 1 (for translation, `ads_mat_x_pt`) or w being 0 (for no translation, `ads_mat_x_vec`). With both functions rotations and scalings are present in the output vector.

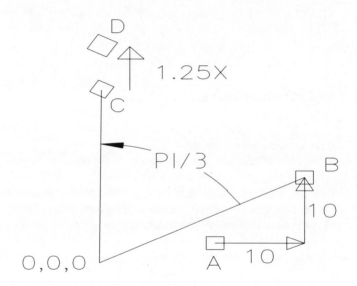

Figure 7.1 A series of transformations, A to B to C to D

Do not be confused by the fact that both vectors and points are called `ads_point`, the way you use them determines whether they are vectors or points.

In LST__7_2.C we ask the user for a point and then translate it by 10,10,0, then rotate it by PI/3, and finally we scale it by 1.25. We create the individual matrices to do each single operation, and then use `ads_mat_x_mat` to create the composite matrix containing all three steps. Note that since premultiplication is used you have to create the composite matrix in what may seem the reverse order. Figure 7.1 is a graphical representation of the composite transformation, operating on a square placed in position A. Position B in the figure is where the square ends up after the composite matrix has been applied to it (all its four corners).

The same sequence using AutoCAD commands would be:

```
MOVE (select the object) 10,10,0
ROTATE (select the object, select origin as rotation center) 60.
SCALE (select the object, and the origin as scaling base) 1.25.
```

There is another example of using `ads_mat_x_pt` in Chapter 9, LST__9_3.C.

A little more background information for three-dimensional geometry is given in Chapter 16 section 16.3.4, which explains normalisation, the dot product and the cross product.

7.4 Listings

```c
//////////////////////////////////////////////////////////////
// LST_7_1.C
//    Illustrates various ads_ geometric utility functions

int test_func (void)
{
    ads_point Point0,Point1 ;   // First line
    ads_point Point2,Point3 ;   // Second line
    ads_point I_Point ;         // Intersection of the 2 lines
    int       Res ;

    // Ask the user for two points, they can both be
    // three dimensional points
    Res = ads_getpoint (NULL,"\nFirst point",Point0) ;
    if (Res != RTNORM) {
        return (RTNORM) ;
    }
    // Use Point0 as "base" for next get (rubber banding)
    Res = ads_getpoint (Point0,"\nSecond point",Point1) ;
    if (Res != RTNORM) {
        return (RTNORM) ;
    }

    // Use ads_distance to find the distance twixt 2 points
    ads_printf ("\nThe distance between these two points in"
                " 3D space is %6.3f",
```

```
                ads_distance(Point0,Point1)) ;

// Draw a line between the two points
(void)ads_command (RTSTR,"_LINE",
                RT3DPOINT,Point0,
                RT3DPOINT,Point1,
                RTSTR,"",
                RTNONE) ;

// Find the angle (in radians) between current UCS and
// the line formed by the two points
ads_printf ("\nThe angle between the line and UCSX"
            " is %6.3f degrees.",
            ads_angle (Point0,Point1) * 360.0/TWOPI) ;

// Draw another line near the first
ads_point_set (Point0,Point2) ;
ads_point_set (Point1,Point3) ;

Point2[X] -= 3.0 ;
Point3[Y] += 3.0 ;
(void)ads_command (RTSTR,"_LINE",
                RT3DPOINT,Point2,
                RT3DPOINT,Point3,
                RTSTR,"",
                RTNONE) ;

// Find the intersection point and draw a POINT at it
Res = ads_inters (Point0,Point1,Point2,Point3,0,I_Point) ;
if (Res == RTNORM) {
    // Print the point of intersection
    ads_printf ("\nThe (infinite) lines"
                " intersect at %6.3f,%6.3f,%6.3f",
                I_Point[X],I_Point[Y],I_Point[Z]) ;

    // Make sure the point will be visible when drawn

    // Set up PointDisplayMODE variable
    Set_Int_Var ("PDMODE",3) ;    // 3 means an "X"

    // Set up PointDisplaySIZE variable
    Set_Real_Var ("PDSIZE",-5.0) ; // -x = x% of vport

    (void)ads_command (RTSTR,"_POINT",
                    RT3DPOINT,I_Point,
                    RTNONE) ;
} else {
    ads_printf ("\nThe lines do not intersect") ;
}
```

```c
        return (Tidy_End(RTNORM)) ;
}
//                      -- end of LST__7_1.C --

/////////////////////////////////////////////////////////
// LST__7_2.C
// A brief example of the use of the matrix and vector
// utilities defined in the rest of this file.

int test_func (void)
{
    int Res ;
    ads_point   Point,X_Late,Scale_Vec ;
    ads_matrix Translate, Rotate, Scale ;
    ads_matrix Rt,Srt ;

    Res = ads_getpoint (NULL,"Input a point:",Point) ;
    if (Res != RTNORM) {
        return (Tidy_End(RTNORM)) ;
    }

    // Make sure points very visible in the drawing
    Set_Int_Var ("PDMODE",3) ;  // points as X
    Set_Int_Var ("PDSIZE",-5) ; // % size of points

    (void)ads_command (RTSTR,"_POINT",
                        RT3DPOINT,Point,
                        RTNONE) ;

    X_Late [X] = 10.0 ;
    X_Late [Y] = 10.0 ;
    X_Late [Z] =  0.0 ;

    // Create a matrix which will shift points by
    // X_Late amount
    ads_mat_xlate (X_Late,Translate) ;

    // Create a matrix which will rotate points
    // about Z by one third PI
    ads_mat_rot (PI/3.0,Z,Rotate) ;

    // Create a matrix which will scale points
    // by 1.25
    Scale_Vec [X] = 1.25 ;
    Scale_Vec [Y] = 1.25 ;
    Scale_Vec [Z] = 1.25 ;
    ads_mat_scale (Scale_Vec,Scale) ;
```

```
        // Create a matrix which will translate and
        // then rotate.
        ads_mat_x_mat (Rotate,Translate,Rt) ;

        // Create a matrix which will translate,
        // rotate and then scale
        ads_mat_x_mat (Scale,Rt,Srt) ;

        // Apply the composite matrix to the point
        ads_mat_x_pt (Srt,Point,Point) ;

        // Show the translated rotated scaled point
        (void)ads_command (RTSTR,"_POINT",
                            RT3DPOINT,Point,
                            RTNONE) ;

        return (Tidy_End(RTNORM)) ;
}


/*****************************************************************/

#include <math.h>
#include "LST__7_2.H"   // Function prototypes

void ads_mat_ident (ads_matrix matrix)
/*
PURPOSE: To set a matrix to the identity matrix,
with, all entries 0 except leading diagonal which
is all 1.
*/
{
    int r,c ;
    for (r = 0 ; r < MSIZE ; r++) {
        for (c = 0 ; c < MSIZE ; c++) {
            if (r == c) {
                matrix[r][c] = 1.0 ;
            } else {
                matrix[r][c] = 0.0 ;
            }
        }
    }
}


void ads_mat_zero (ads_matrix matrix)
/*
PURPOSE: To set a matrix to the zero matrix
*/
{
    int r,c ;
```

```
        for (r = 0 ; r < MSIZE ; r++) {
            for (c = 0 ; c < MSIZE ; c++) {
                matrix[r][c] = 0.0 ;
            }
        }
    }
}

void ads_subvec (const ads_point ap, const ads_point bp,
                 ads_point dp)
/*
PURPOSE: To do   ap - bp  with result in vector   dp
*/
{
    dp[X] = ap[X] - bp[X];
    dp[Y] = ap[Y] - bp[Y];
    dp[Z] = ap[Z] - bp[Z];
}

void ads_addvec (const ads_point ap, const ads_point bp,
                 ads_point dp)
/*
PURPOSE: To do ap + bp with result in vector dp
NOTES:    1) The destination can be one of the sources
*/
{
    dp[X] = ap[X] + bp[X];
    dp[Y] = ap[Y] + bp[Y];
    dp[Z] = ap[Z] + bp[Z];
}

void ads_scalevec (const ads_point sp, ads_real scale,
                   ads_point dp)
/*
PURPOSE: To scale the vector sp by scale, result in dp
NOTES:    1) sp and dp can be the same vector
*/
{
    dp[X] = sp[X] * scale ;
    dp[Y] = sp[Y] * scale ;
    dp[Z] = sp[Z] * scale ;
}

ads_real ads_fabsv (const ads_point ap)
/*
PURPOSE: To return the absolute size of the vector
*/
{
    return (sqrt(ap[X]*ap[X] + ap[Y]*ap[Y] + ap[Z]*ap[Z]));
}
```

```
void ads_mat_ixlate (const ads_point vec, ads_matrix result)
/*
PURPOSE: To set up a matrix to do an inverse translation.
*/
{
    ads_mat_ident (result);
    result[X][T] = -vec[X];
    result[Y][T] = -vec[Y];
    result[Z][T] = -vec[Z];
}


void ads_mat_xlate (const ads_point vec, ads_matrix result)
/*
PURPOSE: To set up a matrix to do a translation.
*/
{
    ads_mat_ident (result);
    result[X][T] = vec[X];
    result[Y][T] = vec[Y];
    result[Z][T] = vec[Z];
}


void ads_mat_rot (ads_real angle, int axis, ads_matrix m)
/*
PURPOSE: To create a pure rotation matrix. axis should be
one of X,Y,Z which specifies about which axis you want to
do the rotation.
*/
{
    int axp1, axp2;

    axp1 = (axis + 1) % 3;
    axp2 = (axis + 2) % 3;
    ads_mat_ident(m);
    m[axp1][axp1] =   m[axp2][axp2] = cos(angle) ;
    m[axp1][axp2] = -(m[axp2][axp1] = sin(angle)) ;
}


void ads_mat_scale (const ads_point Scale, ads_matrix m)
/*
PURPOSE: To create a pure scaling matrix
*/
{
    ads_mat_ident(m);
    m[X][X] = Scale[X] ;
    m[Y][Y] = Scale[Y] ;
    m[Z][Z] = Scale[Z] ;
}
```

```
void ads_mat_x_pt (const ads_matrix mat, const ads_point pin,
                   ads_point pout)
/*
PURPOSE: Transform point. Multiply matrix by a given point.
         Note that it does translation too.
NOTES:   1) Uses an internal 'temp', so 'pin' and 'pout' can
         be the same vector without causing problems.
*/
{
    int i;
    ads_point temp;

    for (i = X; i <= Z; i++) {
        temp[i] = mat[i][X] * pin[X] + mat[i][Y] * pin[Y] +
                  mat[i][Z] * pin[Z] + mat[i][T];
    }
    (void)memcpy(pout, temp, sizeof(ads_point));
}


void ads_mat_x_vec (const ads_matrix mat, const ads_point pin,
                    ads_point pout)
/*
PURPOSE: Transform vector, to multiply a matrix by a vector.
         There is no translation.
NOTES:   1) pin and pout can be the same vectors with
            no problems
*/
{
    int i;
    ads_point temp;

    for (i = X; i <= Z; i++) {
        temp[i] = mat[i][X] * pin[X] + mat[i][Y] * pin[Y] +
                  mat[i][Z] * pin[Z];
    }
    (void)memcpy (pout, temp, sizeof(ads_point));
}


void ads_mat_x_mat (const ads_matrix mata,
                    const ads_matrix matb,
                    ads_matrix matout)
/*
PURPOSE: Multiply two matrices.  Any or all arguments may
         point to the same array.
*/
{
    ads_matrix t;
    int i, j, k;
```

```
        ads_real sum;

        for (i = 0; i < 4; i++) {
            for (j = 0; j < 4; j++) {
                sum = 0.0;
                for (k=0; k<4; k++) {
                    sum += mata[i][k] * matb[k][j];
                }
                t[i][j] = sum;
            }
        }
        (void)memcpy (matout, t, sizeof(ads_matrix));
}
//                      -- end of LST__7_2.C --


//////////////////////////////////////////////////////////////
// LST__7_2.H
// H file to be inlcuded whenever you use one of the
// functions listed below, whose definitions are in
// LST__7_2.C

#define MSIZE 4 // Size of an ads_matrix

void ads_mat_ident (ads_matrix matrix) ;
void ads_mat_zero (ads_matrix matrix) ;
void ads_subvec (const ads_point ap, const ads_point bp,
                 ads_point dp)  ;
void ads_addvec (const ads_point ap, const ads_point bp,
                 ads_point dp) ;
void ads_scalevec (const ads_point sp, ads_real scale,
                   ads_point dp) ;
ads_real ads_fabsv (const ads_point ap) ;
void ads_mat_ixlate (const ads_point vec, ads_matrix result) ;
void ads_mat_xlate (const ads_point vec, ads_matrix result) ;
void ads_mat_rot (ads_real angle, int axis, ads_matrix m) ;
void ads_mat_scale (const ads_point Scale, ads_matrix m) ;
void ads_mat_x_pt (const ads_matrix mat, const ads_point pin,
                   ads_point pout) ;
void ads_mat_x_vec (const ads_matrix mat, const ads_point pin,
                    ads_point pout) ;
void ads_mat_x_mat (const ads_matrix mata,
                    const ads_matrix matb,
                    ads_matrix matout) ;

//                      -- end of LST__7_2.H --
```

Blocks and polylines

8

8.1 Introduction

In this Chapter I will describe blocks and polylines, how you can construct them and how to find out about their internals. I also describe external references. I introduce two functions for creating blocks, comparing the advantages and disadvantages of both.

8.2 Using blocks to save space and time

Blocks are used in AutoCAD as a way of grouping together several entities to form another entity. This has several advantages:

- The user can move (or delete or rotate, etc.) all the entities that form the block as one entity.
- Multiple insertions of a block reduce the size of a drawing compared with having all the individual entities copied.
- File reading and writing speed are increased.
- The same block can be inserted with different scale factors and rotation angles.
- Blocks can have "attributes", this is no longer so important with the introduction of extended data in Release 11.

To create a block the user types "BLOCK", types in the block name, selects the base point for the block and then chooses the entities he wants to include in the block. When he has finished selecting entities they disappear and the block is placed in the drawing. To insert the block the user types "INSERT", the block name, the insertion point, the scale factors (in X and Y) and the rotation angle.

Block definitions can include references to other blocks, but *cannot* reference themselves. This would give rise to an infinite recursive loop, and since computers are finite machines AutoCAD would crash.

Block names, like layer names, *cannot* include spaces, and any lowercase letters will be changed to uppercase.

8.3 A function to create blocks

LST__8_1.C shows a function which creates blocks, and how to use it. This listing mimics what the user does to create blocks, i.e. it puts the entities into the drawing first, then selects them to make the block. Section 8.6 explains a function which is more direct, using `ads_entmake()`.

The listing starts with the prototype of the function:

```
void Create_Block (const char* Name,
                   ads_name First, ads_name Last) ;
```

The first parameter is the name of the block, the last two parameters are the range of entities you want to select. The function includes all entities in the database between `First` and `Last` in the block.

In test_func we create two circles and a line joining their centers. These entities will become the components of our block. After creation of the first circle we call `ads_entlast()` to get hold of its `ads_name()`. Remember that `ads_entlast()` returns the `ads_name` of the last entity inserted. Then we insert another circle and a line. After inserting the line we get hold of its `ads_name` by calling `ads_entlast()` again.

Now we have all the elements we need to call `Create_Block()`, which we do with the name "MYBLOCK".

In `Create_Block()` the first thing we do is see if a block of the same name already exists, because if it does the `ads_command()` sequence will be different than when it is a new block. `Table_Object_Exists()` is defined in Chapter 5.

If the block *does* exist then we must respond "yes" to AutoCAD's question of whether or not we want to redefine it. If the block does not already exist then the parameters to the `ads_command()` miss out the "yes" reply. One of these two calls to `ads_command()` starts the "_INSERT" command, defines the name, and adds the `First` entity to the block.

In the middle part of `test_func()` we do-loop over all the remaining entities up to `Last` inclusive, stopping when `ads_name_equal (Next, Last)` becomes true.

When all the entities have been added we terminate the command by calling `ads_command()` with the null string, just as a user would terminate the selection by hitting ENTER instead of picking another entity. This will cause all the entities to disappear from the screen.

Finally we insert the block we have just created by calling "_INSERT".

As explained in the previous section, each block has a "base point". This is the point used by AutoCAD when you are inserting the block, the point the crosshairs are centered on. It the "local origin" of the block. In LST__8_1.C the base point is assumed to be 0,0,0. This is fine in this example because the group of entities we are using to create the block is centered on 0,0,0. If the group of entities is not centered on 0,0,0 you should move the User coordinate System (see Chapter 9) to a reasonable point before calling `Create_Block()`.

When you experiment with this function you should start with an empty drawing zoomed in on the window -20,20 to 20,20. Also remember to switch off any object snap or grid snap options. You can use the `Save_User_State()` and `Restore_User_State()` functions described in Chapter 6.

8.4 External drawings as blocks, XREFs

A block can be an "external reference", an XREF, which means that it is in fact another drawing file. External references help in reducing file size and in sharing drawings among several users. You may not be responsible for a certain block, but you want to use it, so you make an "external reference" to the drawing created by a colleague.

External references can be "bound" into the current drawing using the command XBIND.

Normally DXF files (see Chapter 18) do not have external references, and all XREFs are resolved into internal blocks when the DXF file is written.

The blocks used as examples in this chapter are all normal "internal" blocks.

8.5 Creating names for blocks

For your convenience in debugging and handling blocks you need to give blocks names which the user will probably never see. For example you may have to create a block which is a graph or figure created automatically. You should use a base name, like "GRAFX", and add on counts for each new version of the block, for example "GRAFX1", "GRAFX2", "GRAFX3" and so on.

Each time you have to make a new version of the same block use `ads_tablesrch()` to see if GRAFX1 exists, and if it does search for GRAFX2 and so on until you find a block name which is not already present in the table.

It is worthwhile starting from GRAFX1 every time because it is possible that the original GRAFX1 is no longer used and has been PURGEd by the user at some time. This would mean that though GRAFX1 is no longer present, GRAFX2 *is*.

The easiest C function to use to create the names is `sprintf()`, here is an example:

```
Create_Name (char* Name)
{
    static int Count = 0 ; // Increases with every call
    sprintf (Name, "GRAFX%d", Count) ;
    Count++ ;                 // Increase count
}
```

8.6 A faster block creating function

LST__8_2.C shows another way of creating blocks, this time using `ads_entmake()`. It is faster in execution than the `Create_Block()` function described above, but you need to be more careful with the input parameters. The speed increase is only noticeable if the block contains many entities or is called very often. The function prototype for the faster function is:

```
void Rb_Create_Block (const char* Name,
                      const struct resbuf* E_List[]) ;
```

`Name` is the name you want to give to the block, and `E_List` is a list of pointers to result buffers describing the entities you want to form the block. The end of the list should be marked with a `NULL`.

In `test_func` we use `ads_buildlist()` to create three result buffer lists

Table 8.1:	Flags for BLOCK entities	
Value	Symbol (LST__5_1.H)	Meaning
16	XREF_DEPENDENT	Block depends on an XREF
32	XREF_RESOLVED	16 set and XREF is resolved
64	REFERENCED	The block is referenced in *this* drawing

describing two circles and a line just as in the previous example. Note the difference; in the LST__8_1.C we actually put the entities into the drawing before adding them to the block. In LST__8_2.C we create result buffer lists which describe the entities; they are not actually put in the drawing. The last entry in `E_List` is NULL.

Note also that while in `ads_command()` we used the string "_CIRCLE" to allow the program to run on non English-language versions of AutoCAD (see Chapter 13 section 13.4), with `ads_buildlist()` we *must* use "CIRCLE" the name of the entity type (in any language). "_CIRCLE" is a command, "CIRCLE" is an entity type.

Blocks consist of a BLOCK entity followed by a list of sub-entities, and are ended with an ENDBLK entity. The BLOCK entity *must* have a name, a layer, and a flags entry. The flags can be left at zero in this example. When you *read* the flags entry of a BLOCK the bits have the meanings shown in Table 8.1 (see also LST__5_1.H).

The BLOCK entity is created successfully; we go on to add all the sub-entity result buffers passed to us in E_List by calling ads_entmake(). After each addition we free the result buffer list. If you do not do it here you would have to do it in test_func(), it is a matter of programming style which you prefer. When all the sub-entities have been added we end the block definition by creating an ENDBLK entity.

The entity we have just created is then inserted into the drawing using the INSERT command.

When you use ads_entmake to create a BLOCK (or a PLINE, see the next section) you must only create one BLOCK at a time. This is because AutoCAD uses an external temporary file to record the sub-entities, and only one of these files can exist at any one time. So do not try to create a second BLOCK while you have not finished creation of a first block. Block creation ends when you add the "BLKEND" entity.

Another warning about using ads_entmake(). It will overwrite any block with the same name. If you want to avoid this you should check if the block already exists by using a function like Table_Object_Exists(), Chapter 5.

By the way the AutoCAD manual says that when you create the end block (Tail_Rb in LST__8_2.C) ADS will return RTKWORD, not RTNORM. As you can see in the listing I have not found that this is true yet, but if you *do* come across RTKWORD instead of RTNORM, it is not an error!

When creating entities like this you should *always* check the return values of ads_buildlist() and ads_entmake(), printing the ERRNO if an error occurs. Creating entities like this is very error-prone, and you need all the help you can get when debugging.

When you try this function start with the same sort of drawing as you did in the previous section.

8.7 Reading block data

Sometimes you would like to find out what is inside a block; LST__8_3.C is an example of how to do this. The function prompts the user to select an INSERT and then lists the INSERT properties and the BLOCK properties.

Now we must be clear about the difference between a BLOCK and an INSERT. An INSERT is the placing of a BLOCK in a drawing. You could think of the INSERT as a *call* to the BLOCK. BLOCKs can be INSERTed at different angles with different scale factors, but the internals of the BLOCK always stay the same.

LST__8_3.C gives the user two sorts of information, *how* the block was inserted (insert position, scale, angle and so on), and *what* the block consists of.

The first thing we do is ask the user to select a single object by calling `ads_entsel()`. This belongs to the same family of functions as `ads_getxxx()` (see Chapter 4). It is also possible to use `ads_initget()` and keywords with `ads_entsel()`. The function prototype is:

```
int ads_entsel (const char* Str, ads_name Ent, ads_point Pt_Res);
```

This function prompts the user with `Str`, if `Str` is NULL then it prompts the user with the standard AutoCAD "Select object:" message. The ads_name of the entity selected is returned in `ent`, and the *place* (three-dimensional coordinate) where the mouse was clicked is returned in `Pt_Res`. This is ignored in this example, but for some applications it can be useful, telling you where a user wants to cut a line or add in an object for example. As with `ads_getxxx()` functions, the return value of `ads_entsel()` will normally be RTNORM, RTCAN, or RTKWORD.

Next we call the function `Entity_Is()` which simply returns 1 if the entity is of the type specified in the single parameter, in this case "INSERT". I explain the workings of this function below. If the selected object *is* an INSERT we call `Print_Insert_Data()` and return.

`Print_Insert_Data()` gets hold of the result buffer list for the insert using `ads_entget()`, and calls `Print_Rb_Data()` to show it to the user, printing among other things the insert position as shown in the example below

```
(10 -- 4.5 6.8 0.0)        --- position
(41 -- 2.0)                --- x scale
(42 -- 2.0)                --- y scale
(43 -- 1.0)                --- z scale
```

By the way you will soon get used to remembering that 10 is the code for insertion point and 42 the code for the scaling in y and so on. AutoLISP programmers already know these numbers of by heart!

One of the things the insert result buffer list `I_Rb` in LST__8_3.C will contain will be the name of the block, that is the name the user specified when he created the block. `Get_Insert_Name()` retrieves this name, which is then used with `ads_tablesrch()` to get the result buffer for the block.

This *second* result buffer list, `Block_Rb`, contains an entity name specified by a -2 DXF code, in the listing it is called BLOCK_EN_CODE. We get hold of this ads_name, `B_En` in the listing, by stepping along `Block_Rb` in the do-while loop until we find BLOCK_EN_CODE as a restype. We use `B_En` to get hold of a *third* result buffer list, which this time is what we are really after.

We use the ads_name `B_En` as a parameter to `ads_entget()` in the last part of the function. B_En can now be treated just as entities are treated in the main drawing, even though it is in fact a block definition in a BLOCK table, see

Chapter 6. So we use `ads_entget()` and `ads_entnext()` to go over the components of the block. Each result buffer, which is a component of the block, is printed out using `Print_Rb_List()`.

There is a pause at the top of the printing loop, and if the user hits Escape (under Windows or control-C under DOS) the loop is abandoned, if he hits any other key the next result buffer is printed out. This is useful for blocks containing many entities. It is very frustrating for the user (or you the programmer) to have to sit through maybe five minutes of debugging prints when he has already found out what he wanted to know.

The two helper functions `Entity_Is()` and `Get_Insert_Name()` both scan the result buffer list obtained from the ads_name passed to them. `Entity_Is()` looks for the result buffer containing the type of the entity, `ENTITY_TYPE_CODE` in `LST__5_1.H`. `Get_Insert_Name()` looks for the buffer `BLOCK_NAME_CODE`, checking on the way that we have passed it an INSERT by looking at `ENTITY_TYPE_CODE` too.

A better block lister would recurse when it comes across a BLOCK inserted inside another BLOCK. You could do this by modifying `Print_Rb_List()` to call `Print_Insert_Data()` whenever it comes across an INSERT as a component of a BLOCK. This is left as an "exercise for the reader".

While all this is not complicated it is intricate, so here is a summary of how to get to internal block data:

1. Get hold of the ads_name of the INSERT. This is done most often by selecting the entity either manually (`ads_entsel()`, `ads_ssget()` etc.) or by scanning the drawing from within the program (`ads_ssget()` with filters).
2. Get the name of the BLOCK which has been INSERTed. You do this by doing an `ads_entget()` on the name found in step 1 and scanning the resulting result buffer list for a `BLOCK_NAME_CODE` buffer. In `LST__8_3.C` this is done by `Get_Insert_Name()`.
3. Use the name found in step 2 above to get a result buffer for the block from the tables section of the file. You do this by using `ads_tablesrch()`.
4. Scan the result buffer list found in the previous step for a `BLOCK_EN_CODE` result buffer. This is the ads_name of the *first* entity inside the block.
5. Starting with the ads_name of step 5 use ads_entget to get the result buffer for each internal entity and `ads_entnext()` to move onto the *next* internal entity.
6. Continue scanning till either you find the thing you are looking for or until `ads_entnext()` does not return RTNORM.

8.8 Polylines

An AutoCAD polyline is a sequence of points joined by lines; it is a single entity. The polyline data format is also used to contain three-dimensional meshes. Polylines can be two or three-dimensional and are created with the _PLINE and _3DPOLY commands respectively.

Polylines are constructed in much the same way as blocks, as you can see from LST__8_4.C. The function `Create_Polyline()` takes three parameters, the number of points, the list of points and a flags integer. The flags integer is used to specify if the polyline is closed (the first and last points are joined by a line) or open.

As with creating blocks there is a main entity, a list of sub-entities, and an entity to end the sequence. For a polyline these correspond to POLYLINE, a list of VERTEX entities and a ENDSEQ entity. The POLYLINE entity requires the layer name, the vertices follow flag, a dummy point, and the polyline flags, as shown in the call to `ads_buildlist()` for the creation of `Pline_Rb()` in LST__8_4.C. (The dummy point is not really used these days, but it needs to be there for compatibility and historical reasons.)

Once the polyline main entity has been created with a call to `ads_entmake()` we for-loop over the array of ads_point, adding in a vertex to the polyline for each entry in P_List. To end the list of points and finish the creation of the polyline entity we call `ads_entmake()` with a SEQEND result buffer.

You should try this function in an empty drawing, experimenting with the OPEN and CLOSED flags.

8.8.1 Modifying polylines

If you want to modify rather than create a polyline then you can use the following two functions. The first, `Get_Vertex()`, returns the current coordinates of a vertex, the second `Move_Vertex()` adds an offset to the vertex and calls `ads_entmod()` to update the database.

```
int Get_Vertex (ads_point Vert, ads_name en)
// Return TRUE if en is an polyline vertex and put it in Vert.
{
    char    E_Type [MAX_CHARS] ;
    struct  resbuf* ebf ; // First result buffer of assoc list
    struct  resbuf* ebn ; // 'Next' result buffer in assoc list
    ebf = ads_entget (en) ; // Get the root of its assoc list
    /* Look at its association list... */
    for (ebn = ebf ; ebn != NULL ; ebn = ebn->rbnext) {
        switch (ebn->restype) {
            case ENTITY_TYPE_CODE :
                (void)strcpy (E_Type,ebn->resval.rstring) ;
```

```
                    break ;
            case 10 :
                memcpy (Vert,ebn->resval.rpoint,
                        sizeof(ads_point)) ;
                break ;
        }
    }
    (void)ads_relrb (ebf) ;
    return (strcmpi (E_Type,"VERTEX") == 0) ;
}

int Move_Vertex (ads_name en, ads_point Offset)
// Return TRUE if En is a vertex and if we it by Offset
{
    char    E_Type [MAX_CHARS] ;
    struct  resbuf* ebf ;  // First result buffer of assoc list
    struct  resbuf* ebn ;  // 'Next' result buffer in assoc list
    int     Moved ;

    ebf = ads_entget (en) ; // Get the root of its resbuf list
    Moved = FALSE ;
    /* Look at its association list */
    for (ebn = ebf ; ebn != NULL ; ebn = ebn->rbnext) {
        int c ;
        switch (ebn->restype) {
            case ENTITY_TYPE_CODE :
                (void)strcpy (E_Type,ebn->resval.rstring) ;
                break ;
            case 10 : // The COORDS, move them...
                for (c = X ; c <= Z ; c++) {
                    ebn->resval.rpoint[c] += Offset[c] ;
                }
                break ;
        }
    }
    if (strcmpi (E_Type,"VERTEX") == 0) {
        // Yes, really a vertex, modify this entity
        (void)ads_entmod (ebf) ;
        Moved = TRUE ;
    }
    (void)ads_relrb (ebf) ;
    return (Moved) ;
}
```

Of course you can modify the vertex coordinates in other ways, mirror them in some line or scale them or rotate them. Move_Vertex() above is only an example. Note also that though we add the offset to the coordinates the vertex will be modified only if we call ads_entmod().

WARNING: When you use `ads_entmod()` on VERTEX entities you must be sure that the last polyline header (i.e. the POLYLINE entity) that you read or wrote belongs to the VERTEX that you want to change. Autodesk does not explain why, but it has probably got something to do with that bane of C programs: the use of global variables.

8.9 Listings

```
////////////////////////////////////////////////////////////////
// LST__8_1.C
// Using ads_command to create blocks

void Create_Block (const char* Name,
                   ads_name First, ads_name Last) ;

static int test_func (void)
{
    int Res ;
    ads_name First_En,Last_En ; // Of the block
    ads_point Center1 = {-10.0, 0.0, 0.0 } ;
    ads_point Center2 = { 10.0, 0.0, 0.0 } ;

    (void)ads_command (RTSTR,"_CIRCLE",
                       RT3DPOINT,Center1,
                       RTREAL, 5.0,
                       RTNONE) ;

    // Get hold of the ads_name of the circle
    // just inserted.
    Res = ads_entlast (First_En) ;
    if (Res != RTNORM) {
        ads_printf ("\nERROR in ads_entlast") ;
        return (Tidy_End(RTNORM)) ;
    }

    (void)ads_command (RTSTR,"_CIRCLE",
                       RT3DPOINT,Center2,
                       RTREAL, 5.0,
                       RTNONE) ;

    (void)ads_command (RTSTR,"_LINE",
                       RT3DPOINT,Center1,
                       RT3DPOINT,Center2,
                       RTSTR,"",
                       RTNONE) ;
```

```
    // Get hold of the ads_name of the line
    // just inserted.
    Res = ads_entlast (Last_En) ;
    if (Res != RTNORM) {
        ads_printf ("\nERROR in ads_entlast") ;
        return (Tidy_End(RTNORM)) ;
    }

    Create_Block ("MYBLOCK", First_En, Last_En) ;

    return (Tidy_End(RTNORM)) ;
}

void Create_Block (const char* Name,
                   ads_name First, ads_name Last)
/*
PURPOSE: To create a block called Name
NOTES   1) We use all the entities from First to Last
           inclusive.
        2) If a block with the same name exists
           it will be redefined.
        3) If you want the insertion point to be in
           a sensible place be sure to set the UCS to
           one of the entities comprising
           the block before calling this function.
*/
{
    int      Res ;
    ads_name En,Next ;
    int Finished,Block_Exists ;
    ads_point Zero = {0.0,0.0,0.0} ; // A useful vector

    // See if the blocks already exists, this
    // function is defined in Chapter 5 of the book.
    Block_Exists = Table_Object_Exists ("BLOCK",Name) ;

    if (Block_Exists) {
        // ACAD will ask if we want to redefine it
        Res = ads_command (RTSTR,"_BLOCK",
                           RTSTR,Name,
                           RTSTR,"_Y",      // Yes, redefine
                           RT3DPOINT,Zero, // Position
                           RTENAME,First,  // 1st ent added
                           RTNONE) ;
    } else {
        // Straight forward block creation
        Res = ads_command (RTSTR,"_BLOCK",
                           RTSTR,Name,
                           RT3DPOINT,Zero,  // Position
```

```
                            RTENAME,First,    // 1st ent added
                            RTNONE) ;
    }
    if (Res != RTNORM) {
        ads_printf ("\nERROR in Create_Block(%s).",Name) ;
        return ;
    }

    /*
     * Loop from First to Last adding in the entities to
     * the block definition
     */
    Finished = FALSE ;

    // Initially put First in En
    ads_name_set (First,En) ;
    do {
        Res = ads_entnext (En,Next) ;
        if (Res != RTNORM) {
            // End of the database
            Finished = TRUE ;
        } else {
            Res = ads_command (RTENAME,Next,RTNONE) ;
            if (Res != RTNORM) {
                ads_printf ("\nWARNING,Create_Block(%s)"
                            ", ads_command failure.",
                            Name) ;
                break ;
            }
            // Compare the Next and Last
            if (ads_name_equal (Next,Last)) {
                // Last entity has just been added
                Finished = TRUE ;
            } else {
                // Get ready to look at next entity
                ads_name_set (Next,En) ;
            }
        }
    } while (!Finished) ;

    /*
     * Terminate the command
     */
    Res = ads_command (RTSTR,"",RTNONE) ;
    if (Res != RTNORM) {
        ads_printf ("\nWARNING,Create_Block(%s)"
                    " terminate did not work <%s>.",Name) ;
    }
```

```
    /*
     * Insert the block where you found and created it
     */
    Res = ads_command (RTSTR,"_INSERT",
                        RTSTR,Name,
                        RT3DPOINT,Zero,  // Position
                        RTREAL,1.0,      // X scale
                        RTREAL,1.0,      // Y scale
                        RTREAL,0.0,      // Rotation angle
                        RTNONE) ;

    if (Res != RTNORM) {
        ads_printf ("\nERROR,Create_Block (%s)"
                    "did not work",Name) ;
    }
}

//                      -- end of LST__8_1.C --

//////////////////////////////////////////////////////////
// LST__8_2.C
// Using ads_entmake to create a block


ads_point Zero    = {  0.0, 0.0, 0.0 } ;

// Function prototype
void Rb_Create_Block (const char* Name,
                      const struct resbuf* E_List[]) ;

static int test_func (void)
{
    int Res ;
    ads_point Center1 = {-10.0, 0.0, 0.0 } ;
    ads_point Center2 = { 10.0, 0.0, 0.0 } ;

    struct resbuf* E_List[4] ; // 2 circles, a line, and a NULL

    E_List[0] = ads_buildlist (RTDXF0,"CIRCLE", // not _CIRCLE!
                               CENTER_CODE,Center1,
                               RADIUS_CODE,5.0,
                               RTNONE) ;
    E_List[1] = ads_buildlist (RTDXF0,"CIRCLE",
                               CENTER_CODE,Center2,
                               RADIUS_CODE,5.0,
                               RTNONE) ;
    E_List[2] = ads_buildlist (RTDXF0,"LINE",   // not _LINE!!!
                               LINE_START_CODE,Center1,
                               LINE_END_CODE,Center2,
```

```
                                  RTNONE) ;
        E_List[3] = NULL ;

        // Strictly speaking you should check all the return
        // values of the three calls above

        Rb_Create_Block ("YOURBLK",E_List) ;

        Res = ads_command (RTSTR,"_INSERT",
                           RTSTR,"YOURBLK",
                           RT3DPOINT,Zero, // Position
                           RTREAL,1.0,      // X scale
                           RTREAL,1.0,      // Y scale
                           RTREAL,0.0,      // Rotation angle
                           RTNONE) ;


        if (Res != RTNORM) {
            ads_printf ("\nERROR,could not insert.") ;
        }


        return (Tidy_End(RTNORM)) ;
}


void Rb_Create_Block (const char* Name,
                      const struct resbuf* E_List[])
/*
PURPOSE: To create a block using the entities described
in the list of result buffers in E_List. The end of the
list should be marked with a NULL pointer.
Note that the result buffers are assumed to be created
with ads_buildlist, i.e. dynamically created, and we
free them here, assuming they are of no more use
to the caller.
*/
{
    int Res,i ;
    struct resbuf* Head_Rb ;
    struct resbuf* Tail_Rb ;

    // Start the block with the BLOCK main entity
    Head_Rb = ads_buildlist (RTDXF0,"BLOCK",
                             BLOCK_NAME_CODE,Name,// Required
                             LAYER_NAME_CODE,"0", // Required
                             INSERT_COORD_CODE,Zero,
                             BLOCK_FLAGS_CODE,0,  // Required
                             NULL) ;
    if (Head_Rb == NULL) {
```

```
        ads_printf ("\nERROR building head of list,"
                        " ERRNO=%d.",Get_Int_Var ("ERRNO")) ;
        return ;
    }
    Res = ads_entmake (Head_Rb) ;
    if (Res != RTNORM) {
        ads_printf ("\nERROR with ads_entmake, Res=%d,"
                        " ERRNO=%d",Res,Get_Int_Var("ERRNO")) ;
    }


    /*
     * Once the main BLOCK entity has been made we can
     * add in sub-entities, which are the components
     * of the block...
     */
    i = 0 ;
    while (E_List[i] != NULL) {
        Res = ads_entmake (E_List[i]) ;
        if (Res != RTNORM) {
            ads_printf ("\nERROR, ads_entmake(E_List[%d]),"
                        " Res=%d, ERRNO=%d",i,
                            Res,Get_Int_Var("ERRNO")) ;
        }
        (void)ads_relrb (E_List[i]) ;  // Free the buffer
        i++ ;  // Get next result buffer
    }


    /*
     * Each BLOCK entity needs a matching ENDBLK,
     * here it is.
     */
    Tail_Rb = ads_buildlist (RTDXF0,"ENDBLK",NULL) ;
    if (Tail_Rb == NULL) {
        ads_printf ("\nERROR building tail of list") ;
        return ;
    }
    Res = ads_entmake (Tail_Rb) ;
    if (Res != RTNORM) {
        ads_printf ("\nERROR with ads_entmake(Tail), Res=%d,"
                        " ERRNO=%d",Res,Get_Int_Var("ERRNO")) ;
    }

    (void)ads_relrb (Head_Rb) ;
    (void)ads_relrb (Tail_Rb) ;
}
//                      -- end of LST__8_2.C --

////////////////////////////////////////////////////////////
// LST__8_3.C
```

```
//      Showing how to list the contents of a block
//      selected by the user.

// Function prototypes
void Print_Insert_Data (const ads_name En) ;
int  Entity_Is (const char* Thing, const ads_name Entity) ;
void Get_Insert_Name (char* Name, const ads_name Entity) ;

static int test_func (void)
/*
PURPOSE: To list the contents of a user selected block,
*/
{
    int        Res ;
    ads_name   E_Name ;
    ads_point  Sel_Pnt ;

    /*
     * Get the user to select an object. You could use
     * ads_initget here for keywords and restricted input
     * if you wanted to
     */
    Res = ads_entsel (NULL,E_Name,Sel_Pnt) ;
    if (Res != RTNORM) {
        return (Tidy_End (RTNORM)) ;
    }

    // Check that the selected entity is an insert
    if (!Entity_Is ("INSERT",E_Name)) {
        ads_printf ("\nEntity is not an INSERT.") ;
    } else {
        Print_Insert_Data (E_Name) ;
    }

    return (Tidy_End (RTNORM)) ;
}


void Print_Insert_Data (ads_name I_En)
/*
PURPOSE: Print the data about the INSERT, i.e. insertion
point, scaling, layer and so on (you'll have to learn
the codes for these, e.g. 41,42,43 = block scaling
factors, 50 = insert angle and so on), and also print
the internals of the BLOCK.
*/
{
    struct resbuf*  I_Rb ;      // The insert's result buffer
    struct resbuf*  Block_Rb ;  // The block's result buffer
    struct resbuf*  Sub_Rb ;    // Sub-entity pointer
```

```
struct resbuf*   Rb ;          // A temp
ads_name         B_En ;        // The ads_name of the block
ads_name         Next ;        // A temp
char Block_Name [MAX_CHARS] ; // The name-string of block
int              No_Ben,Res ;

// Get the root of the INSERT's list
I_Rb = ads_entget (I_En) ;

// Print out the INSERT data
Print_Rb_List (I_Rb) ;

// Free the ram used for the list
(void)ads_relrb (I_Rb) ;

/*
 * Now print out the BLOCK's data. Don't confuse a
 * BLOCK with an INSERT.
 */
ads_printf ("\nNow for the internals...") ;

Get_Insert_Name (Block_Name,I_En) ;

Block_Rb = ads_tblsearch ("BLOCK",Block_Name,0) ;
if (Block_Rb == NULL) {
    ads_printf ("\nWARNING, could not find <%s>"
                " block in tables ",Block_Name) ;
    return ;
}

/*
 * Loop over the Block_Rb list until we find the
 * entity name for this block
 */
No_Ben = 1 ; // Not yet found it
Rb      = Block_Rb ;
do {
    if (Rb->restype == BLOCK_EN_CODE) {
        ads_name_set (Rb->resval.rlname,B_En) ;
        No_Ben = 0 ;   // Found it!
    } else {
        Rb = Rb->rbnext ; // Look at next buffer
    }
} while (No_Ben) ;

(void)ads_relrb (Block_Rb) ;

do {
    // Pause for the user
```

```
        char Dummy[MAX_CHARS] ;
        if (ads_getstring (0," HIT A KEY:",Dummy) == RTCAN) {
            return ; // User abandons print out
        }

        // Show the data for this entity
        Sub_Rb = ads_entget (B_En) ;     // Get it
        Print_Rb_List (Sub_Rb) ;         // Print it
        (void)ads_relrb (Sub_Rb) ;       // Release it

        Res = ads_entnext (B_En,Next) ; // Get next entity
        ads_name_set (Next,B_En) ;
    } while (Res == RTNORM) ;
}


int Entity_Is (char* Thing, ads_name Entity)
/*
PURPOSE: To return 1 if the Entity is a Thing
*/
{
    struct  resbuf* ebf ;  // First result buffer of list
    struct  resbuf* ebn ;  // 'Next' result buffer in list
    int     Is_A_Thing,ETC_Found ;

    Is_A_Thing = 0 ;
    ETC_Found  = 0 ;

    /* Get the root of it's  list */
    ebf = ads_entget (Entity) ;

    /* Look at it's  list */
    for (ebn = ebf ; ebn != NULL ; ebn = ebn->rbnext) {
        if (ebn->restype == ENTITY_TYPE_CODE) {
            ETC_Found = 1 ;
            if (strcmpi (ebn->resval.rstring,Thing) == 0) {
                Is_A_Thing = 1 ;
            }
            break ;  /* Found out what we wanted to */
        }
    }

    if (!ETC_Found) {
        ads_printf ("\nWARNING,EI, ETC not found") ;
    }

    (void)ads_relrb (ebf) ;

    return (Is_A_Thing) ;
}
```

```
void Get_Insert_Name (char* Name, const ads_name en)
/*
PURPOSE: To get the name of the INSERT, i.e. which BLOCK
has been inserted. This name will appear in the BLOCK table
of the drawing.
*/
{
    struct  resbuf* ebf ;  // First result buffer of  list
    struct  resbuf* ebn ;  // 'Next' result buffer in  list
    int     Error ;

    Name[0] = (char)0 ;
    Error   = FALSE ;

    // Get the root of it's  list
    ebf = ads_entget (en) ;

    // Look at it's  list
    for (ebn = ebf ; ebn != NULL ; ebn = ebn->rbnext) {
        switch (ebn->restype) {
            case BLOCK_NAME_CODE :
                (void)strcpy (Name,ebn->resval.rstring) ;
                break ;
            case ENTITY_TYPE_CODE :
                if (strcmpi (ebn->resval.rstring,"INSERT")!=0) {
                    Error = TRUE ;
                    // Not really an error,
                    // but certainly not an INSERT
                }
                break ;
        }
    }

    // Free the ram used for the list
    (void)ads_relrb (ebf) ;

    if (Error) {
        Name[0] = (char)0 ;
    }
}
//                      -- end of LST__8_3.C --

///////////////////////////////////////////////////////
// LST__8_4.C
// Using ads_entmake to create a 2D polyline
ads_point Zero_Point = {0.0,0.0,0.0} ;

// Function prototype
```

```
void Create_Pline (const int N_Points,
                   const ads_point P_List[],
                   const int Flags) ;

static int test_func (void)
{
    #define N_POINTS 6
    ads_point P_List[N_POINTS] = {{0.0, 0.0, 0.0 },
                                  {1.0, 0.0, 0.0 },
                                  {1.0, 1.0, 0.0 },
                                  {0.0, 1.0, 0.0 },
                                  {0.0, 1.5, 0.0 },
                                  {1.5, 1.5, 0.0 }} ;

    Create_Pline (N_POINTS,P_List,OPEN_PLINE) ;
    // Try also sending the flag CLOSED_PLINE

    return (Tidy_End(RTNORM)) ;
}

void Create_Pline (const int N_Points,  // Number of points
                   const ads_point P_List[], // in this List
                   const int Flags)      // Closed or open
/*
PURPOSE: Creates a 2D polyline, either open or closed
         depending on the Flags value.
*/
{
    int Res,i ;
    struct resbuf* Pline_Rb ;
    struct resbuf* Seqend_Rb ;
    struct resbuf* Pnt_Rb ;

    // Start the block with the POLYLINE main entity
    Pline_Rb = ads_buildlist (RTDXF0,"POLYLINE",
                              LAYER_NAME_CODE,"0",
                              VERTS_FOLLOW_CODE,1, // Required
                              VERTEX_COORD_CODE,Zero_Point,
                                  // A required dummy point
                              PLINE_FLAGS_CODE,Flags,
                              RTNONE) ;
    if (Pline_Rb == NULL) {
        ads_printf ("\nERROR building head of list,"
                   " ERRNO=%d.",Get_Int_Var ("ERRNO")) ;
        return ;
    }
    Res = ads_entmake (Pline_Rb) ;
    if (Res != RTNORM) {
        ads_printf ("\nERROR with ads_entmake, Res=%d,"
```

```
                          " ERRNO=%d",Res,Get_Int_Var("ERRNO")) ;
    }
    /*
     * Once the main entity has been made we can
     * add in sub-entities, which are the vertices of
     * of the polyline...
     */
    for (i = 0 ; i < N_Points ; i++) {
        Pnt_Rb = ads_buildlist (RTDXF0,"VERTEX",
                                LAYER_NAME_CODE,"0",
                                VERTEX_COORD_CODE,P_List[i],
                                RTNONE) ;
        if (Pnt_Rb == NULL) {
            ads_printf ("\nERROR adding point,"
                        " ERRNO=%d.",Get_Int_Var ("ERRNO")) ;
            return ;
        }
        Res = ads_entmake (Pnt_Rb) ;
        if (Res != RTNORM) {
            ads_printf ("\nERROR, ads_entmake(Pnt_Rb),"
                        " Res=%d, ERRNO=%d",i,
                          Res,Get_Int_Var("ERRNO")) ;
            return ;
        }
        (void)ads_relrb (Pnt_Rb) ;  // Free the buffer
    }

    /*
     * Each POLYLINE entity needs a matching SEQEND entity,
     * here it is.
     */
    Seqend_Rb = ads_buildlist (RTDXF0,"SEQEND",RTNONE) ;
    if (Seqend_Rb == NULL) {
        ads_printf ("\nERROR building tail of list") ;
        return ;
    }
    Res = ads_entmake (Seqend_Rb) ;
    if (Res != RTNORM) {
        ads_printf ("\nERROR with ads_entmake(Tail), Res=%d,"
                    " ERRNO=%d",Res,Get_Int_Var("ERRNO")) ;
    }
    (void)ads_relrb (Pline_Rb) ;
    (void)ads_relrb (Seqend_Rb) ;
}
//                      -- end of LST__8_4.C --
```

Drawing in 3D and 3D coordinate systems

9

9.1 Introduction

In this chapter we will start some serious drawing in three dimensions. I will discuss two ways of adding entities to the AutoCAD database, which can be used as a base for both 2D and 3D drawing.

I will cover three-dimensional lines and points, while Chapter 10 introduces objects which are inherently three-dimensional, like MESHES and 3DFACEs. I will explain the User coordinate System and the World Coordinate System, and how they can be used to simplify some three-dimensional graphics programming problems.

9.2 A comparison of two methods for adding entities

LST__9_1.C shows two different ways of adding entities to a drawing, using `ads_command()` and `ads_entmake()`. We have used both in the previous chapters, but here we will consider in more detail the differences between the two methods.

At the top of the listing is an include of TIME.H which contains declarations of the timing function clock and the timing type clock_t used later in the listing. Next we come to the prototypes for the line and circle drawing functions defined after test_func.

For programmers new to C the line

```
#define COMMAND_WAY 0   // Change 0 to 1 to see entmake way.
```

may need some explanation. Although this is a normal define we will later use it to control "conditional compilation", which means we can decide which parts of the program will be compiled. This is the same technique we used in Chapter 3 for making a file compilable both in and out of the ADS environment.

The main function simply calls the line and circle drawing function in a for loop and prints the amount of time taken. Just before the for loop we call clock() and store the current time in Start_Time, and after the loop we call clock again storing the current time in End_Time. The units or ticks which the clock uses are of no interest to us here because we are making comparisons. The important thing is that the for loop is long enough that more than a few tens of ticks pass between the start and end of the loop. What we print at the very end of test_func() depends on the value of COMMAND_WAY:

```
#if COMMAND_WAY
    Restore_User_State () ; // Dear reader: ignore this for now
    ads_printf (" using ads_command method") ;
#else
    ads_printf (" using ads_entmake method") ;
#endif .
```

This is where the conditional compilation comes in. If COMMAND_WAY is non-zero then the first ads_printf() will be compiled, otherwise the second one is compiled, thus informing the user which version of the program he has loaded.

Now if you look at the definition for Acad_Line() you will again the use of conditional compilation. The first half of Acad_Line() uses the ads_command() method of creating entities, while the second half (after the #else) uses the ads_entmake() method. Only one half will be compiled, which one depending on the value of COMMAND_WAY. As the source is shown here COMMAND_WAY is 1, so the first half will be compiled. The rest of the definition of Acad_Line() should be clear enough.

Program_State() is used to speed up and make safer the execution of the ads_command() function. It saves some variables which the user has probably set to his liking, and then sets them to values more useful to the application. Speed is gained by switching off command echoing. Speed can also be gained by switching off the drawing of the UCS (User coordinate System) icon. In this simple program it is not the case, but complex applications which change the UCS often will benefit by turning off the icon. Lastly we switch off all object snap modes, because we do not want our lines snapping off-course to endpoints, do we?

The same tricks are used in Acad_Circle(), with conditional compilation used to decide whether ads_command() or ads_entmake() will be used.

If you compile and test the program (in a *new* drawing each time) as shown in LST__9_1.C, with COMMAND_WAY defined as 1 you will get the number of ticks it takes to draw a series of lines and circles using ads_command(). Note that number. Now change the definition of COMMAND_WAY to 0, recompile and re-test the program (in an *new* drawing), again noting the number of ticks taken.

It is most likely that the second test is the faster, taking fewer ticks, than the first. The actual difference depends on your computer, the version of AutoCAD you are using, whether you ran it under Windows or not, and whether you are using "pure" ADS or rxADS.

The obvious conclusion is that when you are looking for speed you should use ads_entmake(). You should also be aware however that there advantages and disadvantages to both methods, and as Donald Knuth says in his book "Literate Programming": "Premature optimisation is the root of all evil (or at least most of it) in programming".

The advantages of using ads_command() are as follows:

- It is easy to understand. If you can make AutoCAD do what you want from the command line you can do the same thing using ads_command().
- Some of the details of constructing objects are hidden from you; the defaults set by the user or AutoCAD are those used when you call ads_command().
- It is easier to contruct some three-dimensional objects using ads_command() and changing the UCS (User coordinate System) compared with using ads_entmake().
- User interaction can be an integral part of the construction of the object; more direct interactivity between the program and the user.

The advantages of using ads_entmake() are as follows:

- Speed, ads_entmake() is almost always faster than ads_command().
- Three dimensional objects are constructed in the WCS (World Coordinate System) and the UCS is ignored.
- There is no need to switch off command echoing and snapping to grids and objects etc. This is partially an advantage in speed, but it is also an advantage in programming (writing) time.

It should be clear that both methods have their place. One last point to make is that if you are careful you can start by using ads_command() to get your program going, and then when the customer starts asking for speed you can start converting to ads_entmake()!

Both ads_command() and ads_entmake() draw objects onto the current layer and/or with the current color. If you, or the user, never change the UCS from the WCS then methods give the same results. However if you or the user starts playing about with the UCS then there will be differences.

Try this experiment with the two versions of LST__9_1.C. Go into a new drawing, make a new layer and rotate the UCS by 45 degrees around X (if you do not know how to do this see the following section). Now run "test" of the COMMAND_WAY defined as 1 version. Save the drawing, exit AutoCAD and make the ads_entmake version of the program (COMMAND_WAY defined as 0). Return to AutoCAD with the same drawing and run "test" again. You will a new series of lines and circles in different positions from the first. This is because, as explained above, `ads_command()` uses the UCS while `ads_entmake()` uses the WCS. Only if the UCS and the WCS are the same will the commands produce the entities in the same positions.

9.3 Coordinate systems in AutoCAD

9.3.1 The user coordinate system

This UCS is a coordinate system which the user (or programmer for that matter) can change to make to make certain operations easier. Imagine trying to draw a rectangular window 1 meter wide by 1.5 meters high set into a roof which is angled at 30 degrees to the horizontal, see Figure 9.1.

To draw the window in three dimensions using the World Coordinate System would mean calculating the heights of the four corners of the window. You would also have to take into account that a window of height 1.5 meters, projected onto the floor (the WCS) has an extension of (cosine (30) * 1.5 =) 1.299 meters. It is easiest to change the coordinate system to coincide with the angle of the roof, and then draw the window in two dimensions, see.

(You will never actually see a screen as shown in the figure because there is only ever one UCS active at one time. The figure shows two to give you the idea of a User coordinate System and a World Coordinate System.)

The AutoCAD command to change the UCS is "UCS", and with it you can:

- Rotate the UCS around the X Y or Z axis by any amount, by typing "X", "Y" or "Z" and then specifying the number of degrees or rotation.
- Change the origin of the UCS, that is where 0,0,0 of the UCS is, by typing "O" and the specifying the coordinates.
- Move the UCS to a plane by typing "3" and specifying three points in the plane, either from the keyboard or with the mouse or digitizer.
- Set the UCS to the coordinate system of an entity, by typing "E" and selecting the entity. For example the Entity Coordinate System (ECS) of a two-dimensional polyline will be in the plane of the polyline.
- Set the UCS to the current view, by typing "V". This is useful if you have a three-dimensional object but want text to be "flat" on the screen or plotted drawing
- Save a UCS under a name by typing "S" and the name, for later restoration with the "R" option when you want to use it again.

In the above example, the roof runs lengthways along X; to have the UCS *parallel* to the roof we would rotate it (the UCS) around X by 30 degrees. To make the UCS coincide with the roof we would change the origin of the UCS to a corner of the roof, maybe using object snapping options to snap to the end point of one of the four lines of the roof.

An alternative method would be to use the "3" option of the UCS command to specify three coordinates in the plane that you want to align the UCS with. In the example the three points could be three of the four corners of the roof, easily selectable using the "snap to end point" mode of AutoCAD.

There are also several UCS variables, UCSFOLLOW, UCSICON, UCSNAME,

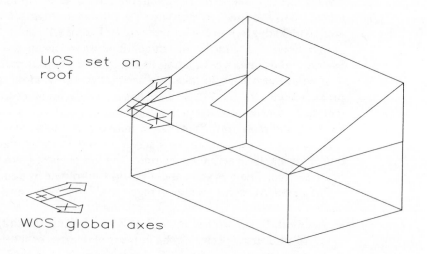

Figure 9.1 An example use of the UCS

UCSORG, UCSXDIR and UCSYDIR. Note that there is no need for a UCSZDIR because the cross product of UCSXDIR and UCSYDIR will give you the Z direction.

Every three-dimensional coordinate system has, once the X and Y directions have been established, a choice of two directions for Z. The standard AutoCAD Z direction follows the right hand rule, if the thumb of your *right* hand represents the X axis, the pointing index finger represents the Y axis and the middle finger, perpendicular to your right palm, represents the Z axis.

9.3.2 The UCS icon

To help you find your way around three-dimensional space there is the UCS icon, shown in Figure 9.2 in its various forms. The X and Y directions need no explanation, the Z direction is towards you (out from the screen) when you can see the square, away from you (i.e. pointing into the screen) when you cannot.

If there is a "+" visible in the icon then it is at the origin of the UCS; it is showing you graphically the 0,0,0 point of the coordinate system. If there is no "+" visible then the UCS icon is only showing you directions; the origin of the current UCS is probably off screen.

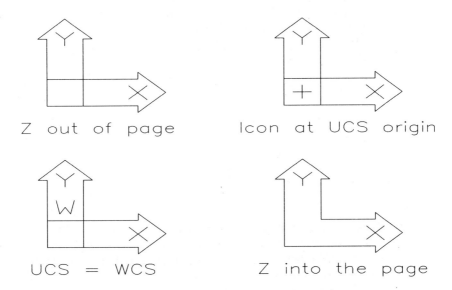

Figure 9.2 The UCS icon in various forms

Table 9.1: Meanings of the two UCSICON variable bits	
Bit	Meaning
0	UCS icon visible if this bit set
1	UCS icon placed at origin if possible if this bit set

If you see a "W" in the icon then the current UCS coincides with the WCS.

The UCS icon can be set on and off, at the origin etc. by using the UCSICON command. You can also change it by setting the AutoCAD variable UCSICON; see Table 9.1.

9.3.3 The world coordinate system

The world coordinate system is the global coordinate system, the final reference system for your drawings. The UCS is helpful for drawing in three dimensions, but they exist in the WCS and are stored as objects in the WCS. In Figure 9.1 you can clearly see the origin and direction of the WCS as indicated by the icon at the bottom left.

The WCS is also the basis for defining other coordinate systems.

It is useful to know that you can override the current UCS when specifying coordinates from the keyboard (or from an ads_command) by preceding the first coordinate by an asterisk. For example

```
ads_command (RTSTR,"_POINT",
             RTSTR,"3,3,0",    // In current UCS
             RTNONE) ; ,
```

draws a point in the current UCS, which may or may not coincide with the WCS, while

```
ads_command (RTSTR,"_POINT",
             RTSTR,"*3,3,0",    // In the WCS
             RTNONE) ; ,
```

draws a point in the WCS taking no account of the current UCS.

Some AutoCAD commands (VPOINT is a good example) switch temporarily to the WCS when asking for coordinates, and you may see this as the UCS icon changes position and the "W" appears inside it. If you do not like this behaviour you can stop it by setting the variable WORLDVIEW from the default of 1 to 0. Personally I prefer the default, always setting the viewpoint in world coordinates.

9.3.4 The entity coordinate system

The ECS is linked very closely to the arbitrary axis algorithm, a terrible animal best left alone unless you really need it. It was invented to provide a compact way of representing flat objects (for example circles, two-dimensional polylines or text) which have been rotated *out* of the two-dimensional X-Y plane. When AutoCAD first appeared it had to run in 640Kbytes of RAM on a dual floppy disk computer; these restrictions created the arbitrary axis algorithm. The extrusion vector (which has the DXF group code 210 that you have been seeing in the various result buffer examples of previous chapters) completely defines the ECS of the entity.

You may find it necessary sometimes to convert from the ECS to the WCS or UCS, because ECS coordinates are practically useless until transformed into a more "user friendly" system.

For flat two-dimensional entities which are *in* the X-Y plane the ECS and the WCS are the same; these entities have an extrusion vector equal to the unit Z direction vector. Obviously these entities most often occur in two-dimensional drawings, like printed circuit board layouts or schematic tubing diagrams and so on.

9.3.4 The model coordinate system

The MCS applies only to nested (that is blocked) entities and is not the same as the ECS described above. The origin of the MCS is the insert point of the block and the orientation is that of the UCS when the block was created. Model coordinates are returned by the ADS functions `ads_nentsel()` and `ads_nentselp()`.

9.4 3D lines and 2D lines.

Constructing three-dimensional lines and points in AutoCAD is just as easy as doing it in two dimensions, all that changes is that the Z coordinate is no longer always 0.

To make things easier when programming for 3D objects you may often find it easier to change the UCS. LST__9_2.C is an example of how to draw lines in three dimensions with and without changing the UCS. It is a parametric program which constructs a tent and sets a window into one of the sides. In this context "parametric" means that the object is created according to the parameters supplied by the user, length width and height.

The listing starts with the prototypes of four functions defined later in the program. You may want to put the last three of these four functions in your main program or library after you have tested them. The same goes for the two constants which follow the prototypes.

`test_func()` itself starts by calling `Get_Tent_Parameters()`, which returns 1 if the parameters have been obtained OK, 0 otherwise. Putting this in a separate function means that while at the moment we are just using `ads_getxxx()` functions, in the future you can change this function to use menus and dialog boxes. The working of the function itself should be fairly obvious to you, using the techniques covered in Chapter 4. Note that it is called in a way similar to the ads_getreal function, returning a value to indicate success of failure, and putting the three results (`Length`, `Width`, `Height`) in the parameters. We have to take the address of the parameter that we want to modify, e.g. `&Length`. Once inside the function, however, there is no need to take the address, because `Len`, `Wid`, and `Hi` are already addresses of (pointers

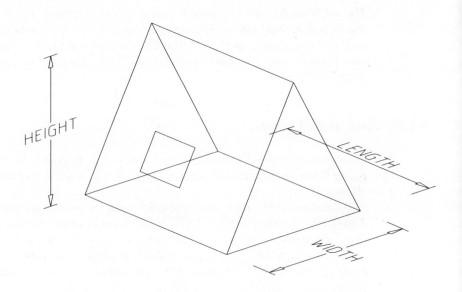

Figure 9.3 A parametric tent

to) `ads_real` variables.

If `Get_Tent_Parameters()` goes well we draw the nine lines which are our tent. Here I have defined a function `XYZ_Acad_Line()` which takes 6 parameters, which are the 3 coordinates each of the start and end points. It is a programming convenience which makes the code easier to understand.

Once the tent has been drawn we calculate one of the top corners of the tent. This is then used to set the UCS using the 3 point method. The three points we use are the origin (of the world and of the tent) the X_Dir and the Tent_Apex(). So we set the UCS in much the same way as shown in Figure 9.1 for the roof of the house.

Set_UCS_3Point() is a very simple function, using ads_command() to call the UCS command, and sending it the three points we want the UCS to be set to. Set_UCS_To_WCS() is very similiar and also defined in LST_9_1.C.

Once the UCS is set to the side of the tent all we have to do is draw a rectangle the size of the window we want to insert. In the program the window size and position are arbitrary, but you get the idea. Note that all the Z coordinates of the lines are 0, even though we are drawing in three-dimensional space. We have fixed the UCS to have an origin at the tent origin, to have its X axis along the length of the tent, and to have its Y-axis from the origin up to the apex.

You should try running this program in an empty drawing; Figure 9.3 is an example output.

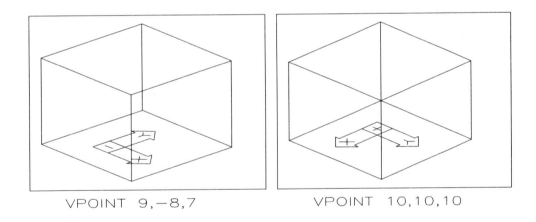

VPOINT 9,−8,7   VPOINT 10,10,10

Figure 9.4 Avoiding visual ambiguity with VPOINT

This is a simple example, but the same technique can be used for more complex problems, for example drawing contour lines on inclined surfaces. Stress analysis programs have to draw contour lines joining equal areas of stress on the object. The object is represented as many flat facets, and the contours can be drawn by setting the UCS to each of these facets and then drawing two-dimensional lines.

A tip for viewing three-dimensional objects, use the AutoCAD command VPOINT, and specify the coordinates 9,-8,7. Do this after the tent has been made and you will get a general 3D view. If you set the point of view to (for example) 10,10,10 or 1,2,1 then the view can be confusing with regular three-dimensional objects such as cubes and rectangles and pyramids. The coordinates 9,-8,7 (or 7,-8,9 for that matter) offset the viewpoint from any special angles which could confuse the eye. This viewpoint also retains the general position of the world coordinate system, with X going off roughly to the right, Y roughly upwards.

You might like to try making the following improvements to the program:

1. In Get_Tent_Parameters() use ads_getdist() so that the mouse can be used to define the sizes.
2. Allow the user to specify an origin point for the tent, so he can place it where he wants using the mouse.
3. Allow the user to specify the size of the window using ads_getdist() (mouse interaction again), checking for (and rejecting) windows too big to fit.
4. Blocking the tent when it is finished and inserting it.

9.5 Local and global object positions

9.5.1 The function ads_nentselp()

In this section I will illustrate the use of ads_nentselp() with an example taken from robotics simulation. ads_nentselp is used to get the user to select and object, often an INSERT, and returns data about where the object was selected, which object was selected, and if the object selected is inside a block. The function prototype is:

```
int ads_nentselp (const char*     Prompt,
                  ads_name        Picked_Ent,
                  ads_point       Picked_Pnt,
                  int             Prog_Pick,
                  ads_matrix      Mcs2Wcs,
                  struct resbuf** Containers);
```

The first three parameters are equal to those of ads_entsel(), see Chapter 8, except that the picked entity can actually be part of a block. If you picked an INSERT with ads_entsel() the ads_name would be set to the INSERT; with ads_nentselp it would be the part of the block, for example a LINE or a CIRCLE which is contained within the block. Another difference to be aware of is that ads_entsel() returns the main entity selected (block or polyline) whereas ads_nentselp() returns sub-entities (block component or VERTEX).

As with `ads_entsel()` the `Picked_Pnt` is the position of the point selected by the user with the mouse.

If you are using this function to get the user to select an entity `Prog_Pick` should be 0. If, on the other hand, the caller specifies the pick point and the user is not consulted, then `Prog_Pick` should be 1.

The matrix `Mcs2Wcs` is a matrix which will transform objects found in the block selected from the block's local coordinate system to the World Coordinate System.

Finally the result buffer list `Containers` is a list of entity names; these are the blocks which *contain* the entity picked. For example if you pick a line which is in BLOCKA, which itself is in BLOCKB, then this list will consist of two buffers, the first being BLOCKA, the second BLOCKB. To the *last* block in this list is the one INSERTed into the drawing.

Note that `Containers` is a pointer to a pointer to a result buffer. Many ADS functions return the result buffer pointer directly, but here it is returned in a parameter, so we need to pass the function the *address* of the place where we want the result buffer pointer to go.

You can specify keyword input as with the `ads_getxxx()` functions described in Chapter 4.

(There is also a function called `ads_nentsel()`, which is older and less flexible than `ads_nentselp()`. Autodesk advises not using `ads_nentsel()`. These two functions can be used to overcome a strange limitation, that you "cannot use the mouse or digitizer to point in perspective mode" as the error message helpfully tells you. If you want to be able to obtain coordinates of a point on an existing entity then using `ads_nentselp()` does allow it.)

9.5.2 Distances to robot sensors

Imagine that you want to simulate an environment containing several robot arms, each with a sensor. You would like to know the distance from a given point to each robot sensor. We will represent robots in the program (and in the drawing) as blocks of any shape, and sensors are represented as points within the blocks, see Figure 9.5, which shows two very simplified robot arms and a line and a point. Note that there are three points visible, one in global space, and two inside the two blocks. Remember to set PDMODE to 3 (corresponding to an "X" and) and PDSIZE to -3 (corresponding to a point size of 3% of the screen). This will make the sensors and ordinary points more visible.

LST__9_3.C is an application which asks the user to specify a point, and then repeatedly asks the user to select a robot arm. It then prints the distance from the sensor to the point. The listing begins with three prototypes of functions defined later in the file. `test_func()` itself is very short; it simply asks the user for a point and then calls `User_Probes_Arms()`.

`User_Probes_Arms()` repeatedly asks the user to select a robot arm. If the user cancels the operation then we jump straight out of the loop. If the user selects an object which is not an inserted block we tell him his mistake and jump to the start of the loop (continue) and ask him for another. We know that the object is not a block because `Containers` is `NULL`. In other words the entity

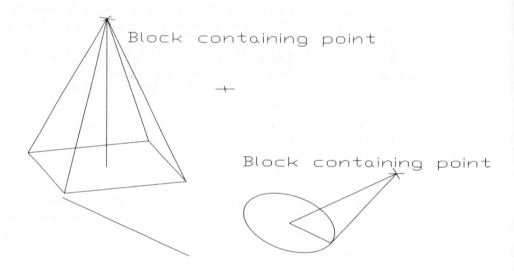

Figure 9.5 Two simple robot arms, with sensors

selected, line, circle, ellipse, point, or whatever, is not part of (contained in) a block. This will happen if in Figure 9.5 the user selects the point or the line. We print the result buffer list of the picked entity to show that it is in fact a part of the block, and not the block itself. This part of the function is not necessary, but it will help you understand `ads_nentselp()`.

Next we call `Get_Sensor_Pos()` which returns the position of the point within the block, in terms of the model coordinate system, i.e. in the coordinate system of the block. We print this position and then transform it, using the matrix initialised for us by `ads_nentselp()`, into the global world coordinate system. Finally we print the distance between this global sensor position and the position first selected by the user. `ads_mat_x_pt()` is explained in more detail in Chapter 7.

I have introduced a simple function `Print_Point()` which is useful when you have to print many `ads_points`. You pass it a message, a format and the point itself. It saves space in listings and is less clumsy than using ads_printf.

Not so simple, however, is the function `Get_Sensor_Pos()`. You should compare it with `Print_Insert_Data()` in LST__8_3.C, Chapter 8; the structure is similar. It follows the six steps for finding internal block data enumerated in the previous chapter. We pass `Get_Sensor_Pos()` the container list, and it should initialise `Pos` with the local position of a point found in the block defined in the container.

The first thing we do is search the container list. It should only have one result buffer of type E_NAME. There will be more result buffers if the object selected is an entity inside a block which is itself inside one or more further blocks. We have specified that our robot arms should consist of a single block containing a point, so there should only be one result buffer in this container list.

Next we get the name of the block using `Get_Insert_Name()` already defined and explained in Chapter 8. Then we search the BLOCK table for the entity name which in turn will gives us *another* entity name which we use to get hold of the result buffer list of the contents of the block. It is all very long winded but finally we get to the do-loop which scans the block result buffer looking for a POINT entity.

The do-loop ends either when we get to the end of the block result buffer list or if at the first POINT entity we find. `Got_Point_Coords()` will return TRUE if the entity it is given is a POINT, and in its `Pos` parameter will be the position of the point.

`Got_Point_Coords()` simply scans the result buffer list looking for two things; the code which says that this is a POINT, and the coordinates of that point. When it has scanned the list it checks to find that both conditions have been satisfied, and returns TRUE if they have been.

When you run the application remember to use the *.xy filters* of AutoCAD which allow you to specify a three-dimensional coordinate by first clicking with the mouse and then specifying the z coordinate from the keyboard. See your AutoCAD manual for more information on filters, which can be very useful in three-dimensional construction. You should prepare a drawing with several robot arms, i.e. blocks each containing a single point, and you should insert them in various places and orientations in the drawing. A good test would be to insert at least one of these blocks after having rotated the UCS about X by 67 degrees and Y by 31 degrees (for example). You can also insert the blocks with non uniform scalings, for example scaling x by 1.3 and y by 2.2.

Having constructed the drawing as explained above, return to the WCS and run the application by typing to the WCS and type "test" at the command line. You will be asked to specify a point, then asked to pick a robot arm, and the distance between the point and the sensor of the robot arm will be printed.

9.6 Transformations in ADS

This section is about transforming from one coordinate system to another, for example from the World coordinate system to the display coordinate system (DCS)or from the current UCS to the world coordinate system. ADS has a function to do this:

```
int ads_trans (const ads_point      In_Point,
               const struct resbuf* From,
               const struct resbuf* To,
               int                  Disp,
               ads_point            Out_Point);
```

In_Point is the original point, the result of the transformation is placed in Out_Point. From specifies the original coordinate system and To specifies the destination coordinate system. If Disp is 0 then the points are treated as points, or else they are treated as displacement vectors.

An example in pseudocode will help to explain ads_trans():

```
ads_trans (Roof_Origin, ROOF_UCS, WCS, 0, WCS_Roof_Origin) ;
```

The above statement would transform the point Roof_Origin in the UCS ROOF_UCS to the WCS, putting the coordinates of the transformed point into WCS_Roof_Origin. Imagine that in Figure 9.1 ROOF_UCS is shown by the UCS icon on the roof. Roof_Origin in the ROOF_UCS is 0,0,0. In the world coordinate system, however, it will be something like 1,6,7 if the corner of the roof where the UCS icon is at 1, 6 and 7 units above ground. With these conditions WCS_Roof_Origin would be set to 1,6,7.

Unfortunately the call to ads_trans() is not so simple, as you can see from the function prototype. You need to specify the From and To coordinate systems as result buffers. The result buffer will be one of the following:

- An integer where restype == RTSHORT and the integer is one of the values specified in Table 9.1.
- An entity name where restype == RTENAME. In this case the coordinate system is the ECS of the entity.
- An extrusion vector where restype == RT3DPOINT, this also specifies the ECS of an entity.

LST__9_4.C is a simple example of the use of ads_trans(). It transforms a point in the WCS to a point in the DCS. One use for this is when you want to label a three-dimensional drawing, but you want the labels to appear "flat" on the screen, that is on the display coordinate system. So the label of the three-dimensional object has to be *visibly* close to the object, yet in the plane of the screen.

In LST__9_4.C Transpoint is a "wrapper" function for `ads_trans()`, making it easier to use so that the caller does not have to worry about result buffers and so on, he simply passes the point to be transformed and the integer codes of the two coordinates systems.

To test this program you should draw a flat rectangle (in the WCS) and then get a three-dimensional view of it by typing in the following commands:

```
VPOINT 9,-8,7
ZOOM 0.9x
```

Now run the application and respond to the prompt for a three-dimensional point by moving the mouse to 4,3,0 and clicking. The reply from the program will be that this point in the DCS is at X,X,X. Now you should change to the view DCS:

```
UCS V
```

and place the cursor at that point you will find that it is in the same place (on the screen) as the point you previously specified in the world DCS. If, while still in the DCS you draw some text at this point, then move to another viewpoint you will see the text (which was once "flat" on your screen) hanging in three-dimensional space.

Another possible use for the technique in LST__9_4.C continues our robotics sensor example of the previous section. The sensor could be a camera and DCS could represent the plane of the CCD (charge coupled device, a lightweight semiconductor image sensor used in robotic applications). In this way you could

Table 9.1: `ads_trans()` coordinate system codes	
Code & define	Coordinate system
0 WCS_TRANS_CODE	World (WCS)
1 UCS_TRANS_CODE	User (current UCS)
2 DCS_TRANS_CODE	Display: DCS of current viewport when other code is 0 or 1
	Display: DCS of current modelspace viewport when other code is 3
3 PCS_TRANS_CODE	Paper space DCS, PSDCS, used only when other code is 2

work out which pixels of the camera would be activated by which objects, if at all. The situation is a more complicated in this case because a camera gives a *perspective* view, while the standard AutoCAD view is orthogonal. Setting up the viewing parameters is covered in the next chapter.

9.7 Listings

```
/////////////////////////////////////////////////////////
// LST__9_1.C
//    Showing two different ways of inserting entities
//    into the database and timing them.
//

#include <time.h> // Defines clock and clock_t

void Acad_Line (const ads_point Start, const ads_point End) ;
void Acad_Circle (const ads_point Center,
                  const ads_real Radius) ;
void Program_State (void) ;
void Restore_User_State (void) ;

#define COMMAND_WAY 1   // Change from 1 to 0 to see entmake way

int test_func (void)
{
    ads_point Start = {12.3, 7.6, 0.0} ;
    ads_point End   = { 8.7, 5.4, 0.0} ;
    ads_real Radius = 5.0 ;
    int i ;
    clock_t Start_Time, End_Time ;

#if COMMAND_WAY
    Program_State () ; // Save user stuff, impose mine
#endif

    Start_Time = clock () ;
    for (i = 0 ; i < 200 ; i++) {
        Acad_Line (Start,End) ;
        Acad_Circle (Start,Radius) ;
        Start[X] += 0.15 ;
        Radius /= 1.01 ;
    }
    End_Time = clock () ;

    ads_printf ("\nIt took %d ticks to do",
                (int)(End_Time - Start_Time)) ;
#if COMMAND_WAY
    Restore_User_State () ;   // Get user state back
    ads_printf (" using ads_command method") ;
#else
    ads_printf (" using ads_entmake method") ;
#endif
```

```
        return (Tidy_End(RTNORM)) ;
}

void Acad_Line (const ads_point Start, const ads_point End)
{
#if COMMAND_WAY

    if (ads_command (RTSTR,"_LINE",
                     RT3DPOINT,Start,
                     RT3DPOINT,End,
                     RTSTR,"",
                     RTNONE) != RTNORM) {
        ads_printf ("\nERROR, ads_command(LINE) did not work") ;
    }

#else

    struct resbuf* Line_Rb ;
    int            Res ;

    Line_Rb = ads_buildlist (RTDXF0,"LINE",
                             LINE_START_CODE,Start,
                             LINE_END_CODE,End,
                             RTNONE) ;
    if (Line_Rb == NULL) {
        ads_printf ("\nERROR, buildlist(LINE) failure:"
                    "ERRNO=%d",Get_Int_Var("ERRNO")) ;
    }

    Res = ads_entmake (Line_Rb) ;
    if (Res != RTNORM) {
        ads_printf ("\nERROR with ads_entmake(l), Res=%d,"
                    " ERRNO=%d",Res,Get_Int_Var("ERRNO")) ;
    }


    if (ads_relrb(Line_Rb) != RTNORM) {
        ads_printf ("\nERROR, LINE, could not free resbuf") ;
    }

#endif
}

void Acad_Circle (const ads_point Center,
                  const ads_real Radius)
{
#if COMMAND_WAY

    if (ads_command (RTSTR,"_CIRCLE",
```

```
                        RT3DPOINT,Center,
                        RTREAL,Radius,
                        RTNONE) != RTNORM) {
        ads_printf ("\nERROR,AL,ads_command(CIRCLE) failed") ;
    }

#else

    struct resbuf* Circle_Rb ;
    int            Res ;

    Circle_Rb = ads_buildlist (RTDXF0,"CIRCLE",
                               CENTER_CODE,Center,
                               RADIUS_CODE,Radius,
                               RTNONE) ;
    if (Circle_Rb == NULL) {
        ads_printf ("\nERROR,AC,buildlist failure:"
                    "ERRNO=%d",Get_Int_Var("ERRNO")) ;
    }

    Res = ads_entmake (Circle_Rb) ;
    if (Res != RTNORM) {
        ads_printf ("\nERROR with ads_entmake(CIRCLE),"
                    " Res=%d,ERRNO=%d",
                    Res,Get_Int_Var("ERRNO")) ;
    }


    if (ads_relrb(Circle_Rb) != RTNORM) {
        ads_printf ("\nERROR, CIRCLE,could not free resbuf") ;
    }
#endif
}


// Short variables in which to save the user state
short User_Cmd_Echo, User_Osmode, User_Ucsicon ;

void Program_State (void)
/*
PURPOSE: To save the variables as the user has set them
and to set them for a quicker and safer execution of the
ads_command() function. Here we save only three, but you
could easily save others
*/
{
    // Save the users vars
    User_Cmd_Echo = Get_Int_Var ("CMDECHO") ;
    User_Osmode   = Get_Int_Var ("OSMODE") ;
    User_Ucsicon  = Get_Int_Var ("UCSICON") ;
```

```
    // Set the programs
    Set_Int_Var ("CMDECHO",0) ; // stops echo
    Set_Int_Var ("OSMODE",0) ; // stops snapping
    Set_Int_Var ("UCSICON",0) ; // stops UCS icon
}

void Restore_User_State (void)
// Restore the users variables, as saved by the above func
{
    Set_Int_Var ("CMDECHO",User_Cmd_Echo) ;
    Set_Int_Var ("OSMODE",User_Osmode) ;
    Set_Int_Var ("UCSICON",User_Ucsicon) ;
}

//                      -- end of LST__9_1.C --

/////////////////////////////////////////////////////////////
// LST__9_2.C
//    Showing how to use the UCS to your own advantage to
//    ease some three dimensional programming tasks.
//    The example here is the parametric construction of a
//    tent with a (non parametric!) window in one side.

// Function prototypes
int Get_Tent_Parameters (ads_real* Len, ads_real* Wid,
                         ads_real* Hi) ;
void Set_UCS_3Point (const ads_point Origin,
                     const ads_point X_Axis,
                     const ads_point Y_Axis) ;
void Set_UCS_To_WCS (void) ;
void XYZ_Acad_Line (const ads_real x0,
                    const ads_real y0,
                    const ads_real z0,
                    const ads_real x1,
                    const ads_real y1,
                    const ads_real z1) ;

// Some useful 3D constants
const ads_point Zero_Point = {0,0,0} ;
const ads_point X_Dir      = {1,0,0} ;

int test_func (void)
/*
*/
{
    ads_real  Length,Width,Height ;
    ads_real  Win_Wide,Win_High ;
    ads_point Tent_Apex ;
```

```
if (!Get_Tent_Parameters (&Length,&Width,&Height)) {
    return (Tidy_End (RTNORM)) ;
}

/*
 * Draw four base lines of the tent
 */
XYZ_Acad_Line (0,0,0,                Length,0,0) ;
XYZ_Acad_Line (Length,0,0, Length,Width,0) ;
XYZ_Acad_Line (Length,Width,0,  0,Width,0) ;
XYZ_Acad_Line (0,Width,0,              0,0,0) ;

/*
 * Draw the two inverted V s at the ends of the tent
 */
XYZ_Acad_Line (0,Width/2.0,Height,  0,Width,0) ;
XYZ_Acad_Line (0,Width/2.0,Height,      0,0,0) ;
XYZ_Acad_Line (Length,Width/2.0,Height, Length,Width,0) ;
XYZ_Acad_Line (Length,Width/2.0,Height, Length,0,0) ;

/*
 * Draw the pole along the roof of the tent
 */
XYZ_Acad_Line (0,      Width/2.0,Height,
               Length,Width/2.0,Height);

/*
 * Calculate an apex of the tent
 */
Tent_Apex [X] = 0.0 ;
Tent_Apex [Y] = Width/2.0 ;
Tent_Apex [Z] = Height ;


/*
 * Set the UCS to be in the same plane as one of
 * the sides of the tent
 */
Set_UCS_3Point (Zero_Point,X_Dir,Tent_Apex) ;

/*
 * Arbitrarily set the size of the window to
 * be put in the side of the tent. You could
 * write another function like Get_Tent_Parameters
 * if you don't like the arbitrariness of this!
 */
Win_Wide = Width / 3.0 ;
Win_High = Height / 4.0 ;
```

```
    /*
     * Draw the rectangular window. Note that tho the
     * side of the tent is (obviously) not flat on the floor
     * all these lines have Z coords 0
     */
    XYZ_Acad_Line (Win_Wide,     Win_High,      0,
                   Win_Wide*2.0,Win_High,      0) ;
    XYZ_Acad_Line (Win_Wide*2.0,Win_High,      0,
                   Win_Wide*2.0,Win_High*2.0, 0) ;
    XYZ_Acad_Line (Win_Wide*2.0,Win_High*2.0, 0,
                   Win_Wide,    Win_High*2.0, 0) ;
    XYZ_Acad_Line (Win_Wide,    Win_High*2.0, 0,
                   Win_Wide,    Win_High,      0) ;

    /*
     * Restore the UCS to the World
     */
    Set_UCS_To_WCS () ;

    return (Tidy_End (RTNORM)) ;
}


int Get_Tent_Parameters (ads_real* Len, ads_real* Wid,
                         ads_real* Hi)
/*
Ask the user for the parameters of a tent to be constructed.
Putting these questions into a separate function means we can
later change this function to use menus and dialog boxes
without changing the main application.
*/
{
    int Res ;

    ads_initget (RSG_NONEG | RSG_NONULL, NULL) ;
    // Len is already an address, so no need to do &Len here
    Res = ads_getreal ("\nLength of tent (X) :",Len) ;
    if (Res == RTCAN) {
        return (0) ;
    }

    ads_initget (RSG_NONEG | RSG_NONULL, NULL) ;
    Res = ads_getreal ("\nWidth of tent (Y) :",Wid) ;
    if (Res == RTCAN) {
        return (0) ;
    }

    ads_initget (RSG_NONEG | RSG_NONULL, NULL) ;
    Res = ads_getreal ("\nHeight of tent (Z):",Hi) ;
```

```
    if (Res == RTCAN) {
        return (0) ;
    }

    return (1) ; // User answered all questions
}

void XYZ_Acad_Line (const ads_real x0,
                    const ads_real y0,
                    const ads_real z0,
                    const ads_real x1,
                    const ads_real y1,
                    const ads_real z1)
/*
Draw a line with the coordinates supplied. Uses ads_command
and therefore draws the line in the current UCS
*/
{
    ads_point Start,End ;

    Start[X] = x0 ; Start[Y] = y0 ; Start[Z] = z0 ;
    End   [X] = x1 ; End   [Y] = y1 ; End   [Z] = z1 ;

    if (ads_command (RTSTR,"_LINE",
                     RT3DPOINT,Start,
                     RT3DPOINT,End,
                     RTSTR,"",
                     RTNONE) != RTNORM) {
        ads_printf ("\nERROR, ads_command(LINE) did not work") ;
    }
}


void Set_UCS_3Point (const ads_point Origin,
                     const ads_point X_Axis,
                     const ads_point Y_Axis)

/*
PURPOSE: Set the current UCS to the plane defined by the
three points in the parameter list
*/
{
    if (ads_command (RTSTR,"_UCS",
                     RTSTR,"3",
                     RT3DPOINT,Origin,
                     RT3DPOINT,X_Axis,
                     RT3DPOINT,Y_Axis,
                     RTNONE) != RTNORM) {
        ads_printf ("\nWARNING could not Set_UCS_3Point") ;
```

```
        }
    }

void Set_UCS_To_WCS (void)
/*
PURPOSE: Set the current UCS to the WCS
*/
{
    if (ads_command (RTSTR,"_UCS",
                     RTSTR,"_W",
                     RTNONE) != RTNORM) {
        ads_printf ("\nWARNING could not Set_UCS_To_WCS") ;
    }
}
//                       -- end of LST__9_2.C --

/////////////////////////////////////////////////////////////
//   LST__9_3.C
//          An example program showing the use of ads_nentselp
//          and model to world transforms. We pretend that the
//          drawing contains several robot arms, each of which
//          has a sensor. Robot arms are defined to be any
//          block with a "POINT" in it, the point being the
//          sensor.

void Print_Point (const char*     Msg,
                  const char*     Format,
                  const ads_point Point) ;
void User_Probes_Arms (const ads_point Test_Point) ;
int  Get_Sensor_Pos (ads_point Pos, struct resbuf* Rb) ;

static int test_func (void)
{
    int       Res ;
    ads_point Test_Point ;

    Res = ads_getpoint (NULL,"\nSelect a point:",Test_Point) ;
    if (Res == RTNORM) {
        User_Probes_Arms (Test_Point) ;
    }
    return (Tidy_End(RTNORM)) ;
}

void User_Probes_Arms (const ads_point Test_Point)
/*
PURPOSE: Given a Test_Point we continually ask the
user to select robot arms and print the distance
from the sensor at the end of the robot arm to
the point in question
```

```
*/
{
    int Res ;
    ads_point Picked_Pnt,Pos ;
    ads_name  Picked_Ent ;
    ads_matrix Mcs_Wcs_Mat ;
    struct resbuf* Contain_Rb;
    struct resbuf* Picked_Rb ;

    do {
        Res = ads_nentselp ("\nPick a robot arm : ",
                            Picked_Ent,
                            Picked_Pnt, // In the WCS
                            FALSE,      // User picks
                            Mcs_Wcs_Mat,
                            &Contain_Rb) ; // Address of!!
        if (Res == RTCAN) {
            // User cancelled operation, get out of loop
            return ;
        } else if (Contain_Rb == NULL) {
            // User did not select an INSERT
            ads_printf ("\nPick a robot arm please.") ;
            continue ; // Goto top of do-loop
        }

        /*
         * Get the result buffer list of the object picked
         * and print it.
         */
        Picked_Rb = ads_entget (Picked_Ent) ;
        if (Picked_Rb == NULL) {
            ads_printf ("\nads_entget failed") ;
            (void)ads_relrb (Contain_Rb) ;
            return ;
        }
        Print_Rb_List (Picked_Rb) ;

        /*
         * Get and print the position of the sensor
         * in the robot arm, both locally and globally
         */
        if (Get_Sensor_Pos (Pos,Contain_Rb)) {
            ads_point Glob_Pos ;
            Print_Point ("\nSensor is at ","%6.3f",Pos) ;
            ads_printf (" on the robot arm") ;
            // Transform to WCS
            ads_mat_x_pt (Mcs_Wcs_Mat,Pos,Glob_Pos) ;
            Print_Point ("\nSensor is at ","%6.3f",Glob_Pos) ;
            ads_printf (" in global space (WCS)") ;
```

```
            ads_printf ("\nThe sensor is %6.3f from"
                        " the test point ",
                        ads_distance (Test_Point,Glob_Pos)) ;
        } else {
            ads_printf ("\nCould not get sensor data") ;
        }

        // Free the ram used for result buffers
        (void)ads_relrb (Picked_Rb) ;
        (void)ads_relrb (Contain_Rb) ;
    } while (TRUE) ;
}

void Print_Point (const char*    Msg,
                  const char*    Format,
                  const ads_point Point)
/*
 *  A simple function to help out printing points
 */
{
    int c ;
    ads_printf ("%s [",Msg) ;
    for (c = X ; c <= Z ; c++) {
        ads_printf (Format,Point[c]) ;
        ads_printf (" ") ; // a bit of space
    }
    ads_printf ("]") ;
}

int Get_Sensor_Pos (ads_point Pos, struct resbuf* Rb)
/*
PURPOSE: Assuming that Rb is the result buffer of the
INSERT selected by the user we find out the local position
of a POINT within the BLOCK. This POINT is assumed to
be the position of a sensor in a robot arm.
See LST__8_3.C for a similar function
*/
{
    int             c ;
    ads_name        Ename ;
    struct resbuf*  Block_Rb ;
    struct resbuf*  Sub_Rb ;   // Sub-entity pointer
    ads_name        B_En ;     // The ads_name of the block
    ads_name        Next ;     // A temp
    char Block_Name [MAX_CHARS] ; // The name-string of block
    int             No_Ben,Res,Goddit ;

    /*
     * Get the ads_name of the entity in the container,
```

```
 * this is the entity which contains the object
 * selected by the user
 */
c = 0 ;
while (Rb != NULL) {
    if (Rb->restype == E_NAME) {
        ads_name_set (Rb->resval.rlname,Ename) ;
    } else {
        ads_printf ("\nERROR, not an E_NAME") ;
        return (FALSE) ;
    }
    c++ ;
    Rb = Rb->rbnext ;
}
/*
 * In this simple example there should only be
 * one container
 */
if (c != 1) {
    ads_printf ("\nERROR, too many containers") ;
    return (FALSE) ;
}

/*
 * The container should be a block,
 * get it's name. This function defined in LST__8_3.C
 */
Get_Insert_Name (Block_Name,Ename) ;

/*
 * Get the result buffer list for the block
 */
Block_Rb = ads_tblsearch ("BLOCK",Block_Name,0) ;
if (Block_Rb == NULL) {
    ads_printf ("\nWARNING, could not find <%s>"
                " block in tables ",Block_Name) ;
    return (FALSE) ;
}

/*
 * Loop over the Block_Rb list until we find the
 * entity name for this block. This entity name
 * will later be used to get hold of the list
 * of entities within the block
 */
No_Ben = TRUE ; // Not yet found it
Rb     = Block_Rb ;
do {
    if (Rb->restype == BLOCK_EN_CODE) {
```

```
                ads_name_set (Rb->resval.rlname,B_En) ;
                No_Ben = 0 ;  // Found it!
            } else {
                Rb = Rb->rbnext ; // Look at next buffer
            }
        } while (No_Ben) ;

        (void)ads_relrb (Block_Rb) ;

        /*
         * Now loop over the entities in this block
         * looking for a point and getting the coordinates
         * of the point within the block
         */
        Goddit = FALSE ;
        do {
            Sub_Rb = ads_entget (B_En) ;  // Get it

            Goddit = Got_Point_Coords (Pos,Sub_Rb) ;

            (void)ads_relrb (Sub_Rb) ;    // Release it

            if (Goddit) {
                break ; // Got all the data we want
            }

            // Get the next entity within the block
            Res = ads_entnext (B_En,Next) ;
            ads_name_set (Next,B_En) ;

        } while (Res == RTNORM) ;

        if (!Goddit) {
            ads_printf ("\nERROR, robot arm does"
                        " not contain a sensor.") ;
            return (FALSE) ;
        }

        return (TRUE) ;
}

int Got_Point_Coords (ads_point Coords, struct resbuf* Rb)
/*
Test the result buffer to see if it is a POINT, and if so
return the coordinates of the point. If this function is
used within a BLOCK it returns coords relative to the
else it returns global coords.
*/
{
```

```
        int Is_Point, Got_Coords ;

        Is_Point = FALSE ;
        Got_Coords = FALSE ;

        while (Rb != NULL) {
            if (Rb->restype == ENTITY_TYPE_CODE) {
                if (strcmpi ("POINT",Rb->resval.rstring)!=0) {
                    // This is not a point
                    return (FALSE) ;
                } else {
                    // Yep, this is a point alright
                    Is_Point = TRUE ;
                }
            } else if (Rb->restype == POINT_COORD_CODE) {
                ads_point_set (Rb->resval.rpoint,Coords) ;
                Got_Coords = TRUE ;
            }
            Rb = Rb->rbnext ;
        }

        if (Is_Point && Got_Coords) {
            return (TRUE) ;
        } else {
            return (FALSE) ;
        }
    }

//                       -- end of LST__9_3.C --

/////////////////////////////////////////////////////////////
//  LST__9_4.C
//        An example program showing the use of ads_trans.
//        In this case the transformation is from the WCS
//        to the DCS.

void Transpoint (ads_point To_Pos,
                 const int To_Cs,
                 const ads_point From_Pos,
                 const int From_Cs) ;

static int test_func (void)
{
    int         Res ;
    ads_point G_Point,Dcs_Point ;

    Set_UCS_To_WCS () ; // defined in LST__9_2.C

    Res = ads_getpoint (NULL,"\nSelect a 3D point:",G_Point) ;
```

```
    if (Res != RTNORM) {
        return (Tidy_End(RTNORM)) ;
    }


    Transpoint (Dcs_Point,DCS_TRANS_CODE,  // To
                G_Point,WCS_TRANS_CODE) ;  // From

    // Print_Point defined in LST__9_3.C
    Print_Point ("\nThe WCS coords are:","%6.3f",G_Point) ;
    Print_Point ("\nThe DCS coords are:","%6.3f",Dcs_Point) ;

    return (Tidy_End(RTNORM)) ;
}

void Transpoint (ads_point To_Pos,
                 const int To_Cs,
                 const ads_point From_Pos,
                 const int From_Cs)
/*
*/
{
    struct resbuf From,To ;
    int Res ;

    From.restype     = RTSHORT ;
    From.resval.rint = From_Cs ;
    To.restype       = RTSHORT ;
    To.resval.rint   = To_Cs ;
    Res = ads_trans (From_Pos,&From,&To,0,To_Pos) ;
    if (Res != RTNORM) {
        ads_printf ("\nads_trans failure, Res=%d,"
                    "ERRNO=%d",Get_Int_Var("ERRNO")) ;
    }
}

//                       -- end of LST__9_4.C --
```

3D objects and rendering

10

10.1 Introduction

In this chapter I introduce two intrinsically three-dimensional objects and how to render scenes with these objects in three dimensions. One of the benefits of AutoCAD is that the "rendering engine" is already included in the software, you only have to create the object and specify how to look at it (from where and in what direction) and how to render it (using which shading algorithm).

There are three sorts of what could roughly be called rendering:

- Hidden line removal, the object looks solid but has no coloring or shading. The internals of 3DFACEs are obviously opaque, but not coloured. While not as spectacular as shading or rendering it is well adapted to plotting or printing on devices of only one or two colours.
- Shading, where objects have visible surfaces of definite colors, and there is a certain amount of shadowing, giving a better feel for depth than simple hidden line removal.
- True rendering, where the properties of the materials of the objects are taken into account when creating the image.

This chapter concentrates on the second sort, shading.

10.2 The 3DFACE entity

A 3DFACE is an entity which usually a flat with three or four sides. It is different from a SOLID (which creates a two-dimensional triangle or quadrilateral) in that it was created to be used in three-dimensional drawings.

When you use the "shade" command on a three-dimensional drawing SOLIDs are transparent (despite their name!) whereas 3DFACEs are opaque, you cannot see through them. This opacity only becomes apparent (if you will excuse the phrase) when you shade or render the drawing, when you first insert the 3DFACE it looks just like a closed polyline, i.e. it is transparent.

If you have ever tried exploding (using the AutoCAD "EXPLODE" command) the three-dimensional entities such as bowls, spheres and boxes which were under the Release 12 3D objects menu, you will have found that they become collections of 3DFACEs. Also exploding AME (Advanced Modelling Extension, a solid modeller, for those of you using Release 11 or 12) objects produces collections of 3DFACEs.

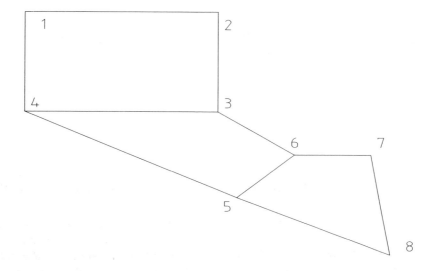

Figure 10.1 The sequence to create multiple 3DFACEs

The command 3DFACE can create several 3DFACE entities without exiting from the command, rather like the LINE command. The sequence of points you have to supply to create three connected 3DFACEs is shown in Figure 10.1.

Note that though all the faces were created together, they do not form a single entity; you can move and erase the faces individually just as you can LINE entities.

The parametric tent we built in Chapter 9 was transparent, built of lines. If we had built it using 3DFACEs it would hide, shade or render into an apparently solid object; see Figure 10.2. Note that the appearance of lines, circles and ellipses etc. does not change with the SHADE command, but they may be hidden behind solid objects. Text cannot be hidden behind solid shaded objects, it appears to "shine through" them.

LST_10_1.C is a simple application which creates a circus tent. It asks the user

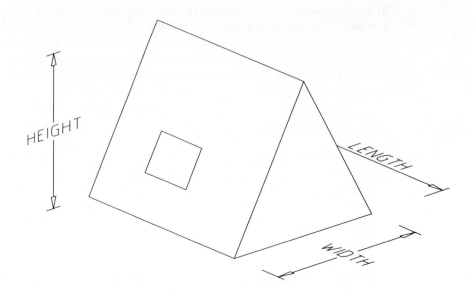

Figure 10.2 The parametric tent created with 3DFACEs

for the center point and radius of the tent and the number of sides, and it creates the tent using these parameters. The application assumes that the tent is two-thirds the radius high and it constructs the tent using 3DFACE entities.

Two "helper" functions are defined in the listing, the first is Insert_3DFACE(), which you should understand completely by now. Note the extra

```
RTSTR,"",    // end 3DFACE command.
```

to end the 3DFACE command, just as we do when using ads_command() to draw LINE entities. Insert_3DFACE() can create 3 or 4 sided faces, and the current UCS is used.

The second helper function is Standard_3D_View(), which is simple but useful. It is the atomisation of the trick explained in section 9.4 of the previous chapter. It puts the viewer in an unambiguous position, and also pulls back a little bit so that edges of objects are not touching the edge of the screen.

The VPOINT command in `Standard_3D_View()` will cause the drawing to regenerate, doing a ZOOM EXTENTS at the same time. After a ZOOM EXTENTS the zoom is such that some parts of the objects in the drawing touch the edges of the screen. These objects may not be clearly visible because they merge with the borders of the viewport. So `Standard_3D_View()` then zooms "in" by a factor of 0.9 (or zooms "out" by a factor of 10% depending on how you want to think of it), thus making sure that none of the objects touch the borders of the viewport.

Now on to the main function, `Build_Circus_Tent()`. The input parameters are the center of the tent, the radius and the number of sides. The declarations of `Wall` and `Trig` show that we will use a four sided 3DFACE for the wall and a three sided 3DFACE for the triangles forming the cupola of the tent. You can see from the listing that the first and last corners of each `Wall` section are always at ground level, and the middle two corners are always at one-third of the radius high.

The highest point triangular section from each wall section to the center pole is always at one position, the top of the center pole, and the center pole here is arbitrarily set at two-thirds the radius in height.

Next we go into a for-loop which loops `N_Sides` times. Each loop draws two

Table 10.1: Meaning of SHADEDGE values	
Value	Meaning
0	Faces are shaded with no edge highlighting
1	Faces are shaded faces with the edges highlighted in the background color
2	Face surfaces are in the background color, and visible edges in the object's color. Gives a result similar to the HIDE command
3	Faces are not shaded, but have their original color, and the edges are the background color with no lighting effect. This is the default value

3DFACE entities, a wall and a "roof-triangle". The maths for the location of X and Y coordinates are very similar to those in LST__2_1.C, see Chapter 2.

Once the user has specified the parameters and the circus tent has been drawing `Standard_3D_View()` is called to give a good general view of the object created. Now we can go onto shading, described in the next section. Save this drawing so that you can experiment with the commands and variables described next.

10.3 Shading and rendering

10.3.1 Shading, SHADEDGE and SHADEDIF

The results of the AutoCAD command SHADE depends a lot on the setting of an AutoCAD integer variable called SHADEDGE. It controls if and how edges of objects appear; see Table 10.1.

For options 0 and 1 you need at least a 256 color display to get decent results. This is not a problem with present day graphics cards. Options 2 and 3 are useful for displays with fewer colors, and also if you want a "cleaner" look to the image. Once you have created your circus tent (or several tents) you should experiment by doing four SHADEs, each with one of the four options of SHADEDGE.

There is another variable that you can use to change the aspect of the shaded image, and that is SHADEDIF, the percentage of the surface which reflects diffusely, as opposed to ambient light. To emphasise shading SHADEDIF should be set to 100, to get images with a very "flat" look SHADEDIF should be set to 0 (not very appealing at all). The default value is 70.

10.3.2 The RENDER command

The AutoCAD RENDER command gives you much more control over what you see and the quality of the final image is much higher than SHADE. RENDER is not really a part of AutoCAD as SHADE is, and a programmer has little control over what the user sees. Your application can only set the viewing parameters (explained in the next section) and call RENDER.

For completeness I will briefly explain a few terms of the RENDER dialog box:.

- Flat shading: This is when no attempt is made to smooth out the facets which are used to represent curved surfaces. For example SPHERE or CYLINDER command create objects which if rendered with flat shading seem to be made up of many small flat faces.
- Gouraud shading: This gives a matt finish to the objects
- Phong shading: This gives a glossy plastic finish to the objects.

You should create a drawing with a few cylinders and spheres of different colors and experiment with various settings of the RENDER command.

10.4 Viewing parameters and variables

Your application have total control over the viewing parameters. You should imagine that you have a camera that can view the drawing in perspective and orthogonally, and that you can place this camera where you want and point it in any direction. You can also change the zoom lens of the camera.

Figure 10.3 shows graphically some of the variables that are used for three-dimensional viewing. The example here is when we are in perspective mode. The truncated pyramid is called the viewing frustrum, and luckily AutoCAD handles all the clipping and transformations required to use it. You get into perspective mode using the DVIEW command and changing the distance. To get out of perspective mode use the DVIEW command and type "OFF".

The TARGET variable is a three-dimensional point and is *where* the camera is pointing. The VIEWDIR is also a point variable, and is the *direction* from the

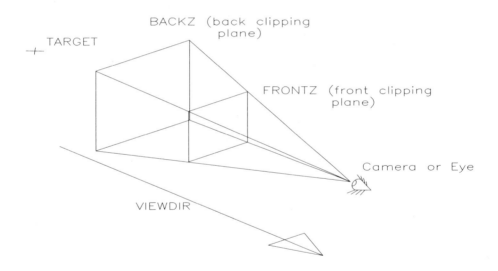

Figure 10.3 The viewing pyramid and view variables

TARGET to the camera. So, strangely enough the VIEWDIR is the direction *from* the target *to* the camera. There is no variable for the camera position; you need to get this by adding the VIEWDIR to the TARGET. You could do this with the following code fragment.

```
ads_point Target, View_Dir, Camera ;
```

```
Get_Point_Var (Target, "TARGET") ;
Get_Point_Var (View_Dir, "VIEWDIR") ;
ads_addvec (Target, View_Dir, Camera) ;
```

FRONTZ and BACKZ are "clipping planes". Only objects, or parts of objects, which fall within FRONTZ to BACKZ will be visible. FRONTZ is a real read-only variable and is the distance from the camera to the front clipping plane. Obviously the bigger this distance the fewer objects (or parts of objects) you will see.

BACKZ is the distance from the camera to the back clipping plane. The bigger this number the more objects or parts of objects you will see.

Table 10.2: Meaning of VIEWMODE bits (a read only variable)	
Bit	Meaning
0	Perspective view if set (DVIEW and a distance)
1	Front clipping is on if set (DVIEW, CLIP, FRONT)
2	Back clipping is on if set (DVIEW, CLIP, BACK)
3	UCSFOLLOW variable is on if set, see Appendix C
4	Front clip is *not* at eye if set, FRONTZ defines the clipping plane

Both FRONTZ and BACKZ can be changed using DVIEW, use the CLIP sub-option and then FRONT or BACK. Use DVIEW CLIP OFF to turn off clipping. It is normal for the user to change these planes using the mouse, though obviously in your application you would have to send real numbers to the ads_command.

VIEWMODE is a read only bit coded integer variable which your application can consult (but not change) to get information about the mode of the current view. You can change the mode of the current view by using DVIEW in ads_command() for example.

Some other viewing variables to look at are VIEWTWIST, VIEWCTR, VIEWSIZE, DISPSILH and ISOLINES; see Appendix C.

One thing you should be aware of when in perspective mode is that when ads_getpoint() will not work, the user will get a message to this effect. You can, however, select objects in perspective mode.

10.5 Meshes

The AutoCAD 3DMESH command is a way of creating a surface. It is actually stored as a special polyline. An example mesh is shown in Figure 10.4. It is one of the entities which, if exploded, becomes a set of 3DFACE objects. It was designed to be created by programs and not users because defining all the points of a mesh by hand is very tedious and error-prone.

To see what ready made 3D meshes look like try a few of the options from the 3D command.

LST_10_2.C shows how to create 3DMESHes. It creates a three-dimensional undulating surface according to some parameters input by the user. The mesh is on a unit square. The parameters are:

- The number of points in the N direction (think of it as X), `N_Points`
- The number of points in the M direction (think of it as Y), `M_Points`
- The frequency of undulation in the X direction, `X_Freq`
- The frequency of undulation in the Y direction, `Y_Freq`
- The size (or amplitude) of the undulations, `Mesh_High`

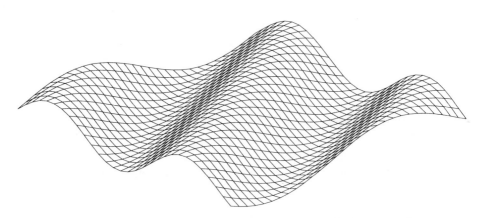

Figure 10.4 A mesh created with the 3DMESH command

- The origin of the mesh, `Origin`.

These parameters are grouped together in a structure type called `Mesh_t` defined at the top of LST_10_2.C. We get these numbers from the user by calling `Get_Parameters()`, which uses the normal `ads_initget()` and ads_getxxx() functions. Note that there is a range of values allowed for the number of points; from 2 to 256 points are allowed, no more, no less.

If the user has not abandoned the command Get_Parameters() returns TRUE and we call Draw_Mesh() , which creates a wavy mesh like the one shown in Figure 10.4 (which has parameters 30,30,10,6,0.2). The function itself is quite simple, it starts the 3DMESH command and sends it the number of N points and M points. (In this example the "directions" N and M correspond to x and y, though this need not be so.)

Next we loop over the points, calculating x and y on a grid within a 1 by 1 square, and calculating z as a sine function whose parameter varies with x and y and X_Freq and Y_Freq. The result is put in Mesh_Point, which is then added to the Origin, to put the mesh at the place specified by the user. Finally ads_command() is used to send the point to the 3DMESH command.

Test this application in an empty drawing and get a good three-dimensional view to look at the results. Try the LIST command on the created mesh, you will find that it lists as a polyline. You should also try the SHADE and RENDER commands on the mesh, but remember to keep the number of points below about 2500 (50 by 50 points) or else the renderer make take an hour or so!

As I said previously meshes need not be on regular grids, they can even be formed into spheres and cylinders or almost any shape you care to think of, just specify the x, y and z coordinates of the points on the surface you want to create. LST_10_2.C would be a good starting point for mapping the height of terrain in a GIS (Geographical Information System) application.

Two other types of mesh you might like to look at are POLYGON meshes and POLYFACE meshes, see the AutoCAD documentation and/or on-line help) for the PFACE mesh command. The REVSURF and TABSURF commands can also be used to produce complex three-dimensional objects quickly.

10.6 Other 3D objects

There are many other objects which you can use to create three-dimensional drawings quickly. Here is a brief list of the commands you can use (in Release 13) to create three-dimensional objects:

- BOX, creates a box or cube
- SPHERE, creates a sphere
- CYLINDER, creates a cylinder
- TORUS, creates a torus (i.e. a donut). Can also be used to create rugby ball shaped objects
- WEDGE, creates a wedge (five surfaces)
- EXTRUDE, used to create three-dimensional objects from two-dimensional outlines, closed polylines, circles, ellipses etc. It can also be used along a

"path line" to create curving tubes with the profile of the selected two-dimensional object. Extrusions can also be tapered

- REVOLVE, used in much the same way as EXTRUDE, two-dimensional objects can be revolved around the X or Y axis to form a solid object
- UNION, used to add any two or more of the above objects to create a third composite object
- SUBTRACT, as with UNION, you can take one object away from another, leaving a hole in the original object
- INTERSECT, used to create an object which is the intersection of two solid objects

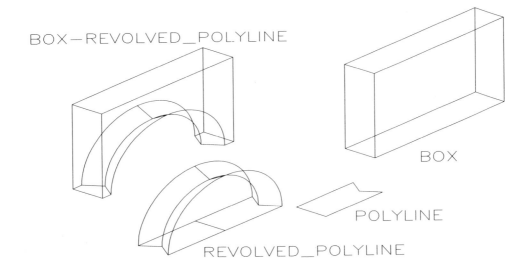

Figure 10.5 Arch created by subtracting revolved PLINE from a box

The objects created with these commands will all seem "transparent" and not "solid". To gain an impression of their solidity you should do a HIDE, SHADE or RENDER. Figure 10.5 shows what you can do with these simple commands. A polyline was drawn, then revolved around itself to produce what looks like a half-pulley. Then a slightly bigger box was created, and the half-pulley was subtracted from the box. In the figure the components have been separated, but in reality they would all have to occupy the same space. The variable which controls the smoothness of shaded and rendered surfaces is FACETRES, see Appendix C.

AME is no longer supported from Release 13 onwards. If you are using Release 12 or 11 you can use `ads_command()` to call AME commands, but for future portability it is better to stick with Release 13 objects. A command AMECONVERT is provided to let you convert old AME objects into Release 13 objects.

10.7 Listings

```c
///////////////////////////////////////////////////////////////////
//   LST_10_1.C
//          Illustrates the creation of a circus tent using
//          3DFACEs
//

#include <math.h> // Important for sin and cos functions

// Prototypes of functions defined later in the file
void Build_Circus_Tent (const ads_point Cen,
                        const ads_real Rad,
                        const int N_Sides) ;
void Insert_3DFACE (const ads_point* Points,
                    const int N_Points) ;
void  Standard_3D_View (void) ;

static int test_func (void)
/*
 * Create a circus tent whose parameters are defined
 * by the user
 */

{
    int       Res,N_Sides ;
    ads_point Center ;
    ads_real  Radius ;

    /*
     * Make sure we start off in the world, not some
     * strange user coordinate system
     */
    Set_UCS_To_WCS () ; // defined in LST__9_2.C

    // Get center point from user, mouse or keyboard
    Res = ads_getpoint (NULL,"\nSelect center of"
                        " tent:",Center) ;
```

```
        if (Res != RTNORM) {
            return (Tidy_End(RTNORM)) ;
        }

        // Get radius by asking for a distance from Center
        // This will do rubber-banding because the first
        // parameter is not NULL
        Res = ads_getdist (Center,"\nRadius of"
                            " tent:",&Radius) ;
        if (Res != RTNORM) {
            return (Tidy_End(RTNORM)) ;
        }

        // Do not accept 0 or negative input for the
        // number of sides of the tent...
        ads_initget (RSG_NONULL | RSG_NONEG,NULL) ;
        Res = ads_getint ("\nNumber of sides :",&N_Sides) ;
        if (Res != RTNORM) {
            return (Tidy_End(RTNORM)) ;
        }

        // Create the tent out of 3DFACES
        Build_Circus_Tent (Center,Radius,N_Sides) ;

        // View the tent
        Standard_3D_View () ;

        return (Tidy_End(RTNORM)) ;
}

void Build_Circus_Tent (const ads_point Cen,
                        const ads_real Rad,
                        const int N_Sides)
/*
Build a circus tent situated at Cen, of Rad radius
and with N_Sides, using 3DFACEs.
*/
{
    int        i ;
    ads_point Wall[4] ;
    ads_point Trig[3] ;

    /*
     * Set the environment to stop snapping and command
     * echoing. You should really save what was there
     * first, and after this function is finished
     * restore it.
     */
    Set_Int_Var ("CMDECHO",0) ;   // No command echo
```

```
Set_Int_Var ("SNAPMODE",0) ; // No snapping
Set_Int_Var ("ORTHOMODE",0) ; // Ortho off
Set_Int_Var ("OSMODE",0) ;    // No Object Snap

// These coords do not change within the for-loop
Wall [0][Z] = 0.0 ;
Wall [1][Z] = Rad / 3.0 ;
Wall [2][Z] = Rad / 3.0 ;
Wall [3][Z] = 0.0 ;

// Neither do these
Trig [2][X] = Cen[X] ;
Trig [2][Y] = Cen[Y] ;
Trig [2][Z] = 2 * (Rad / 3.0) ;
// The above says that the center of the tent is
// two thirds the radius in height

/*
 * Each loop of this for creates a vertical wall
 * and a triangle connecting the wall and the
 * top of the center pole of the tent
 */
for (i = 0 ; i < N_Sides ; i++) {
    ads_real Angle_0, Angle_1 ;

    Angle_0 = (i * TWOPI) / N_Sides ;
    Angle_1 = ((i + 1)*TWOPI) / N_Sides ;

    // first two points equal except for Z
    Wall [0][X] = Cen[X] + (Rad * sin(Angle_0)) ;
    Wall [0][Y] = Cen[Y] + (Rad * cos(Angle_0)) ;
    Wall [1][X] = Wall [0][X] ;
    Wall [1][Y] = Wall [0][Y] ;

    // last two points equal except for Z
    Wall [2][X] = Cen[X] + (Rad * sin(Angle_1)) ;
    Wall [2][Y] = Cen[Y] + (Rad * cos(Angle_1)) ;
    Wall [3][X] = Wall [2][X] ;
    Wall [3][Y] = Wall [2][Y] ;

    // Draw the vertical wall
    Insert_3DFACE (Wall,4) ;

    ads_point_set (Wall[1],Trig[0]) ;
    ads_point_set (Wall[2],Trig[1]) ;

    // Draw the triangle from wall to center pole
    Insert_3DFACE (Trig,3) ;
}
```

```
}

void Insert_3DFACE (ads_point* Coords, int N_Sides)
/*
PURPOSE To insert the 3DFACE passed to us.
*/
{
    if (N_Sides == 4) {
        if (ads_command (RTSTR,"_3DFACE",
                         RT3DPOINT,Coords[0],
                         RT3DPOINT,Coords[1],
                         RT3DPOINT,Coords[2],
                         RT3DPOINT,Coords[3],
                         RTSTR,"",    // end 3DFACE command
                         RTNONE) != RTNORM) {
            ads_printf ("\nERROR, could not do 4"
                    " sided 3DFACE") ;
        }
    } else if (N_Sides == 3) {
        if (ads_command (RTSTR,"_3DFACE",
                         RT3DPOINT,Coords[0],
                         RT3DPOINT,Coords[1],
                         RT3DPOINT,Coords[2],
                         RTSTR,"",    // no 4th point
                         RTSTR,"",    // end 3DFACE command
                         RTNONE) != RTNORM) {
            ads_printf ("\nERROR, could not do"
                    " 3 sided 3DFACE") ;
        }
    } else {
        ads_printf ("\nERROR, N_Sides = %d",N_Sides) ;
    }
}

void Standard_3D_View (void)
/*
 * Sets up an unambiguous and clear view of
 * the three dimensional world.
 */
{
    (void)ads_command (RTSTR,"_VPOINT",  // View from a good...
                       RTSTR,"9,-8,7",   // ...standpoint
                       RTSTR,"_ZOOM",    // Pull back...
                       RTSTR,"0.9X",     // ...a bit
                       RTNONE) ;
}

//                      -- end of LST_10_1.C --
```

```
///////////////////////////////////////////////////////////////
//  LST_10_2.C
//          Illustrates the use of the 3DMESH object.
//

#include <math.h> // Important for sin and cos functions

// A tructure to define a wavy mesh
typedef struct {
    ads_real X_Freq     ; // Prop. to oscillation freq in X
    ads_real Y_Freq     ; // Prop. to oscillation freq in Y
    int      N_Points   ; // Number of points in X
    int      M_Points   ; // Number of points in Y
    ads_real Mesh_High ; // Amplitude of the waves
    ads_point Origin    ; // Origin of the 1 by 1 square
} Mesh_t ;

// Function prototypes
int  Get_Parameters (Mesh_t* Mesh) ;
void Draw_Mesh (const Mesh_t* Mesh) ;

static int test_func (void)
{
    Mesh_t  Mesh ;

    if (Get_Parameters (&Mesh)) {
        Draw_Mesh (&Mesh) ;
    }

    return (Tidy_End(RTNORM)) ;
}

int Get_Parameters (Mesh_t* Mesh)
/*
PURPOSE: To get the user to fill in the Mesh structure.
         Returns TRUE if all goes well, FALSE otherwise
*/
{
    (void)ads_initget (RSG_NONEG | RSG_NOZERO, NULL) ;
    if (ads_getint ("\nN_Points : ",&Mesh->N_Points) != RTNORM) {
        return (FALSE) ;
    } else if ((N_Points < 2) || (N_Points > 256))
        ads_printf ("\nToo few or two many points") ;
        return (FALSE) ;
    }

    (void)ads_initget (RSG_NONEG | RSG_NOZERO, NULL) ;
    if (ads_getint ("\nM_Points : ",&Mesh->M_Points) != RTNORM) {
        return (FALSE) ;
```

```
    } else if ((M_Points < 2) || (M_Points > 256))
        ads_printf ("\nToo few or two many points") ;
        return (FALSE) ;
    }

    (void)ads_initget (RSG_NONEG | RSG_NOZERO, NULL) ;
    if (ads_getreal ("\nX_Freq : ",&Mesh->X_Freq) != RTNORM) {
        return (FALSE) ;
    }

    (void)ads_initget (RSG_NONEG | RSG_NOZERO, NULL) ;
    if (ads_getreal ("\nY_Freq : ",&Mesh->Y_Freq) != RTNORM) {
        return (FALSE) ;
    }

    (void)ads_initget (RSG_NONEG | RSG_NOZERO, NULL) ;
    if (ads_getreal ("\nHigh : ",&Mesh->Mesh_High) != RTNORM) {
        return (FALSE) ;
    }

    if (ads_getpoint (NULL,"\nOrigin : ",Mesh->Origin) != RTNORM)
{
        return (FALSE) ;
    }

    return (TRUE) ;
}

void Draw_Mesh (const Mesh_t* Mesh)
/*
PURPOSE: To draw the mesh passed as a parameter
*/
{
    int     Res,n,m ;

    /*
     * Call the 3DMESH command and tell it how many
     * N and M points there are
     */
    Res = ads_command (RTSTR,"_3DMESH",
                        RTSHORT,Mesh->N_Points,
                        RTSHORT,Mesh->M_Points,
                        RTNONE) ;

    if (Res != RTNORM) {
        ads_printf ("\nERROR starting 3DMESH command") ;
        return ;
    }
```

```
/*
 * Give the 3DMESH command the co-ordinates of
 * all the points.
 */
for (n = 0 ; n < Mesh->N_Points ; n++) {
    for (m = 0 ; m < Mesh->M_Points ; m++) {
        ads_point Mesh_Point ;
        ads_real  x,y,z ;

        // A square grid of points
        x = (ads_real)n / (ads_real)(Mesh->N_Points-1) ;
        y = (ads_real)m / (ads_real)(Mesh->M_Points-1) ;

        // Make waves!
        z = (Mesh->Mesh_High/2.0) *
            sin ((x*Mesh->X_Freq) + (y*Mesh->Y_Freq)) ;

        Mesh_Point[X] = x ;
        Mesh_Point[Y] = y ;
        Mesh_Point[Z] = z ;

        ads_addvec (Mesh_Point,Mesh->Origin,Mesh_Point) ;

        Res = ads_command (RT3DPOINT,Mesh_Point,RTNONE) ;
        if (Res != RTNORM) {
            ads_printf ("\nERROR with 3DMESH command") ;
            return ;
        }
    }
}
//                          -- end of LST_10_2.C --
```

Working with extended data

11.1 Introduction

Extended data was introduced to AutoCAD in version 11, for use with AME (Advanced Modelling Extension) and also for programmers of ADS, which made its appearance at the same time.

In this chapter you will learn about extended data (XDATA) which is supplementary data attached by applications to entities. Any entity can have extended data, lines , blocks, points, text and so on. This chapter covers what you have to do to be able to add extended data to entites, how to write and read the data and some of its limits.

11.2 Why use extended data?

Sometimes you want to attach data to an object which is not graphical. The data is associated with a graphical object, but in itself may not be visible. This has been possible for a long time in AutoCAD by using *attributes*. There are three main disadvantages to using this method:

1. Attributes can only be attached to BLOCK entities, they cannot be attached to LINE or CIRCLE or any other sort of entity.
2. Attributes are awkward to program, being designed initially for the use of a sophisticated designed who does not necessarily know, or want to know, how to program.
3. Attributes can be made visible. You may like to keep the data associated with an object secret.

4. Attributes can be changed by the user. This may be bad if your program relies on the data being present and undamaged.

Extended data solves all the above problems, but what would you use it for? An example could be a lighting layout design program, where short lines represent neons lamps set in a ceiling. You may want to switch the neon lamps on and off so that you can see the different lighting effects.

Another example would be attaching the physical weight of an object to the block representing it as extended data. Other physical values could also be attached, like elasticity, conductivity and so on.

A final example is a printed circuit board layout program, where conversion between the schematic (logical) diagram and the layout requires that the user select which tracks need to be the shortest because they are important signal paths, and which tracks have to be wide because they carry power. Extended data could be used to store this information in the schematic entities, for use in the part of the application which does the (automatic) physical layout.

11.3 The structure of an entity's extended data

Figure 11.1 illustrates the structure of the result buffer list of a circle with some extended data. Extended data always follows the normal data of an entity, and in this example, if you called `Print_Rb_List()` (see Chapter 5, LST__5_1.C) on the result buffer for the circle you would get a print out like this:

```
(-1 - 12345678 87654321)
(0 - "CIRCLE")
(5 - "2F")
(100 - "AcDbEntity")
(67 - 0)
(8 - "0")
(100 - "AcDbCircle")
(10 - 23.4 56.7 0.0)
(40 - 12.9)
(210 - 0.0 0.0 1.0)
(-3 - unknown type)
(1001 - "ATADX-AVORP")
(1000 - "my string xdata")
```

The extended data sentinel, -3 above, (EXTD_SENTINEL in LST__5_1.H) is used to mark the end of ordinary data (radius, center point etc) and the start of extended data. In the above list it has an "unknown type" because it does not have a value as such, it is just a sentinel.

There is only one (if any) extended data sentinel per entity, and every application puts its data in the buffers which follow. The 1001 result buffer (EXTD_APP_NAME) marks the start of extended data, and the string of this buffer contains the "registered name" of the application. What follows is a series of result buffers containing the actual data that the application has associated with the entity. In the above example the application registered as "ATADX-AVORP" has added an extended data string "my string data" to the circle.

The reason for having registred names for extended data is that more than one application can attach extended data to an entity, so we have to have a way of distinguishing between the data of different applications. This is shown graphically in Figure 11.1, where the circle has exteneded data from three applications, XCOMP, MYAPP and COMW, and the line only has extended data from XCOMP. These are the names of the applications registered in the drawing

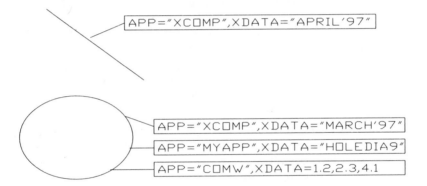

Figure 11.1 Extended data attached to a circle and a line

for extended data. The next section explains how to register your application. In reality of course you will not be able to see the data graphically as in the figure, it is invisible to all but the application program which created it.

11.4 Registering your application, `ads_regapp()`

To be able to write extended data into entities you need to register you application using `ads_regapp()` , the function prototype of which is given below:

```
int ads_regapp (const char* App_Name) ;
```

You pass the name of the application and the function returns RTNORM if all goes well. If RTERROR is returned you should look at ERRNO to see what went wrong. The name of the registered application is stored in the tables section of the drawing; see Chapter 5 section 5.4.

The name of the function *suggests* that every application has a single APPID (*app*lication *id*entifier) in the tables section, but this is not true, and you can register as many names as you want. This allows you to split up the extended data into separate fields. When you use `ads_entgetx()` (explained below) you pass the name that you are interested in.

You must be careful choosing the name you want to register. It can be up to 32 characters long including the 0 terminator, and it must be sufficiently original so that there is not a name clash with another application. If for example you chose "MECH-APP" as the name it is not unlikely that another developer, as lazy as yourself, would choose the same name. So you should choose a long and unusual name for your application. The AutoCAD programming manual gives a complicated method of creating the name by taking the phone number of the phone closest to where you are sitting now, the current time and data and combining them into a unique name. I personally prefer a meaningful though not obvious choice. APPID names, like BLOCK and LAYER names *cannot* contain spaces, and the name will be converted to all uppercase. The names in Figure 11.1 are really too short for a real application, and certainly "MYAPP" is not a good choice for a application's extended data registration!

In LST_11_1.C the function `Register_App()` is called every time the function test_func is run. `Register_App()` contains all the checking you need and prints out how the operation went. You only need to register the application once for every drawing, and in fact registering it twice will cause an error. Hence we first look to see if the name has been registered in the APPID table, and only if it has not we call `ads_regapp()`.

Chapter 2 section 2.2 explains that RQXLOAD is a value passed to your ADS main function every time a new drawing is loaded. This is where you should register the application in the drawing if you are going to use extended data. LST_11_1.C does it in `test_func()` for illustrative purpose only, it is over kill to look so often when once (at drawing load time) would do.

11.5 Reading and writing extended string data

LST__11_1.C is an example of setting and reading extended data. In it we ask the user to select an entity and to type in a string and then we add the string as extended data to that entity. The old value of the string is printed out, if there was one.

We do most of the work in `Set_Xdata_String()` which takes the string to be added and the `ads_name` of the entity to which the string is to be added.

After checking that the string `Val` is not too short or too long we build a result buffer list with `ads_buildlist()` which contains the application name as registered with ads_regapp. This is then used in the call to ads_entgetx(), which is much like `ads_entget()`, but with two parameters instead of one:

```
struct resbuf* ads_entgetx (const ads_name E_Name,
                            struct resbuf* An_Rb) ;
```

`ads_entgetx()` returns all the entity data which `ads_entget()` does (see Chapter 6, section 6.2), plus any extended data associated with the application whose name is in `An_Rb`. So `An_Rb` acts as a filter of extended data. If `An_Rn` is NULL then `ads_entgetx()` behaves just like `ads_entget()`.

`An_Rb` in this example contains a single application name, but it could contain several, and the list returned would contain all the extended data for all the names. Of course the names need to be present in the APPID table.

If `ads_entgetx()` fails, returning NULL instead of a valid result buffer list, you should look at ERRNO to find out what went wrong.

Once we have go the list of entity data, `Rbx`, we create a copy of the string we want to associate with the entity. We have to use a copy and not `Val` itself because the string will become part of the result buffer list which we will free at the end of the function. Inside `Set_Xdata_String()` we do not know where the string `Val` came from, if it is static, or local or global or dynamically allocated. `ads_relrb()` would attempt to free it. By creating a local copy which uses dynamically allocated ram we know that `ads_relrb()` will not have problems freeing it.

We then go over the list looking for any extended data already present, we are looking for an EXTD_SENTINEL followed by an EXTD_STR. We may or may not find these things, it depends on whether extended data from our application has already been attached to this entity.

If we do find the data then we put the old value in `Old_Ptr`, get the address of where we should put pointer to the new value, `Str_Adr`, and print the old value.

When the for-loop ends, if the entity already contains extended data, four conditions should prevail:

1. `Eb_Last` is pointing to the last valid (non NULL) result buffer
2. The extended data sentinel has been found, `Xdata_Sentinel == 1`

3. The old (current) extended data string, `Old_Ptr`, has been initialised
4. The address of where to place the new pointer, `Str_Adr` has been initialised

Note that we only look for the extended data string *after* we have found the

Value	LST_5_1.H	Comments
Table 11.1: Extended data types		
Value	LST_5_1.H	Comments
1000	EXTD_STR	Extended data string, maximum 255 characters
1001	EXTD_APP_NAME	Name of registered application, maxiumu 31 characters
1002	EXTD_CTL_STR	Extended data control string, for example "{" and "}" of AME
1003	EXTD_LYR_STR	Extended data layer name
1004	EXTD_CHUNK	Block of bytes, up to 127. For binary data, use rbinary of resbuf
1005	EXTD_HANDLE	Extended data base handle
1010	EXTD_POINT	Extended data coordinates, general use
1011	EXTD_POS	Extended data 3D world space position
1012	EXTD_DISP	Extended data 3D world space displacement
1013	EXTD_DIR	Extended data 3D world space direction
1040	EXTD_FLOAT	Extended data real number
1041	EXTD_DISP	Extended data distance value
1042	EXTD_SCALE	Extended data scale value
1070	EXTD_INT16	Extended data 16 bit integer
1071	EXTD_INT32	Extended data 32 bit integer (long)

sentinel. Extended data should always start with the sentinel and if you find the string before finding the sentinel something is wrong.

The error check just after for loop should never be TRUE, but it is better to be safe. It is the sort of check that could reveal an error in your program logic as much as an ADS failure in storing extended data.

If `Xdata_Sentinel` is 0 then this entity does not already contain our extended data and we have to create a result buffer for it. We do this with `ads_buildlist()`. Note that `EXTD_SENTINEL` is not the usual type specifier to be followed by a value, it is a value on its own, a *sentinel* or token with no need for a value. Next in the list comes the application identifier string and the string of extended data we want to add. This list is added to the end of the result buffer list of the entity.

If `Xdata_Sentinel` is 1 then extended data from our application, with our application name, already exists, and all we need to do is change the string. First we free the string that was originally there, and then we place in the buffer the string we had allocated at the beginning of the function.

Once the Rxb has been modified, either by adding the extended data or by simply changing the string that was already there, we call ads_entmod() to update the entity. The memory used by Rbx is then freed by a call to ads_relrb().

LST_11_1.C both reads and writes the extended data string, in a real program you should make two different functions, one for reading and one for writing.

You should experiment with this program, adding data to any sort of entity in the drawing, lines, blocks, circles, text etc. Note that even if you exit AutoCAD and then re-enter, the XDATA of entities is preserved.

11.6 Reading and writing other types of extended data

It is possible to write all the types of data listed in Table 11.1 as extended data. The table is in part only for guidance, and the interpretation of what you would use for an EXTD_DISP type depends on your application. A buffer of that type *must* be an ads_point, but its actual meaning depends on how you use it.

LST__11_2.C is an example of setting and reading extended data of two different types, ads_real and long. The structure is very similar to that of LST_11_1.C, except that there is no allocating and freeing of string data.

Although in both the previous examples we have used ads_entmod() to add data to an existing entity, you can use the same techniques as applied here to *create* entities with extended data using ads_entmake(), see Chapter 6, Section 6.4.1.

11.7 Space limits of extended data, ads_xdsize() and ads_xdroom()

There is a limit to how much extended data an entity can have, currently this is 16KB (16,384 bytes). While your own single application may not use very much space it is possible that other applications want to add their own extended data into the entity. The 16KB limits the *sum* of all the data from all the applications. For example if application A created 8KB of data within a single entity and application B wanted to add 9KB it would fail.

There is a function for seeing how much room is left in an entity for extended data:

```
int ads_xdroom (const ads_name Ent, long* Result);
```

You simply give it the name of the entity you are interested in and it puts the room left (in bytes) in Result. Begining C programmers should remember to pass the *address* of Result, as shown for example in LST_11_3.C:

```
Res = ads_xdroom (E_Name,&Amount) ;
```

Amount is a long, and we pass the address of it.

Another function exists for seeing how much room an extended data result buffer list would take:

```
int ads_xdsize (const struct resbuf *Xd_Rb, long* Result);
```

This takes the result buffer list and returns in Result the number of bytes the extended data would occupy if it was added to an entity. Again, remember to pass the *address* of Result .

With these two function you can always check if there is enough room in the entity for more extended data.

In practice it is rare that many applications add so much data to the same entities. You should only really call these functions if you come up with an error when trying to add data using ads_entmod(). If ads_entmod() fails while you are trying to add extended data try looking at the free data room using ads_xdroom() and how much you are trying to add using ads_xdsize(). Calling these two functions only when you need to speeds up your application.

LST_11_3.C is a simple example of using the above two functions; in it we ads_xdroom() an entity and then ads_xdsize() a result buffer, printing the results. You should try this with drawings in which you have added extended data to objects, testing the various entities. Note that LST_11_3.C defines a *third* extended data name, illustrating that several applications can add extended data to the same entity.

11.7.1 Extended data and ARX

With ARX it is possible to use "extension dictionaries" to store non-graphical data. As a general guide, if you are using both ADS and ARX functions, extended data is best for small amounts, 256 bytes or less, because of the low overhead. For larger sizes of extended data use object dictionaries.

If you want to store and read extended data using ARX you need to use the following two member functions of the AcDbObject class:

```
resbuf* xData (const char* App_Name = NULL) const;
Acad::ErrorStatus setXData (const resbuf* xdata);
```

In the first of the above functions the default parameter App_Name=NULL allows you to have all the extended data for this entity. Normally you would pass in the name of the application you are interested in. For more data on ARX and dictionaries see Chapter 17.

It is interesting to note that ASE 2.0 (AutoCAD SQL Extension), which is a database add on to Release 13, was written in ARX but uses ADS style Extended Data to store the database links.

11.8 General non-graphical data

Extended data is for use with entities. To save non-graphical general data associated with a single drawing you could do one of the following:

- Attach the data to an always present but invisible (on a frozen layer) object,a point say
- Use an external file for the data, maybe with the same name as the drawing but with a different extension
- Use "dictionaries" if you are in theARX environment, see Chapter 17.

11.9 Listings

```
///////////////////////////////////////////////////////////
// LST_11_1.C
//    Illustrating adding in an XDATA string to an entity
//    selected by the user

// The name the app is registered under
static char* App_Name="ATADX-AVORP" ;

// Function prototypes
void Register_App (void) ;
int Set_Xdata_Str (const char* Val, const ads_name E_Name) ;

int test_func (void)
/*
Shows how extended data can be written (and incidentally
read) to an entity selected by the user.
*/
{
    int        Res ;
    ads_name   E_Name ;
    ads_point  Sel_Pnt ; // Unused
    char       String[MAX_CHARS] ;

    // Make sure the application is in the APPID table
    Register_App () ;
```

```
        // Ask the user for a single object,
        Res = ads_entsel (NULL,E_Name,Sel_Pnt) ;
        if (Res != RTNORM) {
            // Probably hit ESCAPE or CONTROL-C
            return (Tidy_End (RTNORM)) ;
        }

        // Get a string from the user, the 1 allows spaces
        Res = ads_getstring (1,"\nInput a string: ",String) ;
        if (Res != RTNORM) {
            return (Tidy_End (RTNORM)) ;
        }

        // Put the string in the extended data of the entity
        if (Set_Xdata_Str (String,E_Name)) {
            ads_printf ("\nXdata set ok") ;
        } else {
            ads_printf ("\nXdata NOT set ok") ;
        }

        return (Tidy_End (RTNORM)) ;
}

void Register_App (void)
/*
PURPOSE: To register this application as using extended
data by putting it in the APPID table.
*/
{
    if (Table_Object_Exists ("APPID",App_Name)) {
        ads_printf ("\nApplication already registered.") ;
    } else if (ads_regapp(App_Name) == RTNORM) {
        ads_printf ("\nApplication registered ok.") ;
    } else {
        ads_printf ("\nERROR,could not register app"
                    ",ERRNO=%d",Get_Int_Var("ERRNO")) ;
    }
}

int Set_Xdata_Str (const char* Val, const ads_name E_Name)
{
    int            Res,Len ;
    struct resbuf* Xdata_Rb ;
    struct resbuf* Rbx ;
    struct resbuf* An_Rb ;    // App Name result buffer
    struct resbuf* Ebf ;      // First result buffer of assoc list
    struct resbuf* Ebn ;      // 'Next' result buffer in assoc
list
```

```
    struct resbuf* Eb_Last ; // Last active result buffer
    int Xdata_Sentinel ;
    char*  New_Ptr ;         // New XDATA string
    char*  Old_Ptr ;         // Old XDATA string
    char** Str_Adr ;         // Pointer to Pointer

    // Find length of extended data we will write (change)
    Len = strlen (Val) + 1 ;
    if ((Len > 255) || (Len == 1)) {  // An XDATA string size
limit
        ads_printf ("\nERROR,GSXS,Len = %d",Len) ;
        return (FALSE) ;
    }

    /*
     * Get the extended data of this entity and
     * application
     */
    An_Rb = ads_buildlist (RTSTR,App_Name,NULL) ;
    Rbx = ads_entgetx (E_Name,An_Rb) ; // This ent, this app
    (void)ads_relrb (An_Rb) ; // No more use for it
    if (Rbx == NULL) {
        ads_printf ("\nERROR,SXS,could not get xdata,"
                    " ERROR=%d",Get_Int_Var("ERRNO")) ;
        return (FALSE) ;
    }

    // Allocate memory for the new string, you cannot
    // simply use the input parameter Val, see text.
    New_Ptr = calloc (1,Len) ;
    strcpy (New_Ptr,Val) ;


    /*
     * Go over the list, looking for the XDATA
     * sentinel and the XDATA string which will
     * contain the data we have to change.
     */
    Ebf = Rbx ;
    Old_Ptr = NULL ;
    Xdata_Sentinel = FALSE ; // Not found yet
    for (Ebn = Ebf ; Ebn != NULL ; Ebn = Ebn->rbnext) {
        Eb_Last = Ebn ; // When loop ends Eb_Last = last rb
        switch (Ebn->restype) {
            case EXTD_SENTINEL :
                Xdata_Sentinel = TRUE ;
                break ;
            case EXTD_STR :
                if (Xdata_Sentinel) {
```

```
                        // Sentinel already found, so
                        // get the string
                        Old_Ptr = Ebn->resval.rstring ;
                        Str_Adr = &Ebn->resval.rstring ;
                        ads_printf ("\nOld XDATA = "
                                         "<%s>",Old_Ptr);
                    }
                break ;
        }
    }

    if (Xdata_Sentinel && (!Old_Ptr)) {
        // This is an error
        ads_printf ("\nERROR, sentinel but no string") ;
        return (FALSE) ;
    }

    if (!Xdata_Sentinel) {
        // No extended data yet present in this
        // entity so we must add it.

        Xdata_Rb = ads_buildlist (EXTD_SENTINEL,
                                    EXTD_APP_NAME,App_Name,
                                    EXTD_STR,New_Ptr,
                                    RTNONE) ;
        if (Xdata_Rb == NULL) {
            ads_printf ("\nError,Xdata_Rb,"
                        ",ERRNO =%d",Get_Int_Var("ERRNO")) ;
            return (FALSE) ;
        }

        // Add it to the end of Rbx
        Eb_Last->rbnext = Xdata_Rb ;

        ads_printf ("\nNo XDATA currently present") ;

    } else {
        // We just have to change the string
        free (Old_Ptr) ;
        // Put the new pointer into the resval.rstring
        // slot of the extended data string buffer
        (*Str_Adr) = New_Ptr ;
    }

    Res = ads_entmod (Rbx) ;
    if (Res != RTNORM) {
        ads_printf ("\nERROR,GSXS, could not ads_entmod,"
                "Res=%d, ERRNO=%d ",
                Res,Get_Int_Var ("ERRNO")) ;
```

```
    }

    // Free the ram used for the result buffer list
    if (ads_relrb (Rbx) != RTNORM) {
        ads_printf ("\nERROR,GSXS, ads_relrb(Rbx) failure") ;
    }

    return (TRUE) ;
}

//                          -- end of LST_11_1.C --

/////////////////////////////////////////////////////////////
// LST_11_2.C
//    Illustrating adding in an XDATA long and real
//    to an enity selected by the user.

// The name the app is registered under
static char* App_Name="ATADX-AVORP-ADNOCES" ;

// Function prototypes
void Register_App (void) ;
int Set_Xdata (const ads_real Floater,
               const long     Longer,
               const ads_name E_Name) ;

int test_func (void)
/*
Shows how extended data can be written (and incidentally
read) to an entity selected by the user.
*/
{
    int       Res,Integer ;
    ads_name  E_Name ;
    ads_point Sel_Pnt ; // Unused
    ads_real  Real ;

    // Make sure the application is in the APPID table
    Register_App () ;

    // Ask the user for a single object,
    Res = ads_entsel (NULL,E_Name,Sel_Pnt) ;
    if (Res != RTNORM) {
        // User probably hit ESCAPE or CONTROL-C
        return (Tidy_End (RTNORM)) ;
    }

    // Get a real number
    ads_initget (RSG_NONEG | RSG_NONULL, NULL) ;
```

```
    Res = ads_getreal ("\nInput a positive real number
please:",&Real) ;
    if (Res == RTCAN) {
        return (Tidy_End (RTNORM)) ;
    }

    // Get an integer
    ads_initget (RSG_NONULL,NULL) ;
    Res = ads_getint ("\nInput an integer please:",&Integer) ;
    if (Res == RTCAN) {
        return (Tidy_End (RTNORM)) ;
    }

    // Put the real and the integer in the entity XDATA
    if (Set_Xdata  (Real,Integer,E_Name)) {
        ads_printf ("\nXdata set ok") ;
    } else {
        ads_printf ("\nXdata NOT set ok") ;
    }

    return (Tidy_End (RTNORM)) ;
}

void Register_App (void)
/*
PURPOSE: To register this application as using extended
data by putting it in the APPID table.
*/
{
    if (Table_Object_Exists ("APPID",App_Name)) {
        ads_printf ("\nApplication already registered.") ;
    } else if (ads_regapp(App_Name) == RTNORM) {
        ads_printf ("\nApplication registered ok.") ;
    } else {
        ads_printf ("\nERROR,could not register app"
                    ",ERRNO=%d",Get_Int_Var("ERRNO")) ;
    }
}

int Set_Xdata (const ads_real Floater,
               const long      Longer,
               const ads_name E_Name)
{
    int            Res ;
    struct resbuf* Xdata_Rb ;
    struct resbuf* Rbx ;
    struct resbuf* An_Rb ;    // App Name result buffer
    struct resbuf* Ebf ;      // First result buffer of assoc list
```

```
    struct resbuf* Ebn ;       // 'Next' result buffer in assoc
list
    struct resbuf* Eb_Last ; // Last active result buffer
    int            Xdata_Sentinel ;
    double*        F_Adr ;
    long*          L_Adr ;

    /*
     * Get the extended data of this entity and
     * application
     */
    An_Rb = ads_buildlist (RTSTR,App_Name,NULL) ;
    Rbx = ads_entgetx (E_Name,An_Rb) ; // This ent, this app
    (void)ads_relrb (An_Rb) ; // No more use for it
    if (Rbx == NULL) {
        ads_printf ("\nERROR,SXS,could not get xdata,"
                    " ERROR=%d",Get_Int_Var("ERRNO")) ;
        return (FALSE) ;
    }

    /*
     * Go over the list, looking for the XDATA
     * sentinel and the XDATA itself.
     */
    Ebf   = Rbx ;
    F_Adr = NULL ; // address of floater
    L_Adr = NULL ; // address of longer
    Xdata_Sentinel = FALSE ; // Not found yet
    for (Ebn = Ebf ; Ebn != NULL ; Ebn = Ebn->rbnext) {
        Eb_Last = Ebn ; // When loop ends Eb_Last = last rb
        switch (Ebn->restype) {
            case EXTD_SENTINEL :
                Xdata_Sentinel = TRUE ;
                break ;
            case EXTD_FLOAT :
                if (Xdata_Sentinel) {
                    F_Adr = &Ebn->resval.rreal ;
                    ads_printf ("\nOld FLOAT = "
                                "<%6.3f>",Ebn->resval.rreal);
                }
                break ;
            case EXTD_INT32 :
                if (Xdata_Sentinel) {
                    L_Adr = &Ebn->resval.rlong ;
                    ads_printf ("\nOld INT32 = "
                                "<%d>",Ebn->resval.rlong);
                }
                break ;
        }
```

```
        }

        if (Xdata_Sentinel && ((!F_Adr) || (!L_Adr))) {
            // This is an error
            ads_printf ("\nERROR, sentinel but missing data") ;
            return (FALSE) ;
        }

        if (!Xdata_Sentinel) {
            // No extended data yet present in this
            // entity so we must add it.

            Xdata_Rb = ads_buildlist (EXTD_SENTINEL,
                                    EXTD_APP_NAME,App_Name,
                                    EXTD_FLOAT,Floater,
                                    EXTD_INT32,Longer,
                                    RTNONE) ;
            if (Xdata_Rb == NULL) {
                ads_printf ("\nError,Xdata_Rb,"
                            ",ERRNO =%d",Get_Int_Var("ERRNO")) ;
                return (FALSE) ;
            }

            // Add it to the end of Rbx
            Eb_Last->rbnext = Xdata_Rb ;

            ads_printf ("\nNo XDATA currently present") ;

        } else {
            // The buffers are already there, we just
            // need to change the contents
            (*F_Adr) = Floater ;
            (*L_Adr) = Longer ;
        }

        Res = ads_entmod (Rbx) ;
        if (Res != RTNORM) {
            ads_printf ("\nERROR,GSXS, could not ads_entmod,"
                    "Res=%d, ERRNO=%d ",
                    Res,Get_Int_Var ("ERRNO")) ;
        }

        // Free the ram used for the result buffer list
        if (ads_relrb (Rbx) != RTNORM) {
            ads_printf ("\nERROR,GSXS, ads_relrb(Rbx) failure") ;
        }

        return (TRUE) ;
}
```

```
//                       -- end of LST_11_2.C --

///////////////////////////////////////////////////////////
// LST_11_3.C
//    Illustrating getting data about the ammount of room
//    extended still available in a user selected entity

// The name the app is registered under
static char* App_Name="APP-WEN" ;

static void Register_App (void) ;

int test_func (void)
/*
Shows how to read the amount of data that would be used by
extended data, and the amount of bytes free for extended
data in an entity.
*/
{
    int             Res ;
    ads_name        E_Name ;
    ads_point       Sel_Pnt ; // Unused
    long            Amount ;
    struct resbuf*  Xdata_Rb ;

    Register_App () ;

    // Ask the user for a single object,
    Res = ads_entsel (NULL,E_Name,Sel_Pnt) ;
    if (Res != RTNORM) {
        // Probably hit ESCAPE or CONTROL-C
        return (Tidy_End (RTNORM)) ;
    }

    // Make a dummy XDATA list
    Xdata_Rb = ads_buildlist (EXTD_SENTINEL,
                              EXTD_APP_NAME,App_Name,
                              EXTD_FLOAT,33.3,
                              EXTD_INT32,999,
                              EXTD_STR,"Why high there",
                              RTNONE) ;
    if (Xdata_Rb == NULL) {
        ads_printf ("\nError,Xdata_Rb,"
                    ",ERRNO =%d",Get_Int_Var("ERRNO")) ;
        return (FALSE) ;
    }

    Res = ads_xdroom (E_Name,&Amount) ;
```

```
    if (Res != RTNORM) {
        ads_printf ("\nError,ads_xdroom, Res =%d",Res) ;
        ads_printf (",ERRNO =%d. ",Get_Int_Var("ERRNO")) ;
        return (Tidy_End (RTNORM)) ;
    }
    ads_printf ("\nThis entity still has %d bytes of"
                " extended data room.",Amount) ;

    Res = ads_xdsize (Xdata_Rb,&Amount) ;
    if (Res != RTNORM) {
        ads_printf ("\nError,ads_xdsize, Res =%d",Res) ;
        ads_printf (",ERRNO =%d. ",Get_Int_Var("ERRNO")) ;
        return (Tidy_End (RTNORM)) ;
    }
    ads_printf ("\nThis rb list would occupy %d bytes.",Amount) ;

    (void)ads_relrb (Xdata_Rb) ;

    return (Tidy_End (RTNORM)) ;
}


void Register_App (void)
/*
PURPOSE: To register this application as using extended
data by putting it in the APPID table.
*/
{
    if (Table_Object_Exists ("APPID",App_Name)) {
        ads_printf ("\nApplication already registered.") ;
    } else if (ads_regapp(App_Name) == RTNORM) {
        ads_printf ("\nApplication registered ok.") ;
    } else {
        ads_printf ("\nERROR,could not register app"
                    ",ERRNO=%d",Get_Int_Var("ERRNO")) ;
    }
}
//                      -- end of LST_11_3.C --
```

Dialog boxes and the dialog control language

12.1 Introduction

This chapter is about how to create and use dialog boxes using the Dialog control language (or DCL) You will see how to make your user interface much more modern than the old AutoCAD menu-only interface.

I do not discuss menu files (with extension MNU or MNX) here because they are well covered in the AutoCAD manual and in many books on AutoLISP. Furthermore MNU files are not as tightly bound to the programming language as DCL files are, and are less flexible.

The code to handle dialog boxes in C is not trivial, and AutoLISP programmers migrating to C may consider gaining more experience in C before reading this chapter.

Some dialogs in AutoCAD Release 13 for Windows *are* Windows resources, and some are DCL files. DCL files will run on any platform (UNIX, Extended DOS, Windows 3.1, Windows-95, Windows NT), and so are more flexible than Windows resources. Until both Extended DOS and UNIX accept Windows resource files DCL is the only way or making a portable menu for all platforms.

12.2 What is possible with DCL?

Many of the dialog boxes in AutoCAD Release 12 and Release 13 are created with DCL files. These are text files with the extension DCL which specify the appearance of a dialog box on the screen. You create DCL files with any standard text editor, usually the same editor which you use to write C or AutoLISP programs. Some example DCL dialogs which come with AutoCAD are APPLOAD.DCL, ASISMP.DCL. So anything you see in an AutoCAD dialog box can be done using a DCL file with some C (or AutoLISP) programming. A DCL dialog can contain:

- edit boxes (on their own or in columns or rows)
- text
- buttons (on their own or in columns or rows)
- radio buttons (in columns or rows)
- toggles (on their own or in columns or rows)
- list boxes
- popup lists
- images (loaded from AutoCAD slides or made of vectors)
- sliders

It would take half a book in itself to cover all the possibilities of DCL, I only cover the ones I have found *most* useful: edit boxes, buttons, radio buttons,

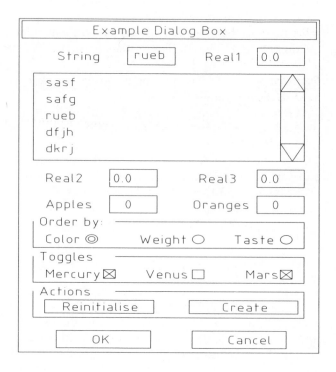

Figure 12.1 An example dialog box.

check boxes and list boxes, see Figure 12.1.

Throughout this chapter I will sometimes refer to "tiles". Tiles are buttons or rows or list boxes or any object which appears in a dialog box. I will use the word "tile" when the actually type of dialog object is not important.

12.2.1 Ready-made DCL files

Two DCL files are very important, BASE.DCL and ACAD.DCL. You should *never* modify BASE.DCL, it contains basic definitions used by all other DCL files. You might want to look at it out of interest, but do not change it.

ACAD.DCL contains the dialog descriptions used by the standard release of AutoCAD. If you really wanted to you *can* change this file, but only when you have finished reading this chapter and only if you are sure of what you are doing. Changing ACAD.DCL only modifies the *appearance* of the standard AutoCAD dialog boxes, you cannot add functionality. As we will see in the rest of this chapter functionality depends on the program (in AutoLISP or C) controlling the dialog box.

12.3 A general and systematic dialog box handler in C

The source files we will use to create a sample dialog box are LST_12_1.C and DIALOG.DCL. These two files are not practical applications, but are designed to show useful features of dialog boxes, and how to handle them. You can imagine a fruit shipping company sending and recieving fruit to and from three planets by a Star Trek-like matter transporter. Do not take this example too seriously, but note how strings, integers, real numbers, buttons and listboxes are handled.

You will learn by example in this chapter, there is no formal defintion of dialog box syntax, which can be found in the AutoCAD documentation.

LST_12_1.C is one of the few listings in this book which is a complete application.

12.3.1 The sample DCL file

DIALOG.DCL, at the end of this chapter, describes the appearance of the dialog box we are going to create. How it actually looks may change from platform to platform, and from graphics card to graphics card, but the overall layout is fixed by this file. As you read the DCL file you should compare it with Figure 12.1.

The first few lines are comments, using the C++ comment symbol //. The line beginning "dcl_settings" is explained in section 12.4.2 The line which starts the description of the dialog box is

```
ex_dlg : dialog {
```

and declares that "ex_dlg" is the name of a dialog. The description of this dialog box starts here and ends with the closing of curly brackets later on at the end of the file:

```
}   // ex_dlg end
```

Going back to the start of the dialog description, the first line after the ex_dlg declaration gives a label to the dialog, which is in fact the title:

```
label = "Example dialog box"; // Visible title
```

When the dialog box appears this will be at the very top of it, the text in the title bar. Next there is a row definition, which says that there are two edit boxes in the row. The row will be below the title. As you read the definition of the dialog box you must imagine that the description goes from the top downwards and from left to right. The two edit boxes in the first row are a box for a string on the left and a box for a real number on the right; see also Figure 12.1.

DCL files do not explicitly support numbers as opposed to text, and it is your program which decides what type goes in what edit box. In other words all edit boxes contain text, and to the DCL file it makes no difference if the text is a series of numerals, or alphabetic characters, or a mixture of both.

Each edit box has a *label*, which is the title of the edit box, visible ot the user, and a *key*, which is what the program uses to identify tiles in the dialog. Keys are not visible to the user. Each edit box also has an *edit_width* (which is the length of the edit box in characters) and an *edit_limit* which is the maximum number of characters the box can contain. It is perfectly possible that an edit box has a width of 4 characters and a limit of 8. The text will scroll automatically as the user enters text beyond the fourth character.

After the first row there is a

```
: list_box {
```

declaration. A list box is simply a list of strings which can be scrolled, and from which you can select an item. Often list boxes are used when selecting file names. The list box in DIALOG.DCL is 40 characters wide, is identified by the application using the key "listbox", and does not allow multiple selections.

So far, from the top heading downwards, we have a title, a row and a list box, just as in the figure.

Next comes another row with two more (real number) edit boxes. This is followed by yet another row with two (integer) edit boxes, Apples and Oranges.

The next item is a "boxed_radio_row". Boxed rows have a containing rectangle and a title. The title (or label) in this example is "Order by:". A radio_row is a collection of "buttons", only one of which can be active and any one time. They are called "radio" buttons because a radio can only be set to a single given waveband at any one time. They are usually circular, and in the figure the radio button labeled "Color" is selected. Again there are labels (visible to the user) and keys (used by the application). Note that both the boxed_radio_row itself and the radio buttons have keys.

Next we have another "boxed_row", this time of check boxes, or toggles, which are usually square. Although these are grouped together they can be switched on and off individually, unlike radio buttons.

Near the end of DIALOG.DCL we have a boxed row of two buttons. Normally buttons are used to trigger some action.

Finally we have the item "ok_cancel", which is a predefined (because often used) DCL structure. Other objects which are predefined are:

- ok_only
- ok_cancel
- ok_cancel_help
- ok_cancel_help_info

The definitions of these tiles can be found in BASE.DCL.

AutoCAD automatically arranges the tiles on the surface of the dialog box, you do not have to specify (exact) positions. You have implicity specified where each tile goes by the top-down, left-right order of the DCL file.

One last point, you can have more than one dialog within a single DCL file. In fact when you start experimenting on your own you will probably start by copying the ex_dlg structure in the same file, and modifying it, leaving ex_dlg as a reference.

12.3.2 A dialog box handler in C

LST_12_1.C illustrates how you can call and interact with DIALOG.DCL. It is a long file because it is very general. After you have understood how this application works you will be able to add your own handlers to LST_12_1.C and you own dialog definitions to DIALOG.DCL.

Along with the normal include files at the top of LST_12_1.C there is ADSDLG.H, which defines the functions and constants used for dialog box interaction.

The first part of this file defines some constants and type definitions which will be used by the dialog box handlers. Here we assume that the program wants the user to change data found in the structure Ex_t (Example_type). It is often the case that a dialog box is most useful where more than one or two values have to be changed. In this case the application wants to use the dialog box to change three reals, four integers and a string.

Two of the integers are special. Tog_Int is an integer where on-off states are stored as individual bits. Three bits have been defined for use in Tog_Int, they are MERC_BIT, VENU_BIT and MARS_BIT. In Release 13 only 32 bit integers are allowed, so you can use as single integer to store up to 32 check box states. In this example we are saying to which planets to send the fruit.

There is also `Radio_Int`, which is used to store a selection (called "radio" because we can only select a single radio band at any one time). Here we are storing a single number, identifying in which order we would like to place the fruit before sending it to one or more planets, by color, by weight, or by taste. Obviously only one order can be selected at any one time, and for this reason we use a radio row here.

Next in the listing come the function prototypes, `main()`, `funcload()` and `dofun()`, all of which are covered in Chapter 2. `Tidy_End()` is covered in Chapter 4, section 4.7. `Dialog_Func()` is the start of our new application. It will be called when the user types "dialog" at the command line.

The first thing `Dialog_Func()` does is to declare and initialise `Data`. This is the data which may (or may not) be changed by the dialog box. When the user ends the dialog box by clicking on OK then `Data` will contain the changes he made. When he clicks on CANCEL then `Data` will not be changed. A simple idea, but if you do not stick to it your users will be very confused.

For AutoLISP programmers new to C note that `Data` is intialised inside `Dialog_Func()`, and so will get the same values every time this function is called. Sometimes you want a structure like this to retain its values between function calls, and in this case you should move the declaration of `Data` outside of the `Dialog_Func()`, thus making it global.

Next we call `Example_Dlg_Func()` three times (inside a for loop). Of course normally you would only call it once, but calling it three times gives you (the programmer) a chance to see the effect of clicking on OK or CANCEL.

The declaration of `Tmp` begins the code which will handle the dialog box. This is a working copy of `Data`, as will be explained later. There follows some tables, the sizes of which set by the seven defines starting with N_REALS. Our dialog box has three reals, so N_REALS is defined to be 3, and so on.

The trick of conditional compilation is used here. If none of your dialog boxes had reals then N_REALS would be 0, and the table would not get compiled:

```
#if N_REALS
....this only compiled if N_REALS > 0...
#endif  // N_REALS
```

This saves memory space in your application.

The first table `D_Real` (Dialog_Real) has three fields for each real. The fields are the name of the dialog to which the real belongs, the key of the real itself (as it appears in the DCL file) and the address of the real. (AutoLISP programmers: read "&" as "address of", and think of it as meaning "the place where the real is stored".)

The same tables can be used for more than just one dialog box, but in our example we are only using "ex_dlg", so all the name fields in all the tables are set to "ex_dlg".

D_Int has a similar structure to D_Real, as does D_Str. Note, however, that D_Str does not need the "&" character, because, in C and C++, a string is an array, and an array is a pointer. The "&" here would be superfluous.

The D_Tog (Dialog Toggles) table is slightly different. This is because we are using a single integer to store up to 32 toggle states. In this example we only use 3 of the 32 bits available. Not only have we got the address of the integer, but also a mask of the bit within the integer each toggle depends on. For example the toggle button "mercury" depends on bit 0, see the definition of MERC_BIT at the start of the file.

Next we have D_Rad (Dialog Radio buttons). There is only one radio row, so the table has only one entry. The dialog box name is "ex_dlg" of course, and the key to the radio row is "order". When the user clicks on the radio buttons the function Order_Fun() is called, and as explained above this function takes a single ads_callback_packet* and returns nothing.

The D_But (Dialog Buttons) table has three fields, the name of the dialog, the key of the button, and a function to call when that button is pressed. This last looks pretty horrible:

```
void (*But_Fun)(ads_callback_packet* Cpak) ;
```

But_Fun is a pointer to (the address of) a function which is called with a single argument of ads_callback_packet* type, and which returns nothing (hence the void keyword at the beginning). But_Fun stores the address of a function of this type. I will explain ads_callback_packet in section 12.3.5. (For more general information on declaring function pointers in this way see Kerningham and Ritchie "The C Programming Language", 2nd Edition, Section 5.11 "Pointers to Functions".) To put it another way: But_Fun points to the function which will be called when one of the action buttons is clicked.

The last table D_List (Dialog Listbox) also has a name, a key, and a function pointer. The function List_Func() will be called whenever the user selects an entry from the list box.

Finally we reach the function Example_Dialog_Func(). This function takes an Ex_t pointer, Dat, as its single parameter, and the first thing it does with it is copy it into Tmp by calling the standard C memcpy function:

```
(void)memcpy (&Tmp,Dat,sizeof(Ex_t)) ;
```

Note that Dat is already a pointer so there is no need for the "&". Tmp on the other hand is a structure, and memcpy wants a pointer, so we need to use the "&" operator. This copies all the bytes of Dat into Tmp. Now Tmp can be used as the working data for the dialog without fear of changing the original data. We will copy Tmp back into Dat only if the user confirms the changes he has made by hitting the OK button.

After copying Dat into Tmp the dialog box is setup, the list box initialised, and ads_start_dialog() is called. Only now will the dialog box become visible.

At this point the user can change numbers and strings, scroll the list box and so on.

When the user has finished he will have clicked either OK or CANCEL. This information is placed in the D_Stat parameter of ads_start_dialog(). If all goes well we unload the dialog file by a call to ads_unload_dialog().

The switch on D_Stat decides whether or not to copy the data from Tmp into Dat. If D_Stat is DLGOK (defined in ADSDLG.H) then we do the copy and set Accepted to TRUE. Or else we do not do the copy and set Accepted to FALSE. Returning Accepted at the end of the function tells the caller (in our case Dialog_Func()) what the user did.

That is the overview of Example_Dlg_Func(), but I have skipped two important function calls, Setup_Dialog_Box() and Init_List(), the first of which is explained in the following section. Init_List() is explained in section 12.3.9.

12.3.3 DCL functions: ads_load_dialog() and ads_new_dialog().

Setup_Dialog_Box() is defined just after the end of Example_Dlg_Func(). It takes three parameters and returns an integer, TRUE if all goes well, FALSE if there was some error in setting up the dialog box. The parameters are:

- char* Name, the name of the dialog box, in our case "ex_dlg".
- int* Dcl_Id, a pointer to an integer which is the "id" of the DCL file, it is set by the call to ads_load_dialog(). Note that it specifies a *file*, not a dialog box.
- ads_hdlg* D_Hndl, a pointer to a handle, (ads_hdlg means "ADS handle to dialog" and is defined in ADSDLG.H). This handle is the "id" of the dialog box we are trying to set up, and is set by the call to ads_new_dialog().

The function ads_load_dialog() tries to load a DCL file, and if it is successful sets Dcl_Id. If the DCL file is not in the current directory you will have to put the full path name in this call.

After we have loaded the dialog file, we must load the individual dialog box. Remember that a single DCL file can have many dialog box definitions. The function ads_new_dialog() is used to load the dialog box. We pass it the name of the dialog *box*, the handle of the dialog *file*, a NULL pointer, and D_Hand. When ads_new_dialog() finishes D_Hand will contain the handle to the dialog created. (The NULL pointer specifies that there is no default action for this dialog box, i.e. we will specify different functions to each tile of the dialog box.)

12.3.4 DCL functions: ads_action_tile() and ads_set_tile()

Now we come onto the meat of `Setup_Dialog_Box()`. We assign to each tile in the dialog box an action, a function. When the user clicks inside an edit box or "pushes" a button or selects an item from the listbox then a given function will be executed. These functions are known as "callback" functions.

The first sort of tiles that we set up are the "real" (floating point number) ones. Again, if N_REALS is defined as 0 then this part of the code is not compiled. In our case N_REALS is 3, so the block is compiled.

The outer for-loop goes over every entry in the `D_Real` table. It compares the name of the dialog box in the table with the name passed to the function. If they are the same then it associates a function with the tile. In our case we only have one dialog box, but if you go on to create other dialog boxes from this model you will have other entries than "ex_dlg".

The tile is "given" a function to execute with the `ads_action_tile()` function:

```
int ads_action_tile (ads_hdlg Dlg, char* Key, CALLB Function) ;
```

The `Dlg` is the dialog box identifier, the `Key` is the key for the tile (for example "real1" or "real2" or "real3" in our case), and the CALLB Function is the function to call when this tile is clicked on. So to assign the function `Get_Real()` to the tile "real2" the call becomes:

```
Res = ads_action_tile (*D_Hndl,"real2",Get_Real) ;
```

To save space in the listing I do not check the return value of `ads_action_tile()`. You may well decide that it is worth looking at `Res` to make sure you have not made a mistake in spelling the tile names.

After we have associated the function `Get_Real` with the tile, we send some data to it, so that the user can see what was originally in `Tmp`. This is done by `sprintf()` putting the contents of the address of the real data into a dummy string (`Dum_Str`) and sending that dummy string to the tile with `ads_set_tile()`. Here is the function prototype to `ads_set_tile()`:

```
int ads_set_tile (ads_hdlg Dlg, char* Key, char* Value) ;
```

The first two parameters are the same as `ads_action_tile()`, but the third, instead of being a function is a string, the string that will be displayed in the tile. Here we see clearly that DCL handles only strings, I cannot send a tile a floating point number directly, but must `sprintf()` it into a buffer (`Dum_Str`) and send that instead. To send "real2" the floating point value 33.3 I would have to do the following:

```
Res = ads_set_tile (*D_Hndl,"real2","33.3") ; // Send a string!
```

What we have done for N_REALS we do for N_INTS, N_STRINGS, N_BUTTONS and N_LISTS. The functions assigned to each type of tile are different of course, and with with N_BUTTONS and N_LISTS there is no "value" to send. What is displayed on the button is the "label" for that button defined in the DCL file, and the listbox is set up by a separate function described in section 12.3.9.

Setting up the toggle buttons (check boxes) is a little trickier. The function assigned to each toggle using `ads_action_tile()` is `Get_Toggle()`. The for-loop in effect does a single loop for each "bit" in the toggle integer. This relies on you having defined each toggle as a single bit in `D_Tog`. We have defined these bits with MERC_BIT, VENU_BIT, and MARS_BIT at the beginning of the file. Remember that, though often grouped together, check boxes operate independently from one another. The status of the Mercury check box does not depend on the status of the Mars check box for example.

The inner block of the for-loop does two things. It compares the mask for the toggle that we are interested in (always "1") with a bit in the toggle integer. If the toggle bit in the integer is one then we copy into `Dum_Str` the string "1", or else we copy in "0". The second thing the inner block does is to send this value to the check box itself. Sending a "1" to a check box checks it (a check or an X will appear inside it). Sending a "0" to a check box causes any check or X inside it to disappear.

Setting up the radio buttons is not so simple either. The trick here is to make sure that in your DCL file any buttons inside a radio_row have the same key as the radio_row itself, with the addition of an integer count attached to the end. In our example DCL file we have a radio_row with a key "order", and the individual buttons within with keys "order0", "order1", "order2". In this way the whole row can be accessed with "order", and the third button can be accessed with "order2".

The inner loop of N_RADIOS associates the `Get_Radio()` func with all radio rows, and sends the name of the active button using `ads_set_tile()`. Lets look closer at that part:

```
i = (*(D_Rad[t].Adr)) ;  // Get value (Tmp.Radio_Int) here
sprintf (Dum_Str,"%s%d",D_Rad[t].Key,i) ; // form "order2"
(void)ads_set_tile (*D_Hndl,D_Rad[t].Key, Dum_Str) ;
```

The first line resolves into `Tmp.Radio_Int`, so "i" will contain that value. The second line forms the key to which radio button we will select; assume that the third and `Dum_Str` will hold "order2". Finally we send to the radio_row ("order") the key of the button we want to select ("order2") using ads_set_tile.

Finally we associate functions to the OK and the CANCEL buttons, with two calls to `ads_set_tile()` using "accept" and "cancel" as the keys. These are standard tiles written as "ok_cancel" in DIALOG.DCL and defined in BASE.DCL.

So now we have written data to every tile so the user can see which initial values are present, and we have assigned a function to call for every tile.

12.3.5 The callback functions and `ads_get_attr_string()`

The functions which are called when a tile is clicked are "callback" functions. This name derives from the fact that you hand over control to the user when you start the dialog box (with `ads_new_dialog()`), and controls comes *back* to you when the user clicks a tile. Clicking a tile calls a callback function.

You will have noticed that CALLB is used in the function prototypes at the top of the file. This is (currently) a blank definition, and you could (currently) leave it out. Autodesk says it helps you identify callback functions, and it may not be blank (empty) in the future.

`Get_Real()` is the callback function which handles edit boxes containing real numbers. All callback functions are handed a single parameter, a pointer to an `ads_callback_packet`. This is defined in ADSDLG.H as:

```
typedef struct {
    ads_hdlg  dialog; // Handle to the dialog box
    ads_htile tile;   // Handle to tile within dialog box
    char*     value;  // Value (string) of the tile
    void*     client_data; // Special data
    int       reason; // Why the CALLB has been called
    long      x, y;   // Location of the tile
} ads_callback_packet;
```

LST_12_1.C uses only the dialog, value and reason members of the packet. The first thing that `Get_Real()` does is see if the reason is CBR_LOST_FOCUS. If it is not we return immediately. If it is CBR_LOST_FOCUS then this means that the user has done something to this tile and then moved on to another. So he has finished typing or editing data in this tile.

We get the key for the tile by using the function `ads_get_attr_string()`, asking for the key of the tile. Then we loop over all the keys we have in D_Real looking for a match. Once we have found it we convert the text value to a floating point number using the standard C function `atof` (Ascii TO Float), store it and send it back to the tile with an `ads_set_tile()`.

Sending back the data to the tile helps confirm what the user has typed and also sets the data inside tiles into a standard form. For example here all real tiles will have the format of "%6.3f", i.e. 6 characters and 3 decimal places.

The expression

```
*(D_Real[i].Adr)
```

looks nasty, but it resolves into "the contents of the ith real pointer in D_Real". In our case these addresses have been set to `Tmp.Real_1`, `Tmp.Real_2`, and `Tmp.Real_3` earlier in the file.

To be really safe you should check that a match is found with the key, and that the text in the tile is a valid floating point number. These checks have been left out to shorten the listing, and are left as an exercise for the reader.

The functions for integers and strings follow the same logic as that for reals. `Get_Toggle()` on the other hand simply looks at the value of the packet (either a "0" or a "1") and sets the bit appropriately.

12.3.6 The ads_done_dialog() function

The last two callback functions are `Dialog_OK()` and `Dialog_Canc()` end the dialog box by calling `ads_done_dialog()`. The two parameters to this function are the handle to the dialog to finish (since more than one dialog box can be open at once) and a symbolic constant to tell the caller if the user hit OK or CANCEL. These are the integers that reappear, as if by magic, in the D_Stat parameter of `ads_start_dialog()` call inside `Example_Dlg_Func()` explained previously in section 12.3.2.

12.3.7 A summary of LST_12_1.C

It has been a long haul, but this very same file can handle as many dialog boxes as you want, and the addition of new buttons and list boxes and tiles becomes a mechanical process. To summarise:

Your top-level dialog box function (in our case `Example_Dlg_Func()`) copies the input data to a temporary and then calls `Setup_Dialog_Box()`. This function loads the DCL file and then loads the dialog box. Then, for every tile defined in the tables, associates a function with a tile and initialise the text in the tile if required. The top-level function then starts the dialog box. Tiles in the dialog box call callback function as the user interacts with them, and these callback functions set data in the temporary data. The user finally clicks either OK or CANCEL, and we return DLGOK or DLGCANCEL in D_Stat. The value in D_Stat is then used to decide whether we should copy the temporary data back into the original, or leave it alone.

12.3.8 Adding a new dialog

To add a new dialog you should first give it a name and design it. Then add the text description of it in DIALOG.DCL. If it is called "plan" for example and has two reals you should add the following two lines to the D_Real table:

```
{"plan", "length",&Tmp.Length} ,
{"plan", "width", &Tmp.Width}
```

and increase N_REALS from 3 to 5. Then you need to write a new top-level dialog box function, using as a template Example_Dlg_Func(). This will include a call to Setup_Dialog_Box() as follows:

```
// Load DCL and dialog, this does NOT show the dialog
if (!Setup_Dialog_Box ("plan",&dcl_id,&D_Hndl)) {
    return (FALSE) ;
}
```

12.3.9 List handling, `ads_start_list()`, `ads_add_list()`, `ads_end_list()`

The only thing missing so far from the description of LST_12_1.C is how the list box is handled. The list box will contain a list of imaginary interplanetary fruits. This list is created and sent to the dialog box in Init_list, called near the start of Example_Dlg_Func() and defined at the bottom of LST_12_1.C.

An array of 33 strings is defined, Alien_List, each of which is initialised, within the first for-loop, to a four character string created randomly using the standard C function rand. The last character of each string is set to 0, to terminate it.

After Alien_List has been initialised we start a list by using the ads function:

```
int ads_start_list (ads_hdlg Hnd, char* Key,
                    short Op, short Index) ;
```

In our example program the key is "listbox", and the operation is LIST_NEW, which means "create a new list box, deleting the old contents", and Index is ignored. Other possibilities for Op in `ads_start_list()` are:

- LIST_CHANGE, changes the contents of the string in the list box at Index position.
- LIST_APPEND, appends an entry to the listbox, Index is ignored.

If `ads_start_list()` returns successfully we repeatedly call `ads_add_list()` in another for loop, sending the string for each fruit to the listbox. Note that `ads_start_list()` has specified which dialog and which tile we are sending the strings to, so `ads_add_list` does not need to specify these things .

When we have finished sending all the strings `ads_end_list()` closes the list.

You can think of this sequence as similar to opening a file, writing data and then closing the file.

Finally there is the callback function for the list box, `List_Func()`. If the reason for the callback is that the user has selected an item from the listbox (reason = `CBR_SELECT`) then we read the index of this selection. The selection made is an integer stored as a string in `Pak->value`. This string is converted into an integer with the standard C-function `atoi()` (Ascii TO Int). This integer is an index into `Alien_Fruit`, and the string at that position is then copied into the string tile of the dialog box and `Tmp.Str`. That is why when the user selects a string in the list box he sees it immediately in the string edit box.

12.4 Other features of DCL

As I mentioned in the introduction, DCL is far to extensive to cover in a single chapter, but this is a book about C and C++ programming, so I will not go into much more details about other aspects of DCL. This section covers a few of the other features of DCL.

12.4.1 Rows and columns

All the DCL groups of tiles in the previous example were organised as rows, though you could have organised them as columns, simply by replacing "row" with "column", "boxed_row" with "boxed_column" and "boxed_radio_row" with "boxed_radio_column".

To put two columns in a single row you should use the following model:

```
row {
    boxed_radio_column {
        . . .
    }
    boxed_radio_column {
        . . .
    }
}
```

12.4.2 Auditing

Auditing makes AutoCAD check the syntax of the DCL file when it is loaded (with `ads_load_dialog()`), and if there are any errors a dialog box will pop up telling you the line number of the error. In our DIALOG.DCL the line which does this is

```
dcl_settings : default_dcl_settings { audit_level = 3; }
```

The higher the audit_level the more checking is done. The range is from 0 to 3. I always use audit_level 3, since it helps me debug both my DCL file and the C functions which drive it. A lower audit level will result in a (not noticeably) faster load, and may let errors slip passed, resulting in malfunctioning dialogs or even a "abnormally terminated" AutoCAD.

12.4.4 Further reading

This chapter has covered, I believe, between 80% to 95% of the useful DCL functionality. For more details see the AutoCAD Customization Manual which has a section about 100 pages long on DCL!

12.5 Listings

```
////////////////////////////////////////////////////////////////
//      LST_12_1.C
//      Illustrating how to load and interact with a DCL
//      file (DIALOG.DCL in this case)

#include <stdio.h>  // Standard C include file
#include <string.h> // Standard C include file
#include <ADSLIB.H> // Interface to ADS library
#include <ADSDLG.h> // Interface to DCL funcs

/*          DATA FOR USE IN THE DIALOG BOX              */

#define MAX_DCL_CHARS      32  // For names & so on...

// This is the Dat used to send and recieve
// data from and to our example dialog box
typedef struct {
    ads_real Real_1,Real_2,Real_3 ;
    int      Int_1,Int_2 ;
    char     Str[MAX_DCL_CHARS+1] ;
    int      Tog_Int ;
    int      Radio_Int ;
} Ex_t ;

// The following used to store toggles in Tog_Int
#define MERC_BIT          0x01  // Bit 0
#define VENU_BIT          0x02  // Bit 1
#define MARS_BIT          0x04  // Bit 2
```

```
// The following for Radio_Int, the order
#define BY_COLOR            0
#define BY_WEIGHT           1
#define BY_TASTE            2


/*                  Function prototpes                    */

int   funcload    (void) ;
int   dofun       (void) ;
int   Dialog_Func (void) ;
int   Tidy_End    (int Ret_Val) ;
int   Setup_Dialog_Box (char* Name,int* Dcl_Id,
                        ads_hdlg* D_Hndl) ;

// These callback functions activated when user clicks
// on tiles
void CALLB Get_Real (ads_callback_packet* Pak) ;
void CALLB Get_Str (ads_callback_packet* Pak) ;
void CALLB Get_Int (ads_callback_packet* Pak) ;
void CALLB Get_Toggle (ads_callback_packet* Pak) ;
void CALLB Get_Radio (ads_callback_packet* Pak) ;
void CALLB List_Func (ads_callback_packet* Pak) ;
void CALLB Create_Func (ads_callback_packet* Pak)  ;
void CALLB Dialog_OK (ads_callback_packet* Pak) ;
void CALLB Dialog_Canc (ads_callback_packet* Pak) ;

int   Example_Dlg_Func (Ex_t* Dat) ;
void Init_List (ads_hdlg Handle) ;
void Init_Func (ads_callback_packet* Pak) ;

#define ELEMENTS(array) (sizeof(array)/sizeof((array)[0]))

struct func_entry {
    char *func_name;     // Name of user command
    int (*func)(void);   // No parameters and returns int
};

struct func_entry func_table[] = {
           {"C:dialog", Dialog_Func}, // Type "dialog"
};

void main (int argc, char* argv[])
{
  short scode = RSRSLT;  // Normal result code (default)
  int stat;

  ads_init (argc,argv);  // Open comms with AutoLISP
```

```
     // For-ever loop
     for ( ;; ) {                  // Request/Result loop

         if ((stat = ads_link(scode)) < 0) {
             printf ("\nERROR,stat=%d",stat) ;
             exit(1);   // < 0 means error
         }

         scode = RSRSLT;               // Reset result code

         switch (stat) {

             case RQXLOAD:  // Load & define functions
                 scode =
                     (funcload() == RTNORM ? RSRSLT : RSERR) ;
                 break;

             case RQSUBR:  // External function request
                 scode = dofun() == RTNORM ? RSRSLT : RSERR;
                 break;

             case RQXUNLD :
             case RQEND :
             case RQQUIT :
                 break ;

             default:
                 break;
         }
     }
}

int funcload (void)
/*
PURPOSE: To tell ACAD the names of functions in the app.
NOTES:    1)  .func_name is what you have to type at the
              keyboard
          2) This is called after EVERY DRAWING LOAD.
*/
{
    int i;

    for (i = 0; i < ELEMENTS(func_table); i++) {
        if (!ads_defun (func_table[i].func_name,(short)i)){
            ads_printf ("\n***funcload failure***\n") ;
            return (RTERROR);
        }
    }
```

```
    return (RTNORM) ;
}

int dofun (void)
{
    int Func_Code ; // Which function to call
    int Ret_Val ;   // Return value of called function

    // Get the function code and check it.
    if ((Func_Code = ads_getfuncode()) < 0 ||
        Func_Code >= ELEMENTS(func_table)) {
        ads_fail("Received nonexistent function code.");
        return (RTERROR) ;
    }

    // Call the function selected
    Ret_Val = (*func_table[Func_Code].func)();
    return (Ret_Val) ;
}

int Tidy_End (int Ret_Val)
{
    (void)ads_usrbrk () ;   // Clear ^C and or ESC flag
    (void)ads_retvoid () ;  // Tell AutoLISP nowt
    return (Ret_Val) ;      // Tell AutoCAD result
}

int Dialog_Func (void)
{
    Ex_t Data ;
    int  i ;

    // Initialise the dialog Dat
    Data.Real_1 = 10.0 ; Data.Real_2  = 20.0 ;
    Data.Real_3 = 30.0 ; Data.Int_1   = 40   ;
    Data.Int_2  = 50   ;
    Data.Tog_Int   = 0 ;
    Data.Radio_Int = BY_COLOR ;
    strcpy (Data.Str,"Sixty") ;

    // Called 3 times to show how OK and CANCEL
    // buttons work, normally you just call once!
    for (i = 0 ; i < 3 ; i++) {
        if (!Example_Dlg_Func (&Data)) {
            ads_printf ("\nChanges abandoned") ;
        } else {
            ads_printf ("\nChanges accepted") ;
        }
```

```
        }
    return (Tidy_End(RTNORM)) ;
}

/******* The following tables for all dialogs *********/

Ex_t Tmp ; // A temp Dat for dialog interaction

// A list of how many things of what type we use
#define N_REALS        3
#define N_INTS         2
#define N_STRINGS      1
#define N_TOGGLES      3
#define N_RADIOS       1 // i.e. # of radio groups
#define N_BUTTONS      2
#define N_LISTS        1

#if N_REALS    // Only compile this if we need to
struct {
    char Name [MAX_DCL_CHARS] ; // Dialog name
    char Key [MAX_DCL_CHARS] ;  // Key within dialog
    ads_real* Adr ;             // Where the real is
} D_Real[N_REALS] = {
                    {"ex_dlg", "real1",&Tmp.Real_1},
                    {"ex_dlg", "real2",&Tmp.Real_2},
                    {"ex_dlg", "real3",&Tmp.Real_3}
                    };

#endif // N_REALS

#if N_INTS
struct {
    char Name [MAX_DCL_CHARS] ; // Dialog name
    char Key [MAX_DCL_CHARS] ;  // Key within dialog
    int* Adr ;                  // Where the int is
} D_Int[N_INTS] = {
                    {"ex_dlg","int1",&Tmp.Int_1},
                    {"ex_dlg","int2",&Tmp.Int_2},
                };
#endif

#if N_STRINGS
struct {
    char  Name [MAX_DCL_CHARS] ; // Dialog name
    char  Key [MAX_DCL_CHARS] ;  // Key within dialog
    char* Str ;                  // Original string
} D_Str[N_STRINGS] = {
                    {"ex_dlg","astring",Tmp.Str}
                    };
```

```
    // Note that & not required, Tmp.Str already an address
    #endif

    #if N_TOGGLES
    struct {
        char Name[MAX_DCL_CHARS] ; // Dialog name
        char Key[MAX_DCL_CHARS] ;  // Key within dialog
        int* Adr ;                 // Adr of toggle int
        int  Mask_Bits ;           // e.g. 0x01 = bit 0
    } D_Tog[N_TOGGLES] = {
            {"ex_dlg","mercury",&Tmp.Tog_Int, MERC_BIT},
            {"ex_dlg","venus",  &Tmp.Tog_Int, VENU_BIT},
            {"ex_dlg","mars",   &Tmp.Tog_Int, MARS_BIT}
                        };
    #endif


    #if N_RADIOS

    #define MAX_RADIOS  32 // Within one row or col

     struct {
        char Name[MAX_DCL_CHARS] ; // Dialog name
        char Key[MAX_DCL_CHARS] ;  // Key within dialog
        int* Adr ;                 // Adr of radio int
    } D_Rad[N_RADIOS] = {
            {"ex_dlg","order",&Tmp.Radio_Int}
                        } ;
    #endif

    #if N_BUTTONS
     struct {
        char Name[MAX_DCL_CHARS] ;
        char Key[MAX_DCL_CHARS] ;
        void (*But_Fun)(ads_callback_packet* Cpak) ;
    } D_But[N_BUTTONS] = {
                        {"ex_dlg","reinit",Init_Func},
                        {"ex_dlg","create",Create_Func}
                        } ;
    #endif

    #if N_LISTS
     struct {
        char Name[MAX_DCL_CHARS] ; // Dialog name
        char Key[MAX_DCL_CHARS] ;  // Key within the fialog
        void (*Func)(ads_callback_packet* Cpak) ;
    } D_List[N_LISTS] = {
                        {"ex_dlg","listbox",List_Func},
                    } ;
    #endif
```

```
int Example_Dlg_Func (Ex_t* Dat)
/*
PURPOSE: To run the dialog box "ex_dlg" in "dialog.dcl"
Returns TRUE if the user clicks OK, FALSE otherwise.
*/
{
    int      dcl_id,D_Stat,Res ;
    ads_hdlg D_Hndl ;
    int      Accepted ;


    // Put the Dat sent to us in Tmp. Tmp will be
    // used as the Tmprary store as the user changes
    // values in the menu. Note that Dat is already
    // an address
    (void)memcpy (&Tmp,Dat,sizeof(Ex_t)) ;

    // Load DCL and dialog, this does NOT show the dialog
    if (!Setup_Dialog_Box ("ex_dlg",&dcl_id,&D_Hndl)) {
        return (FALSE) ;
    }

    Init_List (D_Hndl) ;

    // Now actually visualise the dialog box
    Res = ads_start_dialog (D_Hndl,&D_Stat) ;

    // If you get here the dialog has finished,
    // and it is no longer visible
    if (Res != RTNORM) {
        ads_printf ("\nERROR,ED,Res=%d",Res) ;
        return (FALSE) ;
    } else {
        (void)ads_unload_dialog (dcl_id) ;
    }

    // D_Stat tells us what the user did to end the dlg
    switch (D_Stat) {
        case DLGOK :     // User has finished and wants
                         // the data selected, So copy
                         // the temp working data
                         // into his Dat
            (void)memcpy (Dat,&Tmp,sizeof(Ex_t)) ;
            Accepted = TRUE ;
            break ;

        case DLGCANCEL :      // User has finished
            Accepted = FALSE ; // and is abandoning, no
```

```
                                    // copying to do, leave
                                    // Dat as is
              break ;

          default : // Should never happen!
              ads_printf ("\nERROR,ED,D_Stat=%d",D_Stat) ;
              return (FALSE) ;
      }
      return (Accepted) ;
}


int Setup_Dialog_Box (char* Name, int* Dcl_Id,
                      ads_hdlg* D_Hndl)
/*
PURPOSE: Go through the global Real,Int,String,Radio,
         List and Toggle tables assigning actions to the
         appropriate tiles. I loop over each table
         looking for a match with Name, and then assign
         the actions to the keys themselves.
NOTE:    This does not start the dialog, it initialises
         only.
*/
{
    int  Res,t ;
    char Dum_Str[MAX_DCL_CHARS] ;

    /*
     * Load the DCL file. Change the path below for where
     * you have put DIALOG.DCL. No DCL extension
     */
    Res = ads_load_dialog (
            "D:\\MYBOOK\\ADS_CODE\\DIALOG",Dcl_Id);
    if (Res != RTNORM) {
        ads_printf ("\nERROR,could not load DCL file.") ;
        return (FALSE) ;
    }

    /*
     * Load the particular dialog box which we will use
     */
    Res = ads_new_dialog (Name,*Dcl_Id,NULL,D_Hndl) ;
    if (Res != RTNORM) {
        ads_printf ("\nERROR,SDB,bad load <%s>,",Name) ;
        return (FALSE) ;
    }

    /*
     * Associate to each tile (identified by a key
     * string which corresponds to "key=XXXX" in the
```

```
          *  .DCL file) a function to execute, and set the
          *  initial values of the tiles
          */
#if N_REALS
      // if N_REALS is 0 then this block not compiled
      for (t = 0 ; t < N_REALS ; t++) {
          if (strcmpi(D_Real[t].Name,Name)==0) {
              // An entry found for this dialog,
              // so associate a function with this tile
              (void)ads_action_tile (*D_Hndl,D_Real[t].Key,
                  Get_Real) ;

              // Now write a real number to that tile
              sprintf (Dum_Str,"%6.3f",*(D_Real[t].Adr)) ;
              (void)ads_set_tile (*D_Hndl,D_Real[t].Key,
                  Dum_Str) ;
          }
      }
#endif

#if N_INTS
      for (t = 0 ; t < N_INTS ; t++) {
          if (strcmpi(D_Int[t].Name,Name)==0) {
              (void)ads_action_tile (*D_Hndl,D_Int[t].Key,
                  Get_Int) ;
              sprintf (Dum_Str,"%d",*(D_Int[t].Adr)) ;
              (void)ads_set_tile (*D_Hndl,D_Int[t].Key,
                  Dum_Str) ;
          }
      }
#endif

#if N_BUTTONS
      for (t = 0 ; t < N_BUTTONS ; t++) {
          if (strcmpi(D_But[t].Name,Name)==0) {
              (void)ads_action_tile (*D_Hndl,
                                      D_But[t].Key,
                                      D_But[t].But_Fun) ;
          }
      }
#endif

#if N_LISTS
      for (t = 0 ; t < N_LISTS ; t++) {
          if (strcmpi(D_List[t].Name,Name)==0) {
              (void)ads_action_tile (*D_Hndl,D_List[t].Key,
                  D_List[t].Func) ;
          }
      }
```

```
#endif

#if N_STRINGS
    for (t = 0 ; t < N_STRINGS ; t++) {
        if (strcmpi(D_Str[t].Name,Name)==0) {
            (void)ads_action_tile (*D_Hndl,
                            D_Str[t].Key,Get_Str) ;
            (void)ads_set_tile (*D_Hndl,
                        D_Str[t].Key,D_Str[t].Str) ;
        }
    }
#endif

#if N_TOGGLES
    for (t = 0 ; t < N_TOGGLES ; t++) {
        if (strcmpi(D_Tog[t].Name,Name)==0) {
            (void)ads_action_tile (*D_Hndl,
                        D_Tog[t].Key,Get_Toggle) ;
            /*
             * Set the toggles
             */
            if (D_Tog[t].Mask_Bits & (*(D_Tog[t].Adr))) {
                // This bit set
                (void)strcpy (Dum_Str,"1") ;
            } else {
                // This bit not set
                (void)strcpy (Dum_Str,"0") ;
            }
            (void)ads_set_tile (*D_Hndl,D_Tog[t].Key,
                    Dum_Str) ;
        }
    }
#endif

#if N_RADIOS
    for (t = 0 ; t < N_RADIOS ; t++) {
        if (strcmpi(D_Rad[t].Name,Name)==0) {
            // Found the radio group
            int i ;
            // Associate Get_Radio with the group
            (void)ads_action_tile (*D_Hndl,D_Rad[t].Key,
                    Get_Radio) ;

            // Activate one of the radio buttons
            i = (*(D_Rad[t].Adr)) ;
            sprintf (Dum_Str,"%s%d",D_Rad[t].Key,i) ;
            (void)ads_set_tile (*D_Hndl,D_Rad[t].Key,
                    Dum_Str) ;
        }
```

```
    }
#endif

    // Use standard OK and CANCEL tiles
    (void)ads_action_tile (*D_Hndl,"accept",Dialog_OK) ;
    (void)ads_action_tile (*D_Hndl,"cancel",Dialog_Canc);

    return (TRUE) ;
}

#if N_REALS
void CALLB Get_Real (ads_callback_packet* Pak)
/*
PURPOSE: Gets called when a real number tile is
touched. Pak->reason tells what has happened.
*/
{
    char    Dum_Str[MAX_DCL_CHARS],
            Key[MAX_DCL_CHARS] ;
    int     i ;

    if (Pak->reason != CBR_LOST_FOCUS) {
        return ;
    }

    // Lost the focus, so get data from the tile
    (void)ads_get_attr_string (Pak->tile,"key",Key,
                                MAX_DCL_CHARS) ;

    // Search for which real tile it is
    for (i = 0 ; i < N_REALS ; i++) {
        if (strcmpi (Key,D_Real[i].Key)==0) {
            // Update the data for this tile
            *(D_Real[i].Adr) = atof (Pak->value) ;
            break ;
        }
    }

    // Write to the tile our version of the data
    sprintf (Dum_Str,"%6.3f",*(D_Real[i].Adr)) ;
    (void)ads_set_tile (Pak->dialog,D_Real[i].Key,
            Dum_Str) ;
}
#endif // N_REALS

#if N_INTS
void CALLB Get_Int (ads_callback_packet* Pak)
{
    char    Dum_Str[MAX_DCL_CHARS],
```

```
                    Key[MAX_DCL_CHARS] ;
        int        i;

        if (Pak->reason != CBR_LOST_FOCUS) {
            return ;
        }

        (void)ads_get_attr_string (Pak->tile,"key",
                                   Key,MAX_DCL_CHARS) ;
        for (i = 0 ; i < N_INTS ; i++) {
            if (strcmpi (Key,D_Int[i].Key)==0) {
                *(D_Int[i].Adr) = atoi (Pak->value) ;
                break ;
            }
        }
        sprintf (Dum_Str,"%d",*(D_Int[i].Adr)) ;
        (void)ads_set_tile (Pak->dialog,
                    D_Int[i].Key,Dum_Str) ;
}
#endif  // N_INTS

#if N_STRINGS
void CALLB Get_Str (ads_callback_packet* Pak)
{
    char Key[MAX_DCL_CHARS] ;
    int  i ;

    if (Pak->reason != CBR_LOST_FOCUS) {
        return ;
    }

    (void)ads_get_attr_string (Pak->tile,"key",Key,
                               MAX_DCL_CHARS) ;
    for (i = 0 ; i < N_STRINGS ; i++) {
        if (strcmpi (Key,D_Str[i].Key)==0) {
            (void)strcpy (D_Str[i].Str,Pak->value) ;
            break ;
        }
    }
    (void)ads_set_tile (Pak->dialog,D_Str[i].Key,
                        D_Str[i].Str) ;
}
#endif  // N_STRINGS

#if N_TOGGLES
void CALLB Get_Toggle (ads_callback_packet* Pak)
/*
PURPOSE: To toggle a single bit on or off
*/
```

```
{
    char Key[MAX_DCL_CHARS] ;
    int  i,Not_Bits ;
    int  On ;
    int* Adr ; // Adr of int containing bit to toggle

    if (Pak->value[0] == '0') {
        On = FALSE ;
    } else {
        On = TRUE ;
    }

    /*
     * Find out which tile has been toggled by getting
     * the key attribute of the tile.
     */
    (void)ads_get_attr_string (Pak->tile,"key",Key,
                                MAX_DCL_CHARS) ;
    for (i = 0 ; i < N_TOGGLES ; i++) {
        if (strcmpi (Key,D_Tog[i].Key)==0) {
            Adr = D_Tog[i].Adr ;
            if (On) {
                // Set a single bit
                *Adr = (*Adr) | D_Tog[i].Mask_Bits ;
            } else {
                // Reset a single bit
                Not_Bits = ~D_Tog[i].Mask_Bits ;
                *Adr = (*Adr) & Not_Bits ;
            }
            break ;
        }
    }
}
#endif  // N_TOGGLES

#if N_RADIOS
void CALLB Get_Radio (ads_callback_packet* Pak)
/*
PURPOSE: To get data about a radio box
*/
{
    char    Key[MAX_DCL_CHARS] ;
    int     i,Index ;

    /*
     * Find out which tile has been radioed by getting
     * the key attribute of the tile.
     */
    (void)ads_get_attr_string (Pak->tile,"key",Key,
```

```
                                 MAX_DCL_CHARS) ;

    for (i = 0 ; i < N_RADIOS ; i++) {
        if (strcmpi (Key,D_Rad[i].Key)==0) {
            Index = atoi (Pak->value+strlen(Key)) ;
            (*(D_Rad[i].Adr)) = Index  ;
            break ;
        }
    }
}
#endif

void CALLB Dialog_OK (ads_callback_packet* Pak)
{
    (void)ads_done_dialog(Pak->dialog,DLGOK) ;
}

void CALLB Dialog_Canc (ads_callback_packet* Pak)
{
    (void)ads_done_dialog(Pak->dialog,DLGCANCEL) ;
}

void CALLB Init_Func (ads_callback_packet* Pak)
{
    if (Pak->reason == CBR_SELECT) {
        ads_alert ("\nWould initialise!") ;
    }
}

void CALLB Create_Func (ads_callback_packet* Pak)
{
    if (Pak->reason == CBR_SELECT) {
        ads_alert ("\nWould create!") ;
    }
}

#define N_FRUITS 33

char Alien_Fruit[N_FRUITS][5] ;

void Init_List (ads_hdlg Handle)
{
    int f,c,Res ;

    for (f = 0 ; f < N_FRUITS ; f++) {
        for (c = 0 ; c < 4 ; c++) {
            Alien_Fruit[f][c] = 'a' + ((rand()*20) / RAND_MAX)  ;
        }
        Alien_Fruit[f][4] = (char)0 ;
```

```
    }

    // Initialise the list box, starting with a new empty list
    Res = ads_start_list (Handle,"listbox",LIST_NEW,0) ;
    if (Res != RTNORM) {
        ads_printf ("\nID,ERROR,could not start_list.") ;
        return ;
    }

    for (f = 0 ; f < N_FRUITS ; f++) {
        ads_add_list (Alien_Fruit[f]) ;
    }

    ads_end_list () ;
}

void CALLB List_Func (ads_callback_packet* Pak)
{
    if (Pak->reason == CBR_SELECT) {
        int    m ;
        m = atoi (Pak->value) ; // # of item selected
        // Copy to edit box in dialog
        (void)ads_set_tile (Pak->dialog,"astring",
            Alien_Fruit[m]) ;
        // Copy to temporary data structure
        (void)strcpy (Tmp.Str,Alien_Fruit[m]) ;
    }
}

//                       -- end of LST_12_1.C --

//     DIALOG.DCL
//
//
// DCL file for use with LST_12_1.C
// Illustrates how to interface with the more common
// objects found in dialog boxes
//


// This line tells AutoCAD to check vigorously for
// errors
dcl_settings : default_dcl_settings { audit_level = 3; }

// The following lines describe a dialog box. You can
// have as many dialog boxes as you want within a single
// DCL file. This file has only one, called "ex_dlg".

ex_dlg : dialog {
```

```
label = "Example dialog box"; // Visible title
: row {
    : edit_box {
        label = "String:";
        key   = "astring";
        edit_width = 8 ;
        edit_limit = 8 ;
    }
    : edit_box {
        label = "Real1";
        key   = "real1";
        edit_width = 6 ;
        edit_limit = 6 ;
    }
}  // end of row definition

: list_box {
    key = "listbox";
    width = 40 ;
    multiple_select = false;
}  // end of list box defintion

: row {
    : edit_box {
        label = "Real2:";
        key   = "real2";
        edit_width = 8 ;
        edit_limit = 8 ;
    }
    : edit_box {
        label = "Real3:";
        key   = "real3";
        edit_width = 8 ;
        edit_limit = 8 ;
    }
}

: row {
    : edit_box {
        label = "Apples:";
        key   = "int1";
        edit_width = 6 ;
        edit_limit = 6 ;
    }
    : edit_box {
        label = "Oranges:";
        key   = "int2";
        edit_width = 6 ;
        edit_limit = 6 ;
```

```
        }
    }

    : boxed_radio_row {
        // WARNING: The keys MUST be order0,order1...
        label = "Order by:" ;
        key   = "order" ;
        : radio_button {
            key   = "order0";
            label = "color";
            value = "0";
        }
        : radio_button {
            key   = "order1";
            label = "weight";
            value = "0" ;
        }
        : radio_button {
            key   = "order2";
            label = "taste";
            value = "0" ;
        }
    }

    : boxed_row {
        label = "Toggles" ;
        : toggle {
            label = "on Mercury" ;
            key   = "mercury"  ;
            value = "1"        ;
        }
        : toggle {
            label = "on Venus" ;
            key   = "venus"  ;
            value = "1"        ;
        }
        : toggle {
            label = "on Mars" ;
            key   = "mars"  ;
            value = "1"        ;
        }
    }

    : boxed_row {
        label = "Actions" ;
        : button {
            key   = "reinit" ;
            label = "Reinitialise" ;
        }
```

```
            : button {
                key    = "create" ;
                label  = "Create" ;
            }
        }


        spacer ;
        spacer ;
        ok_cancel ;
}                    // ex_dlg end
```

Practical suggestions for programming AutoCAD

13

13.1 Introduction

In this chapter I give some practical suggestions for programming in C for ADS. It is based on several years of experience in the field and should help you to write tidy and bug free programs. The suggestions cover:

- memory management.
- tidy handling of `ads_function()` return codes
- internationalization
- software copy protection
- unequality of theoretically equal points
- unlocking locked drawings
- why programs refuse to link in multitasking environments
- error handling
- compiling the same sources with multiple compilers.

13.2 Memory management and ADS

13.2.1 Problems with the C standard `malloc()` function

The C standard `malloc()` is the C way of dynamically creating memory space. The idea is that the space is not allocated statically in the program, but allocated only when required. In this way a C program uses less space in the RAM of the computer and also less space on the hard disk in terms of executeable size. An example of its use is:

```
Mystruct_t* Big_Thing ;   // Pointer to a big thing
if (Big_Thing == NULL) {
    printf ("\nERROR, cannot allocate memory for Big_Thing") ;
    ads_exit (1) ; // Only in PURE ADS please
}
// Continue with rest of the program
```

The main problem with `malloc()` is that it can fail. It will fail if there is not enough memory, as shown above. Even if the environment (Windows, Extended DOS, whatever) has a virtual memory manager which uses the disk for RAM, it is possible that the disk is full.

The question is "what do I do if malloc fails?". In C++ there is the try-throw-catch mechanism, but in C the problem is harder to deal with elegantly. The code fragment above suggests the simplest answer to the question above: print an error message and exit. You can only do this in pure ADS, in the rxADS or the ARX environment this would cause AutoCAD to exit! The standard C exit function will close any open files and deallocate any memory previously allocated by the program; see section 13.10 below. Another possibility, if there is a chance of getting the user to help out, is to tell the user that no memory is available and that the action she has selected cannot be completed.

Personally I have found that sophisticated error recovery is not worthwhile and the best thing to do is to print an error message and exit (if possible). Given this decision it was obvious that the whole `malloc()`-check-pointer-write-error-message-exit sequence could be factored into a single function, saving executable space and reading-writing effort; that is what `Safe_Calloc()` does.

13.2.2 `Safe_Calloc()`, a less cumbersome allocator

`Safe_Calloc()` below is based on `calloc()` rather than `malloc()` because the former initialises the memory allocated to all zeroes, which helps maintain repeatability in the case of memory error debugging. It is called with three parameters, the number of items, the size of the items and an error message to print in case of failure.

A call to this function is a single line in your sources and replaces the four lines you would have to write if you checked each `malloc()` individually, along with error message printing and the call to `exit()`. Compare

```
Mystruct_t* Big_Thing ;   // Pointer to a big thing
Big_Thing = Safe_Calloc (1,sizeof(Big_Thing),"Big_Thing") ;
```

with the previous code fragment.

If `Safe_Calloc()` returns then you know that you have the RAM asked for. If it does not return then a more or less useful error message will be printed and the application aborted.

```
void* Safe_Calloc (size_t N_Items, size_t Item_Size,
                   const char* Msg)
/*
Allocates some space just like calloc, but if it can't:
    1) print Msg
    2) abort from app.
*/
{
    void* Ptr ;
    Ptr = calloc (N_Items,Item_Size) ;
    if (Ptr == NULL) {
        ads_print ("\nSafe_Calloc(%lu,%lu,%s) ERROR. ",
            (unsigned long)N_Items,(unsigned long)Item_Size,Msg);
        ads_abort ("...aborting...") ;
    }
    return (Ptr) ;
}
```

13.2.3 Avoiding the "Fatal Error" message, check your memory

Although it is difficult to crash and AutoCAD with an ADS program, it is not impossible! Often the cause of the crash is corrupted memory, for example allocating 511 bytes, but writing 512. Most compilers supply a method for checking the heap, which is the area of memory where `malloc()` gets its bytes. Here is a function which you can call at opportune times during your application to check that all is well with the heap:

```
void Check_Heap (const char* Caller)
/*
PURPOSE: To make sure I have not corrupted occupied or free ram.
If anything nasty is detected I print an error message and abort
my ADS program.
*/
{
    struct _heapinfo H_Info ;
    int    Heap_Status ;
    int    Error ;

    Error = FALSE ;

    // Check that the free entries are ok, setting...
    // ... all free areas to a certain value
```

```
switch (_heapset(0xAA)) {
    case _HEAPBADBEGIN :
        ads_printf ("\nERROR,_HEAPBADBEGIN(1) with"
                        " %s",Caller) ;
        Error = TRUE ;
        break ;
    case _HEAPBADNODE :
        ads_printf ("\nERROR, HEAPBADNODE(1) with"
                        " %s.",Caller) ;
        Error = TRUE ;
        break ;
    case _HEAPEMPTY :
        ads_printf ("\nWARNING, heap empty, %s.",Caller) ;
        break ;
    case _HEAPOK :
        break ;
    default :
        ads_printf ("\nERROR,strange _heapset() with"
                        " %s ",Caller) ;
        Error = TRUE ;
}

if (Error) {
    ads_abort ("\nThere is a HEAP ERROR!") ;
}

// Check that the whole heap is ok
H_Info._pentry = NULL ; /* To start the heapwalk */
do {
    Heap_Status = _heapwalk (&H_Info) ;
    switch (Heap_Status) {
        case _HEAPOK :      /* Carry On Walking */
        case _HEAPEND :     /* Nothing else to do */
        case _HEAPEMPTY :   /* Nothing else to do */
            break ;
        case _HEAPBADPTR :
            ads_printf ("\nERROR,_HEAPBADPTR(2), with"
                            " %s ",Caller) ;
            Error = TRUE ;
            return ;
        case _HEAPBADBEGIN :
            ads_printf ("\nERROR,_HEAPBADBEGIN(2), with"
                            " %s ",Caller) ;
            Error = TRUE ;
            return ;
        case _HEAPBADNODE :
            ads_printf ("\nERROR,_HEAPBADBEGINODE(2), with"
                            " %s ",Caller) ;
            Error = TRUE ;
```

```
                    return ;
             default :
                 ads_printf ("\nERROR, strange Heap_Status(%d)"
                             " with %s ",Heap_Status,Caller) ;
                 Error = TRUE ;
                 return ;
         }
         if (Error) {
             ads_abort ("\nThere is a HEAP ERROR!") ;
         }
    } while ((Heap_Status != _HEAPEND) &&
             (Heap_Status != _HEAPEMPTY)) ;
}
```

The function calls a heap checking function called _heapset() which
initialises the free areas of the heap (those not yet mallocced), and at the same
time checks that the free areas are not corrupt. _heapset() is useful because it
helps keep part of the memory of the computer in a known state; in this case we
set all the free areas to the value 0xAA. This makes bugs a little more
reproduceable.

If the free areas check out OK then the function "walks the allocated heap"
using _heapwalk(). There is no need to go into details here, but this function
looks at every allocated entry in the heap and checks the consistency of it.

You should call the Heap_Check() as shown in the following example:

```
Heap_Check ("\nJust after initialising road-map") ;
```

If there are no errors in the heap at this point then the user will not see
anything printed. If there are, an error message will be printed, along with the
message you put in the call. This way you know roughly what the error was,
and when the error occurred.

Since this function will slow down your application you may like to use
conditional compilation (see section 13.7 in this chapter and Chapter 9 section
9.2 for further example of conditional compilation) to take out the calls to the
function once you are sure all is working well. However remember: early
optimization often makes it difficult to find bugs, so wait until you are sure all
works well before taking out heap checking.

Both Microsoft and WATCOM have these heap checking and walking
functions, Borland C 3.1 has them under another name, see the Borland
documentation (in the index under "heap") for more details.

13.2.4 Free your malloced memory

New comers to C, especially those who use AutoLISP may be tempted not to `free()` the memory allocated with `malloc()` (or `calloc()` or `realloc()` or `strdup()`), thinking that the system will tidy up at the end of the program. This *might* be true in the DOS environment, but is certainly is not always the case in Windows environments.

So you should never lose track of the pointers to allocated memory and you should always free them at the end of the program, earlier if possible.

The problem with not freeing the memory is that as your user runs your ADS functions again and again, without resetting the computer, memory will be eaten up bit by bit, and the whole system could grind to a halt.

13.3 Tidier and shorter listings with `void_ads` functions

Just as it is tempting not to check the return values of `malloc()`, it is tempting to ignore the return values of ADS functions. It is rare that they fail, and if you assiduously check every return value short functions in your application increase in size by between 10% to 50%.

We can use the same sort of trick as that used in the previous section, creating a "wrapper" function for every ads function which returns a value which we are too lazy to check. Consider the following example.

```
void void_ads_relrb (const struct resbuf* rb)
/*
PURPOSE: To replace ads_relrb, checking the return
value but not returning the return value. This makes
you code more readable, while retaining error checks
*/
{
    int Res ;

    Res = ads_relrb(rb) ;
    if (Res != RTNORM) {
        ads_printf ("\nError in ads_relrb, Res = %d",Res) ;
    }
}
```

Now every time you call `void_ads_relrb()` (instead of `ads_relrb()`) you know that the return value will be checked and an error message will be printed. You can write equivalent wrappers for all the ADS functions which rarely if ever fail; for example `ads_sslength()` becomes `void_ads_sslength()`, `ads_ssfree()` becomes `void_ads_ssfree()`.

13.4 Internationalisation

AutoCAD 12 introduced the "_ENGLISHCOMMAND" convention. Whatever language version of AutoCAD every command can be called in two ways. In the Italian version, for example, you can call the circle command by typing either "_CIRCLE" in English, or "CERCHIO" in Italian.

This convention is a great boon to programmers who want to sell their programs in more than one country. ads_command() should always be sent the "_ENGLISH" version of the command.

When you call standard dialog boxes they appear already in the native language of the AutoCAD which is running.

Help files and ads_printf() messages will have to be dealt with in another way. If possible you should construct your program to use external files of help messages which can be customised to each country. "Hard coding" messages into the program is inflexible, and if you ever do find a customer in Belgium it will be you, the programmer, who has to type in the translations rather than your local reseller.

To help you find out what language AutoCAD is using there is a variable called LOCALE, see Appendix C.

The function ads_getcname() may help you as well, see Appendix B.

13.4.1 International date and time

It is often useful to print the date and time in the corner of a drawing to know when it was created and/or last modified. Although AutoCAD has variables which can be used for this purpose, I think you will find the following function much easier to use:

```
#include <time.h>  // required for time and strftime functions
void Make_Date_Time_Strings (char* Date, char* Time)
//PURPOSE: To put in Date & Time string representations of
//         the current date and time
{
    time_t Time_Date ;

    // Get the time
    Time_Date = time (NULL) ;

    // Convert to a string date
    (void)strftime (Date, MAX_CHARS, "%d/%m/%y",
                    localtime(&Time_Of_Day)) ;

    // Convert to a string time
    (void)strftime (Time, MAX_CHARS, "%H:%M",
                    localtime(&Time_Of_Day)) ;
```

```
}
```

This simply gets hold of the current time and date using the standard C `time()` function and converts them into strings using another standard C function `strftime()`, "STRing Format TIME". The format string is very flexible, and you should read the manual of your C/C++ runtime library to find out exactly what is possible. As far as internationalisation is concerned the above date is formatted as DAY-MONTH-YEAR, which is the European and Japanese convention. American readers should change the format string to:

```
"%m/%d/%y"
```

to obtain MONTH-DAY-YEAR format.

With `strftime()` you can also choose whether to print the whole year, or just the last two digits and so on.

13.5 Software protection of your programs

If you want to sell your programs then it is worth considering software protection. Do not be discouraged by the fact that European versions of AutoCAD are software-protected but pirate copies still abound. The illegal market for AutoCAD is huge, so someone somewhere was bound to break the software protection. Your application on the other hand is probably in a niche market where it would cost more to break the protection than buy the orginal program.

The best software protection is afforded by a "hardware lock" or "dongle". This is a piece of electronics in a small plastic box which you usually connect to the printer port of your computer. European users of AutoCAD will be familiar with this device. The application does not run without this hardware lock. Every (paying) customer is given the disks containing the application and a hardware lock. The customer can make as many copies of the disks as he wants, but can only run it on one computer at a time, the one where the hardware lock is.

Computing magazines are full of advertisements for hardware locks, with a wide range of price and features. Some even have a small amount of memory which can be used to count the number of times the application has been run, or the number of hours it has been used. This can be used for "renting" the application to the client.

The hardware lock makers supply a set of libraries which you link to your application. There is usually a function in this library which checks to see if the lock is present, for example:

```
int Lock_Present (const char* Lock_Code) ;
```

Your application should call this to check that the lock is present, it will return 1 if the lock is found, 0 otherwise. If the lock is not found you should print a polite message (maybe using `ads_alert()`) explaining the problem and refuse to run. The lock maker will assign you a code (number or string) which uniquely identifies your application, so that your lock will not allow a different application to run, and another lock will not allow your application to run.

No hardware lock is unbeatable, and determined criminals can break into your application given enough time. You can make it as hard as possible for them by following these tips:

- Take out the debugging information from the release of your application. Programs which contain debugging information can easily be stepped through, and the place where the hardware lock test is called can be found.
- Place the check in many places as possible, testing for the lock at random times.
- Do not *respond* to the lack of the hardware lock immediately. Wait a random period of time or a random number of steps before alerting the user that there is no hardware lock and you will end the application. You should block the application in a part of the program different from where the missing lock condition was found.

I came across one CAD program which used a hardware lock, but only checked for its presence at start up. An "enterprising" company had bought a single copy of the program (hence a single lock) and connected the lock to several computers using a printer sharing switchbox. When a user wanted to run the program he simply switched the box to connect his computer to the hardware lock and the program started. A second (and third and fourth...) user would switch the box to his computer while he started the program!

13.6 When equal points are not

It is possible that two points which should in theory have the same coordinates are not in fact equal. This could happen if originally "snap to node" was used to create key points for different objects (two meshes for example) which were later exploded. A customer once phoned me up with an error of this type, and I had to make a function called `Equal_Points()` to test for near equality, since exact equality could not be guaranteed.

Probably, in a series of floating point operations, AutoCAD does some truncating and/or rounding which changes very slightly the coordinates of the points.

Here is the C function I use to test for three-dimensional points equality. If you get any similar obscure bugs you may like to use it too:

```
int Equal_Points (const ads_point p1, const ads_point p2)
/*
```

```
PURPOSE: To return 1 if the points are "equal",
         i.e. within the given margin.
*/
{
    const ads_real Equality_Margin = (ads_real)0.00000001;
    int c ;

    for (c = X ; c <= Z ; c++) {
        if (fabs(p1[c] - p2[c]) > Equality_Margin) {
            return (0) ;
        }
    }
    return (1) ;
}
```

The only assurances I can give you about the magic number `Equality_Margin` is that the customer has not complained of this problem since I made this change. The application worked in the range from centimeters to tens of meters, and you may have to change `Equality_Margin` to be smaller if your application works in hundredths of an inch or in micrometers.

A similar problem may occur when you are trying to convert a series of lines into a single polyline entity. If the original series of lines comes from a DXF file with low precision (or maybe a CAD system with inherently low precision) then AutoCAD will refuse to join the lines together to form a polyline when you use the PEDIT command.

13.7 Compiling the same sources with different compilers

Sometimes you want the same ADS application to run on two different platforms, and so you may have two different compilers for these platforms. C is a pretty portable language, especially now that most compilers follow the ANSI C definition of the language. However while there may be few differences in language definition, there will often be differences in library functions.

An example is `_dos_findfirst()` and `_findfirst()`. Both these functions are used for searching for files, but they take different parameters and return different values. The first is from WATCOM C when compiling for extended DOS, and the second is from Microsoft Visual C++ when compiling for Windows. The trick which you should use is to use conditional compilation again. All compilers have predefined "defines" which help you identity which compiler is reading the C file. The following program fragment shows you how to exploit these predefines in your C source:

```
#ifdef _MSC_VER   // the Microsoft compiler
...do things with findfirst() ...
#elsif __WATCOMC__  // The Watcom compiler
```

```
...do things with dos_findfirst() ...
#else
#error Neither MSC nor WATCOM compiler is being used
#endif
```

The above fragment of code (obviously with real C statements instead of "...") will compile correctly with Microsoft or Watcom. If neither of these compilers is used the compiler will print the message after #error and stop compiling the file.

Whether you put whole functions or simply customised code-fragments inside the coditional compilation blocks depends on you and the amount of difference between compilers.

13.8 Unlocking locked drawings

It is just *possible* that AutoCAD crashes when you run your application. If this happens the drawing that was open at the time of the crash may be "locked". Drawings are "locked" so that only one user, or session of AutoCAD, can open them at a time. Drawings get unlocked when the drawing is closed from within AutoCAD. Obviously this unlocking of a drawing does not happen if AutoCAD crashes in the middle of an edit.

If, when you restart AutoCAD after a crash, you get the message "drawing locked" then use the menu sequence

File-->Management-->Utilities->Unlock

to unlock it.

13.9 Do not modify your application as it runs!

The advantage of using a multi-tasking system like Windows-95 or Windows NT is that you can quickly switch between applications. For example you could edit and compile the application in one window while testing it in another, where AutoCAD is running.

Problems arise if you try to recompile the application that you have already loaded into AutoCAD. The compiler may give you a message "cannot create XXX.EXE". If this happens simply type

```
(xunload "XXX")
```

at the AutoCAD command line and recompile. In the case of an ARX application you would have to type

```
(arxunload "YYY")
```

but whether this works or not depends on whether you have enabled unloading of your ARX application; see Chapter 15 section 15.3. If unloading has not been enabled you will have to actually exit AutoCAD before you can finish linking your program!

13.10 Which error function to use, ads_fail(), ads_abort(), ads_exit()?

These three functions are used when you realise that something has gone wrong. Here is when you should use them:

Use `ads_fail()` when a recoverable error has occurred, as when the user has typed in an invalid value, or you notice that a non-essential file is missing. The function prototype is :

```
void ads_fail (char* Message) ;
```

It prints the message to the screen, and returns control to your program. You may prefer to use `ads_alert()`; see Chapter 4, which forces the user to acknowledge the error before returning control to the caller.

The function prototype for `ads_abort()` is:

```
void ads_abort (char* Final_Message) ;
```

This will abort only your application, printing whatever message you have called it with; AutoCAD will carry on, and the user will not lose her drawing file. Use `ads_abort()` when there has been a serious error in your application, and you just cannot go on.

The function `ads_exit()` is much like the C function `exit()`. It can be used to suddenly exit the ADS application normally and tidily. It will release all releases assigned by AutoCAD to your application. The prototype is:

```
void ads_exit (int Status) ;
```

If you do not want to signal an error then you should call `ads_exit()` with `Status==0`, or else you should call it with Status some non-zero error code of your choosing.

WARNING: Never call `ads_exit()` (or `exit()` for that matter) in ARX or rxADS applications, you will brutally terminate AutoCAD if you do. There is a function

```
void acrx_abort (const char * format, ...) ;
```

which you can call *if* you *really must* terminate your ARX application. It will terminate AutoCAD as well, but it will give the user a chance to save the drawing file before doing so. The parameters to the function are the same as to `printf()`, which means that you can print an informative message before dying. An example of using `acrx_abort()` is :

```
acrx_abort ("Allocating %u bytes for %s",N_Bytes,Filename);
```

will cause AutoCAD to print a message something like:

```
INTERNAL ERROR: Allocating 200 bytes for GEORGE.TXT
```

As you can see, `acrx_abort()` is to be used with caution, if ever!

Introduction to ARX

14

14.1 Introduction

In this chapter I give an overview of ARX the AutoCAD Run-time eXtension which is third system produced by Autodesk to program, customise, and extend the capabilities of AutoCAD. In Chapter 15 I start to go into the detail of programming ARX applications.

ARX is a huge and dynamic subject, and these three chapters are meant to be a "get you going" introduction to practical programming in this object oriented environment. I have personal experience in trying to find the answers to simple questions just by reading the ARX manuals and documentation. I can say that while all the information is probably present in the official documentation, it is difficult to filter out the simple and important sections from the explanations of esoteric and little-used features of ARX.

A word of warning: Do not try to tackle ARX programming if you are new to C++!

14.2 The goals of ARX

The stated goals of ARX can be summarised as follows:

- ARX uses the C++ class environment. Programs are written in C++ and AutoCAD entites are C++ classes.
- ARX increases execution speed. Calls to ARX and ADS functions are made directly into AutoCAD. In "pure" ADS calls were made using Inter Process Communication (IPC), which is much slower. Other applications can be

called directly, there is no longer a need to use `ads_invoke()` (see Chapter 20), as was required in ADS.

- ARX gives direct access to the internal AutoCAD database, the drawing file in other words. Access in AutoLISP and ADS is via result buffer lists, as we have seen in the first half of this book.
- ARX adds functionality. Things that are impossible to do in AutoLISP or ADS are possible in ARX. An example is that you can connect a "reactor" to an object, and every time the user selects (or moves or tries to erase etc.) that object your own ARX function is called.
- ARX is integrated with ADS and AutoLISP. It is possible to communicate with the other two environments, making re-use of software possible.
- ARX allows a consistent user interface to be created. The best way to illustrate why this is a problem with AutoLISP and ADS would be to think of the old AME (Advanced Modelling Extension) program (which was written in C for ADS). To move an object created by AME (a solid cylinder for example) you had to use a special AME move command called SOLMOVE instead of the standard AutoCAD MOVE command. With ARX you can make all entities react to the *standard AutoCAD* MOVE command in any way you like.
- ARX allows runtime extendibility. Applications do not have to be recompiled to add new functionality to them. This adds the possibility to add functionality to existing classes at run-time.
- ARX gives portability across computing platforms. Although this is a stated goal of ARX (as if it was *not* valid with AutoLISP and C !) the proof of it has yet to be seen. In fact, as I write, only Microsoft Visual C++ can compile ARX programs, and this compiler does not run on UNIX machines. Both AutoLISP and ADS have a greater level of portability across computing platforms, and ARX is the *least* portable of the three. The final aim of Autodesk is to have ARX available on all platforms, and by the time this book is in publication there should be DOS and UNIX ARX extensions, but currently ARX is only available for Windows-95 and Windows NT.
- Multiple database handling. You can access (open, read from and write to) multiple drawing files at the same time, though the user can only see one.

14.3 The ARX implementation and "exposure"

ARX applications are implemented as Dynamic Link Libraries (DLL) familiar to Microsoft Windows programmers. ARX applications share the memory space of AutoCAD itself, and can in fact crash both itself *and/or* AutoCAD.

The ease with which you can crash AutoCAD using ARX (and even rxADS) is a little disappointing if you think about how often 32-bit protected mode programming has been put forward as a way to prevent and/or localise crashes. The idea was that each application ran in its own protected memory space, and was not able to invade the memory space of other applications. Each application could only crash itself. In "pure" ADS this is the case, in both Windows and DOS. A pure ADS application can crash obviously, but it is more difficult to make AutoCAD crash with ADS than with ARX.

On the other hand it is certain that some programming tasks are much easier in ARX than in AutoLISP or ADS, and that applications will run faster.

Another problem to consider if you are programming commercial software is that it is going to be difficult for your client to allocate blame when a crash occurs, has AutoCAD crashed or your application?

So you must be much more careful when you program in ARX or rxADS than you may have been when you programmed in pure ADS or AutoLISP. To be fair to you, the programmer, it is worth saying that it is possible that AutoCAD crashes *your* application as well as the other way round!

Autodesk themselves use the word "exposure". It is a euphemism for "danger". In ARX you are more "exposed", in AutoLISP you are less "exposed". Figure 14.1 summarises the situation. Note that the skill level for ARX programming is the highest not only because it is new and in C++, but also because you need to have a certain familiarity with programming Microsoft Windows.

14.4 Which to use, ADS or ARX?

ADS and ARX are not mutually exclusive, and in many situations you can use both to do the same job. Remember also that ARX needs ADS for user input, entity selection, `ads_printf()`, dialog boxes and so on.

14.4.1 When to use ARX

The following is a list of when you should consider using ARX:
- If you are an experienced C++ programmer.
- If you need the undoubted power of object-oriented programming.
- If you need the speed offered by direct access to the AutoCAD database.
- If you need to create your own custom entities derived from AutoCAD entities.
- If you require the sophistication of "notification"; see section 14.8.

14.4.2 When to use ADS

The following is a list of when you should use ADS as opposed to ARX:

- If you are more familiar with C than C++ .

- If you are moving from AutoLISP to C programming, ADS resbuf handling will be familiar to you.
- User interaction (use of `ads_getxxx()` functions).
- Programs which use dynamic data exchange (DDE) are easier in ADS.
- Programming modeless dialog boxes.
- If you have ADS programs already which work. If the speed is acceptable then there is no need to port them: "if it ain't broke don't fix it"!

14.5 An overview of ARX

ARX applications are C++ programs compiled into dynamic link library files. An ARX application file has the extension "ARX" instead of "DLL", though

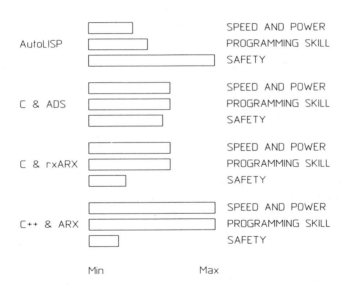

Figure 14.1 Comparison of the four programming environments

otherwise it is a normal DLL. A DLL is a "service provider", it is not a program, and cannot run on its own. AutoCAD loads ARX files to have access to the "services" (functions) provided. ARX applications can communicate with other

ARX applications, AutoLISP applications, ADS applications, and of course AutoCAD itself.

Note that in ARX entities and objects are not the same thing:

- Entities are graphical objects visible to the user and can be manipulated (erased, moved, scaled, changed etc.) by the user.
- Objects may or may not be visible to the user. All entities are objects, but not all objects are entities. Non-graphical objects exist.

14.5.1 The ARX libraries

An ARX application is a C++ program linked to one or more of seven C++ libraries supplied by AutoDESK. These libraries are in themselves DLLs.

The libraries (found under a directory with a name something like \ACAD13\ARX\LIB) are as follows:

- AcRx. A top-level library of classes used for run-time class registration and identification. The base class is AcRxObject which provides run time class identification, object equality testing and object copying (despite my warning above, much of the time for "object" you can read "AutoCAD entity"). AcRxDictionary is also in this library, see section 14.9
- AcEd, in ACEDAPI.LIB. A library of classes for registering native commands and for command notification. The class AcEdCommand is used by your application for defining new commands, which share the same space as AutoCAD commands, and are thus known as "native" commands. The AcEditorReactor class is used to specify how certain objects (e.g. a circle) should react to certain actions (e.g. an erase operation). In this way you can decide to prevent any circle (or certain circles) being erased, whatever the user tries to do.
- AcDb. A library of AutoCAD Database classes giving direct access to drawing entities, symbol tables, header variables and the "named object dictionary". See section 15.4.5 in the next chapter for a partial hierarchy of the AcDb class.
- AcGi. A graphics interface library for drawingAutoCAD entities.
- AcGe, in LIBACGE.LIB. A library of geometry utilities. Provides classes for points, vectors, matrices, curves and surfaces and so on. It also provides functions for converting between ADS geometric types and ARX geometric types.
- AcBr, in ACIS.LIB. A library of classes for inquiring into the "boundary representation" of AutoCAD solids. Solids can be queried with AcDb3dSolid, _es with AcDbBody, regions with AcDbRegion. ACIS is the Release 13 modelling software which replaces AME of Release 12.

Used for user IO, `ads_printf()`, etc.

14.5.2 The ARX view of the AutoCAD drawing

Figure 14.2 shows how ARX views the AutoCAD drawing. There are some similarities to the old DXF structure (there are layers, blocks and variables), but two differences stand out immediately:

- There is no separate ENTITIES section. All entities are in fact contained in one of two blocks, the model space block or the paper space block. These blocks are of course inside the blocks table.
- There is a thing called the "Named Object Dictionary". All objects which are neither entities (which are stored in the blocks table) nor symbols (layers for example) are stored in this dictionary. This dictionary always contains at least two tables, the group table and the MLINE style table.

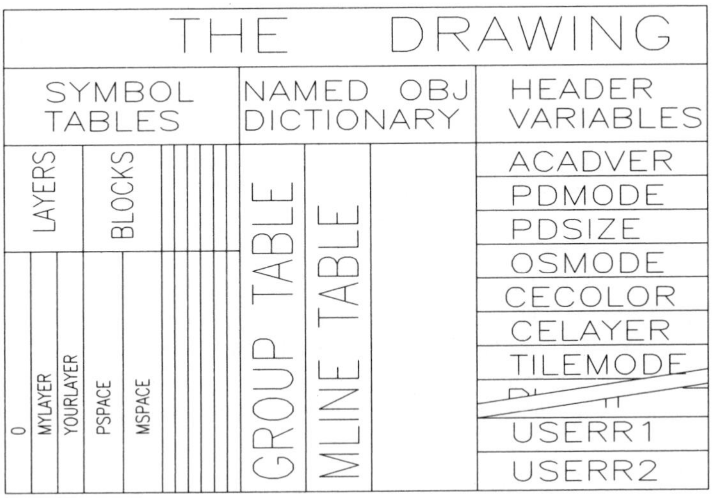

Figure 14.2 The ARX view of the drawing file

(Figure 14.2 is obviously very schematic, it does not show all the symbol tables, only the blocks and layers; it does not show all the blocks, and it does not show all the variables.)

14.7 Deriving custom objects from AutoCAD object classes.

It is possible to create your own objects using as prototypes already defined AutoCAD objects. Remember that objects include entities, and that only entities are visible. Here I will talk about creating new entity types rather than objects in general.

When do you require a new entity type?

- If you need to add intelligence to your entity type
- If you need to store data and functions in your new entity type
- If the available entities do not match exactly what you need
- If you want to hide the implementation of your application
- If you want to save space by using your own simpler entities rather than AutoCAD ones

We could imagine an application used for designing dies for plastic extrusion machines which derives a special object from the normal AutoCAD polyline. This special polyline could be the extrusion profile of the die. This object would have member functions which restrict and/or extend the operations that can be carried out on normal polylines. It might contain member functions which calculate the maximum speed of exit from the die given the extrusion profile, or the area of the extrusion profile and so on.

There are, however, problems with deriving from entities.

- You may have to supply many member functions for drawing the object. For example all `AcDbEntity` have member functions `worldDraw` and `viewportDraw`, which you would have to implement in your new entity type.
- You may have to create functions for writing (and reading) the data inside DXF and DWG files.
- The entity will be useless in the event of AutoCAD running without your application. Entities like this are called *ZOMBIES*. Depending on how your application has been written it may be possible to see the object, but you will not be able to interact with it.
- The programming time to implement the derived object could well run into weeks or months in complex cases.

In Chapter 17 there is a simple program which creates a derived entity.

14.8 Notification and reactors

With notification you can add a sort of active intelligence to your objects. You can create one or more *reactors*, which are objects that respond to *notification* events. Notifiers notify and reactors react to these notifications.

Continuing the example of the previous section you could make your object to react to the user modifying it. In this way you could restict the operations possible on the polyline, for example a polyline used for the extrusion profile cannot self-intersect, and it must always be a closed polyline. Or you could dynamically calculate and display the area of the extrusion profile and the speed of extrusion required.

You decide how objects react to notification events generated by reactors. The reactor is "planted on" the object so that the reactor can become active when a certain event occurs.

There are three sorts of reactor:

- Editor reactors (which are derived from `AcEditorReactor`) are used to respond to events like as loading and unloading a drawing, starting or ending a command, and other user interaction. This is probably the simplest reactor to understand. For example it allows your application to react to the user closing the drawing before he does certain data saving commands required by your application.
- Database reactors (which are derived from `AcDbDatabaseReactor`) are used to respond at the (high) database level, when an object is appended to the database, when an object in the database is modified, or when an object is erased and so on.
- Object reactors (derived from `AcDbObjectReactor`) are used to respond to events at the (lower) object level, such as copying, erasing, or modifying an entity and so on.

There is a further division of reactor types, permanent and transient:

- Persistent reactors are written to .dxf and .dwg files. Persistent reactors placed on objects are saved in the drawing, and will be there when you read the drawing back in.
- Transient reactors are valid only within a single AutoCAD session, they are not stored in the drawing or DXF files.

14.9 ARX dictionaries

Dictionaries in Release 13 are like the symbol tables which we are familiar with from previous releases. We use symbol tables to get an object using the objects text name. For example starting with the line type name "dotted" the line type table will give us the data for that line type. Dictionaries in ARX have a similar purpose; given a string we obtain the object associated with that string.

In Release 13 dictionaries replace symbol tables for new types, while symbol tables are retained for compatibility with Release 12. So had `groups` and `mlinestyles` existed at the time they would have been put in symbols tables in Release 12. They came into being with Release 13, and so have been placed in the group dictionary and the mlinestyle dictionary respectively.

The "named object dictionary" is like a master table of contents for an AutoCAD drawing, which is created when the drawing is created. It always contains at least the two dictionaries mentioned above in `AcDbDatabase`. It can also contain other dictionaries defined by your (or other) applications. Since a dictionary is an object, dictionaries can contain subdictionaries.

Why should you use a dictionary? Well it is a place where you can store non-graphical data within the drawing, for example settings, references to external files, logging data and so on. ARX extension dictionaries (which can be attached to entities) can be considered the evolution of the the extended data of ADS and AutoLISP.

ARX dictionaries are covered in more detail in Chapter 17, with a simple example taken from the GIS world.

First steps with ARX

15

15.1 Introduction

In this chapter you will learn the basics of programming in ARX, the top level structure of an ARX program, how to define new commands for the user, how to create new entities and how to change entities in a drawing. You will also learn how to get and set variables of a drawing in ARX.

For the practicalities of compiling, linking, loading and unloading an ARX program see Appendix A. You will also find things easier if you are well acquainted with Visual C++.

15.2 A minimal ARX program

LST_15_1.CPP shows a minimal ARX program. In this section I will go over the source line by line.

All of the ARX listings have a define as follows:

```
// #define TURN_OLD_ACDB_MEMBERS_OFF 1
```

You should usually leave the define commented as shown above, but if your program does not work you may try removing the comment slashes. It is used to rename some of the member functions from older versions of ARX and AutoCAD.

15.2.1 The include files of an ARX source file

There are three include files in this simple program, and they will be found in a directory with a path something like D:\ACADR13\ARX\INC, it depends on where you have installed AutoCAD. Two of the include files in LST_15_1.CPP are specifically for ARX and one is for ADS. So we see already that ADS co-exists with ARX. In this example our old friend "adslib.h" is included simply for the definition of ads_printf() , but in more complicated programs it would be included for the definitions of ads_getxxx() functions, for example.

The first ARX include file is "RXDEFS.H", which contains mainly constants defined in C++ style, that is enumerations inside a structure. Currently the part of the structure we are interested in is as follows:

```
struct AcRx {
    // ...other things...
    enum  AppMsgCode { kNullMsg = 0,   // Currently unused
                       kInitAppMsg = 1,
                       UnloadAppMsg = 2,
                       kLoadADSMsg = 3,
                       kUnloadADSMsg = 4,
                       kInvkSubrMsg = 5,
                       kCfgMsg = 6,
                       kEndMsg = 7,
                       kQuitMsg = 8,
                       kSaveMsg = 9
                     };
    // ...other things...
};
```

As with ADS include files you should always use the ones supplied by Autodesk; do *not* copy them from this book. It is more than likely that Autodesk will change names or add some definitions during the next year or so.

The above message codes are sent to the application by AutoCAD, as will be explained later in this chapter. C programmers moving to C++ should get used to the idea that #define is (or should be) used much less in C++ than in C to create constants. The structure above creates the constants from AcRx::kNullMsg to AcRx::kSaveMsg.

The second ARX include file is "ACED.H", which stands for AutoCad Editor objects, this in turn includes other H files which define the such things as acedRegCmds and ACRX_CMD_MODAL, both used for creating new commands and explained later in this chapter.

One include file not used directly here, but which contains many constant and type defintions is ADESK.H. For example it defines Adesk::Boolean, and the two boolean values Adesk::kTrue and Adesk::kFalse. It also defines integers of various sizes, Adesk::Int8, Adesk::Int16 and Adesk::Int32. Whenever you see Adesk::X you should look in ADESK.H to see the definition of X.

There are many many more ARX include files than ADS include files, and you will have to get used to long lists of include statements at the start of your C++ source files. We are lucky here in that there are only two ARX includes.

Table 15.1:AcRx message constants	
Constant	When sent to the ARX application
AcRx::kInitAppMsg	When the application is loaded, to open communications between AutoCAD and the application.
AcRx::kLoadADSMsg	When the drawing is opened, to make the ADS library available to the application functions that need it.
AcRx::kUnloadADSMsg	When the user quits a drawing session, to unload the ADS library from memory.
AcRx::kUnloadAppMsg	After the kUnloadADSMsg is sent, to close files, collect garbage, and close the ARX application
AcRx::kInvkSubrMsg	When ads_defun() is called, to evaluate an external function for compatibility with the programs written in the ADS program environment. ARX facilities define direct callback mechanisms and do not need to invoke subroutines to evaluate external functions
AcRx::kSaveMsg	When AutoCAD is saving the drawing, because a SAVE or SAVEAS command was entered.
AcRx::kEndMsg	When AutoCAD ends the drawing, because an END, NEW, or OPEN command was entered.
AcRx::kQuitMsg	When AutoCAD quits the drawing, because a QUIT command was entered.
AcRx::kCfgMsg	When AutoCAD returns from the configuration program.
AcRx::kNullMsg	An empty or zero message, currently unused.

15.2.2 The entry point of an ARX application

After the include files there are the function prototypes of function defined later in the file and then the entry point to the ARX application. This is like the "main" in an ADS application.

The entry point is called "acrxEntryPoint", and you must never change this name. This is also exported in the LST_15_1.DEF file (see section 15.2.5), so that AutoCAD knows where the entry point of your ARX application is. Think of "entry point" as the address of the first function AutoCAD will call to run your application. Your application is a subroutine which is called by AutoCAD, and shares the same memory as AutoCAD.

The line

```
extern "C"
```

is the way of declaring C functions which have to be linked to C++ files. The function in question may look very C++, but it is in fact a normal C function, not, for example, a member function of a class.

`acrxEntryPoint` returns an `AcRx::AppRetCode`, which is a constant defined in "RXDEFS.H" much as `AcRx::AppMsgCode` described in the previous section. Currently there are only two constants defined here:

- `kRetOK`, telling AutoCAD that all went well with the call
- `kRetError`, telling AutoCAD that an error has occurred

`acrxEntryPoint` takes two parameters, the `AcRx::AppMsgCode Msg` and a void pointer (which can be used to pass in pointers of any type). The meanings of the various possibilities of `Msg` are given in Table 15.1. This simple application does not use all the codes.

The first `Msg` case in the switch statement is `AcRx::kInitAppMsg`, which is sent when the application is first loaded, but not when a user loads a drawing. So it is a message normally sent only once for any AutoCAD session. You should use this message as a signal to do one time initialisations and maybe to register your commands. In LST_15_1.CPP `Init_Arx_App()` is called, which I will describe later.

`AcRx::kUnloadAppMsg` is sent when someone or something is unloading the application. You should free memory and destroy any C++ objects created at the start of the application when you get this message.

The next `Msg` case is `AcRx::kLoadADSMsg` which is sent to ARX applications whenever the user loads an existing drawing or starts a new one. You should use this message as a single to do initialisations which have to be done every time a drawing load occurs (maybe getting the name of the drawing or checking the contents of the drawing and so on).

The default case of the switch just prints the number of the message recieved, see Table 15.1 for other possible messages.

One last point about ARX applications in general. You should never use the functions `exit()` or `ads_exit()`, this will cause an exit not only from your application, but also from AutoCAD!

15.2.3 Creating your own commands in an ARX application, command groups

The function `Init_Arx_App()` is called when the application recieves the `AcRx::kInitAppMsg` message, and it is used in our simple application to define a single command. In this example we register two commands.

Commands are registered using a member function of the object `acedRegCmds` as follows:

```
acedRegCmds->addCommand ("MYARX_COMMANDS", // Command group
                 "MYARX1",          // Global command
                 "MIOARX1",         // Italian version
                 ACRX_CMD_MODAL,    // Not transparent
                 &My_Arx_Command1); // Address of cmd
```

The first string says that you are adding a command to a command group, a collection of commands from a specific application. Although it is possible for several applications to share the same command group, it is not recommended.

If you have a later version of AutoCAD Release 13, or the developer's version, you can see what command groups are loaded by using the "ARX" command with the "C" option, this will give you a list of command groups, plus a list of the commands contained within them. In our case the list would be:

```
Command: ARX
?/Load/Unload/Commands/Options: C
Commands registered by extension programs:
Command group "MYARX_COMMAND"
    "MYARX1"
    "MYARX2"
End of List.
```

The second string corresponds to the "global" name of the command. What this really means is the English language name of the command. The third string is the local name of the command, for example the Italian name of the command.

`ACRX_CMD_MODAL` means that the command cannot be invoked transparently. An alternative value you can put in place of `ACRX_CMD_MODAL` is `ACRX_CMD_TRANSPARENT`, which means that your command can be called transparently. An example of a transparent command is ZOOM. If you are inside a command like LINE and you want to zoom in on a detail of the drawing without leaving the line command you can type 'ZOOM, execute the zoom, and the return to the LINE command. If you rummage arround in the include files you will also come across ACRX_CMD_INPROGRESS; this is used by AutoCAD internally.

The last and fifth parameter of `addCommand()` is the address of the function we want to associate with the names. So when the user types "MYARX1" My_Arx_Command1 will be called.

So the two new commands created are MYARX1 and MYARX2, and by typing these at the command line you will get the appropriate messages from the `ads_printf()` calls in the functions.

Finally, when `acrxEntryPoint` recieves the `AcRx::kUnloadAppMsg` message we call `Unload_Arx_App()`, which in turn calls `removeGroup()` to free up the RAM occupied by the ARX application. Obviously once the command group has been removed you cannot use the commands "MYARX1" and "MYARX2".

15.2.4 Definition files

Definition files (with extension .DEF) are used when creating Dynamic Link Libraries, and since our sample ARX program is a DLL it too needs a definition file. In our case it is called LST_15_1.DEF. Here it is in its entirety:

```
DESCRIPTION 'Simple ARX Program'
LIBRARY     lst_15_1
EXPORTS     acrxEntryPoint
            _SetacrxPtp
```

The DESCRIPTION simply inserts a text string in the .ARX library, a place where you could put a copyright notice for example.

The LIBRARY is the name of the library (without the extension). In Windows executable programs (those which are not libraries) this is replaced by a NAME line. This should *always* correspond to the name of the ARX (or DLL) which you are creating. If you start a new application by copying the files of an example application, remember to edit the .DEF file which you copied, because it will contain the LIBRARY name of the example, which you should replace with the name of your application.

The EXPORTS statement tells the compiler what functions (and data) to make available to other Windows applications. In this case we want to make the acrxEntryPoint available to AutoCAD. The _SetacrxPtp is used by AutoCAD for memory management purposes; we do not need to worry about it here, just remember that it has to be present.

The linker will use this definition file to create an ARX library which AutoCAD can use.

15.3 Loading and unloading ARX applications

15.3.1 Manually loading ARX applications

ARX applications can be loaded manually using the AutoCAD "appload" command (as explained in Chapter 2, section 2.1) remembering to select from ARX extension for the file (as opposed to LSP or EXE).

If you like typing (or need to load an ARX application from within an AutoLISP function) you can use the following:

```
(arxload "D:\\MYARX\\LST_15_1")
```

or

```
(arxload "D:/MYARX/LST_15_1")
```

will both load the DLL LST_15_1.ARX. Note that both examples above load the same file, the first uses the C DOS double back-slashes convention to specify the path, and the second uses the LISP UNIX foward-slashes convention.

A third method of loading ARX programs manually is to use the "ARX" command with the "LOAD" option, which like "appload" pops up a dialog box with a list of ARX files which you can load.

15.3.2 Automatic loading of ARX applications

You can load ARX applications automatically by creating a file ACAD.RX similar to the ACAD.ADS files used to automatically load ADS applications. It is a list of ARX application programs, one per line, in your working directory. When AutoCAD starts up in that directory it will load the ARX applications listed in the ACAD.RX file.

For example if your working directory is C:\LAYOUT and you always want to load two ARX applications when you start AutoCAD in that directory you should create a file ACAD.RX in C:\LAYOUT as follows:

```
C:\APPLIX\APPLIX
D:\CALCO\CALCOL
```

This will automatically load APPLIX.ARX and CALCO.ARX whenever you start AutoCAD in C:\LAYOUT.

15.3.3 Unlocking and unloading ARX applications

Normally ARX applications cannot simply be unloaded like AutoLISP and ADS applications. This is because ARX has been designed so that many separate applications can work together, and if one application relies on another we do not want the user unloading them at will.

The simple examples in this book do not have interdependencies like that, so we can use the function:

```
acrxUnlockApplication (void* Ptr) ;
```

The input parameter to this is the pointer which is the second parameter of acrxEntryPoint(). You should call it at initialisation time.

15.4 Creating entities in ARX applications

LST_15_2.CPP (and LST_15_2.DEF) is a simple ARX application which asks the user for two points and draws a line between them, adding the line into the AutoCAD database. The functions `acrxEntryPoint()`, `Initialise_App()` and `Unload_App()` are practically identical to the previous example, LST_15_1.CPP. The really interesing thing about LST_15_2.CPP is how ARX is used to add a line to the database.

15.4.3 The definition of a line as a C++ object

This listing starts with a few more include files than the previous one. The include files we have not seen before are:

```
#include <dbents.h>    // database entities (AcDbLine etc)
#include <dbsymtb.h>   // Block and symbol tables etc
#include <geassign.h>  // ADS to ARX conversions
```

DBENTS.H contains the class definitions for the entity type of AutoCAD, lines, circles, text and so on. It is included in this listing because we create an AcDbLine. If you look in this include file you will find the AcDbLine class definition, complete with constructors, destructors, inspectors (member functions which tell you something about and object) and mutators (member functions which *change* an object).

You should get used to looking inside DBENTS.H to find the member functions of the object entities you want to use.

Here are the current definitions for AcDbLine, with lots missing and slightly re-arranged in order to make the explanation easier:

```
class AcDbLine: public AcDbCurve       // Derived from AcDbCurve
{
public:
    AcDbLine();                        // Default constructor
    AcDbLine(const AcGePoint3d&  start, // Constuctor with start
             const AcGePoint3d&  end);  // and end specified
    ~AcDbLine();                       // Destructor of line

    // Here are the inspectors, note const keyword
    AcGePoint3d  startPoint() const;
    AcGePoint3d  endPoint() const;
    double       thickness() const;

    // Here are the mutators
    void         setEndPoint(const AcGePoint3d&);
    void         setStartPoint(const AcGePoint3d&);
```

```
void          setThickness(double);

... lots of other things...
}
```

There are two constructors: one which takes no parameters and will create a default line (not very useful, a line which starts and ends at the origin), the other allowing the user to specify the start and end points of the line. There is also a destrucor which will free all the memory used by the object when called.

In the above code fragment we have three inspectors, which are const functions (the C++ language guarantees that these three functions will not change the innards of the object) which return to the caller the start, end, and thickness of the line.

The three mutators are used to change the state of the object, again the start, end and thickness of the line.

I will remind you here (as always) that you should *not* use the definitions of AutoCAD include files you find in this book, but use the ones supplied by Autodesk for the target platform and version, usually found on the CD-ROM which comes with the product.

You may also have to get used to reading H files (or using a class browser) rather than manuals. Though the overal layout and philosophy of ARX is well established, it is still in a state of flux as regards member function names, macros, compilers supported and so on.

15.4.4 Creating, opening, deleting and closing objects

The function My_Line, called by the command "MY_LINE", asks the user for the start and end points using two calls to `ads_getpoint()`. The values returned by `ads_getpoint()` are converted from `ads_point` (the ADS environment) to `AcGePoint3d` (a three-dimensional point in the ARX environment) using `asPnt3d()`. This function is defined in the other ARX include file GEASSIGN.H. `AcGePoint3d` is described in more detail in Chapter 16, section 16.3.1.

Now we create the line object by calling the C++ new operator for AcDbLine. When an AcDb entity is created with new it is just a C++ object. It does not yet belong to the drawing database. You can call whatever member functions you want for it: mutators inspectors, whatever.

Now we have to be very careful and clear about opening, creating, deleting and closing objects. If you create an object with new and successfully add it to the database you must not delete it, that is, you should not call its destructor. Once an object has been added to the database it can be "closed", but not before.

Obviously you cannot add an object to the database which is created on the local stack (local variables of a function). It would be perfectly legal C++, but

AutoCAD would in all likelihood crash because once the local environment had disappeared the destructor for that object would be called. Do not do this:

```
void Silly_Func (AcGePoint3D& Start, AcGePoint3d& End)
{
    AcDbLine A_Line(Start,End) ;
    ...append to current drawing model space block table...
    return ; // At this point A_Line dies! and so does AutoCAD!
}
```

So, always use new.

The sequence you should follow is:

1. create the object with new
2. add the object to the database
3. close the object, this updates the entity on the screen.

Note that in the above sequence there is no delete of the object. You should only delete an object if it has not been added to the database. You should not use, in any way, the pointer to the object after it has been closed.

Another way of explaining this is by saying that you own the object until it is added to the database, when the database owns it. If you give AutoCAD the object then you no longer have the right to delete it (using the C++ keyword "delete").

Going back to LST_15_2.CPP, the following five lines of code create the line and add it to the current database:

```
AcDbLine * line = new AcDbLine ;    // Create default line
AcDbDatabase* pDb = acdbCurDwg() ;
line->setDatabaseDefaults (pDb);
line->setStartPoint (Start);        // Call mutator
line->setEndPoint   (End);          // Call mutator
```

`acdbCurDwg()` returns a pointer to the database of the currently open drawing, which is then used to set the line to the database defaults (linetype, layer and so on). `acdbCurDwg()` is an always available global function. Finally we use mutators to set the start and end points of the line. Note how easy this is compared with ADS. In ADS you would have had to traverse several result buffers looking for the DXF types for STARTLINE and ENDLINE, change then and then return the result buffers to ADS. In this listing we do it in two lines!

(Crafty ADS programmers would in fact factorise out the long result buffer sequence into a single function easily called, for example with a function like:

```
Change_Line_Endpoints (const ads_point Start,
                       const ads_point End,
                       ads_name Entity)
```

However even in this case although the code is easier to read, it will run much much than the ARX equivalent.)

We could equally as well have used the other form for the line constructor:

```
AcDbLine * line = new AcDbLine(Start,End) ;
```

not needing to call the mutators, thus saving a couple of lines of source code.

A last, but very important point, when you add entities to the drawing database the coordinate system used is *always* the WCS. ARX does not take account (directly) of the current user coordinate system.

15.4.5 Adding an AcDbEntity to the database

Once we have created our line we want to add it to the database. Entities are added to the database, so we convert the (pointer to) line into a (pointer to) AcDbEntity. As you can see from class hierarchy, AcDbLine is in fact derived from AcDbCurve, which itself is derived from AcDbEntity. Not shown is the fact that AcDbEntity is derived from AcDbObject.

Do not be surprised that a straight line is derived from a curve, mathematically speaking a straight line is a special sort of curve.

```
// Hierarchy of AcDbEntity...
AcDbEntity
  AcDb3dSolid
  AcDbBlockBegin
  AcDbBlockEnd
  AcDbBlockReference
  AcDbMInsertBlock
  AcDbMInsertBlock
  AcDbBody
  AcDbCurve
    AcDb2dPolyline
    AcDb3dPolyline
    AcDbArc
    AcDbCircle
    AcDbEllipse
    AcDbLeader
    AcDbLine
    AcDbRay
    AcDbSpline
    AcDbXline
```

The classes printed in **bold** are abstract classes; that is, classes with virtual functions defined by classes derived from them.

As I have already mentioned, in AutoCAD 13 all entities are in fact inside blocks, and all blocks are inside the block table, see Figure 15.1. Most entities are placed inside the model space block (the LINEs and CIRCLEs etc of Figure 15.1), and this is where we are going to put our newly created line. (A reminder: model space is usually where the real entities (2D or 3D or both) of your drawing go, whereas paper space is used for organising the views into model space and plotting the drawing; paper space is always 2D). We have to open the block table with the following line:

```
Res = pDb->getBlockTable (dbTable, AcDb::kForRead);
```

If there is an error then we exit the function. This member function of the current database opens the block table for read, using the `AcDb::kForRead` constant. The constants `kForRead`, `kForWrite` and `kForNotify` are explained in more detail in the following section.

Note that we have not yet got to the model space block, we have only opened the table of blocks.

Now if all goes well, we open the record that we are after inside the block table:

```
es = dbTable->getAt (ACDB_MODEL_SPACE,
                AcDb::kForWrite,dbRecord);
```

This opens for write the `ACDB_MODEL_SPACE` record and puts a pointer to it in dbRecord. `ACDB_MODEL_SPACE` is actually a string: "*MODEL_SPACE", and you can use either form in your ARX programs. When the user is prompted for a block name, however, if he wants the model space he must type "*MODEL_SPACE", as we will see.

Finally we are in a position to add our line to the model space block. This we do with:

```
AcDbEntity* obj
es = dbRecord->appendAcDbEntity (objId,obj);
```

This does three things, it appends the entity to the database record (adds the entity into the drawing), sets the ownership of the object to the block table record, and returns an object identifier. The object identifier is not used in LST_15_2.CPP, though it is required for the call. Object identifiers and ownership are discussed later in this chapter, section 15.5 and Section 15.6. There is another form of `appendAcDbEntity` which just takes the object pointer. You can use this form when you do not need, or already have, the object identifier; see Chapter 16, section 16.4.1.

To finish the operation you close the record, which you had opened for write with `getAt()`. Next you close the block table which you had opened for read with `pDb->getBlockTable()`, and lastly you close the object which you had opened for write by creating it with the new operator. With this close the line will become visible to the user, and he can list it, move it, erase it, change it and so on.

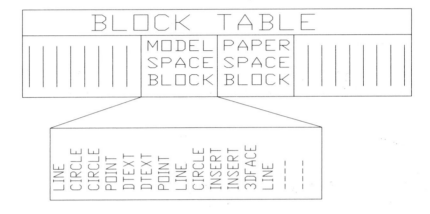

Figure 15.1 Where the model space block is, and what it contains.

15.4.6 Getting variable settings from the database

The very last part of the function illustrates how you can get variable settings of the current drawing. Having opened the database with

```
AcDbDatabase* pDb = acdbCurDwg() ;
```

we can get the header variables using:

```
resbuf rb   ;
pDb->getHeaderVar (&rb,"dwgname");
ads_printf ("\ndrawing name is <%s> ",rb.resval.rstring);
```

(Note that in CPP there is no need for the struct keyword, so we can use `resbuf rb` in CPP files where we would have used `struct resbuf rb` in C files.) Obviously we can also get integer and real variables using the same technique. For example, to read the SNAPMODE variable:

```
pDb->getHeaderVar (&rb,"snapmode") ;
ads_printf ("\nsnapmode =  <%d> ",rb.resval.rint);
```

We can set the variables which are not read only using a similar member function of AcDbDatabase. For example to set the SNAPMODE variable:

```
rb.restype = RTSHORT ;
rb.resval.rint = 1 ;
pDb->setHeaderVar (&rb,"snapmode");
```

Now let us look in a bit more detail at the object identifiers, open constants and the idea of ownership.

15.5 Object identifiers, and ways of opening an object

15.5.1 Object identifiers

An object identifier (or object ID) lets you obtain a pointer to an object so that you can get information about it or change it. Only objects already added to the database have object IDs. In LST_15_2.CPP we get an object ID as soon as we add the line to the database with:

```
es = dbRecord->appendAcDbEntity (objId,obj) ;
```

After the above statement, as long as es == Acad::eOk, objId is a valid identifier for the object in the database. If es is not Acad::eOk then an error has occured.

(Many ARX functions return error codes which are listed in Appendix E. Read this appendix for details about differences between ERRNO values and ARX values for the same error)

A way of getting an object ID from an already existing database drawing entity is to use

```
extern Acad::ErrorStatus acdbGetObjectId (AcDbObjectId& objId,
                                          ads_name    Ename);
```

which is defined in the ARX include file DBMAIN.H. You hand the function an ads_name, and it returns the corresponding object ID, it returns an error status. An Acad::ErrorStatus is one of almost 300 error codes defined as enumerators in ACDB.H. Acad::eOk is the ErrorStatus when nothing went wrong. Appendix E gives more details on other error return values.

The following C++ code fragment shows how you can prompt the user to select a set of objects using the ADS selection set function `ads_ssget()` and then get the object ID for each object selected:

```
ads_name      en   ; // ADS type
AcDbObjectId  eId  ; // Object itentifier
AcDbEntity*   eObj ; // Pointer to actual object
long          len ;
...
rc = ads_ssget (NULL,NULL,NULL,NULL,ss);
if (rc != RTNORM) {
    return ;
}
rc = ads_sslength (Set, &len); // Get num of ents in set
...for safety you should check rc here
for (long i=0; i < len; ++i ) {
    ads_ssname (ss,i,en) ; // Get ith entity name
    if (acdbGetObjectId (eId,en) != Acad::eOk ) {
        ads_printf( "\nERROR! getting object id." );
        return ;
    }
    if (acdbOpenEntity(eObj,eId,AcDb::kForRead) != Acad::eOk ) {
        ads_printf ("\nERROR! opening object for read." );
        return ;
    }
    ...object opened for read, get some data
    ...about it using the eObj pointer...
}
```

Note the difference between these four things:

- ads_name, an ADS type which is used in selection sets and user IO and ADS drawing database programming.
- AcDbObjectId, an ARX class, used to identify objects in the drawing database.
- AcDbEntity*, an ARX class pointer, points to an entity, using the member functions of this entity you can inspect and change the entity. An AcDbEntity* is only valid while the object is open. Once the object is closed it may be written to disk (to save memory), and the pointer will no longer point to the object. The process of writing a closed object to disk to save memory is called "paging out".
- AcDbHandle, an ARX class the handle of object. Handles are stored in the drawing file (and is part of the reason why Release 13 files are bigger than Release 12 files). Handles are not used in LST_15_2.CPP

In ADS only handles and entity names are used, the former being permanent, saved in the drawing, while the latter are valid only for thr drawing session in which they are used.

Another way to get an object ID is to use an iterator see section 15.7 later in this chapter.

15.5.2 Opening an object for read, AcDb::kForRead

An object can be opened for read by up to fifteen readers of an object. You can open any object for read as long as the object is not already open for write or for notify. Once opened for read the object cannot be opened for write (until you close it of course).

See the previous code fragment for an example of opening an object for read. An object opened for read cannot have its internals changed, i.e. you cannot call its mutator member functions.

An object open for read can be quickly re-opened for write using the function upgradeOpen(); see Chapter 16, section 16.4.1.

15.5.3 Opening an object for write, AcDb::kForWrite

If you want to change an object you need to open it for write. You can open an object for write as so long as it is not already open (in any mode). Member functions invoked when an object is opened for write may (or may not) modify the object. Member functions an object class which modify objects are called mutators.

WARNING: If you call an object mutator to change the internals of an object but you have (by mistake) opened the object for read instead of write, you will almost certainly *crash* AutoCAD.

An object created with new is implictly opened for write, as we saw in the previous example.

The following code fragment shows how you could open an object for write, change the color with the mutator setColorIndex, and then close the object:

```
...get entId...
AcDbEntity* E_Ptr;
Acad::ErrorStatus es;
// Open the entity for write
es = acdbOpenEntity (E_Ptr, entId, AcDb::kForWrite) ;
// Change the color
es = E_Ptr->setColorIndex (Color);
es = E_Ptr->close();
```

A color index by the way is a number from 1 to 255, corresponding to the 255 colors you will find in the standard AutoCAD drawings CHROMA.DWG and COLORWH.DWG. Of course you should really look at es to make sure it is Acad::eOk after every one of the three operations above.

15.5.4 Objects opened for notify, AcDb::kForNotify

Notification is a technique for making objects react to actions, a way of giving them some sort of intelligence. Apart from this brief section and Section 14.8 in the previous chapter, notification is not covered in this book.

An object can be opened for notification only when the object is closed, open for read, or open for write, i.e. an object already opened for notify cannot be opened a second time for notify. Objects opened for notification need to already be in the drawing database.

15.6 Ownership of objects and root objects

Every object in the database must have one and only one owner (with ten exceptions, see below). The drawing database is a tree created by this hierarchy of owned objects.

When we used

```
AcDbBlockTable->Record::appendAcDbEntity(),
```

in the listing above we accomplished two things at once, adding the object to the database and assigning ownership. It is possible to add an object to the database without assigning ownership by using:

```
db->addAcDbObject();
```

You should not normally do this.

Root objects are objects which do not have an owner. There are ten root objects:

- AcDbBlockTable, like BLOCKS section in a DXF file
- AcDbDimStyleTable, where dimension styles are stored
- AcDbLayerTable, where layer definitions are stored
- AcDbLinetypeTable, where linetype definitions are stored
- AcDbRegAppTable, where registered applications are stored, see Chapter 11 on extended data, `ads_regapp()`
- AcDbTextStyleTable, where text styles are stored
- AcDbUCSTable, where named UCS are stored

- AcDbViewportTable, where viewport tables are stored. A viewport is a window onto the drawing
- AcDbViewTable, where named views are stored. A named view is the definition of the camera and target and zoom
- The named object dictionary. Groups created by the user are stored in the group dictionary, which itself is stored in the named object dictionary. See Chapter 17

Entities are owned by block table records and symbols are owned by symbol table records. All filing operations begin by filing out the root objects of the database. The AutoCAD "SAVE" command saves all owned objects, so you can see the importance of making sure that the entities you create are owned!

15.7 Changing objects in the database

LST_15_3.CPP (and do not forget LST_15_3.DEF!) is a program which prompts the user to select some objects, then changes any circles selected by increasing their radius by 50%, changes start point of any lines found to the origin, and changes the color of any other objects found. The first part has a familiar look to it and could be from any ADS program, but the second half shows the ease with which objects can be changed in ARX.

`Changer()` is the only function in LST_15_3.CPP which we need to look at, the rest of the file is practically the same as the other two listings in this chapter. In `Changer()` we prompt the user to select some objects with the normal ADS `ads_ssget()` function. If all goes well we use `ads_sslength()` to see how many entities have been selected.

Next we declare the three variables we will need to change the properties of the entities selected. E_Name is an `ads_name` and is set by the call to `ads_ssname()` to each of the entities in the selection set. E_Id is an object identifier, which we find out by calling `acdbGetObjectId` with E_Name as the input parameter. E_Ptr is a pointer to an `AcDbEntity` object. Once we have the object identifier we open the object for write (so we can change it) with `acdbOpenEntity` and E_Ptr is initialised. The sequence is reproduced here (without the error checking included in the listing itself, which in practice is vital):

```
ads_ssname (Set, i, E_Name) ;    // get E_name
acdbGetObjectId (E_Id,E_Name) ;  // get E_Id, the object id
acdbOpenEntity (E_Ptr,E_Id,AcDb::kForWrite); // get E_Ptr
```

The next part of the code illustrates three new member functions, as explained in the following section.

15.7.1 isKindOf(), cast() and desc()

The inside of the for-loop inspects each entity and changes certain properties depending on what is found.

The first test we do is to see if the entity can be cast to an AcDbCircle:

```
C_Ptr = AcDbCircle::cast(E_Ptr) ;
```
If C_Ptr is not NULL then the cast was successful, we have found a circle, and we go on to increase its radius by 50%:

```
double New_Rad ;
New_Rad = C_Ptr->radius() * 1.5 ;    // Call the inspector
C_Ptr->setRadius (New_Rad) ;         // Call the mutator
```

(By the way, compare the last line of the above code fragment with the function Change_Radius() in LST__6_7.C.)

Note how the cast() accomplishes two things at once, test of type, and initialisation of pointer to the object of that type.

If the circle test fails then we look to see if the entity is a line using exactly the same technique:

```
if (NULL != (L_Ptr = AcDbLine::cast(E_Ptr))) {
    L_Ptr->setStartPoint (AcGePoint3d::kOrigin) ;
}
```

If the line test succeeds we set the start point to the origin. Note the use of the AcGePoint3d constant kOrigin.

If both the circle and line tests fail we do a double test to see if the entity is TEXT or MTEXT using isKindOf().

The function isKindOf() is a member of the class AcDbEntity. It is used to see if a given object belongs to a specific class (or is derived from a specific class). The function desc() is a static member function of the class AcDbEntity. It returns an AcRxClass pointer, describing the class. These two functions are used together as follows:

```
E_Ptr->isKindOf(AcDbText::desc()) ;
```

isKindOf() of the object takes the descriptor of AcDbText, and returns a true value if E_Ptr is a sort of AcDbText. "Sort of" means that true may be returned if E_Ptr is an object derived from a AcDbText. In LST_15_3.CPP we test for both AcDbText and AcDbMText with this method.

Why are there two different functions for testing the type of an object? Well it depends on what you want to do. If you need to change specific properties of objects, which are not general to all objects, then you should use cast(). To change the radius of an object, it has to be a circle, so you have to cast it to AcDbCircle. To change the startpoint of an object it has to be a line, so you have to be able to cast it to AcDbLine.

However both lines and circles have color, and so does text and points and 3dfaces. AcDbEntity has a member function to change color, and you need not recast the pointer to a specific type to change the color of an entity. In the LST_15_3.CPP you can see how we change the color of both TEXT and MTEXT in one fell swoop:

```
if ( (E_Ptr->isKindOf (AcDbText::desc())) ||
     (E_Ptr->isKindOf (AcDbMText::desc()))) {
   E_Ptr->setColorIndex (4) ; // TEXT or MTEXT ok
}
```

Just to ram home the point here is another example, transforming any objects which are circles lines or points with one call to transformBy():

```
AcDbEntity* E_Ptr ;
if ((E_Ptr->isKindOf (AcDbCircle::desc())) ||
    (E_Ptr->isKindOf (AcDbLine::desc()))    ||
    (E_Ptr->isKindOf (AcDbPoint::desc()))) {
    E_Ptr->transformBy(....); //  CIRCLE or LINE or POINT ok !
}
```

Back to LST_15_3.CPP. If we do not recognise the entity type we print out its name and change its color anyway. To get the textual name of the object you use:

```
AcDbEntity* E_Ptr ;
...
ads_printf ("\nThis is a %s ",E_Ptr->isA()->name()) ;
```

Whatever the type of the object, we close it at the end of the loop. Finally, before leaving Changes(), we free the selection set created at the beginning.

To test LST_15_3.CPP try it by selecting lots of different types of entities including CIRCLES, LINES, PLINES, POINTS, MTEXT, TEXT and ELLIPSES.

15.8 Listings

```
/////////////////////////////////////////////////////////////////
//   LST_15_1.CPP
//                    A very simple ARX program
//
```

```
// Early versions of ARX (pre-1996) may require this define
#define TURN_OLD_ACDB_MEMBERS_OFF 1

#include <rxdefs.h>  // ARX file AcRx msg codes
#include <aced.h>    // ARX file AcEdStuff
#include <adslib.h>  // ADS file, for ads_printf

// Function prototypes
void My_Arx_Command1 (void) ;
void My_Arx_Command2 (void) ;
void Init_Arx_App(void) ;
void Unload_Arx_App (void) ;

// Here is where control jumps to when an ARX function
// starts up. Note that acrxEntryPoint is "exported" in
// LST_15_1.DEF so that AutoCAD knows where to find the
// entry point for this DLL. The extern "C"  syntax is
// the C++ way of declaring a C function
extern "C" AcRx::AppRetCode
acrxEntryPoint (AcRx::AppMsgCode Msg, void*)
{
    switch (Msg) {
        case AcRx::kInitAppMsg:     // I am starting up
            ads_printf ("\nMYARX: Got kInitAppMsg.");
            Init_Arx_App();
        break;
        case AcRx::kUnloadAppMsg:  // Someone (something)
            Unload_Arx_App();      // is unloading me
            ads_printf ("\nMYARX: Got kUnloadAppMsg.");
        break;
            case AcRx::kLoadADSMsg:
            ads_printf ("\nMYARX: Got kLoadADSMsg.");
            break;
        case AcRx::kUnloadADSMsg:
            ads_printf ("\nMYARX: Got kUnloadADSMsg.");
            break;
            default:
        ads_printf ("\nMY_ARX: Unprocessed Msg<%d>",Msg);
        break;
    }
    return (AcRx::kRetOK) ;
}

void Init_Arx_App(void)
{
    ads_printf ("MYARX, registering the command...\n" );

    acedRegCmds->addCommand ("MYARX_COMMANDS",
                "MYARX1",
```

```
                            "MIOARX1",
                            ACRX_CMD_MODAL,
                            &My_Arx_Command1);

        acedRegCmds->addCommand ("MYARX_COMMANDS",
                            "MYARX2",
                            "MIOARX2",
                            ACRX_CMD_MODAL,
                            &My_Arx_Command2);

        ads_printf ("Type MYARX1 and MYARX2 to test the two
commands") ;
}

void My_Arx_Command1 (void)
{
        ads_printf ("\nMYARX: This is first My_Arx_Command!");
}

void My_Arx_Command2 (void)
{
        ads_printf ("\nMYARX: This is 2nd My_Arx_Command!");
}

void Unload_Arx_App(void)
{
        acedRegCmds->removeGroup("MYARX_COMMANDS");
}

//                      -- end of LST_15_1.C --
```

The following is the definition file for LST_15_1.ARX. All the other ARX applications in this book should have an equivalent definition file, changing the LIBRARY entry to whatever is the name of the ARX application. See section 14.2.1

```
DESCRIPTION 'Simple ARX Program'
LIBRARY     LST_15_1
EXPORTS     acrxEntryPoint
            _SetacrxPtp


////////////////////////////////////////////////////////////
// LST_15_2.CPP
// Illustrating how entities can be added to the
// database using ARX.

// PRE 1996 versions of ARX may require this define
```

```
#define TURN_OLD_ACDB_MEMBERS_OFF 1

#include <aced.h>        // acedRegCmds etc
#include <dbents.h>      // database entities (AcDbLine etc)
#include <dbsymtb.h>     // Block and symbol tables etc
#include <geassign.h>    // ADS to ARX conversions
#include <rxregsvc.h>    // Unlocking function
#include <adslib.h>      // ADS ads_getxxxx etc

void My_Line (void);
void Initialise_App (void* Ptr);
void Unload_App (void);

extern "C" AcRx::AppRetCode
acrxEntryPoint( AcRx::AppMsgCode Msg, void* Ptr)
{
    switch (Msg) {
        case AcRx::kInitAppMsg:
            Initialise_App (Ptr);
            break;
        case AcRx::kUnloadAppMsg:
            Unload_App ();
            break;
        case AcRx::kLoadADSMsg:
            break;
        case AcRx::kUnloadADSMsg:
            break;
        default:
            ads_printf ("\nLST_15_2: unprocessed"
                        " message <%d>. ",Msg);
        break;
    }
    return (AcRx::kRetOK) ;
}


// A function to test adding an entity into the
// AutoCAD database (in this case a line)
void My_Line (void)
{
    int Res ;
    ads_point Dummy ;       // ADS world point
    AcGePoint3d Start,End; // ARX world points

    // get line parameters from user:
    Res = ads_getpoint (NULL,"From : ",Dummy) ;
    if (Res != RTNORM) {
        return ;
    } else {
        // Convert from ADS to ARX type
```

```
        Start = asPnt3d (Dummy) ;
    }

    Res = ads_getpoint (Dummy,"To : ",Dummy) ;
    if (Res != RTNORM) {
        return ;
    } else {
        // Convert from ADS to ARX type
        End = asPnt3d (Dummy) ;
    }

    // Create a new line object. This line is not
    // yet in the database, it is just floating around
    // in memory, a C++ object
    AcDbLine * line = new AcDbLine ; // Create default line

    // Set it's attributes to the database defaults
    // for a line. Use the global acdbCurDwg() func to
    // get a pointer to the currently open database
    AcDbDatabase* pDb = acdbCurDwg() ;

    line->setDatabaseDefaults (pDb);

    // Change the attributes we want to change
    line->setStartPoint (Start); // Call mutator
    line->setEndPoint   (End);   // Call mutator

    // Make the generic AcDbEntity* "obj" point to it
    AcDbEntity* obj;
    obj = line ;

    // Open block table to search for the
    // model space block, where we will put the line
    Acad::ErrorStatus es;
    AcDbBlockTable * dbTable;  // Pntr to block table
    AcDbBlockTableRecord* dbRecord; // To record in table
    AcDbObjectId objId ; // Not really used in this e.g.

    // Use the member func of database to open
    // the block table for read. dbTable will be set
    // by this operation
    es = pDb->getBlockTable (dbTable, AcDb::kForRead);

    if (es != Acad::eOk) {
        ads_printf( "\nCannot open block table." );
        // Close the object for safety reasons
        if (obj->close() != Acad::eOk ) {
            ads_printf( "\nCannot close entity." );
        }
```

```
        return;
    }

    // Use dbTable to open current record in model space
    // block:
    es = dbTable->getAt (ACDB_MODEL_SPACE,
                          AcDb::kForWrite,dbRecord);
    if (es != Acad::eOk ) {
        // Something went wrong, close both the
        // model space block table and the entity
        ads_printf( "\nCannot open model space block." );
        if (dbTable->close() != Acad::eOk) {
            ads_printf( "\nCannot close block table." );
        }
        if (obj->close() != Acad::eOk) {
            ads_printf( "\nCannot close entity." );
        }
    }

    // getAt worked ok, dbRecord is valid
    // append new entity to model space block
    // This also sets the ownership to the block
    // table record
    es = dbRecord->appendAcDbEntity (objId,obj);

    if( es != Acad::eOk ) {
        ads_printf( "\nCannot append entity." );
    }

    // Close the block table record
    if (dbRecord->close() != Acad::eOk ) {
        ads_printf( "\nCannot close database record." );
    }

    if (dbTable->close() != Acad::eOk ) {
        ads_printf( "\nCannot close block table." );
    }

    if (obj->close() != Acad::eOk ) {
        ads_printf( "\nCannot close entity." );
    }


    // Tell the user to which drawing you added the line
    resbuf rb  ;   // No need for 'struct' in CPP

    // Get the header variable of current database
    Res = pDb->getHeaderVar (&rb,"dwgname");
```

```
        // Some early versions of Release 13 do not return
        // Acad::eOk, even tho all went well
        if ((Res == Acad::eOk) || (Res == Acad::eKeyNotFound)) {
            ads_printf ("\nLine added successfully to drawing : <%s>
",
                        rb.resval.rstring);
        } else {
            ads_printf ("\nERROR, Res=%d",Res) ;
        }
}


void Initialise_App (void* Ptr)
{
    ads_printf ("Registering commands...") ;
    acedRegCmds->addCommand("GROUP_15_2",
                            "MY_LINE",
                            "MIA_LINEA",
                            ACRX_CMD_MODAL,
                            &My_Line);
    // Make the application unloadable
    acrxUnlockApplication (Ptr) ;
    ads_printf ("...OK.\nType MY_LINE to test"
                " this application.");
}


void Unload_App (void)
{
    acedRegCmds->removeGroup ("GROUP_15_2");
}
//                      -- end of LST_15_2.CPP --


//////////////////////////////////////////////////////
// LST_15_3.CPP
//     Illustrating how to change attributes of existing
//     entities in a drawing

// #define TURN_OLD_ACDB_MEMBERS_OFF 1

#include <aced.h>        // acedRegCmds etc
#include <dbents.h>      // database entities (AcDbLine etc)
#include <dbsymtb.h>     // Block and symbol tables etc
#include <geassign.h>    // ADS to ARX conversions
#include <adslib.h>      // ADS ads_getxxxx etc

// Function prototypes
void Changer (void);
void Initialise_App (void* Ptr);
void Unload_App (void);
```

```
// Main ARX application entry point
extern "C" AcRx::AppRetCode
acrxEntryPoint( AcRx::AppMsgCode Msg, void* Ptr)
{
    switch (Msg) {
        case AcRx::kInitAppMsg:
            Initialise_App (Ptr);
            break;
        case AcRx::kUnloadAppMsg:
            Unload_App ();
            break;
        case AcRx::kLoadADSMsg:
            break;
        case AcRx::kUnloadADSMsg:
            break;
    }
    return (AcRx::kRetOK) ;
}

// A function which changes the radius of circles and
// the color of lines
void Changer (void)
{
    int       Res ;
    ads_name Set ; // Set of objects selected
    long      Len ; // number of objects selected

    // Get the user to select a set of objects
    Res = ads_ssget (NULL, NULL, NULL, NULL, Set);
    if (Res != RTNORM ) {
        // Error, or used hit ESCAPE
        ads_printf ("\nNothing selected.");
        return ;
    }

    // Len = how many entities selected
    Res = ads_sslength (Set, &Len);
    if (Res != RTNORM) {
        // 0 selected or an error
        ads_printf ("\nInvalid selection set.");
        (void)ads_ssfree (Set);
        return ;
    }

    ads_name     E_Name ; // ADS entity identifier
    AcDbObjectId E_Id ;   // ARX entity identifier
    AcDbEntity*  E_Ptr ;   // Pntr to ARX object

    // Go over all the entities in Set
```

```
for (long i = 0 ; i < Len ; i++ ) {
    // Get the ads_name of the entity
    ads_ssname (Set, i, E_Name) ;

    // Get the object id of the entity
    if (acdbGetObjectId (E_Id,E_Name) != Acad::eOk ) {
        ads_printf( ."\nERROR! getting object id." );
        break ;
    }

    if (acdbOpenEntity (E_Ptr,E_Id,AcDb::kForWrite)
        != Acad::eOk ) {
        ads_printf ("\nERROR! opening object for write.");
        break ;
    }

    ads_printf ("\nThe entity is a ") ;

    AcDbCircle* C_Ptr ;
    AcDbLine* L_Ptr ;
    if (NULL != (C_Ptr = AcDbCircle::cast(E_Ptr))) {
        // Can be cast to AcDbCircle*...
        // ...so change the radius...
        ads_printf ("circle, changing radius...") ;
        double New_Rad ;
        New_Rad = C_Ptr->radius() * 1.5 ;   // Inspector
        C_Ptr->setRadius (New_Rad) ;         // Mutator

    } else if (NULL != (L_Ptr = AcDbLine::cast(E_Ptr))) {
        // Can be cast to AcDbLine...
        // ...change it's start point...
        ads_printf ("line, changing start point...") ;
        L_Ptr->setStartPoint (AcGePoint3d::kOrigin) ;

    } else if ( (E_Ptr->isKindOf (AcDbText::desc())) ||
                (E_Ptr->isKindOf (AcDbMText::desc()))) {
        ads_printf ("text or mtext, changing color...");
        E_Ptr->setColorIndex (4) ;

    } else  {
        // Summat else, say what and change color
        ads_printf ("%s, changing color...",
                    E_Ptr->isA()->name());
        E_Ptr->setColorIndex (1) ;
    }

    // Now close the object, this will update the screen
    if (E_Ptr->close() != Acad::eOk) {
        ads_printf ("\nCannot close entity.");
```

```
                return ;
            }
        }

        (void)ads_ssfree (Set) ;
    }

void Initialise_App (void* Ptr)
{
    ads_printf ("\nRegistering commands...") ;
    acedRegCmds->addCommand("CHANGES", // Cmd group
                            "CHG",     // English
                            "CAMBIA",  // Italian
                            ACRX_CMD_MODAL,
                            &Changer); // Adr of func
    ads_printf ("...OK.\nDraws lines and circles and then type
CHG to test...") ;
}

void Unload_App (void)
{
    acedRegCmds->removeGroup ("CHANGES");
}
//                      -- end of LST_15_3.C --
```

ARX iterators, geometry classes and cloning

16

16.1 Introduction

In this chapter we will see how to use iterators to get hold of the entities in the drawing, and within user-defined blocks. We also have a look at the geometry library which contains classes for points, vectors, matrices and so on. Finally we introduce "cloning", which in reality is simply the ARX word for "copying objects".

In this chapter I will again refer to the include files for ARX classes, which you should find in the directory D:\ACADR13\ARX\INC (assuming you have installed AutoCAD under D:\ACADR13).

16.2 ARX iterators

Iterators are used to step through a list or set of objects. The most obvious use for an iterator is to step through the entities in the model space block to see what the drawing contains. Remember that all entities in a Release 13 drawing are contained in a block, and what we used to think of as the ENTITIES section of the drawing now becomes the model space block.

16.2.1 Listing the contents of the model space

LST_16_1.CPP is an example of how to investigate which entities are in the model space block. I have left out the "standard" parts of the application, all you need to to is use the examples of the previous chapter as a model.

The function Test starts by getting hold of the block table (pBlockTable) of the current drawing. If this works we then open the block that we are interested in for read. There are two possible blocks to open when we are looking at the contents of a drawing, *MODEL_SPACE and *PAPER_SPACE. We open *MODEL_SPACE. Once we have the block we can close the block table.

Now we get hold of an iterator, which will later be used to scan the contents of the model space block. Compressing a little the actual listing, what we do is:

```
pBlockTable->getAt("*MODEL_SPACE",
                   AcDb::kForRead,pBlockTableRecord);
pBlockTableRecord->newIterator (pBlockIterator);
```

getAt() has given us (or rather initialised) pBlockTableRecord, which we in turn use to create a new iterator. A block table record is like a BLOCK in DXF terms. Note the use of the word "new", this is an indication that we will have to delete it at the end of the function.

Once we have an iterator we can close the block table record; we will use the iterator to access it.

The for loop illustrates how nice these iterator objects are:

```
for ( ; !pBlockIterator->done() ; pBlockIterator->step())
```

There is no starting condition, the loop continues while the iterator is not done(), and the iterator moves forward by step(). The iterator has a member function getEntity() , which we can use in the same way as we have previously used getAt(). getEntity() opens the object (for read in this case), and if that works we print the name of the class of the object using the object's class member function name() . We then close the entity and go on to the next iteration.

After we have finished the for-loop we destroy the iterator using the C++ operator delete.

You should try this ARX application on a drawing with a several sorts of entities to see what gets printed. If you create a drawing with two lines and a circle and run the application you will see (maybe in a different order):

```
AcDbCircle
AcDbLine
AcDbLine
```

16.2.2 Changing the internals of a block

LST_16_2.CPP shows how the ARX iterator can be used to get hold of and change the internals of a block. The block can be one of the two predefined blocks ("*MODEL_SPACE" and "*PAPER_SPACE") or any block which has been defined by the user in the drawing.

The function starts by calling the ADS function ads_getstring to ask the user the name of the block he wants to change. "*MODEL_SPACE" and "*PAPER_SPACE" are valid replies, but so are "CHAIR" and "DESK" if these blocks have been defined in the drawing. The users reply is stored in B_Name.

The next few lines of code are almost identical to LST_16_1.CPP except for the call to getAt() :

```
Res = pBlockTable->getAt (B_Name, AcDb::kForRead,
                          pBlockTableRecord);
```

Instead of passing "*MODEL_SPACE" as we did in LST_16_1.CPP we pass the name of the block specified by the user, contained in B_Name. If the block does not exist the return value, Res, will not be Acad::eOk, and in that case we return from the function.

If all goes we close the block table, get a block table record iterator and then close the block table record, just as we did in LST_16_1.CPP. The for-loop which scans the internals of the block has roughly the same structure as before, but this time the getEntity() is called with AcDb::kForWrite. This is because we may want to *change* the contents of the entity.

This time we use only the strictest type checking method for entities, cast() :

```
if (NULL != (C_Ptr = AcDbCircle::cast(E_Obj))) {
    .... yep, really a circle
} else if (NULL != (L_Ptr = AcDbLine::cast(E_Obj))) {
    .... yep, really a line
}
```

The method of changing the radius of a circle is the same as before, except that we half it. If the entity is a line we half its length by setting the end point of the line to its middle point. And here we have a new class of object, an AcGePoint3d, which is from the geometry library, discussed in the next section. The arithmetic of the change in end point should be fairly obvious.

The function ends as before by deleting the iterator.

You should try this application on a drawing with several blocks containing circles and lines already defined. After running the application on a block you may not see any changes immediately, if this happens type REGEN at the AutoCAD command line to update the screen.

16.2.3 Iterating through the vertices of a polyline

The following code fragment shows a function for printing out the coordinates of an AcDb2dPolyline. It illustrates the use of the `vertexIterator` to step through the vertices in the polyline printing out the coordinates. Each vertex is opened for read, if you want to modify the vertices you would have to open each vertex for write.

```
void Print_Pline(AcDb2dPolyline* pline)
{
  AcDb2dVertex*   vert   = NULL;
  AcDbObjectId    vId;
  AcDbObjectIterator *vIter;
  vIter = pline->vertexIterator(); // Create iterator
  for (vId = vIter->objectId(); !vIter->done();
                    vId = vIter->nextAcDbObjectId()) {
      if(Acad::eOk!=pline->openVertex(vert,vId,AcDb::kForRead)){
          ads_printf ("\nERROR opening vertex") ;
          break ;
      }
      ads_printf ("\n") ;
      Print_3d (vert->position()); // Defined in LST_16_3.CPP
      (void)vert->close () ; // Don't forget to close the vertex
  }
. delete vIter; // Destroy iterator
}
```

16.3 The ARX geometry library

The ARX geometry library provides several classes to use when you need to handle points, vectors matrices, arrays and so on.

16.3.1 The difference between AcDbPoint and AcGePoint3d

A class of the geometry library is *not* an entity, it should be considered as a pure representation of a geometrical or mathematical object. For example AcGePoint3d is *not* the same as AcDbPoint. Here is a partial listing of the AcDbPoint declaration, found in DBENTS.H:

```
class AcDbPoint: public AcDbEntity
{
public:
```

```
AcDbPoint();
AcDbPoint(const AcGePoint3d&    position);
~AcDbPoint();
AcGePoint3d position() const;
void        setPosition(const AcGePoint3d& pt);
}
```

Here we can see that it is derived from AcDbEntity (hence it is a class representing an entity) and that it uses AcGePoint3d to supply and set its position. Roughly speaking, AcGePoint3d in ARX corresponds to ads_point in ADS.

Of course this sort of distinction applies to other objects, AcDbLine (database entity) is not the same as AcGeLine3d (geometrical object), and so on.

16.3.2 The three-dimensional point class: AcGePoint3d

As a simple introduction lets look again at the use of AcGePoint3d in LST_16_2.CPP. We change the end point of every line in the block with the following code:

```
AcGePoint3d New_End ;
New_End.x = (L_Ptr->endPoint().x +
            L_Ptr->startPoint().x) / 2.0 ;
New_End.y = (L_Ptr->endPoint().y +
            L_Ptr->startPoint().y) / 2.0 ;
New_End.z = (L_Ptr->endPoint().z +
            L_Ptr->startPoint().z) / 2.0 ;
L_Ptr->setEndPoint (New_End) ;
```

AcGePoint3d is a class defined in GEPNT3D.H. It contains three floating point numbers (the three coordinates) which can be accessed as shown above using .x .y and .z. As you can see from the above code fragment the coordinates can both be read and written.

The components of the point can also be accessed using [ ] just as if it was an ads_point.

```
for (int i = X ; i <= Z ; i++) {
    New_End[i] = (L_Ptr->endPoint()[i] +
                L_Ptr->startPoint()[i]) / 2.0 ;
}
```

Which method you use depends on what you are doing and your personal preferences.

What other things can you do with a `AcGePoint3d`? Well, a quick glance at the include file GEPNT3D.H will show the following member functions (among others):

```
static const AcGePoint3d kOrigin;   // Define origin, 0,0,0
AcGePoint3d  operator +  (const AcGeVector3d&) const;
AcGePoint3d& operator -= (const AcGeVector3d&);
double       distanceTo  (const AcGePoint3d&) const;
Adesk::Boolean operator == (const AcGePoint3d&) const;
Adesk::Boolean operator != (const AcGePoint3d&) const;
AcGePoint3d operator * (const AcGeMatrix3d&, const AcGePoint3d&);
AcGePoint3d operator * (double) const;
```

So you have an origin point which you can access by referring to `AcGePoint::kOrigin`.

You can add a vector `AcGeVector3d` to the point, creating a new point which is offset from the original:

```
AcGeVector3d Offset (1,1,0) ;
AcGePoint3d  Point, Offset_Point ;
Offset_Point = Point + Offset ;
```

Remember that in general vectors are not points. Think of points as positions, and vectors as offsets or movements in a certain direction. That is why there is no operator to add two points, it does not make sense to add two positions, while it does make sense to add a vector to a position, thus creating a new position, or even a vector to a vector.

You can use the `-=` operator to change offset a point negatively:

```
AcGeVector3d Offset (1,1,0) ;
AcGePoint3d  Point, Offset_Point ;
Point -= Vec_Offset ;
```

The `+=` operator exists as well of course.

You can find the distance between the point and another point:

```
double Distance ;
AcGePoint3d Point, Another_Point ;
...initialise the two points...
Distance = Point.distanceTo (Another_Point) ;
```

You can test for equality, and inequality between two points:

```
AcGePoint3d PointA, PointB, PointC ;
....initialise the three points...
if (PointA == PointB) {
    ....
```

```
} else if (PointA != PointC) {
    ....
}
```

You can multiply the `AcGePoint3d` by a matrix, `AcGeMatrix3d`, as follows:

```
AcGeMatrix3d Trans_Mat ;
AcGeVector3d Trans_Vec (0,0,5) ;  // Define a translation vector
Trans_Mat.setTranslation (Trans_Vec); // Setup trans matrix
// Set Point to the origin moved up by 5 in Z
Point = Trans_Mat * AcGePoint3d::kOrigin ;
```

You can scale the point (i.e. all its components):

```
Scaled_Point = Original_Point * 10.0 ;
```

As mentioned in Chapter 15 you can convert from an `ads_point` (maybe obtained from the user with an `ads_getpoint()` call) to an `AcGePoint3D`:

```
ads_point Ads_Pnt ;
AcGePoint3d Arx_Pnt ;
...init the Ads_Pnt...
Arx_Pnt = asPnt3d (Ads_Pnt) ; // Convert from ADS to ARX
```

In converting from `ads_point` to `AcGePoint3d` it is also possible to do a brutal and dangerous cast as follows:

```
AcGePoint3d p ;
rc = ads_getpoint (NULL,"Point : ",(double*)(&p));
```

The third parameter of the function `ads_getpoint()` should be an `ads_point`. In the above code fragment the writer has used the fact that he "knows" that the low level memory layout of the data members of `AcGePoint3d` and `ads_point` are the same. he also "knows" that an `ads_point` can be thought of as a pointer to a double. All these crimes are compressed into this piece of code:

```
(double*)(&p) // casts a AcGePoint3d address to a double pointer
```

Although this example is taken from Autodesk supplied ARX sample code it is *not* good programming practice, and you will do better always to use conversion functions such as `asPnt3d()` . Looking inside the defintion of `asPnt3d()` you will probably see the same sort of cast as above, but if the structure of `AcGePoint3d` changes in the future then so will the code for asPnt3d(). Simply recasting the object as shown in the above code fragment does not protect you from future changes.

All of these operations descrobed above (apart from the tricky and inelegant cast) are illustrated in LST_16_3.CPP. We get the user to give us two points and then perform various operations on them, printing out the results with Print_3d(). Note that there are two definitions of this function, one for vectors and one for points. This is one of the features of C++, two functions can have the same name and different parameters, and the compiler picks the correct function depending on the parameter. The second form will be useful for us in LST_16_4.CPP.

Above I have introduced on the sly two more classes from the geometry library, AcGeVector3d and AcGeMatrix3d; these are discussed in section 16.3.4.

16.3.3 The hierarchy of the AcGe geometry class library

The previous section went into a little detail about the member functions of AcGePoint3d. There are many other geometry classes, and here is the hierarchy of the two-dimensional ones:

```
GePoint2d
GeVector2d
GeMatrix2d
GeEntity2d
    GePointEnt2d
        GePosition2d, GePointOnCurve2d
    GeCurve2d
        GeLinearEnt2d
            GeLine2d, GeRay2d, GeLineSeg2d, GeCircArc2d
        GeEllipArc2d
        GeConic2d
        GePolyLine2d
        GeCubicSpline2d
        GeNurbCurve2d
        GeOffsetCurve2d
        GeCompositeCurve2d
        GePlanarSpaceCurve2d
        GeCurveXCurve2d
```

Indentation indicates inheritance. For example GePosition2d inherits from GePointEnt2d which in turn inherits from GeEntity2d. The **boldface** class names are abstract classes.

There is no space here to go into the details of each class, and you will need to study the ARX include and document files for each class you want to use. The previous section on AcGePoint3d gives you an idea of what to expect and what you will be able to do with the classes. We will now look briefly at two fundamental three-dimensional geometry classes.

16.3.4 The AcGeVector3d and AcGeMatrix3d classes

These two classes implement vectors and matrices used in three-dimensional geometry. The classes are defined in GEMAT3D.H and GEVEC3D.H respectively. With these two classes you can create transformation matrices which operate on vectors or points, as illustrated in LST_16_3.CPP.

Here is a listing of AcGeVector3d, partial and rearranged with explanatory comments:

```
class AcGeVector3d
{
public:
    // Three constructors
    AcGeVector3d();                         // default constructor
    AcGeVector3d(const AcGeVector3d&);      // copy constructor
    AcGeVector3d(double, double, double);   // init constructor
     // Some useful "global" constants
    static const    AcGeVector3d kIdentity; // (0,0,0)
    static const    AcGeVector3d kXAxis;    // (1,0,0)
    static const    AcGeVector3d kYAxis;    // (0,1,0)
    static const    AcGeVector3d kZAxis;    // (0,0,1)

    // Member functions
    AcGeVector3d    normal      () const;
    AcGeVector3d&   normalize   ();
    double          length      () const;
    double          dotProduct  (const AcGeVector3d&) const;
    AcGeVector3d    crossProduct(const AcGeVector3d&) const;
}
```

From the above you can see that you can create a vector in three ways, there are three constructors. The AcGeVector3d constants are sometimes useful in geometry programming, and save you the trouble of defining them yourself. The five member functions shown here (there are many others in the include file) are used as follows:

```
AcGeVector3d Normalised_Vec, Original_Vec, Another_Vec ;
double D_Prod, Length ;
AcGeVector3d C_Prod_Vec ;
Normalised_Vec = Original_Vec.normal() ;
Original_Vec.normalize() ;
Length = Original_Vec.length() ;
D_Prod = Original_Vec.dotProduct (Another_Vec) ;
C_Prod_Vec = Original_Vec.crossProduct (Another_Vec) ;
```

As explained in Chapter 7 this book is not an introduction to geometry but it is worthwhile explaining what some of the perhaps more obscure functions above do.

- Normalisation. This changes the *length* of the vector to be unity, while preserving the direction.
- Dot product. The dot product of two vectors is a scalar (and for that reason it resturns a double in ARX C++). It can be used to indicate how close they are to being parallel. Two parallel unit vectors for example will have a dot product of 1.0. Two perpendicular vectors (of whatever magnitude) will have a dot product of 0.0. A practical application of the dot product would be the effect of wind on an old-style sailing ship. If the wind is parallel to the length of the ship then the force is at its maximum. If the wind is perpendicular to the length of the ship then the force of the wind on the sails is practically zero.
- Cross Product. The cross product of two vectors results in a third vector (in ARX C++ it returns an `AcGeVector3d`) perpendicular to the first two vectors. The size of the third vector is at a maximum when the first two vectors are perpendicular, and it is zero when the first two vectors are parallel. The cross product has applications in physics, among other fields, where is is used to calculate the interaction between electric and magnetic fields.

`AcGeMatrix3d` is just as abundant in the number of member functions as `AcGeVector3d`. Here is a partial listing of the class declaration:

```
class AcGeMatrix3d
{
public:
    // Two constructors
    AcGeMatrix3d();
    AcGeMatrix3d(const AcGeMatrix3d&);

    // The identity matrix
    static const   AcGeMatrix3d    kIdentity;

    // Set a matrix to two others multiplied
    AcGeMatrix3d   operator *      (const AcGeMatrix3d&) const;
    AcGeMatrix3d&  operator *=      (const AcGeMatrix3d&);

    // Invert the matrix itself
    AcGeMatrix3d&  invert          ();
    // Set another matrix to this matrix inverted
    AcGeMatrix3d   inverse         () const;
```

```
        // See if matrices are equal or not
        Adesk::Boolean operator ==      (const AcGeMatrix3d&) const;
        Adesk::Boolean operator !=      (const AcGeMatrix3d&) const;

        // Set the matrix to various useful values
        AcGeMatrix3d&  setTranslation   (const AcGeVector3d&);
        AcGeVector3d   translation      () const;

        // Set the matrix to convert to another coord sys
        AcGeMatrix3d&  setCoordSystem   (const AcGePoint3d& origin,
                                         const AcGeVector3d& xAxis,
                                         const AcGeVector3d& yAxis,
                                         const AcGeVector3d& zAxis);
        // Get the coord sys that this matrix converts to
        void           getCoordSystem   (AcGePoint3d& origin,
                                         AcGeVector3d& xAxis,
                                         AcGeVector3d& yAxis,
                                         AcGeVector3d& zAxis) const;
}
```

As with `AcGePoint3d` and `AcGeVector3d` there is a constant, the identity matrix used in your program like this:

```
Mat = AcGeMatrix3d::kIdentity
```

You can multiply two matrices together, or invert a matrix, test to see if two matrices are equal and so on.

One function is especially interesting. It sets up the matrix to convert from one coordinate system to another, `setCoordSystem()`. This takes four parameters:

* origin, the origin of the new coordinate system
* xAxis, the direction of the X axis in the new coordinate system
* yAxis, the direction of the Y axis in the new coordinate system
* zAxis, the direction of the Z axis in the new coordinate system.

Imagine that we are in the world coordinate system, and we want to set up a new coordinate system relative to this WCS. We use the WCS in this example for simplicity, but any coordinate system would work. Just think that in general of an old coordinate system and a new one. To create a transform matrix to pass from the new coordinate system to the WCS all we have to do is pass the origin and normalised directions of the three axes to the matrix with `setCoordSystem()`, and the matrix will become a transformer for you!

An example will help to clarify this, see LST_16_4.CPP. This imagines a new coordinate system 2 units above the old one (the origin New_Org specifies this), which also swaps the X and Y axes (New_X=(0,1,0) and New_Y=(1,0,0)). The Z axis is left alone. Then we create a point in this new coordinate system at

(1,2,3). Next we call newCoordSystem for the matrix New_Cs and then transform the point with this matrix:

```
Point = New_Cs * Point ;
```

When we print the point we should find that it has been transformed to (2,1,5), which are the coordinates of the point in the WCS. X and Y axes have been swapped and since the new CS is 2 units above the WCS, in the WCS a point at 3 Z units becomes a point at 5 Z units.

LST_16_4.CPP also illustrates another member function of `AcGeMatrix3d`, the invertion function. This will replace the matrix with its inverse, so allowing us to go back to the original point.

16.4 Copying entities with clone and deepClone()

If you want to copy entites in ARX you need to use one of two clone functions, either `clone()` or `deepClone()`. The first is used for simple objects like lines. points, circles, ellipses and so on. The second is used when there is some hierarchy to the object, blocks and polylines come to mind.

16.4.1 Copying simple entities with clone

LST_16_5.CPP illustrates the `clone()` function, it creates a block made up of entities selected by the user. The simple `clone()` function is more dangerous to use than `deepCloneObjects()`, because if you try to `clone()` a polyline, for example, AutoCAD could well crash. This is because you have copied the main polyline entity, but not the sub-entities, the vertices, which belong to the original polyline, not the copy.

We start by asking the user for the name of the block to be created, and then we ask him to select some objects, making sure not to select polylines or blocks. The last question for the user is the insertion point of the block (i.e. the origin of the block to be created).

Next we create a new block table record (remember that this corresponds to a BLOCK in the ADS, AutoLISP and DXF world) and set the name and insertion point of the block:

```
AcDbBlockTableRecord* blockTableRec =
                    new AcDbBlockTableRecord();
blockTableRec->setName (Blk_Name);
blockTableRec->setOrigin (Ins_Pnt);
```

Next we get the block table and add the record to the table, which we then close.

See how we have opened the block table record for write by creating it with new, and note that we do not close it until we have finished adding all the entities to it, after the for-loop, at the end of the function.

Next we go over the entities in the selection set one by one using the for-loop. Within the loop what happens is as follows.

1. Get the ith `ads_name` from the selection set `S_Set` using `ads_ssname()`.
2. Get the object identifier for this entity using the `ads_name()`.
3. Open the entity for read, at the same time getting hold of a pointer to it, `E_Ptr`.
4. Call the `E_Ptr->clone()` function to create a copy of the object pointed at by `E_Ptr`. The clone is pointed at by `Clone_Ptr`.
5. Add the cloned entity (i.e. the copy of `E_Ptr`) to the block record using `appendAcDbEntity (Clone_Ptr)`.
6. Upgrade the original entity, `E_Ptr`, so it will become open for write.
7. Erase the original entity. You can do this because after the previous step, the upgrade, it is open for write, even though it was originally open only for read.
8. Close the original and now erased entity, `E_Ptr`.
9. Close the cloned entity, `Clone_Ptr`.

There are three new things in the above sequence, cloning, upgrading and erasing.

The `AcDbEntity` class has a member function `clone()`, which will return a pointer to a copy of the entity itself:

```
Clone_Ptr = AcDbEntity::cast (Ent_Ptr->clone()) ;
```

Actually `clone()` returns a pointer to `AcRxObject` (from which `AcDbEntity` is derived) and we use the `cast()` function to convert it to a `AcDbEntity` pointer. So copying simple entities is a easy as that. However beware: only simple entities can use `clone()`, complex entities like polyline and block have to use `deepCloneObjects()`, which we examine in the next section.

The pointer which `clone()` returns is a little like the pointer returned by new when used to create a new `AcDbEntity` object. You can regard it as open for write, you can do what you want with it because it is not yet added to the database. As with new entities, if you do not add the cloned object to the database you should free it with delete. If you do add it to the database it is not your job to delete it.

Upgrading an object allows you to increase the access of an object from read only to read or write access:

```
Obj_Ptr->upgradeOpen();
```

If the object was already open for read then after the above call it will be open for write as well.

Objects can be erased by using the function `AcDbObject::erase()` as follows:

```
Obj_Ptr->erase()
```

Only objects open for write (and in the database of course) can be erased. See section 16.5 later in this Chapter. This is as in the original AutoCAD BLOCK command, where entities put into a block are erased. It is not necessary to erase the entity, we have done it like this to re-implement the BLOCK command.

16.4.2 Copying complex entities with deepClone

If you want to be able to copy both simple and complex entites, you will have to use `deepCloneObjects()`. In fact, unless you need very fast execution speed it is always safer to use `deepCloneObjects()`. Unfortunately it is also more complex.

LST_16_6.CPP is an example of the use of `deepCloneObjects()`. Here the user is prompted to select some objects, and we `deepCloneObjects()` them into the model space block. There is no restriction on what the user selects with `deepCloneObjects()`.

This time we do not ask the user to type a block name, but we assume that he wants to copy the objects in ACDB_MODEL_SPACE. As usual we get the selection set, get the length of the selection set, open the current database, and go over the selection set with a for-loop.

We get the object identifier for the ith object selected using the sequence we have already met in previous listings:

```
ads_ssname (S_Set, i, En) ;
acdbGetObjectId (Obj_Id, En) ;
```

Next we declare some variables which will be used when we call `deepCloneObjects()`:

```
AcDbObjectIdArray List ;      // List to clone
AcDbIdMapping     pIdMap ;    // ids of sub entities
AcDbObjectId      Msb_Id ;    // id of main block
AcDbBlockTable*   Blk_Tab ;   // Block table
```

In this example, to keep things simple, `List` , which is an array of object identifiers, will only contain one object, the `Obj_Id` which we found above. You could have created a long list of object identifiers as an alternative to using the for-loop in this listing. The List is intialised with:

```
List.append (Obj_Id);
```

The pIdMap is where the output of deepCloneObjects() is placed, it is the list of objects cloned, including, in the case of a polyline, the polyline vertices. The Msb_Id is the model space block object identifier, and the Blk_Tab is the block table; these are initialised as follows:

```
db->getBlockTable (Blk_Tab, AcDb::kForRead);
Blk_Tab->getAt (ACDB_MODEL_SPACE, Msb_Id) ;
```

First we get the block table (of all blocks in the drawing) then we get the block we are interested in (the model space block). Msb_Id is used to tell deepCloneObjects() where we want to add the cloned entities.

Having got the block we are interested in we close the block table. Then, at last, we call deepCloneObjects():

```
acdbCurDwg()->deepCloneObjects (List,      // To be cloned
                                Msb_Id,    // Where we add, MSB
                                pIdMap); // Ids of cloned objs
```

So the two inputs are List and Msb_Id (which correspond to "what" and "where") and the output is pIdMap and the fact that the objects are copied into the block selected (in this case the model space block). There is in fact a default fourth parameter to deepCloneObjects() , but its use is complex and rare as far as this introduction to ARX is concerned.

This would be the end of the story if we just wanted to copy the object, and we could have ignored pIdMap, but in LST_16_6.CPP we want to print out what has been copied. Remember that although List has only one object identifier, it may produce more than one if there are sub-entities, like vertices of a polyline. We create an iterator which allows us to read (and write if we wanted) the cloned objects. We do this with the following code:

```
AcDbIdMappingIter Iter (pIdMap) ;
ads_printf ("\nDeep cloning %dth object (",i) ;
for (Iter.start(); !Iter.done(); Iter.step()) {
    AcDbIdPair  Id_Pair ;
    AcDbEntity* Ent_Ptr ;
    Iter.get (Id_Pair)) {
    acdbOpenEntity (Ent_Ptr,Id_Pair.value(),AcDb::kForRead) ;
    // Now Ent_Ptr is open for read
    ...
}
```

The AcDbMappingIter constructor requires an AcDbMapping (our pIdMap), which it uses to create, in our case, Iter. Iter is then used in the header of a fot-loop to go over the `pIdMap`, getting hold of the object identifier using `Iter.get (Id_Pair)`. The `.value` field of `Id_Pair` is the object identifier we are after. Note that in the above code fragment lots of error checking has been omitted for clarity, see LST_16_6.CPP in the original. Within the for-loop the only thing we do with the entity that we have opened for read is print its class. Then we close the entity and at the very end of the function we release the selection set created at the beginning.

If you try this function, and select a polyline of three lines (that is with four vertices) and a ordinary line you will get a printout something like this:

```
Deep cloning 0th object (cloned AcDb2dPolyline, cloned
AcDb2dVertex, cloned AcDb2dVertex, cloned AcDb2dVertex,
cloned AcDb2dVertex, cloned AcDbSequenceEnd)
Deep cloning 1th object (cloned AcDbLine)
```

Here you can see that deep cloning a polyline has cloned six entities, while deep cloning a line has produced only one.

(By the way, if you select a block, do not expect to get a list of the components of the block, because what you have really selected is a block *reference*. You would have to program the retrieval of the block *definition* from the block table to get a listing of block components.)

16.5 Erasing and unerasing objects

Any (open for write) object in the database can be erased with the following function:

```
AcDbObject Acad::ErrorStatus
erase (Adesk::Boolean pErasing = Adesk::kTrue);
```

For example:

```
E_Ptr->erase () ;
```

16.5.1 Unerasing objects

Above we used erase() without specifying the default parameter. If you pass erase() Adesk::kFalse then an erased object can be unerased! For example:

```
E_Obj->erase (Adesk::kFalse) ; // unerase the object
```

What erase() actually does is *mark* the object as erased, but it does not actually remove it from the database. So long as you are in the same drawing session as the one in which the object was erased then it is possible to unerase erased object. Objects erased in one session cannot be unerased in following sessions, however. Another way of putting this is to say that erased objects will not be present in DWG or DXF files.

16.5.2 Opening erased objects

You can open an erased object only if unless you specifically ask for it. The last parameter of the `acdbOpenAcDbObject` lets you to specify that you want to open an erased object:

```
Acad::ErrorStatus
acdbOpenAcDbObject(AcDbObject*&    obj,
                   AcDbObjectId    objId,
                   AcDb::OpenMode  openMode,
                   Adesk::Boolean  openErasedObject =
                                   Adesk::kFalse);
```

16.5.3 Opening and unerasing erased objects

LST_16_7.CPP shows how you can erase, open and unerase objects. The user is asked to select some objects, which are then all erased. Then each object type is printed out in turn and the user is asked if he wants to unerase it. Note that to use AcDbEntity::erase() either for erasing or unerasing you have to open the object for write, if you have opened it for read then you should upgrade it as shown in the listing *before* calling `erase()`.

16.6 Listings

```
///////////////////////////////////////////////////////////
// LST_16_1.CPP
// Listing the contents of the drawing (i.e. listing the
// contents of the model space block) using ARX

void Test (void)
{
    int Res ;
    AcDbBlockTable*              pBlockTable;
    AcDbBlockTableRecord*        pBlockTableRecord;
    AcDbBlockTableRecordIterator* pBlockIterator;

    // Open the block table of the current drawing for read
    Res = acdbCurDwg()->getBlockTable(
```

```
                                    pBlockTable,AcDb::kForRead);
if (Res != Acad::eOk) {
    ads_printf("\nOpen of block table failed,"
                " Res:%d\n",Res);
    return ;
}

// Get the model space block, *MODEL_SPACE
Res = pBlockTable->getAt ("*MODEL_SPACE",AcDb::kForRead,
                            pBlockTableRecord);
if (Res != Acad::eOk) {
    ads_printf ("\nOpen of *MODEL_SPACE block failed") ;
    pBlockTable->close();
    return;
}

// Close the block table, don't need it any more
pBlockTable->close();

// newIterator() creates a new iterator which defaults
// to starting at the beginning and skipping deleted
// items
Res = pBlockTableRecord->newIterator (pBlockIterator);
if (Res != Acad::eOk) {
    ads_printf("\nnewIterator failed");
    pBlockTableRecord->close();
    return;
}

// We close the record now that we have an iterator.
Res = pBlockTableRecord->close();
if (Res != Acad::eOk) {
    ads_printf("\nERROR: Block table record close"
                " failed, Res = %d",Res);
    delete pBlockIterator;
}

// Go over all the entries in the model space block
for ( ; !pBlockIterator->done() ; pBlockIterator->step()){
    AcDbEntity* pEntity ;
    Res=pBlockIterator->getEntity(AcDb::kForRead,pEntity);
    if (Res == Acad::eOk) {
        ads_printf ("\n%s",pEntity->isA()->name()) ;
        pEntity->close();
    } else {
        ads_printf("\nEntity open failed, Res=%d",Res);
    }
}
delete pBlockIterator;
```

```
        ads_printf("\n");
}
//                    -- end of LST_16_1.C --

//////////////////////////////////////////////////////////////
// LST_16_2.CPP
//    Changing the contents of any block specified
//    by the user

void Test (void)
{
    int Res ;
    AcDbBlockTable*                pBlockTable;
    AcDbBlockTableRecord*          pBlockTableRecord;
    AcDbBlockTableRecordIterator*  pBlockIterator;
    char                           B_Name[64] ;

    // Ask the user which block to list. It is perfectly
    // valid here for the user to reply "*MODEL_SPACE" or
    // "*PAPER_SPACE" as well as user defined blocks
    Res = ads_getstring (0,"Name of block to list:",B_Name) ;
    if (Res != RTNORM) {
        return ;
    }

    // Open the block table of the current drawing for read
    Res=acdbCurDwg()->getBlockTable(pBlockTable,AcDb::kForRead);
    if (Res != Acad::eOk) {
        ads_printf("\nOpen of block table failed,"
                   " Res:%d\n",Res);
        return ;
    }

    // Get the block table record for B_Name
    Res = pBlockTable->getAt (B_Name, AcDb::kForRead,
                              pBlockTableRecord);
    if (Res != Acad::eOk) {
        ads_printf ("\nOpen of <%s> block failed,"
                    "does this block exist?",B_Name) ;
        pBlockTable->close();
        return;
    }

    // Close the block table, don't need it any more
    pBlockTable->close();

    // newIterator() creates a new iterator which defaults
    // to starting at the beginning and skipping deleted
    // items
```

```
Res = pBlockTableRecord->newIterator (pBlockIterator);
if (Res != Acad::eOk) {
    ads_printf("\nERROR:newIterator failed, Res =%d",Res);
    pBlockTableRecord->close();
    return;
}

// We close the record now that we have an iterator
// into it.
Res = pBlockTableRecord->close();
if (Res != Acad::eOk) {
    ads_printf("\nERROR: Block table record close"
                " failed, Res = %d",Res);
    delete pBlockIterator;
}

// Go over all the entries in the block, reducing
// circle radii and shortening lines...
for ( ; !pBlockIterator->done() ; pBlockIterator->step()){

    AcDbEntity* E_Obj ;
                                        // !!! FOR WRITE !!!
    Res=pBlockIterator->getEntity(AcDb::kForWrite,E_Obj);
    if (Res != Acad::eOk) {
        ads_printf("\nEntity open failed, Res=%d",Res);
        break ;  // An error, get outta the for loop
    }
    AcDbCircle* C_Ptr ;
    AcDbLine*   L_Ptr ;
    if (NULL != (C_Ptr = AcDbCircle::cast(E_Obj))) {
        double New_Rad ;
        New_Rad = C_Ptr->radius() / 2.0 ;
        C_Ptr->setRadius (New_Rad) ;
    } else if (NULL != (L_Ptr = AcDbLine::cast(E_Obj))) {
        AcGePoint3d New_End ;
        New_End.x = (L_Ptr->endPoint().x +
                    L_Ptr->startPoint().x) / 2.0 ;
        New_End.y = (L_Ptr->endPoint().y +
                    L_Ptr->startPoint().y) / 2.0 ;
        New_End.z = (L_Ptr->endPoint().z +
                    L_Ptr->startPoint().z) / 2.0 ;
        L_Ptr->setEndPoint (New_End) ;
    } else {
        ads_printf("\nDid not change the %s",
                    E_Obj->isA()->name());
    }
    E_Obj->close();
}
delete pBlockIterator;
```

```
        ads_printf("\n");
}
//                           -- end of LST_16_2.C --


/////////////////////////////////////////////////////////////
// LST_16_3.CPP
//    Illustrating some of the member functions
//    of the AcGePoint3d class

#include <gemat3d.h> // Required for matrix stuff

void Print_3d (const AcGePoint3d& Pnt) ;
void Print_3d (const AcGeVector3d& Vec) ;

void Test (void)
{
    int Res ;
    ads_point Dummy ;     // ADS world point
    AcGePoint3d Point_1,Point_2 ; // ARX world points

    // Get a point from user:
    Res = ads_getpoint (NULL,"Point_1 please : ",Dummy) ;
    if (Res != RTNORM) {
        return ;
    } else {
        // Convert from ADS to ARX type
        Point_1 = asPnt3d (Dummy) ;
    }

    // Get another point from user:
    Res = ads_getpoint (NULL,"Point_2 please : ",Dummy) ;
    if (Res != RTNORM) {
        return ;
    } else {
        // Convert from ADS to ARX type
        Point_2 = asPnt3d (Dummy) ;
    }

    // Show the selected points
    ads_printf ("\nPoint_1 = ") ;
    Print_3d (Point_1) ;
    ads_printf ("\nPoint_2 = ") ;
    Print_3d (Point_2) ;

    // Show how to use equality test
    if (Point_1 == Point_2) {
        ads_printf ("\nPoint_1 == Point_2") ;
    }
```

```
    // Show how to use unequality test
    if (Point_1 != AcGePoint3d::kOrigin) {
        ads_printf ("\nPoint_1 is not at the origin") ;
    }

    // See how far away the point is from the origin:
    double Distance ;
    Distance = Point_1.distanceTo (AcGePoint3d::kOrigin) ;
    ads_printf ("\nPoint_1 is %6.3f from the origin",
                Distance ) ;

    Distance = Point_1.distanceTo (Point_2) ;
    ads_printf ("\nPoint_1 is %6.3f from Point_2",Distance ) ;

    // Introduce the AcGeVector class and use it to offset
    // a point using the '+' operator.
    AcGeVector3d  Vec (1,1,0) ;
    AcGePoint3d Offset_Point ;

    Offset_Point = Point_1 + Vec ;

    ads_printf ("\nPoint_1 offset by 1,1 is ") ;
    Print_3d (Offset_Point) ;

    // Ilustrate the '-=' operator to offset
    Point_2 -= Vec ;

    ads_printf ("\nPoint_2 negatively offset by 1,1 becomes ") ;
    Print_3d (Point_2) ;

    // Illustrate use of matrices and vectors to create a
    // a translation matrix
    AcGeMatrix3d Trans_Mat ;
    AcGeVector3d Trans_Vec (1,2,3) ;

    Trans_Mat.setTranslation  (Trans_Vec);
    Point_1 = Trans_Mat * AcGePoint3d::kOrigin ;

    ads_printf ("\nThe origin translated by 1,2,3 is ") ;
    Print_3d (Point_1) ;

    // Show how easy simply scaling is...
    Point_2 = Point_1 * 3 ;
    ads_printf ("\nand then scaled by 3 = ") ;
    Print_3d (Point_2) ;
}


void Print_3d (const AcGePoint3d& Pnt)
```

```
/*
PURPOSE: Prints out the values of a point
*/
{
    ads_printf ("[") ;
    for (int i = X ; i <= Z ; i++) {
        ads_printf ("%6.3f ",Pnt[i]) ;
    }
    ads_printf ("]") ;
}


void Print_3d (const AcGeVector3d& Vec)
/*
PURPOSE: Prints out the values of a vector
*/
{
    ads_printf ("[") ;
    for (int i = X ; i <= Z ; i++) {
        ads_printf ("%6.3f ",Vec[i]) ;
    }
    ads_printf ("]") ;
}
//                      -- end of LST_16_3.C --


/////////////////////////////////////////////////////////
// LST_16_4.CPP
//    Illustrating how to set up an AcGeMatrix the
//    to transform from one coordinate system to another

#include <gemat3d.h> // Required for matrix stuff

void Test (void)
{
    AcGeMatrix3d New_Cs ;    // CS transforming matrix
    AcGePoint3d  New_Org (0,0,2) ; // Origin of old CS
    AcGeVector3d New_X (0,1,0) ;   // X axis of old CS
    AcGeVector3d New_Y (1,0,0) ;   // Y axis of old CS
    AcGeVector3d New_Z (0,0,1) ;   // Z axis of old CS
    AcGePoint3d  Point (1,2,3) ;   // A test point

    ads_printf ("\nOriginal point = ") ;
    Print_3d (Point) ;

    // Set New_Cs to a matrix which transforms from
    // one coordinate system to another
    New_Cs.setCoordSystem(New_Org,
                          New_X,
                          New_Y,
                          New_Z) ;
```

```
        Point = New_Cs * Point ; // Transform original point

        ads_printf ("\nXformed point = ") ;
        Print_3d (Point) ; // 2,1,5

        // Invert the matrix
        New_Cs.invert () ;
        // Transform point back into origial CS
        Point = New_Cs * Point ;

        ads_printf ("\nOriginal point,using matrix inverse= ") ;
        Print_3d (Point) ;
}

//                      -- end of LST_16_4.C --

////////////////////////////////////////////////////////////
// LST_16_5.CPP
//      Shows how to create a new block of simple entities
//      using the clone() function.

void Test( void )
{
        AcGePoint3d Ins_Pnt ;
        ads_point   Dummy ;
        char        Blk_Name[80] ;
        ads_name    S_Set ;
        long        Len ;
        int         Res ;

        // Ask name of block:
        Res = ads_getstring (0,"\nNew block name: ",Blk_Name ) ;

        if ((Res != RTNORM) || (Blk_Name[0] == '\0')) {
            ads_printf ("\nRes=%d, Blk_Name=<%s>",
                            Res,Blk_Name) ;
            return ;  // User probably hit ESCAPE key or ENTER
        }

        // WARN the user!
        ads_printf ("\nSelect ONLY lines and circles!") ;

        // Get entities for block:
        Res = ads_ssget (NULL,NULL, NULL, NULL, S_Set ) ;
        if (Res != RTNORM ) {
            return ; // User probably hit ESCAPE key
        }

        Res = ads_sslength (S_Set,&Len);
```

```
if (Res!=RTNORM ) {
    ads_printf ("\nBad selection set.");
    ads_ssfree (S_Set );
    return ;
}

// Get insertion point of block:
Res = ads_getpoint (NULL,"\nBlock insertion point : ",
                Dummy) ;
if (Res == RTNORM ) {
    Ins_Pnt = asPnt3d (Dummy) ;
} else {
    return ; // User probably hit ESCAPE key
}

// Create a new block table record:
AcDbBlockTableRecord* blockTableRec =
                    new AcDbBlockTableRecord();

// Set name and origin of new record:
blockTableRec->setName (Blk_Name);
blockTableRec->setOrigin (Ins_Pnt);

// Get block table
AcDbDatabase* db = acdbCurDwg();
AcDbBlockTable* blockTable = NULL ;

// Get block table from database, open for writing
db->getBlockTable (blockTable, AcDb::kForWrite);

// Add block table record to block table
AcDbObjectId blockTableRecordId; // Required, not used
blockTable->add (blockTableRecordId,blockTableRec);

// Close the block table now that the new block
// record has been added
blockTable->close();

// Declare variables used for cloning...
ads_name     En ;        // Temp for ents in S_Set
AcDbObjectId Obj_Id ;    // Used to open entity
AcDbEntity*  Ent_Ptr ;   // Used to clone(copy) entity
AcDbEntity*  Clone_Ptr ; // New (cloned) entity

// Go over the selection set
for (long i=0 ; i < Len ; i++ ) {

    // Get the ith entity in the selection set
```

```
    ads_ssname (S_Set, i, En );

    // Get the object id of the ith entity
    if (acdbGetObjectId (Obj_Id, En) != Acad::eOk) {
        ads_printf("\nError retrieving object id." ) ;
        break ;
    }

    // Open the entity for READ, because we are NOT
    // going to change it, just clone (copy) it.
    if (acdbOpenEntity (Ent_Ptr, Obj_Id, AcDb::kForRead)
                        != Acad::eOk ) {
        ads_printf ("\nError opening object for read.");
        break ;
    }

    // Clone (copy) the simple object
    if ((Clone_Ptr =
        AcDbEntity::cast (Ent_Ptr->clone()))
        == NULL ) {
        ads_printf ("\nError cloning object." );
        break ;
    }

    // Add cloned entity to the block table record:
    blockTableRec->appendAcDbEntity(Clone_Ptr);

    // Upgrade the original entity so it can be erased
    if (Ent_Ptr->upgradeOpen() != Acad::eOk ) {
        ads_printf("\nError upgrading original obj." );
        break;
    }

    // Now erase and close it (in that order) it
    if (Ent_Ptr->erase() != Acad::eOk ) {
        ads_printf("\nError erasing original obj." );
        break;
    }
    if (Ent_Ptr->close() != Acad::eOk ) {
        ads_printf("\nError closing original obj." );
        break;
    }

    // Close the cloned entity
    if (Clone_Ptr->close() != Acad::eOk ) {
        ads_printf("\nError closing cloned object." );
        break;
    }
}
```

```
        // Release memory used in the selection set
        if (ads_ssfree (S_Set) != RTNORM ) {
            ads_printf("\nError freeing selection set." );
        }

        // Close the block table record (i.e. the BLOCK)
        if (blockTableRec->close() != Acad::eOk) {
            ads_printf("\nError closing block table record." );
        }
}
    //                          -- end of LST_16_5.CPP --

//////////////////////////////////////////////////////////////
// LST_16_6.CPP
//       Illustrating deep cloning of objects. The user will
//       be prompted for whatever objects he wants, some need
//       deep cloning (polylines and blocks) some don't. This
//       app always deep clones the selection set.
//

#include <dbidmap.h> // Database ID mapping and iterating

void Test (void)
{
    AcGePoint3d Ins_Pnt ;
    ads_name    S_Set ;
    long        Len ;
    int         Res ;

    // Get entities to clone
    ads_printf ("\nSelect objects to clone : ") ;
    Res = ads_ssget (NULL,NULL, NULL, NULL, S_Set );
    if (Res != RTNORM ) {
        return ; // User probably hit ESCAPE key
    }

    Res = ads_sslength (S_Set,&Len);
    if (Res != RTNORM ) {
        ads_printf ("\nBad selection set.");
        ads_ssfree (S_Set);
        return ;
    }

    // Get current database
    AcDbDatabase* db = acdbCurDwg();

    // Declare variables used for cloning...

    // Go over the selection set
```

```
for (long i = 0 ; i < Len ; i++ ) {
    ads_name         En ;      // Temp for ents in S_Set
    AcDbObjectId     Obj_Id ;  // Used to open entity

    // Get the ith entity selected
    ads_ssname (S_Set, i, En);

    // Get the object id of the entity
    if (Acad::eOk != acdbGetObjectId (Obj_Id, En)) {
        ads_printf ("Error retrieving object id.\n" );
        break;
    }

    AcDbObjectIdArray List ;     // List to clone
    AcDbIdMapping      pIdMap ;  // ids of sub entities
    AcDbObjectId      Msb_Id ;   // id of main block
    AcDbBlockTable*   Blk_Tab ;  // Block table

    // Start a list of entities
    List.append (Obj_Id); // See DBIDARR.H

    // Get id of block we will add entities to

    // 1) Open the block table for read
    db->getBlockTable (Blk_Tab, AcDb::kForRead);

    // 2) Get the model space block's id in Msb_Id
    if (Blk_Tab->getAt (ACDB_MODEL_SPACE, Msb_Id)
        != Acad::eOk) {
        ads_printf ("\nERROR getAt(ACDB_MODEL_SPACE)") ;
        break ;
    };

    // 3) Now we've got model space, close block table
    Blk_Tab->close();

    // Copy (deepclone) the objects
    acdbCurDwg()->deepCloneObjects (
                    List,     // To be cloned
                    Msb_Id,   // Where we add, MSB
                    pIdMap) ;// Ids of cloned objs

    AcDbIdMappingIter Iter (pIdMap) ;

    ads_printf ("\nDeep cloning %dth object (",i) ;
    for (Iter.start(); !Iter.done(); Iter.step()) {
        AcDbIdPair  Id_Pair ;
        AcDbEntity* Ent_Ptr ;
        if (!Iter.get (Id_Pair)) {
```

```
                        ads_printf ("\nCould not Iter.get()") ;
                        continue ;
                }
                // Open the cloned entity for read
                if (acdbOpenEntity (Ent_Ptr,Id_Pair.value(),
                                AcDb::kForRead) != Acad::eOk ) {
                        ads_printf ("\nError opening id pair value" );
                        continue ;
                }

                // Print what we have cloned
                ads_printf (" cloned %s,",Ent_Ptr->isA()->name());

                // Close the cloned entity
                if (Ent_Ptr->close() != Acad::eOk ) {
                        ads_printf ("\nError closing object" );
                        continue ;
                }
        }
        ads_printf (")") ;
    }

    // Release memory used in the selection set
    if (ads_ssfree (S_Set) != RTNORM ) {
        ads_printf("\nError freeing selection set." );
    }
}
//                          -- end of LST_16_6.C --

///////////////////////////////////////////////////////////
// LST_16_7.CPP
//      Shows how to erase and unerase objects

void Test (void)
{
    ads_name    S_Set ;
    long        Len ;
    int         Res ;

    // Get entities to erase :
    Res = ads_ssget (NULL,NULL, NULL, NULL, S_Set );
    if (Res != RTNORM ) {
        return ; // User probably hit ESCAPE key
    }

    Res = ads_sslength (S_Set,&Len);

    if (Res!=RTNORM ) {
        ads_printf ("\nBad selection set.");
```

```
        ads_ssfree (S_Set );
        return ;
}


// Declare variables used for cloning...
ads_name      En ;         // Temp for ents in S_Set
AcDbObjectId Obj_Id ;      // Used to open entity
AcDbEntity*  Ent_Ptr ;     // Used to clone(copy) entity

// Go over the selection set, erasing all the entities
for (long i=0 ; i < Len ; i++ ) {

    // Get the ith entity in the selection set
    ads_ssname (S_Set, i, En);

    // Get the object id of the ith entity
    if (acdbGetObjectId (Obj_Id, En) != Acad::eOk) {
        ads_printf("\nError retrieving object id." ) ;
        break ;
    }

    if (acdbOpenEntity (Ent_Ptr, Obj_Id, AcDb::kForWrite)
                     != Acad::eOk ) {
        ads_printf ("\nError opening object for write.");
        break ;
    }

    // Now erase and close it (in that order) it
    if (Ent_Ptr->erase() != Acad::eOk ) {
        ads_printf("\nError erasing original obj." );
        break ;
    }

    if (Ent_Ptr->close() != Acad::eOk ) {
        ads_printf("\nError closing erase obj." );
        break ;
    }
}

// Go over the selection set getting data of erased objects
for (i=0 ; i < Len ; i++ ) {

    // Get the ith entity in the selection set
    ads_ssname (S_Set, i, En );

    // Get the object id of the ith entity
    if (acdbGetObjectId (Obj_Id, En) != Acad::eOk) {
        ads_printf("\nError retrieving object id." ) ;
        break ;
```

```
      }

      if (acdbOpenEntity (Ent_Ptr, Obj_Id, AcDb::kForRead,
                          Adesk::kTrue)
                          != Acad::eOk ) {
         ads_printf ("\nError opening object for write.");
         break ;
      }

      ads_printf ("\nThis erased object was a %s",
                  Ent_Ptr->isA()->name()) ;

      char Reply[20] ;
      Res = ads_getstring (0," unerase it (y/n) ?",Reply) ;
      if ((Res == RTNORM) && (Reply[0] == 'y')) {

          // Upgrade the original entity so it can be erased
          if (Ent_Ptr->upgradeOpen() != Acad::eOk ) {
              ads_printf("\nError upgrading original obj." );
              break;
          }

          if (Ent_Ptr->erase (Adesk::kFalse) != Acad::eOk ) {
              ads_printf("\nError unerasing obj." );
              break;
          }
      }

      if (Ent_Ptr->close() != Acad::eOk ) {
          ads_printf("\nError closing original obj." );
          break;
      }
   }


   // Release memory used in the selection set
   if (ads_ssfree (S_Set) != RTNORM ) {
      ads_printf("\nError freeing selection set." );
   }
}

//                    -- end of LST_16_7.CPP --
```

Derived entities and dictionaries

17.1 Introduction

In this chapter I give you a glimpse of some of the possibilities offered by ARX using advanced programming techniques, with a few simple but practical programming examples. The new techniques that ARX offers that are covered in this chapter are:

- inheritance from AutoCAD entities and objects to create your own custom entities. There is an example of deriving from the `AcDbCircle` object
- the `AcEdJig` class, used to help create entites which can be dynamically sized and warped as the user moves the mouse
- dictionaries, used to store non-graphical data either "within" entities (like extended data) or in the drawing itself in what is called the Named object dictionary
- writing and reading custom entities to and from the drawing.

17.2 Using inheritance to create custom entities

It would be impossible for a single CAD company to offer all the entity types that CAD developers would like to use. One of the strong points of ARX is that applications developers can use the standard AutoCAD entities as a base class on which to build their own entities. For example if you need a special sort of polyline, then you can derive it from the standard AutoCAD entity `AcDb3dPolyline`. You then add to it the data members and member functions required to extend its properties and customise it to your application, while still using the member functions of the standard polyline.

In ADS the only way to even attempt to do this is to add extended data to the entity (see Chapter 11). It is very easy to do but lacks the flexibility and power of the object oriented ARX method.

17.2.1 Which member functions to overload when deriving a custom entity?

In general you need to work quite hard to create a new entity type. There is an apocryphal story about an Autodesk employee who decided to (or was told to) "invent" the POLYGON entity. What this means in practice is that while some of the member functions can be inherited from `AcDbEntity` without change, he had to re-write many of them. It took eight weeks of full-time work to get this done. The implementation is sometimes distributed on the AutoCAD CD-ROM under the ARX samples directory, the name of the source file is POLY.CC.

Here is a selection of the simple member functions that you can often leave untouched when you derive an entity:

- `colorIndex()`, `setColorIndex ()`
- `layer()`, `setLayer()`,
- `linetype()`, `setLinetype()`
- other simple "attribute" mutators and inspectors

These are the easy ones. Just some of the more difficult ones which you may have re-write are:

- the constructor for the entity
- the `highlight()` and `unhighlight()` functions, so the user can see when the entity has been selected
- `getGeomExtents()`, which returns an AcDbExtents object. This is a box, flat 2D rectangle or 3D parallopiped, enclosing the object
- `getEcs()` , to get the Entity Coordinate System of the object
- `getOsnapPoints()`, so that the user can SNAP to key points of your new entity type
- `getGripPoints()`, so that grip points can be drawn on the entity
- `intersectWith()`, which calculates all the intersection points of your custom object with the object passed into this function
- the `transformBy()` function, which will transform you object by the `AcGeMatrix3d` passed to it
- `xData()` to get XDATA from the entity
- `setXData()` to put XDATA into the entity
- `worldDraw()` and `viewDraw()` which are used to graphically show your entity on the screen. These functions will use the `AcGi` (graphics interface) classes to help in the drawing of the object
- `explode()` to decompose the entity into its component parts.

AcDbEntity is itself derived from AcDbObject. Remember that an AcDbEntity is simply an AcDbObject which is visible in the drawing. In other words it is a visible database object. If you want your custom entity to be saved, in all its glory and data members, in drawing and DXF files you must also re-write the following member functions for your entity:

- dwgInFields() to read the entity in from a DWG file.
- dwgOutFields() to write the entity to a DWG file.
- dxfInFields() to read the entity from a DXF file.
- dxfOutFields() to write the entity to a DXF file.

In C++ terms the ability to store and retrieve an object this is called giving the object *persistence*, i.e. it is an object that does not just disappear when the program (in this case AutoCAD) ends. Later in this chapter there is an example of deriving from AcDbObject to create a class with persistency.

If you are getting worried about the amount of work to do, I will reassure you; you are not obliged to implement *all* these member functions anew. You could decide, for example, that you are not going to support the DXF file format, in which case you do not need to implement dxfInFields() and dxfOutFields().

One geographical informations systems (GIS) software company which decided to implement an entirely new entity type, basing it on the two-dimensional polyline used to represent state borders. The work was long and difficult but the rewards great. They halved the database size and a speeded up in processing time by 300%.

17.2.2 Zombie classes

A problem with custom entities, not only from the programmer's point of view but also from the user's, arises when a drawing containing entities created by one application is taken to a computer running the correct version of AutoCAD, but *without* the application. Or maybe the application has been deleted from the computer's hard disk. In either case if the ARX application which created the custom entities is not available on the computer which he is using then the user will not be able to move, or edit the entity. In some circumstances he may not even be able to see the entity!

There is a similar, but much less serious, problem with extended data, since only the application which wrote the extended data to the entity knows its format and knows what to do with it. Extended data is, however, always invisible, and the entities to which it is attached are always visible. What about a derived entity which does not know how to draw itself because the application with the drawing code is missing? These entities are called zombies; they are not really dead, but they are not very much alive either.

Zombies even have their own classes: `AcDbZombieObject` and `AcDbZombieEntity`.

Zombies are also created when the application which created the entity has been unloaded before the drawing has been saved. In this case the `dwgOutFields()` member function for that custom entity is no longer present, and so AutoCAD has no idea about how to write the drawing to the file. Zombies are placed in the file as "placeholders".

17.2.3 A simple example of deriving a custom class, a special circle

I am grateful to Markus Kraus for the simple example in LST_17_1.CPP of deriving a custom class. This application derives from `AcDbCircle`, adding functionality at the instant when the user is defining the radius. The radius of the circle is seen as a number close to the center of the circle, dynamically changing as the radius is changed as the user moves the cursor.

The listing starts with the usual bundle of include files, and what they are used for is commented on in the source itself. Then there is a call to the macro:

```
ACRX_CLASS (MkrCircle,AcDbEntity)
```

This macro says that we are to derive an new class, `MkrCircle` from the `AcDbEntity` class. There follows the class declaration, and we see that there is a constructor, a function to list the entity, a function to set the radius and so on. The next macro we see is:

```
ACRX_DXF_CLASS_OBJ_BODY(MkrCircle,AcDbEntity,1,MKRCIRCLE,Mkr);
```

which starts the definition of the body of the class. The arguments to the class are, in order:
- the class name, in this case `MkrCircle`, a Markus Kraus Circle
- the parent class name, here `AcDbEntity`
- the version number, here 0
- the DXF name of the class, i.e. the class's equivalent of the string "CIRCLE", in this case it is "MKRCIRCLE". We will not be saving the entity in DWG or DXF files, so this name is not really used, but the macro needs the parameter
- the name of the application which is creating the class, here it is Mkr

As with all extracts from include files you should follow the examples given with the release of AutoCAD you are using; it is possible that as the months and years go by Autodesk changes the macro names or parameter order or number of parameters. So getting the correct include files is even more important with ARX than with ADS. Despite Autodesk's protestations to the contrary ARX is *less* portable across releases than either AutoLISP or ADS.

After the call to the macro there are the actual bodies of the member functions, most of which are easy enough to understand. The inspector member functions all call the function `assertReadEnabled()` which cause the application (and of course AutoCAD) to crash if you try to write to an `MkrCircle` which is not open for read. A message box will come up explaining why the crash occurred, to help you debug, though it will not help the user very much! Similarly the mutator member functions all have a call to `assertWriteEnabled()` which will cause a crash if the `MkrCircle` is not open for write. This is the standard behaviour of AutoCAD `AcDbEntity`, and derived entities should follow the same rules.

17.2.4 Dynamic sizing of the circle

Jumping over some lines of code to the definition of `Ctest()`. The function works as follows. We ask the user for the center point of the circle and then create a `CircleJig` object. Then we call the acquire() function for this `CircleJig`. Inside `CircleJig::acquire()`, `drag()` is called. Now inside `drag()` the sequence is as follows:

1. AutoCAD calls `CircleJig::sampler()` which sets the `CircleJig::Jig_Rad` data member according to the distance of the cursor from the center of the circle.
2. Acad calls `CircleJig::update()` which actually sets the radius of the `CircleJig::MkrCircle`.
3. AutoCAD calls `CircleJig::entity()`, which returns the `MkrCircle` we have just modified
4. AutoCAD draws the circle using the `MkrCircle::worldDraw()` function. AutoCAD knows about which worldDraw function to call because we handed it the entity in the previous step.

So `CircleJig::sampler()` is used to get information about the position of the cursor. First we call `setUserInputControls()` to set how we should treat input from the user. Most of the flags of `setUserInputControls()` should be fairly obvious except maybe for `kDontUpdateLastPoint`, all this flag does is to prevent the AutoCAD system variable LASTPOINT from being changed during the interaction.

The function gets the distance from the cursor to the center of the circle using:

```
DragStatus stat = acquireDist (dist, Jig_Circ->center());
```

and if the returned status is normal checks for zero distance (not a valid value in AutoCAD for circles). Other functions which we could have used here are `AcEdJig::acquireAngle()` and `AcEdJig::acquirePoint()`. Another check that is made is to see if the distance has changed from the last time we called sampler. This information may not seem important, but it is helpful in speeding up reaction time. If the distance has *not* changed then there is no need to redraw the circle and we signal this with the constant kNoChange. At the end of the function stat has been set to one of the following:

- kNormal, a change has occurred with the cursor and we want to update the image
- kOther, the cursor is in an invalid poistion (in our specific case a circle of zero radius has been specified)
- kNoChange, no cursor movement has occurred.

This return value tells AutoCAD whether it should call MkrCircle::worldDraw() or not.

When CircleJig::update() is called, by AutoCAD, all it has to do is set the radius of the MkrCircle member. This function could be more complicated if the entity we were handling itself was more complicated. For example we could be positioning robot arms as the user moves the cursor, and in that case RobotJig::update() would perhaps have to do some inverse kinematics calculations. In that case we would use acquirePoint() rather than acquireDist(). However all that is left as an exercise for the reader.

AutoCAD also calls CircleJig::entity(), whose duty it is to return the pointer to the entity we are controlling. Finally AutoCAD calls MkrCircle::worldDraw() to draw the changed entity on the screen. Neither update() nor worldDraw() will be called if sampler() does not return a kNormal value.

MkrCircle::worldDraw() simply draws a circle of the appropriate size, documenting the radius by printing it near the center of the circle. Note that worldDraw() does not use the standard AutoCAD entities to draw MkrCircle, but member functions of the Mode passed in as a parameter:

```
Mode->geometry().circle (M_Center,M_Radius,...) ;
Mode->geometry().text (M_Center,...) ;
```

This is because we are not yet adding the object to the database, we are just dynamically displaying it as the user moves the cursor. The possible "geometries" which you can use apart from AcGiWordlDraw::circle() and AcGiWorldDraw::text() are listed in the ARX include file ACGI.H.

Back to CircleJig::acquire(). When the user finally decides that he has go the radius he wants by clicking on the mouse or digitizer drag() returns. The stat it returns will be the last one we returned in sampler(), unless of course we returned kNoChange in which case the stat will be kNormal. If al goes well then we append the entity Jig_Circ to the database, as described in the next section. If drag() does not return kNormal then we delete the Jig_Circ In this case the return value may be kOther (probably because a zero radius was specified) and we print a message to the user telling him that what he specified was not a valid circle.

17.2.5 Handing over entities

Now we do not really want to save the MkrCircle in the database; we just created it for temporary use as the circle was sized by the user. However we have added it to the database with the AcEdJig::append(). It is added to the *current* space, either model space or paper space. What we want to do is swap the MkrCircle with an AcDbCircle of the same size. To do this there is a member function of AcDbEntity called handOverTo() :

```
AcDbEntity* Ent1 ;
AcDbEntity* Ent2 ;
...
Ent1->handOverTo (Ent2) ;
```

This puts Ent2 where Ent1 once was. Ent1 *must* be part of the database, and Ent2 must *not* be part of the database. If the swap takes place OK then it is our responsibility to delete Ent1, which was once part of the database.

Summarising a little:

```
MkrCircle* Mc_Ptr = (MkrCircle*)pLast ;
AcDbCircle* C_Ptr = new AcDbCircle;
C_Ptr->setDatabaseDefaults();
C_Ptr->setRadius (Mc_Ptr->radius());
C_Ptr->setCenter (Mc_Ptr->center());
if (Acad::eObjectToBeDeleted ==  Mc_Ptr->handOverTo(C_Ptr)){
    delete Mc_Ptr ; // All has gone well, I must delete original
}
C_Ptr->close();
```

So this example has shown two things:

- how it is possible to derive from standard entities to create your own custom entities
- how dynamic sizing (or rotation or scaling or whatever) is possible uing the AcEdJig class.

Now let us go on to look at dictionaries.

17.3 Dictionaries

17.3.1 Extension dictionaries

Extension dictionaries store data which is related to a specific `AcDbObject`. If the AcDbObject is an AcDbEntity then you can consider the extension dictionary as a sort of extended data. You usually use extension dictionaries to store non-graphical data associated with graphical entities. It is better to use extended data when the requirements are small (less than 256 bytes per entity per application) and simple.

As with extended data a single object can have several extension dictionaries, maybe each dictionary created by a separate application. This book does not cover extension dictionaries in any more detail.

17.3.2 The named object dictionary

The named object dictionary is a place where you can store data which is relevant to the drawing, but which does not have to be attached to any particular entity. It's name comes from the fact that access to the dictionary is by strings, the strings are also known as *keys*. LST_17_2.CPP is an example of using the Named Objects Dictionary to store data about weather. The application could be a GIS program which needs information on the weather conditions in various seasons or months.

17.3.3 Creating a new dictionary

We create a new dictionary in the Named Objects Dictionaries (or NOD) called WEATHER. We allow the user to insert entries in the WEATHER dictionary, and the keys he could use are "SUMMER" or "APRIL" or "WINTER1994".

Each entry in the WEATHER dictionary stores just two numbers: the number of rainy days in that season and the number of sunny days. Obviously a real application would store more meteorological data, and would be more specific about what a sunny or rainy day is. The entries, objects, in the WEATHER dictionary are of the class `Season`.

`Season` is a non-graphical class derived from `AcDbObject`, and LST_17_2.CPP also shows how you can give persistence to custom objects, by redefining the `dwgInFields()` and `dwgOutFields()` function definitions.

LST_17_2.CPP starts with the usual includes and function prototypes the listing derives an object from `AcDbObject` by using the `ACRX_CLASS` macro:

```
ACRX_CLASS (Season, AcDbObject)
```

```
public:
    Season (void); // Must have default constructor
    Acad::ErrorStatus dwgOutFields (AcDbDwgFiler* Flr) const;
    Acad::ErrorStatus dwgInFields (AcDbDwgFiler* Flr) ;
    void   Show (void) const;
    void   Set_Days (const int Rainy, const int Sunny) ;
private:
    Adesk::Int32 Days_Of_Rain, Days_Of_Sun ;
END_ACRX_CLASS
```

which says that `Season` is derived from `AcDbObject`. The first three member functions are necessary, the constructor (which must not have any parameters), the function to write out the object to the DWG file, and the function to read in the object from the DWG file. The other two functions are simply to print out the Season, and to set the data of the Season. As you can see we do not support reading and writing the object to DXF files, there are no `dxfOutFields()` or `dxfInFields()` declarations.

There are two data members, 32 bit integers, which are used to store the number of rainy and sunny days for any given Season.

The declaration of Season ends with the `END_ACRX_CLASS` macro.

The macro `ACRX_DXF_CLASS_OBJECT_BODY` is used just as it was in LST_17_1.CPP, the parameters being (in this order) class name, parent class name, version number, DXF name and application name:

```
ACRX_DXF_CLASS_OBJ_BODY(Season,AcDbObject,0,WEATHER,
                        Dick_Test);
```

The definition of the `Season` constructor simply initialises the day counts to zero.

17.3.4 Giving custom objects persistence

The function `dwgOutFields()` is used by AutoCAD to store your custom object in the DWG file, and you decide what gets saved and what not, and the format. The first thing the function must do is make sure the object is open for read, hence the call to `assertReadEnabled()`. We are *writing* the object to a file, but we are reading it from the memory of AutoCAD, we are not going to change the object, so it has to be open for *read*, not for write.

Next we must call `dwgOutFields()` for the parent class, which is simply achieved:

```
AcDbObject::dwgOutFields (Filer) ;
```

(AcDbObject is the parent class of Season.) The technique of calling the same method for the parent class is called super messaging, the parent class is also called the super class. Next we write the two items of data:

```
Filer->writeItem  (Days_Of_Rain)  ;
Filer->writeItem  (Days_Of_Sun) ;
```

Here I have omitted the error checking for clarity. In the declaration of the two data items we used `Adesk::Int32` rather than simply `int`, so that we would be sure that when we called writeItem() the correct number of bytes would be written to the file. Remember that definitions like `Adesk::X` are found in ADESK.H. In the listing, after each write, we `assert()` that no error occurred. Finally we return `Acad::eOk` to the caller.

Note that any data members not saved explicity in `dwgOutFields()` will not be saved in the drawing, but this does not mean you cannot create them for temporary use.

The definition of `dwgInFields()` follows the pattern of `dwgOutFields()`, except of course that we make sure that the object (in memory) is open for write, and we read the data from the DWG file into the object.

The definition of `Show()` simply prints out the days of rain and sun (after asserting that the object is open for read), while `Set_Days()` simply changes the private data members `Days_Of_Rain` and `Days_Of_Sun` (after asserting that the object is open for write, of course).

17.3.4 Creating and accessing custom dictionaries

The function which asks the user what he wants to do to the WEATHER dictionary is called `Dick_Test()` and starts by asking if he wants to list the entries, delete or add entries. If he replies with one of the keywords, we call `Get_Dictionary()` and then one of the three functions to do what he has asked.

`Get_Dictionary()` is used to get the object identifier of the WEATHER dictionary. If the WEATHER dictionary does not exist then we create it. First we open the Named Objects Dictionary, the pointer to it is called `Name_List` in the LST_17_2.CPP. This is where our dictionary is or will be stored. Then we try to get the WEATHER dictionary using `getAt()`. If `getAt()` succeeds then `D_Id`, the dictionary object identifer is intialised and we do not have to do anything else except close `Name_List`.

If `getAt()` fails then the WEATHER dictionary does not exist and we create it by calling `setAt()` with a new AcDbDictionary:

```
AcDbDictionary* Name_List;
acdbCurDwg()->getNamedObjectsDictionary(
                Name_List,AcDb::kForWrite);
```

```
if (Name_List->getAt ("WEATHER",D_Id) == Acad::eKeyNotFound){
    AcDbDictionary* Dick = new AcDbDictionary ;
    if (Name_List->setAt ("WEATHER", Dick, D_Id) != Acad::eOk){
        return (Adesk::kFalse) ;
    }
    if (Dick->close() != Acad::eOk ) {
        return (Adesk::kFalse) ;
    }
}
```

The `setAt()` call also initialises the object identifier `D_Id`, which is why we called `Get_Dictionary()` in the first place.

The next function, `Add_To_Dick()`, is called when the user wants to add an entry to the WEATHER dictionary. It has two parts: the first part simply asks for the name of the season and the number of sunny and rainy days. Standard `ads_getxxx()` functions are used for this.

In the second half of `Add_To_Dick()` we get our WEATHER dictionary (using the `D_Id` passed into the function) and add a newly created `Season` to it. Summarising the listing, we have:

```
acdbOpenObject (Dick, D_Id, AcDb::kForWrite) ; // Open our dict
Season* S_Ptr = new Season ;            // Create a new Season
S_Ptr->Set_Days (Rainy,Sunny) ;         // Set Season data members
S_Ptr->Show ();                         // Show user data members
AcDbObjectId Obj_Id ;             // Unused, but required for call
Dick->setAt (O_Name,S_Ptr,Obj_Id) ; // Add to the dictionary
S_Ptr->close() ;                        // Close our Season
Dick->close() ;                         // Close our dictionary
```

You can see that the sequence above is very similar to how we added the dictionary to the Named Objects Dictionary. Remember that once we have given AutoCAD and object by putting into the database we must not delete it, because it is no longer ours!

Note that `AcDbDictionary::setAt()` will *overwrite* any dictionary entry with the same name. If the user adds "WINTER" twice, the first specification is replaced by the second.

`List_Dick()` is called when the user wants to list the entries in the dictionary. First we open our dictionary and then we use a dictionary iterator, to go over the dictionary contents:

```
AcDbDictionaryIterator* i;
for (i=Dick->newIterator(); !i->done(); i->nextElement()){ .
    ...
}
```

The iterator `i` is intialised at the start of the for-loop by a call to the member function of `AcDbDictionary`, `newIterator()`. The for-loop continues until the end of the dictionary is reached (when `i->done()` becomes true). Each step of the for-loop gives us a new entry. The name of the entry is easily found using `i->name()`. This is the name that the user gave the Season when he added it to the WEATHER dictionary. Dictionaries store their contents in alphabetical order, irregardless of the order in which the entries were created.

The object identifier of the dictionary entry is also found using a member function of the iterator, this time `i->objectId()`. We open the object for read and then print out various things about it. In reality we are only interested in calling Show() to see how the season has been defined by the user, but I have placed calls to get and print the object handle and class and so on, to show that it is really an AcDbObject just like any other.

Remember that while object identifiers and entity names change from AutoCAD session to session, handles always stay the same for any given object or entity.

When we have finished listing the contents of the dictionary we destroy the iterator and close the dictionary.

The last new function is `Del_Dick()`, which removes entities from the dictionary. We open the dictionary for write (because we are going to change it) and then ask the user for the name of the entry to delete. Then we call `remove()` and `close()`:

```
acdbOpenObject (Dick, D_Id, AcDb::kForWrite) ;
ads_getstring (1,"\nName of entry to remove: ",O_Name);
Dick->remove (O_Name) ;
Dick->close() ;
```

Again in the above code fragment the required error checking has been omitted to show the sequence succinctly and clearly.

Another way of removing dictionary entries is to `erase()` them:

```
AcDbObject* Obj;
Dick->getAt (O_Name,AcDb::kForWrite,Obj) ;
tObj->erase () ;
tObj->close () ;
```

You can try this application in an empty AutoCAD drawing, and you should check that our WEATHER dictionary is actually written out to the drawing file when you save it. Remember to load the application before loading the drawing, or else your dictionary entries will turn into zombies!

17.3.5 Registering new classes with AutoCAD

One last point before we leave this dictionary example. In `Init_App()` there are the following two calls:

```
Season::rxInit() ; // Add to (register with) run time hierarchy
acrxBuildClassHierarchy () ; // Rebuild with Season
```

The first call registers `Season` as a class in the run time hierarchy of AutoCAD classes, and the second rebuilds the hierarchy, taking account of the new class, `Season`, which we have just added. (Earlier versions of ARX use `initSeason()` to register the `Season` class)

17.4 Dictionaries and ADS

ADS can access dictionaries (which are only present remember from Release 13 onwards) using the functions :

```
struct resbuf* ads_dictnext (ads_name Dict, char* Sym, int Rw);
struct resbuf* ads_dictsearch (ads_name Dict, char* Sym, int Sn);
int ads_namedobjdict (ads_name result);
```

See the appropriate entries in Appendix B for more information.

17.5 Listings

```
/////////////////////////////////////////////////////////////
// LST_17_1.CPP
//      A useful example of deriving custom objects.
//      Thanks to Markus Kraus of Autodesk Software
//      Development Europe for the original of this file
//

// #define TURN_OLD_ACDB_MEMBERS_OFF 1

#include <stdio.h>     // sprintf
#include <aced.h>      // Drawing Editor
#include <adslib.h>    // ADS functions
#include <dbents.h>    // Database entities
#include <acgi.h>      // Graphics Interface, for display
#include <geassign.h>  // ADS-ARX-ADS conversions
```

```cpp
//            derived      parent
ACRX_CLASS( MkrCircle, AcDbEntity )
public:
                    MkrCircle (void);
    AcGePoint3d     center    (void) const;
    void            setCenter (const AcGePoint3d&);
    double          radius    (void) const;
    void            setRadius (double);
    Adesk::Boolean worldDraw  (AcGiWorldDraw*);
private:
    AcGePoint3d M_Center;
    double      M_Radius;
END_ACRX_CLASS

// args are:            derived, parent,    ver, DXFNAME, App
ACRX_DXF_CLASS_OBJ_BODY (MkrCircle,AcDbEntity,1,MKRCIRCLE,Mkr);

// The constructor
MkrCircle::MkrCircle (void) :
            M_Center (0,0,0), M_Radius (0)
{ }

AcGePoint3d MkrCircle::center (void) const
{
    assertReadEnabled(); // Make sure object open for read
    return M_Center ;    // read from it
}

void MkrCircle::setCenter (const AcGePoint3d& pt)
{
    assertWriteEnabled (); // Make sure object open for write
    M_Center = pt ;        // write to it
}

double MkrCircle::radius (void) const
{
    assertReadEnabled (); // make sure object open for read
    return M_Radius ;     // read from it
}

void MkrCircle::setRadius( double rad )
{
    assertWriteEnabled (); // make sure object open for write
    M_Radius = rad ;       // write to it
}

// In this application the following gets called everytime
// the user moves the mouse
Adesk::Boolean
```

```
MkrCircle::worldDraw (AcGiWorldDraw* Mode)
{
    Mode->geometry().circle (M_Center,
                             M_Radius,
                             AcGeVector3d( 0, 0, 1 ) );
    char Tmp[80];
    double T_Size ;

    sprintf (Tmp, "%.2f", M_Radius ) ;

    T_Size = M_Radius / 10.0 ;
    Mode->geometry().text (M_Center,        // Position
                           AcGeVector3d (0,0,1), // Direction
                           AcGeVector3d (1,0,0), // Normal
                           T_Size,  // X size
                           1.0,     // width rel to X size
                           0,       // Oblique flag
                           Tmp);    // text itself
    return Adesk::kTrue;
}

// AcEdJig is a class used for dynamic sizing and warping
// of objects with the mouse. Here we derive a new class
// from it so we can dynamically size the MkrCircle..
class CircleJig : public AcEdJig
{
public:
                    CircleJig (const AcGePoint3d& center);
    void            acquire   (); // Initialization
    AcDbEntity*     entity    () const ;
    DragStatus      sampler   ();
    Adesk::Boolean update     ();

private:
    MkrCircle* Jig_Circ ;
    double     Jig_Rad ;
};

// The constructor of CircleJig
CircleJig::CircleJig (const AcGePoint3d& center)
{
    Jig_Circ = new MkrCircle;
    Jig_Circ->setCenter (center);
    Jig_Circ->setDatabaseDefaults();
}

AcDbEntity* CircleJig::entity (void) const
/*
This function is called by AutoCAD, all we have to do is
```

```
return the entity which is being modified. This is the
entity which will be dragged by "drag" and modified by
"update".
*/
{  return (Jig_Circ) ;  }



// The function starts the interaction with the user,
// prompting for a radius and following the motions of
// the mouse by calling the drag() function
void CircleJig::acquire (void)
{
    setDispPrompt ("Radius:");
    DragStatus stat = drag () ;
    if (stat == kNormal) {
        // finished ok, append to database
        append () ; // Appends to default space...
                    // ....normally Model space
    } else {
        // user did not finish normally, does not
        // want to append to the database
        delete Jig_Circ ;
        if (stat == kOther) {
            // probably a circle of zero radius
            ads_printf ("\nBAD CIRCLE" );
        }
    }
    Jig_Circ = NULL ;
}


// Acquire data about the position of the mouse and set
// a (some) data members of CircleJig.
AcEdJig::DragStatus CircleJig::sampler (void)
{
    AcGePoint3d secondPoint;
    double dist;

    // Set the mode of getting user data
    setUserInputControls((UserInputControls)
        (kNullResponseAccepted|kAccept3dCoordinates|
        kGovernedByOrthoMode|kDontUpdateLastPoint));

    // get distance from cursor to center of circle
    DragStatus stat = acquireDist (dist, Jig_Circ->center());
    if (stat == kNormal) {
        if (0.0 == dist) {
            stat = kOther ; // Circles of zero radius no good
        } else {
            if (dist != Jig_Rad) {
```

```
                    Jig_Rad = dist ;
            } else {
                stat = kNoChange;
                // Signal that we don't need to redraw
            }
        }
    }
    return (stat) ;
}


Adesk::Boolean CircleJig::update (void)
/*
update() is called by AutoCAD when the user moves the mouse.
Update the radius of the circle. After this call AutoCAD
calls entity().
*/
{
    Jig_Circ->setRadius (Jig_Rad) ;
    return Adesk::kTrue;
}



void Ctest (void)
{
    AcGePoint3d basePoint ;
    CircleJig* pJig ;
    int Res ;

    // Ask user for center point of circle
    Res = ads_getpoint (NULL,"Center point:",
                        asDblArray(basePoint)) ;
    if (Res != RTNORM) {
        return ;
    }

    // Create an object which will dynamically show the
    // user the changes as the mouse is moved
    pJig = new CircleJig (basePoint);
    pJig->acquire() ;
    delete pJig ;

    // Get the last object inserted into the DWG
    ads_name lastEnt;
    Res = ads_entlast (lastEnt) ;
    if (Res != RTNORM) {
        return;
    }

    // Get the object id of the last object
```

```
                AcDbObjectId lastId;
                if (Acad::eOk != acdbGetObjectId (lastId,lastEnt)) {
                    return;
                }


                // Open the object for write, getting the object pointer
                AcDbEntity* pLast;
                if (Acad::eOk !=
                        acdbOpenAcDbEntity (pLast,lastId,AcDb::kForWrite)) {
                    return;
                }


                MkrCircle* Mc_Ptr = (MkrCircle*)pLast ;
                if (Mc_Ptr != NULL) {

                        // Create a new circle to take over the place of
                        // the AcDbCircle.
                        AcDbCircle* C_Ptr = new AcDbCircle;
                        C_Ptr->setDatabaseDefaults();
                        C_Ptr->setRadius (Mc_Ptr->radius());
                        C_Ptr->setCenter (Mc_Ptr->center());

                        // Swap the two entities
                        if (Acad::eObjectToBeDeleted ==
                                              Mc_Ptr->handOverTo(C_Ptr)){
                            delete Mc_Ptr ; // All has gone well, it is
                                              // my responsibility to delete
                                              // this
                        }
                        C_Ptr->close();
                }
        }


        // Initialization Function
        void Init_App (void)
        {
            initMkrCircle();
            acrxBuildClassHierarchy();

            // Add some commands to test the AcDb API Library
            acedRegCmds->addCommand("ACDB_TEST",
                                    "CTEST",
                                    "CTEST",
                                    ACRX_CMD_MODAL,
                                    Ctest);

            ads_printf ("\nType CTEST to test new circle command") ;

        }
```

```
// Usual ARX entry points
extern "C" AcRx::AppRetCode
acrxEntryPoint( AcRx::AppMsgCode msg, void* )
{
    switch(msg) {
                case AcRx::kInitAppMsg:
                    Init_App ();
                    break;
                case AcRx::kLoadADSMsg:
                    break;
                case AcRx::kUnloadADSMsg:
                    break;
                case AcRx::kUnloadAppMsg:
            acedRegCmds->removeGroup ("ACDB_TEST");
        default:
                    break;
    }
    return AcRx::kRetOK;
}


//                   -- End of LST_17_1.CPP --


//////////////////////////////////////////////////////////////
// LST_17_2.CPP
//     Illustrating how to create a dictionary of your own in
//     the Named Objects Dictionary (the NOD). The data you
//     place in the NOD is saved in the drawing.

#include <string.h>    // strcmp etc
#include <aced.h>      // registering commands etc
#include <dbsymtb.h>   // AcDbDictionary etc
#include <adslib.h>    // ads_printf, ads_getent etc

// Some pre-1996 versions of AutoCAD require this define
#define TURN_OLD_ACDB_MEMBERS_OFF 1

// Function prototypes
void Dick_Test (void);
Adesk::Boolean Get_Dictionary (AcDbObjectId& D_Id);
void Add_To_Dick (AcDbObjectId& D_Id );
void Del_Entry (AcDbObjectId& D_Id );
void List_Dick (const AcDbObjectId& D_Id);
void Init_App (void);
void Unload_App (void);

// Declare a custom object type derived from AcDbObject...
ACRX_CLASS (Season, AcDbObject)
public:
```

```
        Season (void); // Must have default constructor
        Acad::ErrorStatus dwgOutFields (AcDbDwgFiler* Flr) const;
        Acad::ErrorStatus dwgInFields (AcDbDwgFiler* Flr) ;
        void    Show (void) const;
        void    Set_Days (const int Rainy, const int Sunny) ;
private:
        Adesk::Int32 Days_Of_Rain, Days_Of_Sun ;
END_ACRX_CLASS


ACRX_DXF_CLASS_OBJ_BODY(Season,AcDbObject,0,WEATHER,
                        Dick_Test);

// The constructor, must have no parameters
Season::Season (void)
{
    Days_Of_Rain = 0 ;
    Days_Of_Sun  = 0 ;
}


// This function saves the two data fields of the custom
// class in the drawing
Acad::ErrorStatus
Season::dwgOutFields (AcDbDwgFiler* Filer) const
{
    assertReadEnabled () ;   // Make sure we can read the obj
    Acad::ErrorStatus es;

    // Super messaging...
    es = AcDbObject::dwgOutFields (Filer);
    assert (es == Acad::eOk) ;

    es = Filer->writeItem (Days_Of_Rain) ;
    assert (es == Acad::eOk) ;

    es = Filer->writeItem (Days_Of_Sun);
    assert (es == Acad::eOk);

    return (Acad::eOk) ;
}

// This function retrieves the custom object from the DWG
Acad::ErrorStatus
Season::dwgInFields (AcDbDwgFiler* Filer)
{
    assertWriteEnabled () ; // Make sure we can write the RAM
    Acad::ErrorStatus es;

    // Super messaging...
```

```
    es = AcDbObject::dwgInFields (Filer);
    assert (es == Acad::eOk) ;

    es = Filer->readItem (&Days_Of_Rain) ;
    assert (es == Acad::eOk) ;

    es = Filer->readItem (&Days_Of_Sun);
    assert (es == Acad::eOk);

    return (Acad::eOk) ;
}

// Print what the weather is like
void Season::Show () const
{
                assertReadEnabled();
    ads_printf ("\nDays of sun: %d, of rain %d ",
                Days_Of_Sun,Days_Of_Rain) ;
}

// Set the days of sunshine and days of rain
void Season::Set_Days (const int Of_Rain, const int Of_Sun)
{
                assertWriteEnabled();
    Days_Of_Rain = Of_Rain ;
    Days_Of_Sun = Of_Sun ;
}

// A function to test our seasonal dictionary
void Dick_Test()
{
    int Res;
    char kw[20];
    AcDbObjectId D_Id;

    // Initialise for keyword input
    ads_initget (0, "Add List Delete");
    Res = ads_getkword ("List/Delete/<Add>: ", kw );

    if (Res == RTNONE ) {
        // The user went for the default, Add
        strcpy (kw, "Add");
        Res = RTNORM ; // Ok now
    }

    if (Res != RTNORM) {
        return ;
    }
```

```
        // Get the object Id of the weather dictionary
        if (!Get_Dictionary (D_Id)) {
            ads_printf ("\nError, on opening WEATHER dict.");
            return ;
        }

        if (strcmpi (kw, "Add") == 0) {
            Add_To_Dick (D_Id);
        } else if (strcmpi (kw,"List") == 0) {
            List_Dick (D_Id);
        } else if (strcmpi (kw,"Delete") == 0) {
            Del_Entry (D_Id);
        }
    }


// Initialise D_Id with the object identifier of
// our dictionary, which should be found in the NOD. If it
// is not then we add it. We return true if all goes well
Adesk::Boolean Get_Dictionary (AcDbObjectId& D_Id)
{
    AcDbDictionary* Name_List;

    // Get the names of the objects in the NOD. Name_List
    // will be the thing we get, and we open it for write...
    if (acdbCurDwg()->getNamedObjectsDictionary (Name_List,
                                AcDb::kForWrite) != Acad::eOk){
        ads_printf ("\nUnable to open the NOD.");
        return (Adesk::kFalse) ;
    }

    // Get the particular entry we are interested in
    if (Name_List->getAt ("WEATHER",D_Id) ==
                                        Acad::eKeyNotFound) {

        // Could not find ours, so we will create it...

        AcDbDictionary* Dick = new AcDbDictionary ;

        ads_printf ("\nAdding WEATHER dictionary to NOD.");

        if (Name_List->setAt ("WEATHER", Dick, D_Id)
                            != Acad::eOk ) {
            ads_printf ("\nUnable to add dictionary to NOD.");
            return (Adesk::kFalse) ;
        }
        if (Dick->close() != Acad::eOk ) {
            ads_printf ("\nUnable to close dictionary.");
            return (Adesk::kFalse) ;
        }
```

```
    }
    if (Name_List->close() != Acad::eOk ) {
        ads_printf( "\nUnable to close the NOD. ");
        return (Adesk::kFalse) ;
    }
    return (Adesk::kTrue) ;
}

// Add a Season object to the weather dirctionary
void Add_To_Dick (AcDbObjectId& D_Id)
{
    int             Res,Rainy,Sunny ;
    AcDbDictionary* Dick ;
    char            O_Name[132] ; // Set by the user

    Res = ads_getstring (1,"\nEnter season name:",O_Name);
    if ((Res != RTNORM) || (O_Name[0] == '\0')) {
        Dick->close ();
        return;
    }

    ads_initget (RSG_NONEG,NULL) ; // No negative days
    if (RTNORM != ads_getint ("\nRainy days ? ",&Rainy)) {
        return ;
    }

    ads_initget (RSG_NONEG,NULL) ; // No negative days
    if (RTNORM != ads_getint ("\nSunny days ? ",&Sunny)) {
        return ;
    }

    // User completed the questions, create a new season

    if (acdbOpenObject (Dick, D_Id, AcDb::kForWrite) !=
                        Acad::eOk ) {
        ads_printf ("\nError opening dictionary for write.");
        return ;
    }

    Season* S_Ptr = new Season ;

    S_Ptr->Set_Days (Rainy,Sunny) ;
    S_Ptr->Show ();

    AcDbObjectId Obj_Id ;

    if (Dick->setAt (O_Name,S_Ptr,Obj_Id) != Acad::eOk ) {
        ads_printf ("\nError adding new entry to dict.");
        Dick->close();
```

```
            return ;
        }

        if (S_Ptr->close() != Acad::eOk ) {
            ads_printf ("\nFailed to close new object.");
            Dick->close();
            return ;
        }
        if (Dick->close() != Acad::eOk ) {
            ads_printf ("\nFailed to close dictionary.");
            return ;
        }
}

// List the objects in the WEATHER dictionary
void List_Dick (const AcDbObjectId& D_Id )
{
    AcDbDictionary * Dick;

    if (acdbOpenObject (Dick,D_Id,AcDb::kForRead )
                                            != Acad::eOk ) {
        ads_printf ("\nUnable to open dictionary to read.");
        return ;
    }
    ads_printf ("\n");

    // Use this iterator to go over the entries
    AcDbDictionaryIterator* i;

    for (i=Dick->newIterator(); !i->done(); i->nextElement()){

        ads_printf ("\nName: '%s',   ",i->name());

        AcDbObject* Obj;

        if (acdbOpenObject (Obj,i->objectId(),AcDb::kForRead)
                                            != Acad::eOk ) {
            ads_printf ("Unable to open entry"
                                    " object for reading.\n") ;
        } else {

            // The following lines just to show that the
            // custom object is just like an AcDb object
            AcDbHandle Obj_Handle ;
            char H_Str[20] ;

            Obj->getAcDbHandle (Obj_Handle) ;

            Obj_Handle.getIntoAsciiBuffer (H_Str) ;
```

```
                    ads_printf (" Id %lx, handle %s, class %s,",
                             i->objectId(),H_Str,Obj->isA()->name()) ;


                    // Show what we are really interested in
                    ((Season*)Obj)->Show() ;
                    Obj->close();
            }
    }

    delete i ; // Destroy the iterator

    if (Dick->close() != Acad::eOk) {
        ads_printf ("\nError closing dictionary.");
    }
}

// Delete an entry from the WEATHER dictionary:
void Del_Entry (AcDbObjectId& D_Id)
{
    int Res ;
    AcDbDictionary* Dick ;
    char O_Name[132];

    // Open the dictionary for write, get the pointer
    if (acdbOpenObject (Dick, D_Id, AcDb::kForWrite)
                                        != Acad::eOk ) {
        ads_printf ("\nUnable to open dictionary for write" );
        return;
    }
    Res = ads_getstring (1,"\nName of entry"
                            " to remove: ",O_Name);

    if ((Res!=RTNORM) || (O_Name[0] == '\0')) {
        return;
    }

    if (Dick->remove (O_Name) != Acad::eOk ) {
        ads_printf ("\nError removing dictionary entry.");
    }

    if (Dick->close() != Acad::eOk) {
        ads_printf ("\nError closing dictionary.");
    }
}

void Init_App (void)
{
```

```cpp
    acedRegCmds->addCommand ("CHAP17",
            "DICK","TRACY",
            ACRX_CMD_MODAL,
            &Dick_Test);

    // initSeason() ; // old version
     Season::rxInit() ; // Add to (register with) run
                        // time hierarchy

    acrxBuildClassHierarchy (); // Rebuild with Season

    ads_printf ("\n********************************");
    ads_printf ("\nType DICK to test dictionary app.");
    ads_printf ("\n********************************");
}

void Unload_App (void)
{
    acedRegCmds->removeGroup ("CHAP17");
}

extern "C" AcRx::AppRetCode
acrxEntryPoint (AcRx::AppMsgCode msg, void*)
{
    switch( msg ) {
        case AcRx::kInitAppMsg : Init_App() ; break;
        case AcRx::kUnloadAppMsg : Unload_App() ; break;
    }
    return (AcRx::kRetOK) ;
}

//                 -- End of LST_17_2.CPP --
```

DXF, the drawing exchange format

18

18.1 Introduction

Sometimes it is necessary to transfer data created in your AutoCAD application to another program or another computer. If your program and the program you want to communicate with under the Windows-95 operating system *both* use DDE then this is a possible method. This is often not the case and this is where DXF comes in.

Another possible use of DXF is to analyse the structure of a drawing "by hand", when you are debugging. Since the format is simple ASCII it is possible to read a print-out of it. This can be helpful in understanding how AutoCAD stores its data. This is only a really sensible option in the case of very small drawings or on small sections of large ones.

You may ask "Why not use the AutoCAD file format?" The answer is simple: the AutoCAD file format is not publicly available, and Autodesk does not guarantee that the file format is constant. The format has had many revisions, large and small, during the history of AutoCAD. DXF on the other hand is well documented and widely used and understood. The revisions and additions of the DXF format are also documented.

By the way, the DWG format is not kept "secret" for fear of opening up the format to third parties, but because Autodesk do not want to have to support every DWG format ever created, and they want to be free to change it as the like. It is possible to buy programs and libraries from third parties which read and support DWG files, but they are usually one version behind the current version of AutoCAD, and if there are any problems with these programs or libraries Autodesk can in no way be held responsible. The DXF file format is on the other hand fully supported.

If you really must use the DWG format you should investigate the following two products: AutoLook and Amadeus, both produced by Kovac Software (see Appendix F for the address). Kovac Software have reverse-engineered the .DWG file format and provide these two products to allow your program to read and write .DWG files without having to be in AutoCAD. This reverse engineering is not illegal by the way, just very difficult.

For the programmer it is worthwhile saying that, especially with Release 13 onwards, incorporating a *general* DXF reader (and, to a lesser extent, writer) in a program is not easy. You should think of DXF as a useful format for file exchange where the entities are simple as in lines, polylines, circles ellipses and so on.

This chapter covers how to use the DXF commands in AutoCAD, the DXF format, the differences between DXF in Release 13 and previous releases and shows two example programs for reading and writing DXF files. The arbitrary axis algorithm for the compact representation of flat objects in three-dimensional space is also explained. For very detailed explanations of DXF fields see Appendix D.

18.2 Using DXF files

18.2.1 The DXFIN and DXFOUT commands

DXF is a straightforward ASCII file format which contains *all* the information needed to create or represent a standard 2D or 3D AutoCAD drawing. It is used widely in DOS, Windows (3.1, NT and 95), on the Macintosh and in UNIX. In AutoCAD the commands to use are DXFIN and DXFOUT. ASCII DXF files have the extension *.DXF, binary DXF files have the extension *.DXB.

DXFIN reads in a DXF file created by AutoCAD or another program. For example you would like to edit some solid models created in a mechanical modelling program by a colleague who does not use AutoCAD. Your colleague uses the "create DXF file" command of his program, and gives you the resulting file, for example "MODEL.DXF". You can read "MODEL.DXF" into AutoCAD with the DXFIN command.

If you are bringing in the DXF file into an already existing drawing then only part of the file will be read in. As explained later this may or may not be important to you. However, to make sure that you get ALL the data for the DXF file open a new drawing with *no prototype* and make sure that the first thing you do is the DXFIN command.

DXFOUT is used to write a DXF file. An example of its use is the reverse of the above situation; you have edited the model and would like to give it back to your colleague. You use the DXFOUT command to create the file, say "MODEL1.DXF" and give the resulting file to you colleague. Now he can use her favourite (non AutoCAD) modeller (maybe on a Macintosh or UNIX platform) to view and adjust the changes you made. Most programs which can write DXF files should also be able to read them, though it is not always the case. Many programs which can read DXF files *cannot* write them. For example desktop publishing programs need to read DXF files to be able to use them as technical illustrations, but they do not usually have the capability to write them.

The prompt which appears after you have chosen the filename to write the DXF file will be something like this:

```
Enter decimal places of accuracy (0 to 16 / Entities / Binary
<6>)
```

This gives you the possibility to
1 change from the default accuracy of the DXF ASCII file from 6 decimal places to some other value
2 save only entities which you select (using the normal AutoCAD selection mechanism)
3 save the file as a binary DXF, which preserves full accuracy of the drawing, is smaller than ASCII binary files, but difficult to read by humans and simple DXF programs; in keeping with the rest of this chapter the idea is to keep things simple, so binary DXF files are not covered; it is also more probable that DXF reading programs (desktop publishing and other CAD programs) are able to read ASCII DXF files rather than binary ones; the binary format was introduced in Release 10.

18.2.2 The DXFIX program

DXFIX.EXE is an Autodesk program to allow later versions of AutoCAD to produce DXF files readable by earlier versions, for example to allow a DXF produced by Release 13 to be readable by Release 12. This program reads binary and ASCII files, but by default this creates only binary DXF files. You should read the documentation which comes with the program to see how flexible the program is. It will also give you an idea of how difficult it is to produce a fully fledged DXF reading and writing program.

An example command line, to create a Release 12 ASCII DXF file from a Release 13 binary or ASCII source file, is given below.

```
dxfix  -a6  -tdxfix13  test_r13 test_r12
```

The "-a6" flag says "create output as ASCII with 6 decimal places of accuracy"; then there is "-tdxffix13", which means "use the dxfix13.dxt translation file"; finally come the input and output filenames. The translation file is used to convert from Release 13 to Release 12 entities.

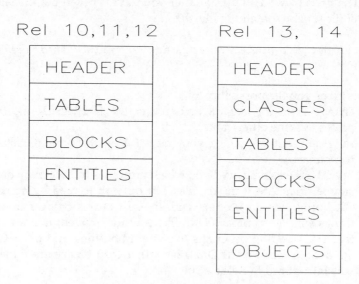

Figure 18.1 The overall format of DXF files

18.3 An example DXF file and some DXF groups

A Release 13 DXF file has seven sections and an end of file marker. The sections are HEADER, TABLES, BLOCKS, CLASSES, ENTITIES and OBJECTS. CLASSES and OBJECTS have been added in version 13, versions 11 and 12 of the AutoCAD DXF format contained had only four sections, see Figure 18.1. For an explanation of what these two new sections are see Chapters 14 and 15. This chapter explains in detail only HEADER, BLOCKS, and ENTITIES sections, since as explained previously writing complete DXF readers and writers is a very heavy programming job. In fact with Release 13 and the fact that third parties can create their own custom entities, some parts of DXF files will be *completely unreadable* by programs which do not have access to third party documentation.

The following is a simple example Release 12 DXF file which has empty HEADER, TABLES, and BLOCKS sections and contains a single line from 0,1,0 to 2,3,0 in the ENTITIES section. Note that the comments on the right do not exist (and should not be placed) in real DFX files.

```
0                      Start of the header section...
SECTION
2
HEADER
0
ENDSEC                 ...end of the header section.
0                      Start of the tables section...
SECTION
2
TABLES
0
ENDSEC                 ...end of the tables section.
0                      Start of the blocks section...
SECTION
2
BLOCKS
0
ENDSEC                 ...end of the blocks section
0                      Start of the entities section...
SECTION
2
ENTITIES
0                      Start of a line description
LINE
8                      The line is on layer...
0                      0
10                     The line's first x coord is
0.000000               0.000000
20                     The line's first y coord is
1.000000               1.000000
30                     The line's first z coord is
0.000000               0.000000
11                     The line's last x coord is
2.000000               2.000000
21                     The line's last y coord is
3.000000               3.000000
31                     The line's last z coord is
0.000000               0.000000
0
ENDSEC                 End of the ENTITIES section
0
EOF                    End of the file.
```

As you can see the DXF format is rather verbose and hard to read. The lines of a DXF file should be read in pairs, and these pairs are called DXF groups. The first line of a group is the group code, and it indicates what sort of data will follow on the second line. Near the end of the above example there is:

```
31
0.000000
```

31 is the GROUP CODE for the z coordinate of the end point of a line, and 0.000000 is the value for that z coordinate.

0 is a very important group code and identifies the start of a section, table entry or entity. The first 4 lines of the example above signify the start of the HEADER section:

```
0                        What follows is a
SECTION                  SECTION
2                        The text value or name of this section is
HEADER                   HEADER
```

Sections end with the group:

```
0
ENDSEC
```

In general group codes identify both *what* the data is, and its *format* (integer, string, floating point etc.). See Appendix D.

Comment lines can be put in like this:

```
999
This is a comment, as is any line which follows the 999 group
code
```

18.4 The DXF sections

18.4.1 The HEADER section

This section contains general information about the drawing, in particular it contains values of the AutoCAD variables. If the file has been made using the AutoCAD DXFOUT command then the values are those found in the drawing itself at the time of the DXFOUT command.

Variable values are stored as 2 groups, 4 lines. Here is an example:

```
9                        What follows is the name of a variable
$OSMODE                  OSMODE is the name of the variable
70                       What follows is an integer value
0                        0 is the value of the integer variable.
```

In other words the above four lines say "OSMODE is currently set to 0".

When your program READS a DXF file produced by AutoCAD with the DXFOUT command you will find that the header is very long, with all the variables specified. You can safely ignore any of the variables which are of no interest to you. It is probably of no interest to you that OSMODE=9 for example. One variable that may be important is ACADVER which tells you which version of AutoCAD created the DXF file. See Appendix C.

When your program *writes* a DXF file to be read by AutoCAD (using the DXFIN command) you can totally ignore any variables which you do not want to set. The simple example file above has in fact an empty HEADER section, but can be read by AutoCAD with no problems.

18.4.2 The TABLES section

This section contains the tables in the drawing. There are tables for linetypes, layers, textstyles, views, User Coordinate Systems, viewports, dimension styles, and application identification tables. The above example has an empty tables section, which is valid.

Even the simplest AutoCAD produced DXF file will have a complex tables section, but as with the HEADER section, your program can probably ignore most of it, skipping all the irrelevant parts and reading only what is necessary.

18.4.3 The BLOCKS section

This section contains block definitions. As mentioned elsewhere, blocks save space in RAM and on disk.

If your application program wants to be sure of reading all the graphic entities in all DXF files you need to be able to read this section.

When your application program *writes* DXF files you can often choose not to use blocks without any great loss of efficiency. For example a DOS program which creates wire-frame fractal mountains would have little use for blocks; there are no copied objects, and thus there is no redundancy to be exploited by using blocks. However a program which uses many repeated symbols, a mapping program for example, should use blocks when writing DXF files to save space. In this example the blocks table would contain the defintions of mapping symbols for churches, triangulation points and so on.

Now this is a tricky point; because handling DXF blocks is not simple, they can be nested, scaled, rotated, on various layers and so on. Before you decide that your program needs to be able to read DXF blocks make sure that is not easier to rewrite the application inside AutoCAD, and let it do all the work!

Writing DXF blocks is much easier than reading them because you have full control over the complexity of the nesting, scaling and so on.

The definition of the internals of blocks follows exactly the same format as that for objects in the ENTITIES section described below. For example, the definition of two lines which form a block will be the same as the definition of the same two lines as two separate entities in the ENTITIES section.

Blocks are inserted into the drawing by putting the INSERT group in the ENTITIES section.

Summarising:

1) Do not use blocks if there is no reason to.
2) When writing (a program to write) DXF files use simple blocks if you would save a lot of disk and memory space by doing so.
3) Expect a lot of work if you want your program to read any DXF file with any sort of blocks in it!

18.4.4 The ENTITIES section

The actual objects (entities) in the drawing are specified in the entities section. This section contains the lines, polylines, circles, text, block inserts, and so on which are actually visible.

18.5 A DXF writing program

The program LST_18_1.C described here illustrates how to write simple DXF files; the entities used are LINEs CIRCLEs and BLOCKs. You can use the functions in the program as components and starting points for you own programs and functions.

Error checking and other refinements have been omitted for the sake of space and clarity, though you should think about adding them in your own version. In particular all entities are placed on layer "0". It would be useful in a mapping program (for example) to contours on one layer and symbols on another.

The program is written using the classical C "function decomposition" method. This makes it more readable, as the sequence of actions is clear and each function is simple. For instance each DXF group, which consist of two lines (group code and group value) has its own function. So DXF strings are written using the function Write_Dxf_String() and DXF integers are written using the function Write_Dxf_Int().

The include file LST__5_1.H, a list of defines for DXF codes, is also used by LST_18_2.C later in this chapter.

The main function of the program simply opens a file with the name passed to it on the command line and creates a DXF file of four sections (omitting the CLASSES section). The name of the file must have the .DXF extension if you want to read it into AutoCAD with the DXFIN command.

The program writes an empty HEADER section (where you many want to place settings for AutoCAD variables in a real program, see the example above of OSMODE), an empty TABLES section, a BLOCKS section with a simple example block definition, and an ENTITIES section with entities defined by the user when the program runs.

In practice AutoCAD's DXFIN will also accept DXF files with only the ENTITIES section, but I have included the other three sections here to illustrate the complete structure. If you have no variables, tables or blocks to write out then you should create a DXF file with only the ENTITIES section.

The `Write_Blocks()` function writes the section header, an example block called "EXAMPLE", and ends the section. The example block is written by `Write_Example_Block()` and shows how to define a block in DXF format. The block definition starts with a BLOCK entity type which is followed by the definition of the layer, flags, and insertion point of the block, all of which are required. The REFERENCED (=64) flag means that the block is referenced in the DXF file (i.e. there is an INSERT "EXAMPLE" group in the ENTITIES section). Next come the actual entities which form the block, in this case a cross mde up of two lines. The end of the block is marked with the ENDBLK group.

Next comes the interactive part of the program: `Write_Entities()`. This simply reads keyboard input looking for C,L,I or ESC keys, corresponding to Circle, Line, Insert and END commands. Both `Write_Dxf_Line()` and `Write_Dxf_Circle()` are self-explanatory, each one writing four groups into the file. Remember that each of these groups corresponds to two lines in the file.

`Write_Dxf_Coords()` writes out the 3 groups (6 lines) to specify a 3 dimensional coordinate. The `Group_Code` specifies the base code of the coordinates. For example a POINT has group codes 10,20,30 (base code = 10), as does the start point of a LINE. The endpoint of a LINE has group codes 11,21,31, (base code = 11) as does the second point of a 3DFACE. The 3rd point of a 3DFACE has group code 12,22,32 (base code 12) and so on.

`Write_Dxf_Real()` writes out the two lines for a real number. Again the `Group_Code` specifies what sort of object the value refers to. Real numbers in a DXF file are used for angles and scale factors and so on. `Write_Dxf_String()` and `Write_Dxf_Int()` follow the same pattern as `Write_Dxf_Real()`.

In all three functions it is possible, and would be advisable, to add error checking on the group codes. For example `Write_Dxf_String()` could check that the group code is within the range 0-9 or 1000-1009, issuing an error message if it is not. This would catch group code errors (easy to make!) early in the debugging process. See Appendix D for ranges of DXF codes.

`Write_Insert()` shows how to insert a block which has already been defined in the BLOCKS section. Note that you can not only specify the position, but also the scaling and rotation of the block inserted. When you test this program remember that DXFIN will read blocks from the DXF file only if the drawing is a new one and has no drawing prototype.

18.6 A DXF reading program

After all I have said about the difficulties of writing programs which read DXF files why would anyone want to try? Here is a practical example. You have written a program that analyses the radiation and conduction of heat from radiators in a room. An architect comes to you with a DXF file of a floor plan of a building he has designed and would like you to help him place the radiators. Assuming that other data exchange methods are not (for various reasons) practicable, you need to add to your program the capability of reading DXF files to get the architect's data.

Now it is obvious that the only data you need to get out of the DXF file is the outline of the floor, so this already simplifies the problem. If we assume that the plan is drawn using LINE entities on layer "0" all you need to do is extract these lines from the DXF file and you have all the data you need. LST_18_2.C is a program that does just that.

So the trick is to find out exactly what you need from the DXF file and ignore the rest.

Near the top of LST_18_2.C is a typedef for groups, Group_t. This is a basic definition and includes an integer for the group code and a string for the group value. A more sophisticated, but unused, version of Group_t is given (in comments) which has a union instead of a string for the group value. This means that integers, real numbers and strings could be stored in a more natural way. LST_18_2.C does not require that level of sophistication.

Then there is main(), practically identical to the main() of LST_18_1.C, except of course that we open the file for reading instead of writing.

The function Skip_To_Entities_Section() reads the file in until it finds the ENTITIES section, ignoring HEADER, TABLES, BLOCKS, CLASSES sections, if they exist. It uses a small function Read_Group which fills in the fields of the Group variable passed to it. The file is read until we find a SECTION with a name ENTITIES.

Next the Print_Lines() function is called, which simply prints out to the screen the start and end coordinates of any lines found in the ENTITIES section. If it finds a LINE entity it calls Print_Line_Coords(), which in turn reads in groups, ignoring most of them and printing only the start and end coordinates. In any actual program these lines would be read in as useful data with which to work.

An important thing to note here is that at both high and low levels of the program the principle "ignore what you are not interested in" is used. This is even more drastic than the "ignore what you do not understand" principle suggested by AutoDESK DXF manuals. At the high level the program ignores all sections it is not interested in. At the low level the LINE groups probably contain the width, type, colour and layer data, and `Print_Line_Coords()` simply ignores these, and looks only for start and end coordinates.

The "ignore what you do not understand" principle ensures that as the DXF format is added to in the coming years, your DXF reading functions will continue to work, though maybe missing new data types.

18.7 Future developments of the DXF format

The DXF format first appeared in 1982, and has changed with the changing versions of AutoCAD ever since, and it will surely change in the future.

Be warned that the Release 13 and 14 DXF specification includes many new entities whose data structure is not documented! The 3DSOLID entity is an example of this. It is an ACIS object (ACIS has replaced AME as the solid modeller in Release 13), and AutoDESK is (currently) not allowed to tell us the structure of the data. It is pure binary data and there is no way of decoding it.

Other entities in the Release 13 and 14 DXF file which may not be documented are entities created by third party applications. It is up to the application developer to decide whether or not to document the DXF representation of his custom entity. Some developers may want to keep the data structure of their entities secret, and so unreadable by a general DXF reader.

It is also possible that the developer has decided not to give a DXF representation of his custom object at all. This means that though the object appears on the screen and in the DWG file, it will be missing from any files created by the DXFOUT command.

18.8 Listings

```
///////////////////////////////////////////////////////////
//   LST_18_1.C
//      Simple (DOS) program to show how to write DXF files
//      which can later be read by the AutoCAD DXFIN
//      command. This program reads line and circle
//      coordinates typed in by the user, and creates a
//      DXF file.
//

#include <stdio.h>
#include <conio.h>
#include "lst__5_1.h"  // DXF codes

/********** Defines and function prototypes **************/

#define ESC_KEY 27
```

```
        void Write_Header (FILE* File) ;
        void Write_Tables (FILE* File) ;
        void Write_Blocks (FILE* File) ;
        void Write_Example_Block (FILE* File) ;
        void Write_Entities (FILE* File) ;
        void Write_Dxf_Circle (FILE* File,
                                double x0, double y0, double Radius) ;
        void Write_Dxf_Line (FILE* File, double x0, double y0,
                                double x1, double y1) ;
        void Write_Dxf_Coords (FILE* File, int Group_Code,
                                double x, double y, double z) ;
        void Write_Dxf_Real (FILE* File, int Group_Code, double x) ;
        void Write_Dxf_String (FILE* File, int Group_Code, char* St) ;
        void Write_Dxf_Int (FILE* File, int Group_Code, int Value) ;
        void Write_Dxf_Insert (FILE* File, double x0, double y0) ;


        int main (int argc, char* argv[])
        {
            FILE* File ;

            // Check command line arguments
            if (argc != 2) {
                printf ("\nUsage:\nwritedxf filename.dxf\n") ;
                return (1) ;
            }

            // Open the file for writing
            File = fopen (argv[1],"wt") ;
            if (File == NULL) {
                printf ("\nError,cannot open %s for write",argv[1]) ;
                return (1) ;
            }

            // The following 4 lines illustrate the overall structure
            // of a release 12 DXF file, readable by release 13.

            Write_Header (File) ;
            Write_Tables (File) ;
            Write_Blocks (File) ;
            Write_Entities (File) ;

            // Write the last 2 lines of the DXF and close it
            Write_Dxf_String (File,ENTITY_TYPE_CODE,"EOF") ;

            fclose (File) ;

            return (0) ;
```

```
}

void Write_Header (FILE* File)
{
    Write_Dxf_String (File,ENTITY_TYPE_CODE, "SECTION") ;
    Write_Dxf_String (File,NAME_CODE,        "HEADER") ;

    // In here you can put code to write AutoCAD variables

    Write_Dxf_String (File,ENTITY_TYPE_CODE, "ENDSEC") ;
}

void Write_Tables (FILE* File)
{
    Write_Dxf_String (File,ENTITY_TYPE_CODE, "SECTION") ;
    Write_Dxf_String (File,NAME_CODE,        "TABLES") ;

    // In here you can put code to write linetypes and so on

    Write_Dxf_String (File,ENTITY_TYPE_CODE, "ENDSEC") ;
}

void Write_Blocks (FILE* File)
{
    Write_Dxf_String (File,ENTITY_TYPE_CODE, "SECTION") ;
    Write_Dxf_String (File,NAME_CODE,        "BLOCKS") ;

    Write_Example_Block (File) ;

    Write_Dxf_String (File,ENTITY_TYPE_CODE, "ENDSEC") ;
}

void Write_Example_Block (FILE* File)
/*
PURPOSE: Writes and example block consisting of two lines
in the shape of an X
*/
{
    Write_Dxf_String (File,ENTITY_TYPE_CODE, "BLOCK") ;
    Write_Dxf_String (File,LAYER_NAME_CODE,  "0") ;

    Write_Dxf_String (File,NAME_CODE,         "EXAMPLE") ;
    Write_Dxf_Int    (File,BLOCK_FLAGS_CODE, REFERENCED) ;
    Write_Dxf_Coords (File,BLOCK_BASE_CODE,  0.0,0.0,0.0) ;
    Write_Dxf_String (File,NAME2_CODE,        "EXAMPLE") ;

    Write_Dxf_Line   (File,-1,-1, 1, 1) ;
    Write_Dxf_Line   (File,-1, 1, 1,-1) ;
```

```
        Write_Dxf_String (File,ENTITY_TYPE_CODE, "ENDBLK") ;
        Write_Dxf_String (File,LAYER_NAME_CODE,  "0") ;
}


void Write_Entities (FILE* File)
/*
Get the user to type in coordinates of circles and lines
and write these entities into the ENTITIES section of
the DXF file.
*/
{
    char Key ;

    Write_Dxf_String (File,ENTITY_TYPE_CODE, "SECTION") ;
    Write_Dxf_String (File,NAME_CODE,        "ENTITIES") ;

    /*
     * Look over the keyboard as the user inputs
     * circles and lines
     */
    do {
        float x0,y0,x1,y1,Radius ;

        printf ("C=circle, L=line, I=Insert, ESC = end\n") ;
        switch (Key=getch()) {
            case 'c' : // Circle
            case 'C' :
                printf ("\nInput x,y,Radius:") ;
                scanf ("%f,%f,%f",&x0,&y0,&Radius) ;
                Write_Dxf_Circle (File,x0,y0,Radius) ;
                break ;
            case 'l' : // Line
            case 'L' :
                printf ("\nInput x0,y0,x1,y1:") ;
                scanf ("%f,%f,%f,%f",&x0,&y0,&x1,&y1) ;
                Write_Dxf_Line (File,x0,y0,x1,y1) ;
                break ;
            case 'i' : // Line
            case 'I' :
                printf ("\nInput insert position x0,y0:") ;
                scanf ("%f,%f",&x0,&y0) ;
                Write_Dxf_Insert (File,x0,y0) ;
                break ;
            case ESC_KEY :
                break ;
            default :
                printf ("C  L  or  ESC please.\n") ;
                break ;
        }
```

```
    } while (Key != ESC_KEY) ;

    // End the entities section
    Write_Dxf_String (File,ENTITY_TYPE_CODE, "ENDSEC") ;
}


void Write_Dxf_Circle (FILE* File, double x0, double y0,
                        double Radius)
/*
Write a CIRCLE group to the DXF File
*/
{
    Write_Dxf_String (File,ENTITY_TYPE_CODE, "CIRCLE") ;
    Write_Dxf_String (File,LAYER_NAME_CODE,  "0") ;
    Write_Dxf_Coords (File,CENTER_CODE, x0,y0,0.0) ;
    Write_Dxf_Real   (File,RADIUS_CODE,Radius) ;
}


void Write_Dxf_Line (FILE* File, double x0, double y0,
                                 double x1, double y1)
/*
Write a LINE group to the DXF File. There are usually 14
text lines to represent a line in an AutoCAD drawing.
*/
{
    Write_Dxf_String (File,ENTITY_TYPE_CODE, "LINE") ;
    Write_Dxf_String (File,LAYER_NAME_CODE,  "0") ;
    Write_Dxf_Coords (File,LINE_START_CODE,x0,y0,0.0) ;
    Write_Dxf_Coords (File,LINE_END_CODE,  x1,y1,0.0) ;
}


void Write_Dxf_Coords (FILE* File, int Group_Code,
                        double x, double y, double z)
/*
PURPOSE: Writes out the 6 lines of a 3D point in a DXF file.
NOTES:   The Group_Code will be 10,11,12 or 13,
         corresponding to the x coordinate of a first second
         third or fourth point. The y and z coord Group_Codes
         are obtained by adding 10 and 20 respectively to
         the Group_Code.
*/
{
    fprintf (File," %d\n%f\n",Group_Code,    x) ;
    fprintf (File," %d\n%f\n",Group_Code+10, y) ;
    fprintf (File," %d\n%f\n",Group_Code+20, z) ;
}


void Write_Dxf_Real (FILE* File, int Group_Code, double x)
/*
```

```
PURPOSE: Writes out the group of a single real number with
         the Group_Code specified.
*/
{
    fprintf (File," %d\n",Group_Code) ;
    fprintf (File,"%f\n",x) ;
}


void Write_Dxf_String (FILE* File, int Group_Code,
                         char* String)
/*
PURPOSE: To write a DXF name or string group. The Group_Code
should always be in the range 0..9
*/
{
    fprintf (File," %d\n",Group_Code) ;
    fprintf (File,"%s\n",String) ;
}


void Write_Dxf_Int (FILE* File, int Group_Code, int Value)
/*
PURPOSE: To write a DXF integer group.
*/
{
    fprintf (File," %d\n",Group_Code) ;
    fprintf (File,"%d\n",Value) ;
}


void Write_Dxf_Insert (FILE* File, double x0, double y0)
/*
PURPOSE: To insert the example block at the given position.
NOTES:   This function assumes default scaling and angle.
*/
{
    Write_Dxf_String (File,ENTITY_TYPE_CODE,"INSERT") ;
    Write_Dxf_String (File,LAYER_NAME_CODE, "0") ;

    Write_Dxf_String (File,NAME_CODE,        "EXAMPLE") ;

    // The insertion point of the block
    Write_Dxf_Coords (File,INS_POINT_CODE,   x0,y0,0.0) ;

    // The scaling factor
    Write_Dxf_Real (File,XSCALE_CODE,1.0) ;
    Write_Dxf_Real (File,YSCALE_CODE,1.0) ;

    // The angle of insertion, in degrees
    Write_Dxf_Real (File,ANGLE_CODE,0) ;
}
```

```
//                        -- end of LST_18_1.C --
//////////////////////////////////////////////////////////////
// LST_18_2.C
//      A program to extract line entities from a DXF file.
//
//

#include <stdio.h>
#include <string.h>
#include "list_5_1.h"  // DXF codes

/* Defines, typedefs and function prototypes */

#define TRUE        1
#define FALSE       0
#define MAX_CHARS 128

// A group consists of two things,
// the group code and it's value
typedef struct {
    int  Code ;
    char Value[MAX_CHARS] ;
} Group_t ;

/*
 A more sophisticated version of Group_t shown below,
 but not used in this program:

typedef struct {
    int  Code ;
    union {
        int    Integer ;
        char*  String ;
        double Real ;
    } Value ;
} Group_t ;
*/

void Skip_To_Entities_Section (FILE* File) ;
void Print_Lines (FILE* File) ;
void Print_Line_Coords (FILE* File) ;
void Read_Group (Group_t* g, FILE* File) ;


int main (int argc, char* argv[])
{
    FILE* File ;
```

```
    // Check command line arguments
    if (argc != 2) {
        printf ("\nUsage:\nreaddxf filename.dxf\n") ;
        return (1) ;
    }

    // Open the file for reading
    File = fopen (argv[1],"rt") ;
    if (File == NULL) {
        printf ("\nError, could not open <%s> for
reading",argv[1]) ;
        return (1) ;
    }

    Skip_To_Entities_Section (File) ;

    Print_Lines (File) ;

    fclose (File) ;

    return (0) ;
}


void Skip_To_Entities_Section (FILE* File)
/*
PURPOSE: Read the file until we get to the ENTITIES section.
Uses the normal "ignore what you do not understand" principle,
skipping HEADER, CLASSES, TABLES, BLOCKS, OBJECTS section, and
taking interest only in the ENTITIES section.
*/
{
    Group_t Group ;
    int     Ent_Sec_Found ;

    Ent_Sec_Found = FALSE ;
    do {
        Read_Group (&Group,File) ;
        if (Group.Code == ENTITY_TYPE_CODE) {
            if (strcmp (Group.Value,"SECTION") == 0) {
                Read_Group (&Group,File) ;
                if (Group.Code == NAME_CODE) {
                    if (strcmp (Group.Value,"ENTITIES")==0) {
                        Ent_Sec_Found = TRUE ;
                    }
                }
            }
        }
    } while (!feof(File) && !Ent_Sec_Found) ;
```

```
        if (!Ent_Sec_Found) {
            printf ("\nERROR,no ENTITIES section found") ;
            exit (1) ;
        }
}


void Print_Lines (FILE* File)
/*
PURPOSE: Read the file, printing all the LINE entities we find
*/
{
    Group_t Group ;

    do {
        Read_Group (&Group,File) ;
        if (Group.Code == ENTITY_TYPE_CODE) {
            if (strcmp (Group.Value,"LINE") == 0) {
                Print_Line_Coords (File) ;
            }
        }
    } while (!feof(File)) ;
}


void Print_Line_Coords (FILE* File)
/*
PURPOSE: Prints out the start end end coords of a line read from
a DXF file
All other data about the line is ignored (LAYER,LINETYPE etc).
*/
{
    Group_t Group ;
    int Printed_1st,Printed_2nd ;

    Printed_1st = FALSE ;
    Printed_2nd = FALSE ;

    // Read in groups until we print find both start and end
points
    do {
        Read_Group (&Group,File) ;
        if (Group.Code == LINE_START_CODE) {
            printf ("\nLine = [%s ",Group.Value) ;
            Read_Group (&Group,File) ;   // Read Y value
            printf (" %s ",Group.Value) ;
            Read_Group (&Group,File) ;   // Read Z value
            printf (" %s] ",Group.Value) ;
            Printed_1st = TRUE ;
        } else if (Group.Code == LINE_END_CODE) {
            printf (" --- [%s ",Group.Value) ;
```

```
            Read_Group (&Group,File) ;    // Read Y value
            printf (" %s ",Group.Value) ;
            Read_Group (&Group,File) ;    // Read Z value
            printf (" %s] ",Group.Value) ;
            Printed_2nd = TRUE ;
        }
    } while (!Printed_1st || !Printed_2nd) ;
}


void Read_Group (Group_t* Group, FILE* File)
/*
PURPOSE: Read in the two lines from the File which
make up a group
*/
{
    char Dummy [MAX_CHARS] ;

    fgets (Dummy,MAX_CHARS-1,File) ;
    Group->Code = atoi (Dummy) ;

    fgets (Group->Value,MAX_CHARS-1,File) ;

    // Strip the \n character from end of line
    Group->Value[strlen(Group->Value)-1] = (char)0 ;
}
//                      -- end of LST_18_2.C --
```

Case studies and applications

19

19.1 Introduction.

In this chapter I present two cases studies of ADS applications that I have personally been involved with, as well as a few details of applications developed by third parties using ADS and ARX. The chapter ends with some ideas (suggestions) for future applications which could exploit the power, flexibility and popularity of the AutoCAD environment.

19.2 Case Study: MOONLITE an interior lighting design package

MOONLITE is a program that I wrote in C and ADS which is used by lighting engineers to layout the lighting scheme of interiors. It is most often used for large environments such as banks, churches and hotels. It was written exclusively for the Martini SpA of Italy, and is used by them internally and by their largest resellers.

The evolution of MOONLITE is interesting, mirroring the evolution of the PC world. Although the final aim was an AutoCAD application (because of the widespread use of AutoCAD) it started as a DOS application created with Borland C V3.0 (16 bit DOS executable). This was simply because I did not want to take on three fairly heavy tasks at the same time. The tasks were:

- writing the lighting calculation functions (ray-tracing and radiosity)
- designing the data structures and storage
- designing the user-interface.

So the DOS version was written to experiment with, and confirm, the correct working of the lighting calculations. There was practically no user interface, the rooms were always rectangular, and the output of the program was isolux contours (lines of equal brightness or luminance) drawn within a rectangle on a VGA graphics board.

If you have some old engineering or scientific program, written in C for DOS or UNIX, which works correctly, but requires a better user interface, you could do worse than consider AutoCAD.

The next step was to port the DOS Borland C program to AutoCAD Release

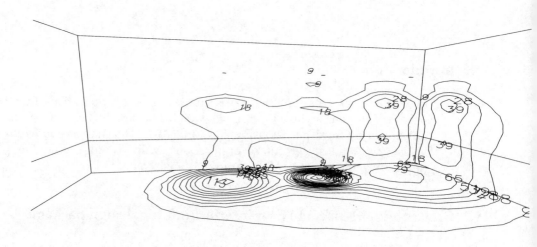

Figure 19.1 Isolux (equal light intenisty) contours in a room

11 (as it was then). I used WATCOM C 386 Version 9.0, after considering Metaware High C. The problem with the latter was that it cost *more* than WATCOM *and* you had the added cost of to buy the PHARLAP Assembler and Linker. In the DOS and AutoCAD world WATCOM has served me well.

It is interesting to note that from this point onwards the "core" of the program, the lighting calculation, changed very very little, and the heaviest work was in creating an easy to use interface and the functions that wrote and read the data from the drawing (the positions and sizes of walls, the positions and angles of the lights and so on). Remember this: your users do not only want a program which gets the right results, but also one which is easy to use.

There is a theory that the user interface to your program should be "consistent", always behaving in the same way. This is fine if you are writing a program from scratch, but AutoCAD has a long history and sometimes you have to stick to traditional ways of doing things. This may mean using old style menus because the users likes them, or at least she is used to them, or even more important she can customise them without any programming knowledge. Slowly you can introduce DCL and Windows dialog boxes. It is a three way compromise between tradition, consistency and modernity.

While visualisation can be achieved relatively easy with widely available graphics libraries, or even using the Windows API (Application Programmers Interface), the functions which open windows and draw lines and print text and so on), what is more difficult to program is the selection and manipulation of objects ("entities" in AutoCAD DWG parlance). This is one of the most

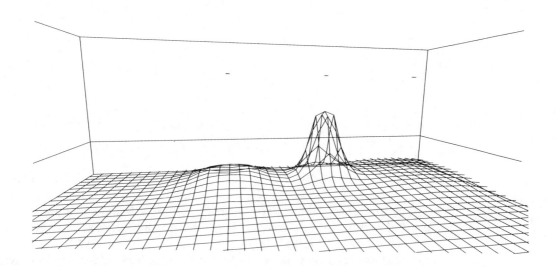

Figure 19.2 A different representation of figure 19.1

important things that AutoCAD offers programmers, *interactivity*.

If you can show the results of a lighting calculation, but you cannot change the angling of a lamp (or switch it off or change it's photometric curve) then the program is not very interactive. Interactivity is a two way process, simple visualization is a one way process. The ADS ads_getxxx() and selection set functions make interactivity easier to program.

Then there is the data storage. The first version of MOONLITE used "attributes" to store data about lamps and wall surfaces. The problem with attributes is that they can only be associated with BLOCK entities. Lines and circles for example cannot have attributes. With Release 12 I moved over to the easier to use (from a programmers point of view) extended data associated to individual entities.

A second part of the MOONLITE was the renderer. This was an Extended DOS application (using WATCOM again) which creates photorealistic images using a mixture of ray tracing and radiosity. Radiosity is becoming important in the architectural simulation world because many lamps these days give indirect or diffuse lighting; that is, they shoot light at a white ceiling which is reflected downwards to give an pleasant and even "skylike" distribution of light. Radiosity is particularly suited to calculate the diffuse interaction of light.

This level of control on the lighting calculation cannot be achieved with the commercially available renderers. Another thing that they lack is the possibility to define of the photometric curve of the lamp.

The AutoCAD application and the Extended DOS application share the same

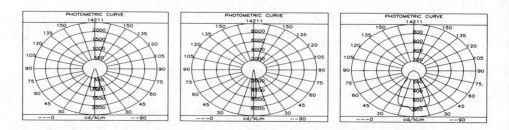

Figure 19.3 Photometric curves of lamps used in Figures 19.1 and 19.2

lighting calculation source code, so that any errors found there are corrected immediately for both programs. This is where the IN_ADS definition helps when compiling for "multiple targets"; see Chapter 3, Section 3.2.2.

The application was never ported to AutoCAD Release 13 for Windows which is rather slow. It *was* ported to AutoCAD Release 12 for Windows using the WATCOM windows extender.

The WATCOM Extended DOS version by the way runs perfectly well with AutoCAD Release 13 for Extended DOS, without even recompiling with the new Release 13 libraries.

MOONLITE consists of 83 C source files and more than 40000 lines of code. The initial development took several months of programming time. It also makes extensive use of DCL dialog boxes and traditional AutoCAD menus.

19.3 Case study: DRILLDWG.EXP, a PCB drill hole plotter

LST_19_1.C was written as a response to the emergency of a colleague who could not read a file which specified the sizes and positions of holes in a PCB (Printed Circuit Board). He needed to see where the holes were and how big they were, after which he could program his numerically controlled drilling machine to do the job.

LST_19.1.C is part of the application which does this, written in a hurry in a few hours. I have tidied it up a little, but not much, for presentation in this book.

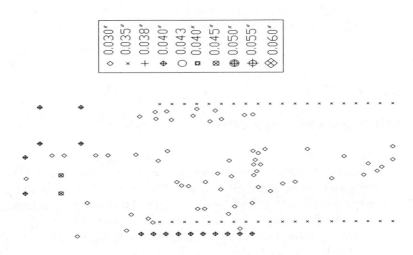

Figure 19.4 A drilling plan for a printed circuit board

I did not have a formal description of the file format, just two examples. It was fairly clear that each line in the file represented a hole; here is a sample:

```
ASCII(0.0300,2.3250,5.9375)
```

The first number is the diameter, the second two are the x y coordinates of the hole. I simply had to read all of the lines from the file in and draw a symbol at the given position.

The program asks the user for the file name (it would have been better to use the file selection dialog box described in Chapter 4 Section 4.6.2), and then calls Read_In_Holes, which opens the file, reads it line by line, putting the data into Holes. When all the data has been read in Draw_Hole is called in a for-loop to plot the holes in the AutoCAD drawing.

I decided to take a short cut with the symbols. Each diameter of hole would have a different symbol, an X or a + or an X with a circle and so on. Each symbol was a block. (I could not use the PDMODE and PDSIZE variables because they apply to *all* points in a drawing). The name of each block would be "HB", standing for Hole Block, plus the diameter of the hole. For example "HB3000" was the Hole Block representing the diameter 0.0300.

I did not have time to write the function to create these symbols (BLOCKs) automatically, so what I did was read the file in several times, and each time Table_Object_Exists failed because an "HBXXXX" block was not present, I created that block by hand. See the comment towards the end of Draw_Hole in LST_19_1.C. Once the particular HBXXXX block was deined I would load the ASCII the file in again and and see of any other blocks had to be defined.

The results can be seen in Figure 19.4

19.4 Back to LISP

19.4.1 LISP2C, going from AutoLISP to C automatically

LISP2C is not an ADS or ARX application, but it is well worth a mention in any book on AutoCAD programming. LISP2C is a program which creates ADS C programs from AutoLISP sources. The idea is that the AutoLISP programmer does not have to throw away years of AutoLISP programming experience to move to C; he simply lets the LISP2C convertor to it for him!

The C code output by this program is pretty grim as regards human readability, but that does not really matter, since it was designed to be read only by compilers.

See Appendix F for the address BASIC, the Slovenian company which created LISP2C.

19.4.2 5 VITAL LISP, a LISP compiler for AutoCAD

Vital LISP is an application *written* in C for ADS, but is is actually a LISP compiler. According to the publicity it is 100% compatible with AutoLISP while being at the same time 5 times faster. It also has an integrated development environment including an editor, a debugger and "watch windows" to see exactly how the variables in your application change while the application is running.

This shows that if you have your own favourite computer and language, and the experience to create a compiler or interpreter for it, you can create your very own programming environment inside AutoCAD. I am sure that there must be some FORTH or SMALLTALK programmers out there who would like to have a try.

You could even invent you own language which is suited to the field in which you work, fine-tuned for heat distribution calculations or the automatic design of fractal buildings.

19.5 GIS, geographical information systems

GIS is an ever expanding field; modern computers massage enormous ammounts of data quickly, and graphics is a way to present the data in an easily understandable way. There are some AutoLISP GIS applications but the data and processing requirements of GIS are so large that ADS and ARX are much better suited.

Some of the things which GIS applications do are:
- display of population densities and movements
- display of the variation in housing and office prices across a city
- analysis of polution data
- analysis of satellite or aerial photographs, often superimposed on vector-based maps
- road, traffic, telephone and electricty cable planning for local authorities
- three dimensional geological analysis for mining and oil drilling
- "geomarketing", where should we advertise which product at which price?
- Route planning

If you intend to write a GIS application using AutoCAD as your base software you should study in detail the commands which handle the input of raster images and the variables which control them:
- TIFFIN, a command which imports TIFF (Tagged Image File Format) images. These images normaly have a .TIF extension. The TIF image format is rather complicated.
- PSIN, a command which imports encapsulated Postscript image files, which have an .EPS extension.
- PSOUT, the reverse of PSIN, saves a drawing as a encapsulated postscript image.
- GIFIN, a command which imports GIF (Graphics Interchange Format) images, which have a .GIF extension. GIF was developed by CompuServe in 1987.

- SAVEIMG, a command which is used to save a drawing file as a raster image. The file can be saved in TGA, GIF, or TIFF formats.
- RIASPECT and other Raster Input variables. See Appendix C.

You should be aware that raster images imported into AutoCAD can occupy a lot of memory space and that in the worst case each pixel in the image becomes a SOLID entity in the drawing. I don't mean SOLID in the terms of a three dimensonal solid, but a 2D SOLID entity used by AutoCAD to represent flat filled objects. AutoCAD tries to group similarly colored pixels into single SOLID entities, this saving space, but making the writing of functions to process the image more difficult.

19.6 Medical engineering CAD

CAD systems which handle three dimensional solid models are ideal for medical CAD. For example the placement of an internal prosthesis can be simulated before an operation. This way the surgeon will have a better idea of what to expect and can plan the operation accordingly.

Reconstruction of three dimensional body scans is also a good application of CAD systems. The virtual reconstructed body can then be rotated, sliced, and viewed and processed at will.

The superposition of x-rays images over drawing files is also possible, with the same commands for raster import explained in the section on GIS above.

One dental application, DentaCAD, by PIAFLORLO is described in CAD User April 1991. It is an application for the design of false teeth, and also controls a laser operated 3D stereolithographic processing cell which creates the plate out of a special plastic!

19.7 Constructing models for virtual reality

It may be hard to believe but one of the hardest and most tedious tasks when a virtual world is made is creating the objects to put in it. Most virtual reality systems have a DXF input function, so you could write an AutoCAD ADS or ARX application to create your worlds semi-automatically and then export them using the DXFOUT command.

For example the creation of a three dimensional landscape with rivers and mountains and trees could be fully automated, and each time the application is run a random number controls the placement, type and number of the objects in the world. This is a way of creating hundreds and thousands of different worlds automatically.

Trees are good subjects for automatic creation; a recursive function could be written which starts from a trunk, and then splits into two or more branches, which in turn split again. The angles of the splits and the length of the successive branches could be parameters into the `Make_Tree()` function, or `Tree` class constructor.

The same argument applies to buildings in virtual reality, though the application would have to be more intelligent than the one which creates landscapes. Natural landscapes may or may not be suited to man, but buildings must be created for human use, and there would have to be well defined constraints on the sort of building created.

An emerging standard for a virtual reality file format is VRML, The virtual reality modelling language. The idea is that models can be transmitted over the Internet and viewed interactively with World Wide Web viewers like Netscape, Mosaic and MS Explorer. An ADS or ARX program to convert between DWG files and VRML files would be very useful to a lot of people.

19.8 Exersises for the reader

Here is a list of possible applicatiions that you might wish to write:
- an application for planning the best motion and path of machine tools
- an application to help set up and sequence stage lighting in theatres
- an application to take the physical dimensions of a transistor and predict and draw the power rating solid
- an application to help in the design of car seats according to modern ergonomic theories
- an application for finite element analysis of mechanical parts
- a garden designers program
- a program which directly controls robot arms and physically creates the object designed by the user with AutoCAD
- AutoCAD interface to machine tools to produce models
- an appliaction to help and guide in the design of moulds
- an application to automtically design origami animals
- an application which designs furniture parametrically, for example an oval table with six round legs to seat between 6 and 8 people, in the style of Guzzini
- an application to design racing yachts (or cars or bikes) and to simulate their performance in various conditions
- an application to visualise the reconstruction of vanished or damaged buildings and cities.

Some of these applications already exist for AutoCAD, some exist; but not for AutoCAD; and some have yet to be written. ARX programmers have another road to fame and fortune, that of inventing a very useful custom object and selling the rights to companies to use it, see Chapter 17. Take up the challenge to invent a better mousetrap! (Ah, I had not thought of that one.)

19.9 Listings

```
//////////////////////////////////////////////////////////
//      LST_19_1.C
//      Plotting the postions and sizes of holes in a printed
//      circuit board.

#include <stdio.h>     // Standard C include file
#include <string.h>    // Standard C include file
#include <math.h>      // Standard C include file
#include <ADSLIB.H>    // Interface to ADS library

#define MAX_HOLES   350
#define MAX_CHARS   200

typedef struct {       // The Hole Type structure
    ads_point Pos ;    // Where
    ads_real  Diam ;   // What size
} Hole_t ;

// Declare functions used in this file
static int funcload   (void) ;
static int dofun      (void) ;
static int ddwg_func (struct resbuf *rb) ;
static int Read_In_Holes (Hole_t* Holes,
                          const char* File_Name) ;
static void Draw_Hole (Hole_t* Hole) ;

// Definition to get an array's element count
#define ELEMENTS(array) (sizeof(array)/sizeof((array)[0]))

struct func_entry {
    char *func_name;
    int (*func) (struct resbuf *);
};

// Define the array of function names & handlers.
static struct func_entry func_table[] = {
        {"C:ddwg", ddwg_func}  // User types "DDWG"
};

/*
 * Here you place the functions:
 *   main()
 *   funcload()
 *   dofun()
 * as defined in LST__2_1.C.
 * You will also need to add the functions
```

```
*     Table_Object_Exists   (Chapter 5 Section 5.4.2)
*     Set_Int_Var           (LST__3_1.C)
*/

// This big global is NOT elegant or efficient, but I
// was in a hurry!
static Hole_t Holes[MAX_HOLES] ;

static int ddwg_func (struct resbuf* inrb)
{
    int    Res,h,N_Holes ;
    char   Name[MAX_CHARS] ;

    // Get all the data required to draw the drill holes...
    Res = ads_getstring (0,"Input name of NCD file:  ",Name) ;
    if (Res == RTCAN) {
        return (RTNORM) ;
    }

    N_Holes = Read_In_Holes (Holes,Name) ;

    // Tell user a bit what is going on
    ads_printf ("\nRead in %d lines from %s.",N_Holes,Name) ;

    // Switch off command echoing to speed up drawing
    Set_Int_Var ("CMDECHO",0) ;

    // Draw N_Holes
    for (h = 0 ; h < N_Holes ; h++) {
        Draw_Hole (&Holes[h]) ;
    }

    // Switch command echoing back on
    Set_Int_Var ("CMDECHO",1) ;

    return (RTNORM) ;
}

static int Read_In_Holes (Hole_t* Holes, const char* File_Name)
{
    FILE*   File ;
    char    Line[MAX_CHARS+1] ;
    int     Count ;
    Hole_t* Hole ;

    File = fopen (File_Name,"rt") ;
    if (File == NULL) {
        PRINT ("\nERROR,Could not open %s.",File_Name) ;
        return (0);
```

```
        }

        Hole  = Holes ;
        Count = 0 ;

        while (!feof(File)) {
            float Diam,x,y ;
            (void)fgets (Line,MAX_CHARS,File) ;   // Get a single line
            if (3 == sscanf (Line,"ASCII(%f,%f,%f),",&Diam,&x,&y)) {
                Hole->Pos[X] =  x ;
                Hole->Pos[Y] = -y ;
                Hole->Diam   = Diam ;
                Count++ ;
                Hole++ ;
            } else {
                ads_printf ("\nERROR, line =<%s>",Line) ;
                return (0) ;
            }
        }
        return (Count) ;
}


static void Draw_Hole (Hole_t* Hole)
{
        char Blockname[MAX_CHARS] ;
        int Res ;

        // Create a hole block whose name is "HBXXX" where
        // XXX is the diameter of the hole
        sprintf (Blockname,"HB%d",(int)(Hole->Diam*10000.1)) ;
        if (Table_Object_Exists ("BLOCK",Blockname)) {
            Res = ads_command (RTSTR,"_INSERT",
                                RTSTR,Blockname,      // Name
                                RT3DPOINT,Hole->Pos,// Position
                                RTREAL,1.0,          // X scale
                                RTREAL,1.0,          // Y scale
                                RTREAL,0.0,          // Angle
                                RTNONE) ;
            if (Res != RTNORM) {
                ads_printf ("\nCould not insert <%s>.",Blockname) ;
            }
        } else {
            // Message to me to create this block by hand!
            ads_printf ("\nBlock <%s> does not yet exist",
                        Blockname) ;
        }
}
//                          -- end of LST_19_1.C --
```

AutoLISP and ADS communications

20

20.1 Introduction

In this chapter I will explain how your ADS application can communicate with AutoLISP, and also how several ADS applications can communicate with each other. We will also see a different way of registering external functions using the ADS functions `ads_regfunc()`

20.2 Communicating with AutoLISP

LST_20_1.C is a function which illustrates how to send and receive parameters to and from AutoLISP functions.

Why would you want to do this? Well, if you are an experienced AutoLISP programmer you may feel that only part of your application needs to be ported to C or C++. For example the user interface and top level parts of your AutoLISP application could be left in AutoLISP, while time-consuming calculations could be ported to C to speed them up.

20.2.1 Sending data from AutoLISP to ADS

The first thing `test_func()` does is get hold of the arguments sent by AutoLISP by calling `ads_getargs()`. This returns a pointer to a result buffer containing the arguments. Here is the function prototype:

```
struct resbuf* ads_getargs (void) ;
```

There can be from zero to many arguments. If there are zero arguments then `ads_getargs()` will return a `NULL` pointer, and in this case our `test_func()` returns straight away. If there are one or more arguments then the result buffer list contains these arguments, and it is printed using `Print_Rb_List()` (see Chapter 5 and LST__5_1.C).

So the arguments of the AutoLISP function are not passed directly to `test_func()`; you have to get hold of them by calling `ads_getargs()`.

Unlike the result lists returned by many other ADS functions, the list returned by `ads_getargs()` is managed by ADS itself, and you do not need to call `ads_relrb()` to release the list. If you need more than temporary access, the data in the list should should make a copy of it.

20.2.2 Returning data from ADS to AutoLISP

To return data to AutoLISP you use the `ads_retxxx()` functions; see Appendix B for a full list. For example you use `ads_retint()` to return an integer, `ads_retreal()` to return a real, `ads_rett()` to return a TRUE value and so on.

In LST_20_1.C the type of return value depends on the type of the first argument passed in to us. This is an arbitrary choice, but it illustrates what is possible. The mapping is as follows:

- If we are passed a real we return a result buffer list consisting of the original real minus 1, a string "A LIST", and a 16 bit integer (i.e. a short) equal to 99). The list is created with the ads function `ads_buildlist()`; see Chapter 6 section 6.3.5.
- If we are passed a string we try to convert it to a real using `atof()`, add one to it and return it with `ads_retreal()`.
- If we are passed a 16 bit integer we add 66 to it and return it with `ads_retint()`.
- Other types are ignored, and we use `ads_retvoid()` to tell AutoCAD we are returning nothing.

20.2.3 Testing LST_20_1.C

If you go into AutoCAD and load this ADS application you should be able to repeat the following sequence of AutoLISP calls (do not type in the comments which follow the // characters!):

```
Command: test                          // as if a normal ACAD cmd
No arguments sent to this function
Command: (c:test)                      // AutoLISP calls C:test
No arguments sent to this function
```

```
Command: (setq ss (ssget))          // AutoLISP
Select objects:                     // select some objects
<Selection set: 1>                  // ss = the selection set
Command: (c:test ss)                // pass test_func a sset
The args are as follows:
(5007 -- pick set 1 25412374)
No return value for this input
Command (c:test "ransen")           // pass test a string
The args are as follows:
(5005 -- "ransen")
1.0                                 // tries to convert to real
Command: (c:test "3.0")
The args are as follows:
(5005 -- "3.0")
4.0                                 // Succeeds
Command: (c:test 1)                 // Pass an integer
The args are as follows:
(5003 -- 1)
67                                  // +66, and return it
Command: (c:test 1.0 2 "three")     // Send 3 parameters
The args are as follows:
(5001 - 1.000)
(5003 - 2)
(5005 - "three")
(0.0 "A LIST" 99)                   // resbuf list returned
```

So you can see that the exchange of parameters between AutoLISP and C is very simple and flexible.

We have defined the name of the function in the listing as "C:TEST", which means that the user can type in "TEST" to call it, see Chapter 2 Section 2.2, but AutoLISP calls it with the name "C:TEST".

20.3 Communication between ADS applications

It is possible for ADS applications to call functions in other ADS applications. This section described LST_20_2.C and LST_20_3.C, the latter contains a function which calls another function in the former.

A quick reminder of the terminology: In ADS and ARX an "external function" is one which can be called (by the user or another application) from outside the application in which it is defined.

First let us look at LST_20_2.C. This is a simple but complete ADS program. The initialisation is quite different from our "template" file LST__2_1.C. First of all there is only one external function defined, Called_Func(), so I have removed the for-loop which goes over all the functions. The switch in the main is different too, it only has one case! I have taken out the RQXUNLD, RQEND, RQQUIT and default cases since they are never used. The RQSUBR (request to run subroutine) case is present but commented out. This is because we use a different function to register the calls available, `ads_regfunc()`:

```
int ads_regfunc (int (*Func)(), int Func_Code) ;
```

`Func()` is the function that we want to register and `Func_Code` is the code number we assigned to the function with `ads_defun()`. Take a look at `funcload()`, `ads_defun()` associates the code number 0 with the string `"Called_Func"`, and `ads_regfunc()` associates the code number 0 with the address of `Called_Func()`. Now AutoCAD and other applications are able to call `Called_Func()` directly without going through the switch in `main()`. That is why RQSUBR need not be handled any more.

Now on to `Called_Func()` itself. Note that we have not defined it as a user callable command, there is no `"C:"` prefix in the call to ads_defun. `Called_Func()` gets the parameters sent to it by using `ads_getargs()`, just as in the LST_20_2.C when interfacing with AutoLISP. It checks that there are at least two arguments, though it ignores any after the second, and it also checks that they are of the right type. If any of these checks fail it returns nothing to the caller with ads_retvoid(), and also tells AutoCAD that things have not gone well by returning RSERR (Request for Subroutuine ERRor). `Func()` in the above function prototype must always return one of these two codes.

If all goes well, `Called_Func()` takes the real value and the string value and adds them together (assuming that the string value contains a real number string). This sum is returned to the caller using `ads_retreal()`, just as we saw with the previous AutoLISP example.

So this is the first "server" program. It compiles to LST_20_2.EXE and is loaded normally.

The second program, LST_20_3.EXE, the "client", is going to call the "server". Let us look at LST_20_3.C. It too has only one function and uses `ads_regfunc()` to register it. This time, however, the function is callable by the user, because the call to `ads_defun()` includes the "C:" prefix.

The function is `Caller_Func()` and has the same code as `Called_Func()`, 0. The two programs run separately and there is no conflict between them because they have the same code. Think of it as AutoCAD's way of saying "the zeroth function of LST_20_2.EXE is `Called_Func()`, and the zeroth function of LST_20_3.EXE is `Caller_Func()`". Had `Called_Func()` been the fifth function it would have had number 4. Both functions have number 0 simply because they are each contained in an ADS program with only one function.

There *would* be a conflict, however, if both functions had the same name, so be careful when you choose the names for your external functions. Choose names that reflect not only what the function does, but what the whole application does. For example two architectural applications HEATLOSS and LAYOUT could both have external functions called CALC. It would be sensible to prefix each one with the application name: HL_CALC and LA_CALC.

Back to LST_20_3.C. We build a result buffer list of the name of the external function that we want to call, followed by just the arguments that `Called_Func()` wants (a real and a string). Then we *invoke* `Called_Func()` with:

```
int ads_invoke (const struct resbuf* Call_Rb,
                      struct resbuf** Reply_Rb);
```

This function invokes an external function defined in another ADS application. The `Call_Rb` argument is a result-buffer list that specifies the external function call, plus any parameters required. The `Reply_Rb` argument is the address of a result-buffer pointer which contains the external function's return values when `ads_invoke()` returns. Note that the second parameter is the *address* of `Reply_Rb`, because `ads_invoke()` will modify it:

```
Res = ads_invoke (Call_Rb,&Reply_Rb) ;
```

If all goes well `ads_invoke()` then we will find the results of `Called_Func()`'s calculation in the first (and presumably only) result buffer. We check the return value and the number and type of the `Reply_Rb` , there should be one real there. If these check out OK we print the result with `ads_printf()`

Finally, when we have finished using them, we free both result buffers with `ads_relrb()`, it being the callers responsability to do this.

Obviously for this mechanism to work you must know the name of the external function you want to call, and the order and type of the parameters it is expecting, and will return. In this simple example `Called_Func()` accepts two arguments and returns only one; it could could easily be more complicated, expecting three arguments and returning seven for example. Argument number and type errors are checked for in both LST_20_2.C and LST_20_3.C, and you would be wise to follow this example.

`Caller_Func()` also assumes that `Called_Func()` is loaded. If it is not `ads_invoke()` will return with an error code and `Reply_Rb` set to NULL .

20.4 Listings.

```
////////////////////////////////////////////////////////////////
// LST_20_1.C
//     Illustraying how to exchange data between ADS and
//     AutoLISP

static int test_func (void)
{
    struct resbuf* In_Rb ; // Will hold what is passed in
```

```
            struct resbuf* Out_Rb ; // Will hold what we return
            ads_real New_Real ;
            short    New_Int ;

            // Get the arguments sent to us
            In_Rb = ads_getargs () ;
            if (In_Rb == NULL) {
                ads_printf ("\nNo args sent to this function") ;
                ads_retvoid () ;   // No args, no return value
                return (RTNORM) ;
            } else {
                // Show the args to the user
                ads_printf ("\nThe args are a follows:") ;
                Print_Rb_List (In_Rb) ;
                ads_printf ("\n") ;
            }

            // Depending on the arg type return something
            // to the caller...
            switch (In_Rb->restype) {
                case RTREAL :
                    // Return a list of values
                    New_Real = In_Rb->resval.rreal - 1.0 ;
                    Out_Rb = ads_buildlist (RTREAL,New_Real,
                                            RTSTR,"A LIST",
                                            RTSHORT,99,
                                            RTNONE) ;
                    ads_retlist (Out_Rb) ;
                    break ;
                case RTSTR :
                    // Return a single real
                    New_Real = atof (In_Rb->resval.rstring) + 1.0 ;
                    ads_retreal (New_Real) ;
                    break ;
                case RTSHORT :
                    // Return a single integer
                    New_Int = In_Rb->resval.rint + 66 ;
                    ads_retint (New_Int) ;
                    break ;
                default :
                    // Do not return anything
                    ads_printf ("\nNo return value for this input") ;
                    ads_retvoid () ;
                    break ;
            }
            return (RTNORM) ;
        }

    //                -- End of LST_20_1.C --
```

```
//////////////////////////////////////////////////////////////////
// LST_20_2.C
//     Showing how ADS applications can communitare with
//     each other using ads_regfunc() and ads_invoke(). This
//     file contains a function Called_Func() which will be
//     called from a function in LST_20_3.C. Obviously both
//     apps have to be loaded for this to work!
//

#include <stdio.h>      // Standard C include file
#include <string.h>     // Standard C include file
#include <ADSLIB.H>     // Interface to ADS library

// Function prototypes
static int funcload (void) ;
static int Called_Func (void) ;

// Entry point
void main (int argc, char* argv[])
{
  short scode = RSRSLT;        // Normal result code (default)
  int stat;

  ads_init (argc,argv);        // Open comms with AutoLISP

  // For-ever loop
  for ( ;; ) {                 // Request/Result loop

      if ((stat = ads_link(scode)) < 0) {
          printf ("\nERROR,stat=%d",stat) ;
          exit(1);  // < 0 means error
      }

      scode = RSRSLT;               // Reset result code

      switch (stat) {

          case RQXLOAD:             // Load & define functions
              scode = funcload() == RTNORM ? RSRSLT : RSERR;
              break;

#if 0
// This case is not need if all your functions are
// registered using ads_regfunc
          case RQSUBR:
              scode = dofun() == RTNORM ? RSRSLT : RSERR;
              break;
#endif
```

```
            case RQXUNLD :
            case RQEND :
            case RQQUIT :
                break ;

            default:
                break;
        }
    }
}


static int funcload (void)
/*
PURPOSE: To tell AutoCAD the names of the functions in
this file. There is only one function in this case and
we use ads_regfunc. Compare this function with the one
of the same name in LST__2_1.C
*/
{
    int Res;

    if (!ads_defun ("Called_Func",0)) {
        ads_printf ("\nads_defun (Called_Func) failure") ;
        return (RTERROR);
    }

    // We have defined the function ok, so now register
    // it with AutoCAD. this will allow a direct call of
    // it from this and other applications using ads_invoke.
    Res = ads_regfunc (Called_Func,0) ;
    if (Res != RTNORM) {
        ads_printf ("\nads_regfunc (Called_Func) failure.") ;
        return (RTERROR) ;
    }
    return (RTNORM) ;
}


static int Called_Func (void)
/*
This simple example shows how a function should behave when
it is called by another ADS function. This function expects
a real number and a string. The string should be a real number
too (e.g. "1002.56"). The sum is calculated and returned
to the caller.
*/
{
    struct resbuf* Rb ;
    struct resbuf* Second_Rb ;
    struct resbuf* Out_Rb ;
```

```
    ads_real Num1,Num2 ;

    // Get args of caller
    Rb = ads_getargs () ;

    // Check that there are two result buffers
    if ((Rb == NULL) || (Rb->rbnext == NULL)) {
        ads_printf ("\nERROR, Called_Func called with "
                    " too few arguments") ;
        ads_retvoid() ;
        return (RSERR) ;
    }

    // Check that the first buffer contains a real
    if (Rb->restype != RTREAL) {
        // First parameter not correct
        ads_printf ("\nERROR, Calc_Func called with bad"
                    " first argument") ;
        ads_retvoid() ;
        return (RSERR) ;
    }

    // Check that the second buffer contains a string
    Second_Rb = Rb->rbnext ;

    if (Second_Rb->restype != RTSTR) {
        ads_printf ("\nERROR, Called_Func called with bad"
                    " 2nd argument") ;
        ads_retvoid() ;
        return (RSERR) ;
    }

    Num1 = Rb->resval.rreal ;

    // Convert string buffer to a real number
    Num2 = atof (Second_Rb->resval.rstring) ;

    // Build a resbuf list with the sum of two numbers
    Out_Rb = ads_buildlist (RTREAL,Num1+Num2,RTNONE) ;
    if (Out_Rb == NULL) {
        ads_printf ("\nERROR. ads_buildlist failed") ;
        ads_retvoid () ;
        return (RSERR) ;
    }

    (void)ads_retlist (Out_Rb) ;

    // No need to release the either Rb or
    // Out_Rb result buffers because it is the
```

```
        // caller's responsibility

        return (RSRSLT) ; // Indicate that a result is returned
}

//                 -- End of LST_20_2.C --

//////////////////////////////////////////////////////////////
// LST_20_3.C
//      Showing how ADS applications can communicate with
//      each other using ads_regfunc() and ads_invoke(). This
//      listing contains a function which calls another
//      function in LST_20_2.C using ads_invoke().
//


#include  <stdio.h>      // Standard C include file
#include  <string.h>     // Standard C include file
#include  <ADSLIB.H>     // Interface to ADS library

// Function prototypes
static int funcload  (void) ;
static int Caller_Func (void) ;

// manin entry point for ADS application
void main (int argc, char* argv[])
{
  short scode = RSRSLT;        // Normal result code (default)
  int stat;

  ads_init (argc,argv);        // Start comms with AutoLISP

  // For-ever loop
  for ( ;; ) {                 // Request/Result loop

      if ((stat = ads_link(scode)) < 0) {
          printf ("\nERROR,stat=%d",stat) ;
          exit(1);  // < 0 means error
      }

      scode = RSRSLT;              // Reset result code

      switch (stat) {

          case RQXLOAD:            // Load & define functions
              scode = funcload() == RTNORM ? RSRSLT : RSERR;
              break;

          default:
```

```
                    break;
            }
      }
}

static int funcload (void)
/*
PURPOSE: See comments in LST_20_2.C
*/
{
   int Res;

   if (!ads_defun ("C:Caller_Func",0)) {
        // C: makes the function callable from the command line
        ads_printf ("\nads_defun (Caller_Func) failure") ;
        return (RTERROR);
   }

   // We have defined the function ok, so now register it.
   Res = ads_regfunc (Caller_Func,0) ;
   if (Res != RTNORM) {
        ads_printf ("\nads_regfunc (Caller_Func) failure.") ;
        return (RTERROR) ;
   }
   return (RTNORM) ;
}

static int Caller_Func (void)
/*
This function "knows" that another function exists in
another ADS application called  "Called_Func". The other
function sums a real number and a string. We call it
and print the result
*/
{
    struct resbuf* Call_Rb ;
    struct resbuf* Reply_Rb ;
    int Res ;

    // Some test values
    ads_real Num_1   = 3.3 ;
    char      Num_2[] = "4.4" ;


    // Create the function name and argument list
    Call_Rb = ads_buildlist (RTSTR,"Called_Func", // funcname
                             RTREAL,Num_1,         // first arg
                             RTSTR,Num_2,          // 2nd arg
                             RTNONE) ;
```

```
        if (Call_Rb == NULL) {
            ads_printf ("\nERROR. ads_buildlist failed") ;
            return (RTNORM) ;
        }

        // Call the other function, his reply will be in Reply_Rb
        Res = ads_invoke (Call_Rb,&Reply_Rb) ;
        if (Res != RTNORM) {
            ads_printf ("\nBad call to ads_invoke, Res=%d. ",Res) ;
            return (RTNORM) ;
        }

        if ((Reply_Rb == NULL) || (Reply_Rb->restype != RTREAL)) {
            ads_printf ("\nBad reply") ;
            return (RTNORM) ;
        }

        // Got what seems to be a good reply, print it
        ads_printf ("\n%6.3f + %s = % 6.3f",Num_1,Num_2,
                    Reply_Rb->resval.rreal) ;

        ads_retvoid () ;

        // The callers responsability to release these....
        ads_relrb (Reply_Rb) ;
        ads_relrb (Call_Rb) ;

        return (RTNORM) ;
}

//                  -- End of LST_20_3.C --
```

Appendix A Compilers and environments.

A.1 Introduction

This appendix explains how to compile ADS and ARX applications with various compilers and in various environments. Although this is a very technical and nitty gritty appendix; it also has a very personal slant because I will only cover compilers and environments that I have personally used. If the compiler and or environment you are using is not in this appendix you will be able to find the information you need, plus BAT files, MAKe files and so on on the AutoCAD CD-ROM.

If you are just starting with C and AutoCAD you may want to use the Extended DOS version of AutoCAD, either Release 12 or Release 13. Compiling for Windows-95 (or Windows 3.1 or Windows NT) just adds complications to what will already seem a very complex process.

This appendix covers:

- Borland C\C++ V 3.x for AutoCAD Release 12 DOS platform.
- Borland C\C++ V 4.x for AutoCAD Release 12 DOS platform.
- Watcom C\C++ V 10.0 for AutoCAD Release 12 DOS and Release 13 DOS.
- Microsoft VC++ V 2.2 and V4.0 for AutoCAD Release 13, Windows-95.

In this appendix I use "DOS" and "Extended DOS" interchangeably; from AutoCAD Release 11 onwards only Extended DOS was supported

If you have the source code disk then read README.TXT on the disk for the latest information about compilers settings and header files.

A.1.1 Installing the compiler and AutoCAD

When you install the compiler, remember to install any ADS files if asked. Your compiler may ask you, or let you indicate via a menu, whether or not you want the ADS support files. When using 16 bit DOS compilers (For example Borland 3.x or Borland 4.x) make sure you install the LARGE memory model.

Before trying to compile a program for AutoCAD you should try compiling and running normal programs with your compiler, to be sure that the compiler is installed correctly. You should also be sure that AutoCAD is running correctly by making, saving and changing a few simple drawings.

When installing AutoCAD you may be asked if you want to include ADS or ARX files, reply "YES".

Only when you are sure that both AutoCAD and your compiler are working correctly should you try to compile ADS or ARX programs.

A.2 ADS for Extended DOS AutoCAD Release 12

Many users of AutoCAD are still using Release 12 rather than Release 13 (even though they may have bought the Release 13 upgrade) because Release 12 creates much smaller drawing and DXF files and is faster. For this reason I am including some general information on compiling for Release 12 Extended DOS. Release 12 does not have ARX support, you can only write *pure ADS* applications.

A.2.1 Compiling the example programs

Go into your AutoCAD directory (usually something like C:\ACAD12) under the ADS subdirectory (e.g. C:\ACAD12\ADS) and you will find several BAT files. Each BAT file is for compiling the example AutoCAD ADS applications with a different compiler. You will also find the sources of C programs used as examples. The BAT files will have names more or less as follows:

- makesamp.bat   -- compiles examples using Metaware High-C
- msc6samp.bat   -- compiles examples using Microsoft C V 6.0
- tbc3samp.bat   -- compiles examples using Turbo-C V 3.0
- w90samp.bat   -- compiles examples using Watcom V 9.0
- z30samp.bat   -- compiles examples using Zortech V 3.0

The actual number of BAT files and their names may vary, but by reading the contents of the BAT file you can find out which is for your compiler.

Once you have found the name of the BAT file for your compiler, type it in at the DOS command line (e.g. TBC3SAMP.BAT for Borland C version 3). The BAT file should compile all the C files in the directory, creating .EXE of .EXP files which you can later load into AutoCAD as applications.

Depending on the compiler, an EXE or an EXP file will be created. The difference is that .EXE files are 16 bit applications while .EXP files are 32 bit applications. Borland-C will create 16 bit EXE files while WATCOM will produce 32 bit EXP files.

Note also that though Borland creates 16 bit ADS applications they run perfectly well within Release 12 Extended (32 bit) DOS environment.

32 bit applications are required when the program is complicated and/or uses lots of memory, while 16 bit applications are for small and medium scale projects. Sometimes, however, 16 bit applications run faster than 32 bit applications, so it is not always true that "bigger is better".

Release 12 gave you the choice to make 16 or 32 bit ADS applications. In Release 13 you can only make 32 bit applications. 32 bit Release 12 applications for the DOS environment may well run without recompilation for Release 13 DOS, for example my Watcom 10.0 applications compiled for Release 12 Extended DOS run without modification on Release 13 Extended DOS. This is called "binary compatibility" between versions.

If you have problems when you run the BAT file the most likely cause is a missing or incorrect SET in the BAT file. First make sure that you are using the correct BAT file, if you are using a Watcom compiler it is no good running the Borland BAT file. Sometimes the BAT files will give you a message like:

"You must edit z30samp.bat and change the variable ZORTECH"

This means that the BAT file has been written assuming that (for example) your ZORTECH environment variable is (for example) C:\ZORTECH, but maybe you have installed it in (for example) D:\ZTEK. If you get that message change the BAT file appropriately, changing the line

```
set ZORTECHc:\zortech
```

to

```
set ZORTECH=d:\ztek
```

When the BAT file of your choice has finished you should confirm that the EXE or EXP files have been created; list the executables using the normal

```
DIR *.EXE
```
or

```
DIR *.EXP
```

and make sure that the time and date of the files listed are now and today. You should find many files, the one we are interested in is MAGNETS.EXE or

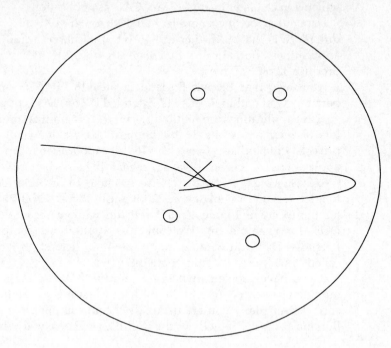

Figure A.1 Output of the magnets ADS applications

MAGNETS.EXP, which is a simulation of a free hanging pedulum swinging between some magnets on the floor. Once you have found MAGNETS.EXE go up one directory into your AutoCAD directory (e.g.C:\ACAD12), run AutoCAD, and open a new drawing. Now you are ready to load and run the pendulum simulation.

Type

```
(xload "ads/magnets")
```

at the AutoCAD command line (remembering the bracket and the quotes) then type "demo" and then "run". You will see on the screen a plan view of the magnets on the floor and the path of the pendulum as it swings erratically between them; see Figure A.1.

For those of you who already program in AutoLISP the (xload) command will be seem very similar to the AutoLISP (load) command, and in fact (xload) load an ADS executable into AutoCAD just as (load) loads an AutoLISP program.

The opposite of (xload) is (xunload). This takes the application out of the memory of AutoCAD. There is no need for the full path name, just the name of the application. For example

(xunload "MAGNETS")

will take MAGNETS.EXE out of AutoCAD, and the commands defined within MAGNETS.C will no longer be available to the user.

Note the sense of the slash in (xload "ads/magnets"), it is a *forward* slash, not a backward slash. The backward slash is commonly used in DOS and Windows to define directories, but in AutoLISP and ADS the forward slash is used. Another way of loading the program would be:

```
(xload  "/ACAD12/ADS/MAGNETS")
```

If you want to use the backward slash you have to use two of them:

```
(xload  "\\ACAD12\\ADS\MAGNETS")
```

There are several example programs in the ADS directory, supplied by Autodesk to illustrate ADS programming techniques. Try compiling and loading the others to see what happens. The examples do not always give instructions when loaded, so you may have to read the corresponding C source files to understand the commands to type in at the AutoCAD command line. For example MAGNETS.C contains descriptions of other commands, apart from the "DEMO" and "RUN" described above.

A.3 Compiling for Release 12 Extended DOS

The Borland compilers use an IDE (Integrated Development Environment) where you set the compiler options via easy to use menus and dialog boxes. Borland C/C++ V3.x has both DOS and Windows IDE. When compiling for ADS it is best to use the DOS IDE to save entering and exiting from Windows. Unfortunately the Borland C/C++ V4.x *only* has the Windows IDE, which means that if you have to run AutoCAD under DOS you have to enter and exit Windows every time you want to change your program.

If you have both versions of Borland C/C++ (3.x and 4.x) you may find it best to use version 3.x DOS hosted IDE for AutoCAD DOS ADS applications. If you own only version 4.x you have no choice, you *have* to use the Windows-based IDE.

The Watcom compiler version 9.x does not have an IDE, while version 10.x has an IDE which runs only under Windows. Both versions 9.x and 10.x have a DOS command line style too, and I suggest using this when compiling for AutoCAD ADS. This means that options are selected either on the command line, in the make file or via DOS SET environment variables.

Release 12 ADS programs are made up of 2 basic components, your own code and the ADS library. There is a different ADS library for each compiler. In what follows it is assumed that you have installed AutoCAD in C:\ACAD12. Substitute the actual installation directory (for example D:\AC) if this is is not C:\ACAD12 on your PC.

For BORLAND 3.x (using DOS hosted IDE):

1) Open a project file called for example BC3_ADS.PRJ (Project->Open Project).
2) In the project file window and add BC3_ADS.C (Project->Add Item).
3) Add also the ADS library C:\ACAD12\ADS\TBCADS3.LIB as you did in step 2.
4) In the INCLUDE options add the C:\ACAD12\ADS path. This will allow the compiler to find the include file ADSLIB.H (Options->Directories->Include).
5) Set the 80186/80286 option on (Options->Compiler->Advanced Code Generation).
6) Set the f287 floating point co-processor on (Options->Compiler->Advanced Code Generation).
7) Choose the LARGE memory model (Options->Compiler->Code Generation).
8) In the DEFINES option of the compiler add "__TURBOC__ PROTOTYPES=1 RMADS ADS" (Options->Code Generation->Defines).

Some versions of the appload dialog do not accept EXE as an extension to an application (they want LSP or EXP). If you have trouble loading the program with the appload dialog box you will have to use the manual version:

```
(XLOAD "\\BOOKSRC\\BC3_ADS\\BC3_ADS")
```

which should work.

For BORLAND 4.x (using Windows hosted IDE)

1) Open a new project using the PROJECT, NEW PROJECT menus.
2) The NEW TARGET dialog box will pop up, type BC4_ADS as the name of the new project.
3) Still in the NEW TARGET dialog box select the platform to be DOS STANDARD, the LARGE memory model, deselect the class library, select the RUNTIME library, and select floating point, not emulation.
4) The IDE will create a default project with BC4_ADS.EXE as the target (i.e. the program we want to create, the target we want to "build") and BC4_ADS.CPP as the (only) source component. We will be programming in C (not in C++ yet!), so we should delete any BC4_ADS.CPP entry (using the DEL key) and add a new node called BC4_ADS.C using the INS key.

5) Now you want to add the second component of the program, the ADS library. Go into the project window and hit the INS key to add a component, and type in C:\ACAD12\ADS\TBCADS3.LIB.
6) Now get the OPTIONS PROJECT dialog box, and in DIRECTORIES add C:\ACAD12\ADS in the DIRECTORIES INCLUDE text box.
7) In the COMPILER DEFINES add TURBOC=1 PROTOTYPES=1 RMADS ADS

For WATCOM 9.0 and 9.5 (DOS command line):

First you have to create the ADS library compatible with Watcom 9.0 and 9.5 and AutoCAD. This involves converting the Autodesk library to a format compatible with WATCOM. The chapter "Creating an AutoCAD Application" in the Watcom "Users Guide" explains what to do. Here is a summary:

1) Go into the \ACAD12\ADS dir (or your equivalent).
2) Type "REN WCADS.LIB OWCADS.LIB".
3) Type "WLIB WCADS +OWCADS.LIB".

Now you have \ACAD12\ADS\WCADS.LIB compatible with Watcom and AutoCAD ADS. You need do the above procedure once only.

To create the EXP ADS application:
1) Add the C:\ACAD12\ADS path to the SET INCLUDE statement of your AUTOEXEC.BAT file. For example if it was originally: "SET INCLUDE=C:\WC10\H" then you should change it to : "SET INCLUDE=C:\WC10\H;C:\ACAD12\ADS"
2) Use the following to compile and link:
    WCL386 /l=ads /fpi87 /3s \ACAD12\ADS\WCADS.LIB LST__2_1

Now you should do a "DIR *.EXP" to see if the LST__1_1.EXP was created.

All three of the above procedures create "pure ADS" applications.

Release 12 also has example BAT files to create EXE files for Release 12 under Windows. Using Microsoft and Borland it is possible to create 16 bit Windows ADS applications; using Watcom 9.01 you can create 32 bit Windows applications.

A.4 ADS for Windows 3.1 and Windows-95, AutoCAD 12, WATCOM 9.0

Though this situation may seem rather out of date it is worth at least mentioning. It is possible to create a 32 bit ADS application which runs under Windows 3.1 and Windows-95 with AutoCAD 12. You need WATCOM 9.0X. I use WATCOM 9.01, and the documentation recommends WATCOM 9.01d.

What actually happens is that the WATCOM compiler/linker compiles for Windows and links to its own 32 bit extender designed to run under 16 bit Windows. You should see the example files in the AutoCAD 12 for Windows directories and the WATCOM manual for creating 32 bit applications to run in 16 bit Windows.

A.5 ADS for Windows 3.1 and Windows-95, AutoCAD 12, Borland 3.X,4.X

This environment is well illustrated in the BAT and make files which come under the AutoCAD 12 for Windows ADS directory. The files generated are 16 bit executables.

A single BAT file (BCMAKE.BAT) recompiles all the examples, and uses WINADS.BC as the makefile. The make file uses the command line compiler and linker. The resulting executables can be loaded into AutoCAD 12 for Windows using the normal (XLOAD ...) command or from the applications dialog box (found under the FILES menu).

Using the Borland C 4.0 IDE you should get the example programs going first. Here are some hints:

- Create a new IDE project as a 16 bit Windows executable.
- In Project Options Directories add the C:\ACADWIN\ADS (or whatever it is called on your installation) path in the include and library edit boxes.
- In Project Options Compiler Defines add the three lines "ADS=1   WIN=1 __MSC=1".
- In Project Options 16bit Compiler Processor set the 80286 radio box.
- In Project Options 16bit Compiler Memory Model set the Large radio box.
- In Project Options Linker and Project Options Librarian switch off all case-sensitive buttons.
- Remember to Add Node the .RC file and the .DEF file of the example you are recreating. If you do not do this the application will compile but you will get an "EXE is invalid" message when you load it into AutoCAD for Windows. If you start writing your own ADS programs basing them on the example remember to copy the .DEF and RC files supplied by Autodesk (for example ADS_PERR.DEF and ADS_PERR.RC) into your working directory.
- In the DEF file change the NAME to MYAPP (or whatever).

•In the RC files change the single string in the STRINGTABLE to MYAPP (or whatever). Unfortunately you may have to reset the computer if you get the invalid EXE message before you are able to compile it again.

• Add C:\ACADWIN\ADS\WINADS.C as a source node in the project window.

• Add C:\ACADWIN\ADS\WINADSBC.LIB as a library in the project window.

A.6 ADS for Releases 12 & 13, DOS, using WATCOM 10.X

As mentioned previously, applications compiled with Watcom Release 10.x should run without modification with both Release 12 and Release 13 DOS platform AutoCADs. Using Watcom 10.0 and 10.5 you can create 32 bit pure ADS applications for use with Extended DOS AutoCAD.

If we imagine that you have two C source files and one CPP source file (SPIRA.C, SPIRA1.CPP and SPIRA2.C) and one include file (SPIRA.H) which form your ADS application you should create a make file (called SPIRA.MAK) as shown below:

```
#               WATCOM C 10.0 / 10.5 make file for
#               S  P  I  R  A  .  E  X  P
#               running under DOS Extended AutoCAD ADS
#               This version 8th July 1995

wcc_options  = /fpi87 /fp5 /s /4s /w3 /we /dIN_ADS=1 /za /fo=OBJ\
no_ansi_options  = /fpi87 /fp5 /s /4s /w3 /we /dIN_ADS=1 /fo=OBJ\

#SPIRA.EXP depends on (is created from) the following 3 OBJ files
SPIRA.EXP : OBJ\SPIRA.OBJ OBJ\SPIRA1.OBJ OBJ\SPIRA2.OBJ
        WLINK @SPIRA.LNK

#SPIRA.OBJ depends on SPIRA.C and SPIRA.H
OBJ\SPIRA.OBJ : SPIRA.C SPIRA.H
  WCC386 $(wcc_options) SPIRA.C

#Note here we use a CPP file and a different command line
OBJ\SPIRA1.OBJ : SPIRA1.CPP SPIRA.H
  WPP386 $(no_ansi_options) SPIRA1.CPP

OBJ\SPIRA2.OBJ : SPIRA2.C SPIRA.H
  WCC386 $(wcc_options) SPIRA2.C
```

The make file is simply a listing of all the components of the program and what you have to do to create the program. Each indented line is an instruction of what to do if the first component of the line above is older than any of the rest of the files on the line. Comment lines start with #.

The link file (called SPIRA.LNK) should look like this:

```
system   ads
name     SPIRA.EXP
file     OBJ\SPIRA OBJ\SPIRA1 OBJ\SPIRA2
library  \ACAD12\ADS\WCADS
```

Here we are assuming that the Watcom ADS library is called WCADS is in the directory \ACAD12\ADS. To make the above example you simply type:

```
WMAKE -f MYPROG.MAK
```

at the DOS command line. See your Watcom linker and make manuals for more details.

One word about how to call CPP functions from C files and vice versa. Imagine that SPIRA.C contains a call to Cpp_Func() in SPIRA1.CPP, which in turn calls a C_Func() in SPIRA2.C. In this case Cpp_Func() is declared in SPIRA.C as:

```
extern void Cpp_Func (void) ;
```

In SPIRA2.CPP we have to allow Cpp_Func() to be visible to C files. We also have to let C functions be called from the CPP file. This is done as shown in the code fragment below:

```
// PART OF SPIRA1.CPP...

// Make the Cpp_Func visible in (callable from) other C files
extern "C" void Cpp_Func (void) ;

// Make the C_Func visible in (callable from) this CPP file
extern "C" void C_Func (void) ;

void Cpp_Func (void) { C_Func() ; }  // Cpp_Func calls C_Func
```

So extern "C" is used in both directions, C to CPP and CPP to C. When mixing C and CPP programming another thing to be aware of is that usually the macro _cplusplus is defined automatically by the compiler when it is compiling a CPP file. This can help you conditionally compile parts of your header files.

A.7 ADS for Release 13 under Windows-95 compiled using Visual C++

In this section I assume that you are using Windows-95 as both your *development platform* (where you create the application) and as the *target platform* (where you run the application). The procedure for creating and running applications under Windows NT will be similar.

You should find your AutoCAD directory:

\ACADWIN\ADS\SAMPLE

This contains several BAT and MAKE files. The file which compiles the examples is called WINADS.BAT, and you will have to change the following statements of WINADS.BAT:

```
set MSVCPATH=\msvc32s
set ADSINC=\acadr\ads
set ADSLIB=\acadr\ads
```

These lines tell the Microsoft compiler where library and header files are located. For example if you had installed the compiler in D:\MSCV2 and AutoCAD Release 13 in E:\ACADWIN you should change the above three lines as follows:

```
set MSVCPATH=D:\MSCV2
set ADSINC=E:\ACADWIN\ADS
set ADSLIB=E:\ACADWIN\ADS
```

I recommend copying WINADS.BAT to another file, MYWINADS.BAT (in the same directory) and making the changes there. In this way if you make a mistake you can go back to the original WINADS.BAT and start again.

Once you have make the changes you can compile which ever of the sample programs by going into a DOS shell of Windows-95 and typing:

```
mywinads fact
```

or

```
mywinads magnets
```

which will compile fact.c and magnets.c respectively. These are pure ADS applications, and are loaded with (xload). You can then run your Windows AutoCAD and load the programs with:

```
(xload "E:/WINADS/ADS/SAMPLE/FACT")
```

or

```
(xload "E:/WINADS/ADS/SAMPLE/MAGNETS")
```

You should look at the source files of these applications to see what they do and how to use them. Magnets.c is explained briefly in section A.2.1 above.

A.8 rxADS for Windows-95 compiled using Microsoft Visual C++

Currently the directories of this environment are included only on special CD-ROMs supplied by AutoCAD to developers, though they may be included on the standard AutoCAD Release 13 CD-ROM by the time you read this. You should contact your closest AutoCAD office if you cannot find them on your CD-ROM.

The directory will be something like \ACADWIN\ADSRX\SAMPLE, and you should find MKARX.BAT. Copy it to your own BAT file (named for example MYMKARX.BAT) and change the following lines to suit your own environment. If the original lines are:

```
set MSVCPATH=\msvc
set ARXPATH=\acad\adsrx
set ADSINC=\acad\ads
```

you should change them to

```
set MSVCPATH = D:\MSVC20
set ARXPATH  = E:\ACADWIN\ADSRX
set ADSINC   = E:\ACADWIN\ADS
```

In the above we assumed that you have installed AutoCAD Release 13 for Windows in E:\ACADWIN, and your Microsoft compiler is in D:\MSVC20. Now type

```
MYMKARX fact
```

in DOS (or a DOS shell) and fact.arx will be created. If there is an error you should check the modifications you made to the three lines above. To make sure that it is *your* version of fact.arx look at the date and time of fact.arx. If it does not correspond to today and now delete fact.arx and run the bat file again.

Now when you run AutoCAD you can load fact by typing:

```
(arxload "/ACADWIN/ADSRX/SAMPLE/FACT")
```

Note that you have to use *(arxload)*, not (xload), because this is an *rxADS* application, not a pure ADS application. Alternatively you can load the application with the "appload" dialog box, found under the "TOOLS->APPLICATIONS..." menu.

If you are running under a DOS shell of Windows-95 you may get the following message:

```
This program cannot be run in DOS mode.
```

If this happens you should change the properties of the DOS shell as follows:

1. click the *right* mouse button on the "START" button of Windows-95
2. click the *left* mouse button on "OPEN"
3. Open the "programs" group
4. find the icon for the shell which you use to run the compiler
5. click the right button on this icon and select "properties"
6. under "PROGRAM->Advanced Program Settings" click the check box for "Prevent MS-DOS based programs from detecting Windows" so that it is *not* checked.
7. close everything and run the batch file from the shell as before.

A.9 ARX for Windows-95 compiled using Microsoft Visual C++

As with rxADS (explained in the previous section) the directories of this environment are currently included only on a special CD-ROM supplied by Autodesk to developers. They should be included on the standard AutoCAD Release 13 CD-ROM by the time you read this.

ARX is very new and is changing quite quickly. You should find that while the principles which are explained in this book always hold, some changes in macro names and object member names may occur. Thus it is very important that you base your programs on examples supplied by Autodesk. Bear in mind that currently only Microsoft Visual C++ is supported by Autodesk for ARX development. Be sure to read the README file which come with AutoCAD relative to ARX development.

I will refer to the two versions of Microsoft Visual C/C++ used as MSVC 2.2 and MSVC 4.0. As of writing, only MSVC 2.2 is *officially* supported by Autodesk, though the programs can be compiled and run correctly with MSVC 4.0. No doubt official support will move to MSVC 4.0 in time. To get the MSVC 4.0 to link the ARX libraries you will have to click the FORCE option under Build->Settings->Customise->Force file output. It is likely that as you link you will get several "multiply defined symbol" errors. The force option makes the linker ignore these errors and create an ARX file anyway. Be careful using FORCE though, see errors LNK2001, LNK4006, LNK4088 and LNK4098 in section A.7.2 below.

I am concentrating on Windows-95 rather than Windows NT because it is likely that for the near future Windows-95 will outsell Windows NT. To be honest it is probably better to *develop* on Windows NT, even though your application will run under Windows-95.

Your first step in creating your own ARX programs is to see if you can compile at least a few of the examples supplied by Autodesk. You do this working in the Visual C++ IDE (Integrated Development Environment). The examples will be found in a directory with a name something like \ACAD\ARX\SAMPLE. Simply load the make file for each example (which will have the extension .MAK) and rebuild it (under the "project" menu of MSVC 2.2, under the "Build" menu of MSVC 4.0). As with rxADS check the time and date of the resulting .ARX file, and if it is old delete it and rebuild it.

If you are bringing an example written for MSVC 2.2 into the MSVC 4.0 environment you should open the project workspace (File->Open Workspace) with the 2.2 .MAK file. MSVC 4.0 will ask if you want to convert it into a version 4.0 project, you reply "YES" of course.

Now you can load the program into Autocad using "(arxload)" or "appload", see the previous section.

When you have succesfully got some ARX example programs to run you can start to write your own. If you copy an example to another directory, changing the file names in the process, remember to change the following :

- The output file name of the project. This is under "project-->settings->link->Output Filename". ("Build->settings->Link->General->Output Filename" in MSVC 4.0.) If the example you copied was "ARXEX3" and the program you are creating is called "MYARX", then the output filename should be changed from "ARXEX3.ARX" to "MYARX.ARX".
- The definition file (e.g. ARXEX3.DEF). This definition file will contain the line "LIBRARY ARXEX3", which you should change to "MYARX". If you forget to include the definition file in the project, and the project compiles and links successfully, when you try to load it into AutoCAD you may well get the following error message: "File MYARX.ARX is invalid."
- The link options. In the MSVC 2.2 "project->settings->link->object library modules" edit box there will be a long list of libraries which need to be linked to your ARX application. The ones supplied with the example may have relative path names. If you are developing your application in a different directory from the example you will have to change these relative path names to absolute ones. In MSVC 4.0 the menu is "Build->Settings->Link->Object/library modules".
- The include directories. You may have to insert the full path to the include directories required by ARX applications by changing the edit box "project->settings->c++->preprocessor->additional include directories". In MSVC 4.0 the menu is "Build->Settings->Preprocessor->Additional include directories", or under "Tools->Options->Directories->Include files".

A.10 Tips and tricks for ADS and ARX programmers

A.10.1 Searching for examples and class definitions source files

Often when a new programming language or library arrives a good way of really start getting to grips with it (apart from reading books of course!) is to look at example programs and include files. The same goes for newcomers to established languages.

I have found that in DOS the Borland utility "grep" (which should be supplied with your Borland compiler) is useful for searching files for keywords. For example if you want to search the current directory and all sub-directories for the word "ads_textpage" you should type in the following command:

```
grep -id ads_textpage *.C
```

The -i option says "ignore case" and the -d options says "look in sub-directories too.

If you have not purchased a Borland compiler you may be able to find other free versions of "grep" on the Internet or in programmers shareware CD-ROMs.

If you are using Microsoft Visual C++ then there is a utility very much like grep but using a dialog box, "Find in Files". It is under the "SEARCH" menu of the IDE of MSVC 2.2. Just to keep you on your toes, under MSVC 4.0 it is under the "FILES" menu.

Again, users of Visual C++ should become familiar with class browser to find and read ARX class declarations. The MSVC 4.0 class browser is much better than the MSVC 2.2 one.

A.10.2 Debugging with Visual C++

To be able to debug an ARX program you should activate the debugging options in the project settings and also change the executable program to run. This latter you can do with the menu sequence: "Project->Settings->Debug->Executable For Debug Session" (MSCV 2.2) or: "Build->Settings->Debug->Executable For Debug Session" (MSVC 4.0) . In this edit box type the full pathname of the AutoCAD executable, for example:

```
E:\ACADWIN\ACAD.EXE
```

When you have compiled the program use the menu sequence Debug->Go. The compiler may well say "No debug information in ACAD.EXE, proceed anyway?", reply YES. Of course you will be able to debug *your* application but not AutoCAD itself!

A.10.3 Common Visual C++ errors

Here are a few errors (and tips about how to eliminate them) which you may encounter as you start playing with ARX and Visual C++ programming. Some of them are simple, but having them listed here may save you time when you start programming ARX.

- C1083: If the include file cannot be found add its path using "Tools->Options->Directories->Include->Add"
- C2229, C2296: Bad left or right operands. What seems a perfectly correct C++ statement is not because you are forgetting (for example) that radius is a function of a class, not a field of a structure:

```
New_Rad = C_Ptr->radius * 1.5 ; // !!!WRONG!!!
New_Rad = C_Ptr->radius() * 1.5 ; // Ok
```

- LNK1104: Cannot find a library because it may not be in the library path. Add it using "Tools->Options->Directories->Libraries->Add" or "Project->Settings...->Link->Object/Library Modules". In MSVC 4.0 this dialog is under "Build->Settings->Link->General".
- LNK1104: Maybe you are compiling and linking an executable already in use, (xloaded) or (arxloaded) by AutoCAD. You will have to (xunload) it or (arxunload) before you can re-create the exe or arx.
- LNK1120, LNK2001: Unresolved externals: If the names of the functions unresolved are functions which you have written maybe you have misspelled them (either in the call or in the definition). If you do not recognise the names of the unresolved functions there are probably some missing library files. You can add the missing library following the sequence outlined for the error LNK1104 above. To find out *which* library file is missing you will have to search the standard AutoCAD ARX or ADS include files. *Never* ignore this warning by using the FORCE option, see LNK4088 below. If you are mixing C and CPP files you may need to use the extern "C" way of showing C functions to CPP files and vice versa. See A.5 above.
- LNK2001: See also LNK1120. May occur also if you are mixing C and CPP files, remember to use the extern "C" way of importing variables from C into CPP files.
- LNK4006: Muliply defined malloc, free and so on. This could happen if you are using MSVC 4.0 with ARX libraries and examples designed for MSCV 2.2. According to Autodesk you can ignore it. If you are using MSVC 2.2, however, you should try to get rid of these errors.
- LNK4070: This may happen when you are creating an ARX DLL by copying and renaming the files from an example program. It means that what the DLL thinks it is called (inside itself) and its real filename are different. You should put this right by making sure that they are both the same:
  1) "Project->Settings...->Link->Output" ("Build->Settings.." in MSVC 4.0) filename in General subsection should be set to ARX0.ARX for example.
  2) The definition (.DEF) file should have a line: LIBRARY ARX0

- LNK4088: An ARX has been created because you used the FORCE option, but it may not run, and you could even crash AutoCAD. You can ignore this warning only if you do *not* get warning LNK2001 described above. The linker may suggest that you use the use /NODEFAULTLIB flag; you can safely ignore this suggestion.
- LNK4098: Caused for similar reasons to LNK4006 above. Ignore if you are using MSVC 4.0 with ARX for MSVC 2.2.
- U1073: This may occur if you have misspelled a source file name, so it does not exist. For example I added "TEST" to a make file (TEST.C and TEST.OBJ), but in fact I should have added "TESTS".
- Internal Link Error during Pass 1. This bug caused me hours of fun, no ARX file was generated. It seems to be a problem when creating any DLL files (not just ARX files) when you have made a CDROM installation of MSVC 4.0. If this is the case you should try installing the software on your hard disk. The problem went away when I tried it. It may not be a problem under Windows NT.

Appendix B Catalog of ADS functions

B.1 Introduction

This chapter gives an alphabetical listing of ADS functions. Functions described in the text are present here only as a function prototype, with a reference to the chapter and section where the function is covered.

Often the functions return a value to indicate if they finished successfully or not. Usually success is indicated with RTNORM, and usually if the return value is not RTNORM you should look at the environment variable ERRNO to find out what went wrong. To aid you in understanding errors Autodesk supplies two files, OL_ERRNO.H, a symbolic listing of error codes, and ADS_PERR.C, which prints a text description of a given error code. You can adapt these two files to your own program.

B.2 Alphabetical listing of ADS and ARX function

```
void acrx_abort (const char * format, ...);
```
(ARX only.)

Terminates an ARX application, and prompts the user to save changes to the drawing up to the beginning of the current command. The `acrx_abort()` function takes a format control string and optional additional arguments (the prompt) like `ads_printf()`. Calling this function will cause AutoCAD to exit with a message "INTERNAL ERROR". See Chapter 13, Section 13.10. You should probably never call this function.

```
void ads_abort(const char *str);
```

(ADS only)

See Chapter 13, section 10. This prints an error message and abandons your application.

`int ads_action_tile(ads_hdlg hdlg, char *key, CLIENTFUNC tilefunc);`

    See Chapter 12, section 12.3.4.

`int ads_alert (const char *str);`

    See Chapter 4, section 4.6.1.

`ads_real ads_angle (const ads_point pt1, const ads_point pt2);`

    See Chapter 7, section 7.2 and remember that the angle measured is the angle between the UCS X axis and the line from `pt1` to `pt2`. The answer comes back in *radians*, not degrees. If you are using a Microsoft compiler for Release 12 then you should be aware that `ads_angle()` has problems and you should use another method. If your are not using Microsoft for Release 12 and you get strange results try setting the UCS to the WCS.

`int ads_angtof (const char Str, int Unit, ads_real* v);`

    Converts `Str`, which represents an angle in the display format specified by unit, into an `ads_real`. The result is in radians and put in v. Unit specifies the units in which the string is formatted, see Appendix C, the AUNITS values. If Unit is -1 AUNITS itself is used. Try the AutoCAD command UNITS to get an idea of the possibilities.

    If successful RTNORM is returned.

`int ads_angtos(ads_real v, int Unit, int prec, char *str);`

    The complementary function of angtof (see above), converts an ads_real to a string. Units is either -1 (where AUNITS is used) or a valid AUNITS value.

`int ads_arxload (const char* App);`

    Loads an ARX module into an ADS or ARX application. Corresponds to the AutoLISP (arxload). This function returns an error code when App does not specify an existing file or when the file cannot be loaded for some reason.

`struct resbuf* ads_loaded (void);`

    Returns a pointer to a list of the external ARX applications that are currently loaded. The name of each application is returned as a string in its own result buffer, resval->rstring. When no external applications are loaded, `ads_arxloaded()` returns NULL. You should call `ads_relrb()` to release the list that `ads_arxloaded()` returns, unless of course the list is NULL.

`int ads_arxunload (const char* App);`

    Unloads an ARX module from an ADS or ARX application. Corresponds to the AutoLISP (arxunload). This function returns an error code when App does not specify a loaded ARX application or when the program to be unloaded has

AutoCAD Programming in C/C++

dependents. "Dependents" are applications which need the ARX module you are trying to unload.

struct resbuf* ads_buildlist (int rtype, ...);

See Chapter 6, section 6.3.5, and for creating blocks see Chapter 8, section 8.5. For returning lists to AutoLISP see Chapter 20, section 20.2.

int ads_cmd (struct resbuf *rbp);

Very similar to the ads_command() function, see Chapter 3, section 3.2, but uses a list of result buffers (maybe created with ads_buildlist()). It is better than ads_command() because the list of commands can be built at run-time, but has the disadvantage that it runs a little slower.

WARNING: Can only be called only in ARX when AutoCAD sends the message kInvkSubrMsg to the application.

int ads_command (int Rtype, ...);

See Chapter 3, section 3.2.

WARNING: Can only be called only in ARX when AutoCAD sends the message kInvkSubrMsg to the application.

int ads_cvunit (ads_real old_val, const char *oldunit,
**   const char *newunit, ads_real* new_val);**

Converts an ads_real, in units specified by oldunit, into the units specified by newunit, and sets new_val to the converted value. The oldunit and newunit arguments are strings matching the unit specifications found in the file acad.unt. RTNORM is returned if all goes well, else RTERROR.

int ads_defun (const char *sname, short funcno);

See Chapter 2 section2.2.

struct resbuf* ads_dictnext (ads_name dict, char *sym, int rewind);

Scans the dictionary specified by dict, and returns either the next entry (if rewind is 0 or the first entry (if rewind is 1) as a result-buffer list. This function is similar to ads_tblsearch(), see Chapter 5, section 5.4.

A dictionary is a container object that is like a symbol table. An optional DXF sequence stores the current object's dictionary handle, so arbitrary drawing database objects can be attached to any object in a drawing. For more on dictionaries see Chapter 17.

WARNING: Only one global iterator is maintained for this function. If the program passes a new dictionary name to ads_dictnext() after traversal of the dictionary has begun, the original program pointer location is lost.

To obtain the master entity name use ads_nameobjdict().

The dict argument is an entity name, unlike the tblname string argument to ads_tblsearch(). The sym string can be in lowercase, ads_dictsearch() will convert it to uppercase before passing it to AutoCAD.

When `ads_dictnext()` is called repeatedly, it normally returns the next entry in the specified table each time. If there are no more entries in the dictionary, `ads_dictnext()` returns NULL. It never returns deleted dictionary entries.

If the `rewind` argument is nonzero, the dictionary is rewound and `ads_dictnext()` returns the first entry in the dictionary. When you begin scanning a table, supply a nonzero rewind argument to rewind the table and find its first entry.

A dictionary entry is returned as a linked list of result buffers with DXF group codes and values.

When `ads_dictnext()` fails, it sets the system variable ERRNO to a value that indicates the reason for the failure.

struct resbuf* ads_dictsearch (ads_name Dict, char* Sym, int Setnext);

Scans the dictionary specified by `Dict` for `Sym`. If it finds `Sym`, it returns its entry as a result-buffer list. The Setnext argument specifies whether the `ads_dictsearch()` call will affect the next call to `ads_dictnext()`. This function is similar to `ads_tblsearch()`.

To obtain the entity name of symbol table entry, call `ads_tblobjname()`.

The `Dict` argument is an entity name, unlike the tblname string argument to `ads_tblsearch()`. The `Sym` string can be in lowercase; `ads_dictsearch()` will convert it to uppercase before passing it to AutoCAD. To obtain the master entity name, call `ads_nameobjdict()`.

If `ads_dictsearch()` finds sym, it returns the entry as a linked list of result buffers with DXF group codes and values. If it does not find sym, `ads_dictsearch()` returns NULL. It cannot find dictionary entries that have been deleted.

Normally, `ads_dictsearch()` has no effect on the order of entries retrieved by `ads_dictnext()`. However, if `ads_dictsearch()` is successful and the `Setnext` argument is nonzero, the `ads_dictnext()` entry counter (for the specified table) is adjusted so that the next `ads_dictnext()` call will return the entry that follows the one returned by `ads_dictsearch()`.

If `ads_dictsearch()` fails, look at ERRNO for the reason for the failure.

ads_real ads_distance (const ads_point pt1, const ads_point pt2) ;

See Chapter 7, section 7.2.

int ads_distof(const char *str, int Unit, ads_real *v);

Converts `str`, containing a real value in the display format specified by unit, into an ads_real, v. If Unit is -1, the variable LUNITS is used (see Appendix C), or else it should be a valid value for LUNITS. Try the AutoCAD command UNITS to get the hang of AutoCAD units.

If successful RTNORM is returned.

ads_done_dialog(ads_hdlg hdlg, int status);

See Chapter 12, section 12.3.6

```
int ads_draggen(const ads_name ss, const char* Prompt, int Cursor,
        int (*Scnf), (ads_point pt, ads_matrix mt),
        ads_point p);
```
Allows the user to drag a selection set. Prompt should be a prompt message or NULL. The cursor argument specifies the form of cursor to display while the user drags the selection set. Scnf is a pointer to a function called whenever the user moves the cursor. Keyword entry can be setup as with ads_getxxx() functions (see Chapter 4).

Cursor should be :

- 0 = Display the normal crosshairs
- 1 = Don't display a cursor (no crosshairs)
- 2 = Display the entity-selection target cursor

The Scnf is a pointer to a function with a prototype (name can be different):

```
int my_sample_fcn(ads_point pt, ads_matrix Matrix);
```

Scnf() is called every time the user moves the cursor, Scnf() should change Matrix, which will then be used to change the selection set.

The Scnf() function must return:
- RTNORM if Matrix is modified
- RTNONE if Matrix is not modified
- RTERROR if it wants to terminate the transformation. In this case ads_draggen() returns RTCAN.

ads_draggen() distinguishes between a keyword and arbitrary input by returning RTKWORD when it receives a keyword and RTSTR for arbitrary input. Use ads_initget() to enable these options.

The return values are:
- RTNORM = success
- RTERROR = failure, look at ERRNO to find out why.
- RTCAN = user cancelled or if Scnf() returned RTERROR.
- RTNONE, RTKWORD, or RTSTR set up by a prior call to ads_initget().

```
int ads_end_list (void);
```
See Chapter 12, section 12.3.9

```
int ads_entdel (const ads_name ent);
```
See Chapter 6, section 6.4.3.

```
struct resbuf* ads_entget (const ads_name ent);
```

See Chapter 6, section 6.2, to get data about entities in the drawing, see Chapter 8 section 8.8 to getting data about components of block definitions.

struct resbuf* ads_entgetx (const ads_name ent,const struct resbuf *apps);
See Chapter 11, section 11.5.

int ads_entlast (ads_name result);
See Chapter 5, section 5.2 and Chapter 8, section 8.3.

int ads_entmake (const struct resbuf *ent);
See Chapter 6 section 6.4.1 and Chapter 8 section 8.4. See also LST__6_6.C.

int ads_entmod (const struct resbuf *ent);
See Chapter 6, section 6.4.2, and LST__6_7.C.

A good way of using this function to modify entities is in co-operation with ads_entget(). ads_entget() will return a result buffer list, you scan this list looking for the property of the entity you want to change (the radius of a CIRCLE or the color of a LINE for example). Once you have found the result buffer you are looking for you modify its value (changing the radius or color in the above example) and then pass the modified list to ads_entmod() .

Summarising:
1. Get result buffer of entity to modify using ads_entget() .
2. Modify part(s) or result buffer as you require.
3. Call ads_entmod() with modified result buffer.

int ads_entnext (const ads_name ent, ads_name result);
See Chapter 6, section 6.2, Figure 6.1, and Chapter 8 sections 8.3 and 8.8.

int ads_entsel (const char *str, ads_name entres, ads_point ptres);
See Chapter 8, section 8.6. If the user selects a complex entity, the polyline or block header is returned. Compare with ads_nentselp(), which returns the nearest block attribute or polyline vertex.

int ads_entupd (const ads_name ent);
This function redraws (updates) the specified entity. If ent is in a block definition you need to do a REGEN to see the changes. On success RTNORM is returned, else RTERROR, you should look at ERRNO to find the reason for the failure.

void ads_exit (int status);
(Pure ADS only.)
See Chapter 13, section 13.10, a clean way of suddenly leaving a C ADS program. Does *not* cause AutoCAD to exit, just the pure ADS application from which it is called.

void ads_fail (const char* Str);

See Chapter 13, section 10, prints a gentle error message, but does not exit from your application.

int ads_findfile (const char* Fname, char* Result);

Searches for the file specified by Fname, and sets Result to its full path name.

For safety (and portability with operating systems with long file names, e.g. Windows-95) Result should be 512 characters long. You can qualify Fname by specifying a drive or directory prefix otherwise the search is made according to the current AutoCAD library path see Chapter 2, section 2.4.1. A return value of RTNORM means the file has been found, else RTERROR is returned.

void ads_free(void* buff);

(New in Release 13.)

Releases memory allocated by ads_malloc(), ads_realloc(), or ads_calloc() pointed to by buff. See your C library manual for the standard C function free().

int ads_get_attr_string (ads_htile tile, char *attr,
                          char *value, int len);

See Chapter 12, section 12.3.5.

int ads_getangle (const ads_point pt, const char *prompt,
                 ads_real* result);

See Chapter 4, section 4.2.

char* ads_getappname (void);

Returns the file name of the current ARX application, needed to unload the application. In the ADS program environment, the global variable ads_appname() is referenced to return the file name.

struct resbuf* ads_getargs (void);

See Chapter 20, section 20.2.

int ads_getcname(const char* Cmd, char **Result);

Gets the localised or English name of an AutoCAD command after allocating memory for it. The first parameter is a constant symbol set to the name of a command, such as the following:

const char *cmd = "LINEA";   // Italian LINE command

The length of Cmd must be 64 characters or less. Result contains a pointer to the destination for the string result, which for the Italian command LINEA would be LINE.

Returns RTNORM if all goes well, otherwise an error code.

int ads_getcorner (const ads_point Base, const char* Prm, ads_point Rslt);

See Chapter 4, section 4.2.

```
int ads_getdist (const ads_point Base, const char* Prm, ads_real* Rslt);
```
  See Chapter 4, section 4.2.

```
int ads_getfiled (const char *title, const char *default,
                  const char *ext, int flags, struct resbuf *result);
```
  See Chapter 4, section 4.6.2

```
int ads_getfuncode(void);
```
  See Chapter 2 section 2.2.

```
int ads_getinput (char* str);
```
  See Chapter 4, section 4.6.

```
int ads_getint (const char *prompt, int *result);
```
  See Chapter 4, section 4.2.

```
int ads_getkword (const char *prompt, char *result);
```
  Prompts the user for a keyword (Prompt must be a message string or NULL), and puts the result in Rstl, the maximum length of which will be 512 characters (including the NUL terminator). See Chapter 4, section 4.5 for other functions which can use keyword input.

   Unlike other `ads_getxxx()` functions `ads_getkword()` function does *not* return RTKWORD, it knows that is what it will (should) get. The return values are:
- RTNORM if it succeeds
- RTERROR if it fails
- RTCAN if the user cancels the request.
- RTNONE can be enabled by a prior call to `ads_initget()`, see Chapter 4, section 4.3

  See LST_17_2.CPP for an example use of `ads_getkword()`.

```
int ads_getorient (const ads_point Base, const char* Prm,
          ads_real* result);
```
  See Chapter, 4 section 4.2

```
int ads_getpoint  (const ads_point Pt2, const char* Prmpt, ads_point Pt1);
```
  See Chapter 4, section 4.2

```
int ads_getreal (const char *prompt, ads_real *result);
```
  See Chapter 4, section 4.2

```
int ads_getstring (int Cronly, char* Prmpt, char* Res);
```
  See Chapter 4, section 4.2

```
int ads_getsym (const char* Sym_Name, struct resbuf** Sym_Val);
```

Retrieve the value of an AutoLISP symbol. The value is placed in the single result buffer Sym_Val (NB: the extra level of indirection). Even when Sym_Name is not found the function returns RTNORM. If the function fails for some other reason RTERROR is returned and you should look at ERRNO.

WARNING: Note that you can use this function in ARX only after AutoCAD sends the message kInvkSubrMsg.

`int ads_getvar (const char *sym, struct resbuf *result);`

See Chapter 5, section 5.3.2

`int ads_graphscr (void);`

Makes the display to switch from the text screen to the graphics screen for single screen (extended) DOS computers. In windowed systems opens or switches to the AutoCAD text window.

`int ads_grclear (void);`

Clears the current viewport. Call ads_redraw to refresh it. Returns RTNORM unless a critical error occurs.

`int ads_grdraw (const ads_point Fr, const ads_point To,`
`            int Col, int Hi_Lite);`

Draws a vector between two points in the current viewport and in the current UCS. If Color is -1 then the vector is drawn in XOR, or else it should be a color number from 0 to 255. If the Hi_Lite argument is 1, the vector is highlighted; if Hi_Lite is 0, the vector is drawn in normally. The vector is clipped to fit the screen. Returns RTNORM unless a critical error occurs.

WARNING: The vector is *not* added to the drawing database.

A good example of the use of this function is given in the MAGNETS.C program which comes as an ADS example with AutoCAD.

`int ads_grread (int track, int *type, struct resbuf* Result);`

Used to directly read input devices, almost at the hardware level. You should *not* use this function unless you really really need to. See the AutoCAD ADS manual.

`int ads_grtext (int Box, const char *text, int Hi_Lite);`

Used to writes the text string to the graphics screen area specified by Box. The menu boxes are numbered beginning at 0. The Hi_Lite argument controls the highlighting of menu items. When Box is a valid screen box (see the variable SCREENBOXES in Appendix C):

- Hl < 0: Text is displayed in that box. If the value of Box is greater than the SCREENBOXES-1 the call to ads_grtext() usually has no effect.
- Hl > 0: The text of the box highlighted. Any box previously highlighted will be turned off. Text argument is ignored.
- Hl = 0: If the box is highlighted, ads_grtext() turns highlighting off. The Text argument is ignored.

If Box equals -1, ads_grtext() writes the text into the mode status line, Hi_Lite is ignored. The length of the mode status line differs from display to display, but it is usually least 40 characters.

If Box equals -2, ads_grtext() writes the text into the coordinate status line, Hi_Lite is ignored. If coordinate tracking is on, any value written into this field is overwritten as soon as the coordinates are updated by mouse movement.

For any value of Box is less than -2 the text areas on the screen are restored to their standard values.

Returns RTNORM id the box number is in range, else it returns RTERROR.

int ads_grvecs (const struct resbuf* Vlist, ads_matrix Matrix);

Used to draw a list of vectors specified in Vlist. Vlist can contain:

- A pair of points (RTPOINT or RT3DPOINT) that specify the endpoints of the vector, expressed in the current UCS; these can be three-dimensional points. You must pass pairs of vectors in two successive result buffers.
- A color (resbif type RTSHORT) that applies to all succeeding vectors until another color is encountered. vlist specifies another color. Colors from 0 to 255 are normal AutoCAD color indices, above 255 signifies XOR, below 0 signifies highlighted.

The Matrix is a 4x4 as described in Chapter 7, section 7.3. NULL signifies the identity matrix. Returns RTNORM unless it encounters a bad result buffer, when it returns RTERROR.

WARNING: The vectors are *not* added to the drawing.

int ads_handent (const char *handle, ads_name entres);

Finds the entity with the specified handle, and sets entres to its current entity name. Handles must be turned on in the current drawing. In Release 13 handles are always on.

An entity's name changes whenever AutoCAD opens the drawing, but the entity's handle is constant throughout its life. An ADS application that manipulates a specific database can use ads_handent() to obtain the current name of an entity that the application must manipulate. Once the name is obtained, the entity can be handled by using the other entity functions.

The ads_handent() function will find entities deleted during the current editing session. Another use of this function is to find such entities and undelete them, if necessary, with the ads_entdel() function.

If ads_handent() succeeds RTNORM is returned. If handles are disabled, if handle is not a valid handle string, or if handle cannot be found in the current database RTERROR is returned. When ads_handent() fails, it sets the system variable ERRNO to a value that indicates why.

Apart from giving a permanent identifier to objects in the drawing database handles are also useful for connecting separate objects. For example if two objects have always to be paired, but they cannot be placed in a single BLOCK, then one (or both) of the objects can be given XDATA containing the handle of the other. An example in a lighting program would be a spotlight which must always point at a given object. The spotlight object's XDATA would contain the handle of the object at which it must always point. The program can retrieve this handle from the spotlight and use `ads_handent()` to get the (current) entity name of the object.

`int ads_help (char* Filename, char* Topic, int command);`

Provides help. On the Windows or NT platform, if filename is a Windows help file, then Windows help is provided. If filename is an AutoCAD platform-independent help file, AutoCAD help is provided. To request a particular help topic, pass its topic ID string (called context ID in the Winhelp documentation) to `ads_help()` in the topic argument, and pass 0 in the command argument.

You should use `ads_help()` to make a call for help from a dialog box button and `ads_setfunhelp ()` to define a call for command line help.

On the Windows or Windows NT platform, if filename is a Windows help file and command is not equal to 0, the three `ads_help()` parameters are passed directly to `Winhelp()` in the Microsoft Windows API. The topic parameter is cast to the DWORD `dwdata` parameter of `WinHelp()`. See the Microsoft Windows SDK documentation for a complete description of `Winhelp()`. For a complete definition of the command parameter, include the SDK header file windows.h for Win16 or winuser.h for Win32.

AutoCAD platform-independent help

If filename is an AutoCAD platform-independent help file, then only the following subset of the Winhelp API command values is recognised.

- HELP_CONTENTS   Displays the first topic
- HELP_HELPONHELP   Displays help on using help
- HELP_PARTIALKEY   Displays the Search dialog box

The ads_help() function returns RTNORM if it is successful. It returns RTERROR is the help file is not found. Your application does not have to generate error messages, because both WinHelp and AutoCAD platform-independent help report errors directly to the user.

Here are some help examples:

```
// Bring up help for the TRIM command in AutoCAD
// platform-independent help (by default Windows=acad.hlp
// DOS/UNIX = acad.ahp
ads_help (NULL, "trim", 0);
// Bring up help for the topic my_dialog in the file myfile.ahp
ads_help("myfile.ahp", "my_dialog", 0);
// Bring up the Search dialog box for AutoCAD help.*/
ads_help(NULL, "", HELP_PARTIALKEY);
```

`int ads_init(int argc, char *argv[]);`

See Chapter 2, section 2.2.

`int ads_initget (int Val, const char* Key_Word_List);`

See Chapter 4, section 4.3.

```
int ads_inters (const ads_point From1, const ads_point To1,
                const ads_point From2, const ads_point To2,
                int Test_On, ads_point Result);
```
See Chapter 7, section 7.2.

```
int ads_invoke (const struct resbuf *args, struct resbuf **result);
```
See Chapter 20, section 20.3.

```
int ads_isalnum(int c);
int ads_isalpha(int c);
int ads_iscntrl(int c);
int ads_isdigit(int c);
int ads_isgraph(int c);
int ads_islower(int c);
int ads_isprint(int c);
int ads_ispunct(int c);
int ads_isspace(int c);
int ads_isupper(int c);
int ads_isxdigit(int c);
```
All the above are the ADS equivalent to the standard C functions `isalnum()...isxdigit()`. See the C library manual of your compiler for more details

```
int ads_link (int Code);
```
(ADS only.)
See Chapter 2, section 2.2.

```
struct resbuf* ads_loaded (void);
```
Returns a resbuf list (see Chapter 5) of the external ARX applications that are currently loaded in AutoCAD. The name of each application is returned as a string in its own result buffer (`resval->rstring`). Returns NULL if there are no external applications.

Remember to release the resbuf with `ads_relrb()` once you have used it (as long as it is not NULL).

```
int ads_load_dialog (char *dclfile, int *dcl_id);
```
See Chapter 12, section 12.3.3.

```
struct resbuf* ads_loaded (void);
```
Returns a result buffer list of the external ADS applications currently loaded. The names are placed in `resval->rstring` of each buffer. You should call ads_relb when you have done with the list.

```
void* ads_malloc (int sz);
```
(New in Release 13.)

See your C library manual for the standard C function "malloc()". May use AutoCAD memory instead of memory from the standard environment. If you use ads_malloc to allocate memory, then you should use ads_realloc to reallocate it and ads_free() to free it. That is do not mix AutoCAD supplied memory with standard C environment supplied memory.

int ads_menucmd (const char *str);

Activates one of the submenus of the current AutoCAD menu. The str argument consists of two parts, separated by an equal sign, in the following form:
```
"section=submenu"
```
where section specifies the menu section and submenu specifies which submenu to activate within that section.

See the AutoCAD customisation manual for more details.

int ads_mode_tile (ads_hdlg hdlg, char *key, short mode);

Sets a DCL tile's mode. The key argument specifies the tile. The mode argument is an integer value whose meaning is:
- 0, MODE_ENABLE,Enable tile
- 1, MODE_DISABLE,Disable tile
- 2, MODE_SETFOCUS,Set focus to tile
- 3, MODE_SETSEL,Select edit box contents
- 4, MODE_FLIP,Flip image highlighting on or off

int ads_msize (void *buff);

(New in Release 13.)

Returns the size of the Buffer. Buffer should have been previously allocated by ads_malloc(), by AutoCAD, or by another ARX application (which in turn had used AutoCAD or a call to ads_malloc()).

int ads_namedobjdict (ads_name result);

(New in Release 13)

Returns the name of the named object dictionary, which is the root of all nongraphical objects in the current drawing. Using this name   with ads_dictsearch() and ads_dictnext(), a program can access nongraphical objects.

ads_name_clear (ads_name Name) ;

Not actually a function but a macro defined in ADS.H as

```
#define ads_name_clear(name) name[0]=name[1]=0
```

and used to set both components of the ads_name to zero.

ads_name_equal (const ads_name Name1, const ads_name Name2) ;

Not actually a function but a macro defined in ADS.H as
```
#define ads_name_equal(name1, name2) (name1[0]==name2[0] \
```

```
                                        && name1[1]==name2[1])
```

and used to check if the two names are equal (that they both refer to the same AutoCAD entity). Returns a non-zero value if the names are equal, zero otherwise. For an example of use see Chapter 8, section 8.3.

ads_name_nil (ads_name Name) ;

Not actually a function but a macro defined in ADS.H as

```
#define ads_name_nil(name) (name[0] == 0 && name[1] == 0)
```

and returns a non-zero value if the entity name is {0.0}.

ads_name_set (const ads_name from, ads_name to) ;

Not actually a function but a macro defined in ADS.H as

```
#define ads_name_set(fr,to) (memcpy(to, fr, sizeof(ads_name)))
```

and used to copy the first ads_name from the first parameter to the second.

int ads_nentselp (const char *str, ads_name en, ads_point pt,
               int pk, ads_matrix x,
               struct resbuf **refstkres);

See Chapter 9, section 9.5.1, and LST__9_3.C for an example of use.

int ads_new_dialog (char *dlgname, int dcl_id,
                CALLB def_callback, ads_hdlg *hdlg);

See Chapter 12, section 12.3.3,

struct resbuf* ads_newrb (int Type);

Allocates memory for a result buffer and sets its restype field to Type. An ADS application is must release the memory it has allocated with ads_newrb by calling `ads_relrb()`. See Chapter 4, section 4.6.2, and LST__4_4.C for an example of use.

int ads_osnap (const ads_point pt, const char*mode,
             ads_point result);

Applies the Object Snap modes specified by mode to the point pt, and passes back the closest point it finds in result. Both pt and result are three-dimensional points. The mode argument contains one or more Object Snap identifiers, spelled as they are at the AutoCAD prompt line (abbreviations are allowed). If mode specifies more than one snap mode, the identifiers are separated by commas.

The system variable APERTURE determines the allowable proximity of a selected point to an entity when using Object Snap.

If `ads_osnap()` can find a point, it returns RTNORM; otherwise, it returns an error code.

void ads_polar (const ads_point Base, ads_real Angle,
             ads_real Dist, ads_point New_Point) ;

Uses `Angle` and `Dist` as polar coordinates to calculate `New_Point`. Angle is in radians, 0 radians is along the X axis, increasing angle is counterclockwise.

int ads_printf (const char *format,...);

> Almost identical to the normal C `printf()`, with all the normal formatting characters for doubles, ints, strings and so on. What it prints should not exceed 132 characters. You should never call the normal C `printf()` function in an ADS program.
>
> For printing in the current units in ARX or rxADS you can use a magic formatting formula:
>
> ```
> ads_real Real_Num ;
> ads_printf ("%-9.16q0",Real_Num) ;
> ```
>
> Try the above several times while changing the "UNITS..." menu settings.

ads_point_set (const ads_point From, ads_point To) ;

> Not actually a function but a macro defined in ADS.H for Release 13 as
>
> ```
> #define ads_point_set(fr,to)   (memcpy(to,fr,sizeof(ads_point)))
> ```
>
> and used to copy an `ads_point` from the first parameter to the second.

int ads_prompt (const char* Prompt);

> Prints `Prompt` on the command line of AutoCAD screen.as a message to the user

int ads_putsym (const char *Sym_Name, struct resbuf *Sym_Val);

> Sets the value of an AutoLISP symbol. The list must contain values of types that are valid in AutoLISP, or else if it fails. If you want to set the value of a symbol to nil use the special resbuf type RTNIL as follows:
>
> ```
> value->restype = RTNIL;
> ```
>
> If `Sym_Name` does not exist then a new AutoLISP symbol is created, and `Sym_Val` assigned to it.
>
> Returns RTNORM if all goes well, or else RTERROR.
>
> Note that this command can only be used in ARX if AutoCAD sends the kInvkSubrMsg to the application.

int ads_redraw (const ads_name Ent, int Mode);

> Used to redraw an entity or a graphics viewport (when `Ent==NULL`). If Ent is a valid entity and Mode is not 0, then ads_redraw draws only `Ent`. `Mode` has the following effect on the redraw:
> 1. Redraw `Ent`
> 2. Undraw `Ent` (blank it out)
> 3. Highlight `Ent`
> 4. Unhighlight `Ent`

If negative modes are sent (-1, -2, -3, or -4) then the headers and sub-entities of polyline and block entities are redrawn. If positive modes are sent then only the headers are redrawn.

RTNORM is returned if all goes well, else RTERROR, see ERRNO to see what went wrong.

```
int ads_regapp (const char *appname);
```
See Chapter 11, section 11.4.

```
int ads_regfunc (int (*fhdl) (), int fcode);
```
See Chapter 20, section 20.3.

```
int ads_relrb (struct resbuf *rb);
```
Release the memory allocated to the rb, and all result buffers in the chain of which it may form the head. See Chapter 4, section 4-6-2 for an example.

RTNORM is returned if all goes well, else an error code.

```
int ads_retint (int ival);
int ads_retlist (const struct resbuf *rbuf);
int ads_retname(const ads_name aname, int type);
int ads_retnil();
int ads_retpoint(const ads_point pt);
int ads_retreal(ads_real rval);
int ads_retstr(const char *s);
int ads_rett();
int ads_retval(const struct resbuf *rbuf);
```
For all the above see Chapter 20, section 20.2 These functions are used in mixed language programming (C, C++ and AutoLISP).

```
int ads_retvoid (void);
```
Returns nothing AutoLISP, usually used to stop ADS commands from printing "nil" on the command line. This function always returns RTNORM. See also Chapter 4 section 4.7, and Chapter 20 section 20.2.

```
int ads_rtos (ads_real Val, int Unit, int Prec, char* Str);
```
"Prints" an ads_real Val in the String. If Unit is -1 the current LUNITS setting is used (see Appedix C), else Unit must be one of the valid codes for LUNITS. Prec is the number of decimal places in the the result.

RTNORM is returned if all goes well, RTERROR otherwise.

```
int ads_set_tile(ads_hdlg hdlg, char *key, char *value);
```
See Chapter 12, section 12.3.4

```
int ads_setfunhelp (char *sname,
                char *filename, char *topic, int command);
```
Defines a help call that should be made if transparent help is requested during a command line prompt for the function named sname. The other three parameters for ads_setfunhelp() are the same parameters as for

ads_help(); see above. You should use ads_setfunhelp() to define a call for command line help and ads_help() to make a call for help from a dialog box button. The ads_setfunhelp() function is typically called immediately after ads_defun(), using the same function name supplied to ads_defun(). The ads_defun() function clears any previously registered help for the given command.

Command line help can be registered only for external functions using the "C:" prefix, i.e. those which are called from the AutoCAD command line.

int ads_setvar (const char *sym, const struct resbuf *val);

See Chapter 5, section 5.3.2.

int ads_setview (const struct resbuf *view, const int vport);

(New in Release 13.)

Establishes a 3D view for a specified viewport. The first parameter, view, is a chain of resbufs formatted like the chain returned by ads_tblnext() when applied to the VIEW symbol table. The second parameter, vport, identifies which viewport should receive the new view. The viewport number is like the number returned by the system variable CVPORT. If vport is 0, the current viewport receives the new view.

WARNING: This command can be used in the ARX program environment only when AutoCAD sends the message kInvkSubrMsg to the application.

Returns RTNORM if successful, otherwise RTERROR.

int ads_snvalid(const char *tbstr, int pipetest);

(New in Release 13.)

Tests a symbol table name for validity, including symbol table names with out-of-code-page escape sequences. A symbol table name is valid if it is non-NULL and is not more than 31 characters long. Characters have to be alphanumeric, $, -, or _. The | character (vertical bar) is allowed for symbol table names with external references, but it cannot be the first or last character. The first parameter is a null-terminated table name declared as a const symbol, as follows:

```
const char *tbstr = "LAYER\0" ;
```

The second parameter is TRUE or FALSE. TRUE allows the pipe character (|) in the table name, and FALSE does not. An application that reads a symbol table name from the keyboard should not accept a name containing |, because other functions would not accept this name.

Returns RTNORM if the symbol table name is valid, otherwise OL_ESNVALID.

int ads_ssadd (const ads_name Ent, const ads_name Set, ads_name New_Set);

Make a new selection set or adds Ent to an existing selection set. If both `Ent` and `Set` are NULL, then a new empty selection set is created in `New_Set`. If `Ent` is not NULL and `Set` is NULL, a new selection set is created in `New_Set` with a single member, `Ent`. If `Ent` is not NULL and Set is not NULL then Ent is added to `Set`, the resulting set being put in `New_Set`.

`Set` and `New_Set` can be the same selection set. This is the best way to add entities to existing selction sets. If you use ads_ssadd with a Set = NULL, the you must later release the set with `ads_ssfree()`. If all goes well RTNORM is returned, else you should lok at ERRNO to see what went wrong.

`int ads_ssdel (const ads_name ename, const ads_name ss);`

Remove Ent from the Set. On success RTNORM is returned, else look at ERRNO to see what went wrong.

`int ads_ssfree(const ads_name sname);`

See Chapter 6, section 6.3 See also the two warnings to the function `ads_ssget()` below.

`int ads_ssget (const char* Str, const void* Pt1, const ads_point Pt2,`
`const struct resbuf* Entmask,  ads_name S_Set);`

See Chapter 6, section 6.3.

WARNING: Do not make the mistake of thinking that this function is like `ads_getxxx()` functions where the first parameter is the prompt. With `ads_ssget()`, Str it is the selection method, and setting it to NULL prompts the user with the standard AutoCAD "select objects" message.

WARNING: Even if the returned selection set is empty you should free it with `ads_ssfree()` after use.

`int ads_ssgetfirst(struct resbuf** grip_set, pResbuf*`
`pickfirst_set);`

Determines which objects are selected and gripped. Upon return, grip_set points to a resbuf that contains a selection set consisting of all objects with grips. If no objects have grips, grip_set is null. The pickfirst_set points to a resbuf that contains a selection set consisting of all the objects selected (while AutoCAD is at the command prompt) but not gripped. If no objects are selected or gripped, pickfirst_set is null.

Neither the contents of grip_set nor pickfirst_set should point to resbufs before calling ads_ssgetfirst(). Call ads_ssfree() to deallocate memory allocated for the returned selection sets. Call `ads_relrb()` to deallocate memory allocated for the resbufs.

Only entities from the current drawing's model space and paper space, not nongraphical objects or entities in other block definitions, are seen by this function. Returns RTNORM or RTREJ.

`int ads_sslength (const ads_name sname, long *len);`

See Chapter 6, section 6.3.2.

```
int ads_ssmemb (const ads_name Ent, const ads_name Set);
```
Returns RTNORM if it finds Ent in Set, else it returns RTERROR.

```
int ads_ssname(const ads_name ss, long i, ads_name entres);
```
See Chapter 6, section 6.3.2.

```
int ads_ssnamex(struct resbuf** rbpp, const ads_name ss,  const long i);
```
(New in Release 13.)

Retrieves information on how a selection set is created. Upon return, the rbpp points to a resbuf that contains the object name of the i th element in the selection set ss. If i is -1, rbpp points to a list of the object names of all members of the selection set and data describing how selections were made.

Only selection sets with entities from the current drawing's model space and paper space, not nongraphical objects or entities in other block definitions, are seen by this function.

Call ads_relrb() to deallocate resbufs pointed to by rbpp.

Returns RTNORM if successful, otherwiseRTERROR.

```
int ads_ssetfirst (const ads_name grip_set, const ads_name pickfirst_set);
```
(New in Release 13.)

Sets which objects are selected and gripped. The function returns an error if any object in grip_set is also in pickfirst_set. Otherwise, when the function returns the objects in grip_set are given grips, and the objects in pickfirst_set are selected but not gripped.

Do not call ads_ssetfirst() when AutoCAD is in the middle of executing a command.

```
int ads_start_dialog(ads_hdlg hdlg, int *status);
```
See Chapter 12, section 12.3.2.

```
int ads_start_list (ads_hdlg hdlg, char* key, short op, short indx);
```
See Chapter 12, section 12.3.9

```
int ads_tablet (const struct resbuf *args, struct resbuf** result)
```
Depending on the first item in args, ads_tablet() either retrieves the current digitizer (tablet) calibration or sets the calibration. The first item in args must be an integer (RTSHORT) whose value is either 0 or 1. If args begins with 0, ads_tablet() retrieves the current calibration and returns it in the result list. If args begins with 1, it must also specify the new calibration arguments. The elements of args and result have the same meanings, as follows:

code: An integer code (RTSHORT). If the code you pass in args equals 0, ads_tablet() retrieves the current calibration in result; in this case you must not provide the other arguments. If the code you pass in args equals 1, ads_tablet() sets the calibration according to the arguments that follow; in this case you must provide the other arguments. The code returned in result always equals 1.

row1, row2, row3: Three three-dimensional points (RT3DPOINT). These arguments specify the three rows of the tablet's transformation matrix.

direction: A three-dimensional point (RT3DPOINT). This is the vector (expressed in the world coordinate system, or WCS) that is normal to the plane that represents the surface of the tablet.

When you retrieve a tablet calibration (the code in args equals 0), you should declare result as a **resbuf. The ads_tablet() function allocates the items in the result list. You should release it later with a call to ads_relrb().

When you set a tablet calibration (the code in args equals 1), you can pass the result argument as NULL. This tells ads_tablet() to set the calibration "silently," without returning the new calibration values. If you set the calibration but pass result as a declared resbuf pointer, ads_tablet() sets result to the new calibration. The values returned in result should equal the values specified in args, with the following possible exceptions:

- If the direction specified in args is not normalized, ads_tablet() corrects it, so the direction it returns when you set the calibration may differ from the value you passed.
- In a similar way, the third element in row3 (row3[Z]) should always equal 1. The ads_tablet() function returns it as 1 even if the row3 in args specified a different value.

When you call ads_setvar() to set the tablet mode, make sure that the call was successful even if it returned RTNORM by using ads_getvar() to get the value of the TABMODE system variable and by checking that TABMODE is no longer 0.

If ads_tablet() succeeds, it returns RTNORM; otherwise, it returns an error code, and you should look at the system variable ERRNO.

```
struct resbuf* ads_tblnext (const char* tblname, int rewind);
```
See Chapter 5, section 5.4.2. Remember to free the returned resbuf after you have finishished with it.

```
int ads_tblobjname (char* tblname, char* sym, ads_name objid);
```
Returns by reference in objid, the name (from a symbol table) of an entity of type ads_name, which can be passed to ads_entget() or ads_entgetx(). These functions obtain a pointer to the entity. The first argument tblname, is the name of the symbol table where the entity's name is listed. The second parameter, sym, is the entity's name as written in the symbol table.

Useful for changing LAYERs and other symbol tables.

```
struct resbuf *ads_tblsearch(const char* tname, const char* Sym, int Sn );
```
See Chapter 5, section 5.4.2. Remember to use ads_relrb() to free the returned result buffer after you have finished using it.

int ads_term_dialog (void) ;

        Terminates all current DCL dialog boxes as if the user had canceled each of them. If an application terminates while any DCL files are open, AutoCAD automatically calls ads_term_dialog. Used mainly for aborting nested dialog boxes.

int ads_textbox (const struct resbuf* ent, ads_point p1, ads_point p2);

        Finds the coordinates of a box that encloses the text entity ent. The ent argument must specify a text definition in the form of a result-buffer list (of the kind returned by ads_entget()). The ads_textbox() function sets the p1 argument to the minimum (X,Y) coordinates of the box and the p2 argument to the maximum (X,Y) coordinates. It assumes that the origin is (0,0) and the rotation is 0 (or 270 if the text is vertical). If the text is located at a different point or is rotated, your program must handle these values explicitly.

        If the text is horizontal and is not rotated, p1 (the bottom-left corner) and p2 (the top-right corner) describe the bounding box of the text. The coordinates are expressed in the ECS of ent, with the origin (0,0) at the left endpoint of the baseline. (The origin is *not* the bottom-left corner if the text contains letters with descenders, such as g,p,q,y etc. Some upper case letters have unexpected descenders, such as Q.) If the text is vertical or rotated, p1 and p2 still observe the left-to-right, bottom-to-top order; the offsets are negative, if necessary.

        If the result-buffer list passed in ent begins with a -1 (entity name) group, this group must name an existing text, attdef, or attrib entity. No further groups need to be present, but if the list contains further groups, these override the entity's actual attributes.

        If the result-buffer list does not begin with a -1 group, it must begin with a 0 (entity type) group, and it must contain a group that contains the string itself. This is a 1 (value) group for a text or attrib entity, or a 2 (tag string) group for an attdef entity. Other values are assumed to be the default values unless they are explicitly specified. The defaults are as follows:

- Style (group 7). Defaults to the current text style.
- Size (group 40). Defaults to the size of the style if that is fixed; otherwise, defaults to the current default size of the style.
- Width factor (group 41). Defaults to the default width of the style.
- Obliquing angle (group 51). Defaults to the default angle of the style.

If ads_textbox() succeeds, it returns RTNORM, else RTERROR.

int ads_textpage (void);
int ads_textscr (void);

        Makes the display switch from the graphics screen to the text screen, clearing the text screen in the process. In Windows the text window is popped up, and these two functions are identical. In Extended DOS ads_textpage() clears the text screen, ads_textscr() does not. Both functions return RTNORM on success.

```
int ads_tolower (int c);
int ads_toupper (int c);
```
> See your C compliers standard C function library, look under "tolower" and "toupper."

```
int ads_trans (const ads_point pt, const struct resbuf *from,
               const struct resbuf *to, int disp, ads_point result);
```
> See Chapter 9, section 9.6.

```
int ads_undef (const char *sname, short funcno);
```
> Undefines an external function that was previously defined by a call to ads_defun(). The sname argument is the name of the function, and funcno is the nonnegative integer code of the function. Both of these arguments must be identical to those supplied in the ads_defun() call. If AutoLISP does not recognise both arguments as identifying the same external function, it returns an error status and leaves the function defined.
>
> The ADS application that calls ads_undef() must be the same program that originally defined the function with ads_defun().
>
> It is not necessary to call ads_undef() in response to an RQXUNLD request. This function is provided for applications that need to manage the use of function names explicitly.
>
> If ads_undef() succeeds, it returns RTNORM, otherwise it returns an error code.

```
int ads_unload_dialog(int dcl_id);
```
> Chapter 12, section 12.3.2.

```
int ads_usrbrk();
```
> See Chapter 4, section 4.7. Note that while it is necessary to use this command you should be judicial in its use. It takes quite a lot of time under DOS to look at the keyboard, and even longer under Windows. In one of my applications I found that ads_usrbrk() was dominating the calculation time! I shifted the call out a loop and while the apparent responsiveness to control-C did not change, the calculation speed improved dramatically. You will have to experiment.

```
int ads_vports(struct resbuf **result);
```
> Sets result to point to a list of viewport descriptors for the current viewport configuration. Each viewport descriptor is a sublist consisting of the viewport identification number and the coordinates of the viewport's lower-left and upper-right corners.
>
> If the AutoCAD system variable TILEMODE is set to 1 (on), the returned list describes the viewport configuration created with the AutoCAD VIEWPORTS command. The corners of the viewports are expressed in values between 0.0 and 1.0, with (0.0, 0.0) representing the lower-left corner of the display screen's graphics area, and (1.0, 1.0) representing the upper-right corner.

If TILEMODE is 0 (off), the returned list describes the viewport entities created with the MVIEW command. The viewport entity corners are expressed in paper space coordinates. Viewport number 1 is always paper space when TILEMODE is off.

The current viewport's descriptor is always first in the list.

If it succeeds, ads_vports() returns RTNORM else RTERROR. Call ads_relrb() to deallocate memory for the contents of result.

int ads_wcmatch(const char *string, const char *pattern);

Attempts to match a wild-card pattern to a string. The string argument is the string to scan, and the pattern specifies which character patterns to scan for. The ads_wcmatch() function returns RTNORM if the string matches the pattern, and RTERROR if it does not. By default does a *case sensitive* compare.

Alphanumeric characters in the pattern are treated literally. If characters are enclosed in brackets, ads_wcmatch() matches a single character (for example, [fo] matches the letter foro). Within brackets, you can use a hyphen (-) to specify a range of letters or digits (for example, [A-D] matches A, B, C, or D). A leading tilde (~) negates the characters; that is, ads_wcmatch() reports a match if the string does not correspond. The pattern string can include multiple patterns, separated by commas. Other special characters also have particular meanings; see the table that follows.

If a tilde is not the first character within brackets, it is treated literally. To specify a literal hyphen as an option within brackets, make it the first or last bracketed character (for example, [-ABC] or [ABC-]), or the first character to follow a leading tilde (as in, [~-ABC]). To specify a literal right bracket (]) within brackets, make it the first bracketed character or the first to follow a leading tilde (as in []ABC] or [~]ABC]).

Other special characters may be defined in future releases, so use a leading reverse quote (') to escape all special characters that are not used as described in this section.

Wild card characters are:
- # (Pound) Matches any single numeric digit.
- @ (At) Matches any single alphabetic character.
- . (Period) Matches any single nonalphanumeric character.
- * (Asterisk) Matches any character sequence, including an empty one. You can use an asterisk anywhere in the search pattern, at the beginning, middle, or end.
- ? (Question mark) Matches any single character.
- ~ (Tilde) If it is the first character in the pattern, then it matches anything except the pattern.
- [...] Matches any one of the characters enclosed.
- [~...] Matches any single character not enclosed.
- - (Hyphen) Uses inside brackets to specify a range for a single character.
- , (Comma) Separates two patterns.

- ' (Reverse quote) Escapes special characters (reads next character literally).

```
int ads_xdroom (const ads_name ent, long *result);
```
See Chapter 11 section 11.7.

```
int ads_xdsize (const struct resbuf *xd, long *result);
```
See Chapter 11 section 11.7.

```
int ads_xformss(const ads_name ssname, ads_matrix genmat);
```
Applies a transformation matrix, genmat, to the selection set specified by ssname. The genmat argument is a 4x4 matrix. If genmat does not do uniform scaling, ads_xformss() returns RTERROR. To do uniform scaling, the elements in the scaling vector must all be equal [S XS YS Z]; in matrix notation, [M 00 = M 11 = M 22].

Applying a transformation to a selection set is a means of scaling, rotating, or moving the entities in the selection set without using ads_command(), ads_cmd(), or ads_entmod().

If it succeeds, ads_xformss() returns RTNORM; otherwise, it returns RTERROR. If ads_xformss() fails, it sets the system variable ERRNO to a value that indicates the reason for the failure.

```
int ads_xload(const char *app);
```
Loads the external (ADS) application specified by the app string. The ads_xload() function searches for the specified application according to the current AutoCAD library search path. This is the same search path used by the AutoLISP (xload) and ads_findfile() functions. If the application is successfully loaded, its external functions can be called by ads_invoke().

On success ads_xload() returns RTNORM else RTERROR. See the ERRNO system variable for the reason for the failure.

```
int ads_xunload(const char *app);
```
Unloads the external (ADS) application specified by the app string. The ads_xunload() request fails if the application tries to unload itself, or if the other application has been nested by means of calls to ads_invoke().

If it succeeds, ads_xunload() returns RTNORM; it returns RTERROR if it cannot find or unload the specified file. When ads_xunload() fails, it sets ERRNO indicate the reason for the failure.

Appendix C AutoCAD system variables

C.1 Introduction

This appendix gives an alphabetical listing of all the system variables used in AutoCAD Release 13. When Release 14 comes out you should look under the "new in Release 14" section of the manuals to see if any new variables have been added.

For each variable listed the type and the DXF code are also listed. If there is no DXF code it means that this variable is not saved in the drawing file, and of course is not saved in DFX or DXB files.

For more on how to access and change variables see Chapter 5. See Appendix D, section D.3 on the format of the variables in a DXF file.

Note that while in DXF a point (and other coords) is defined by the three group codes 10, 20 and 30, in ADS result buffers only the 10 is used. So in ADS a 10 group contains three coordinates in the ads_point. In this list of variables all three group codes are given (you may need to know them if you program for DXF), but ADS only uses the first. The same applies to group codes such as 11,21,31 and so on.

Some variables, marked in the list as "read-only", cannot be changed directly using ads_setvar(), but they can be changed with an AutoCAD command. LENSLENGTH is a variable which can only be changed using the DVIEW command. Other variables cannot be changed at all, for example HANDLES, these also are marked as "read-only".

Some variables are practically commands; for an example see the REINIT variable which can be used to regenerate the drawing.

Just as it is worthwhile scanning the "Contents" pages of manuals you may find it useful to scan this list of variables every now and then to refresh your memory about what obscure modes (and commands) are available.

C.2 AutoCAD system variables

ACADPREFIX, string.
The directory path set by the ACAD environment variable.

AFLAGS, integer.
Flags for the ATTDEF command
- 0 = All modes off
- 1 = Invisible
- 2 = Constant
- 4 = Verify
- 8 = Preset

ACADVER, string, DXF code 1.
The AutoCAD drawing database version number:
- AC1006 = R10,
- AC1009 = R11 and R12
- AC1011 = R13

ANGBASE, real, DXF code 50.
Angle 0 direction. The user may change this, so in your application you should store the current value, set it to zero, and restore it at the end of the application.

ANGDIR, integer, DXF code 70.
Direction of positive angle measure:
- 1 = clockwise angles
- 0 = counterclockwise angles
As with ANGBASE you should store it, set it to the direction you want, and restore it, because the user may have changed it for his own use.

APERTURE, integer.
Sets the size (in pixels) of the box (drawn around the cross-hair cursors) used for object snapping.

AREA, real, read only.
Stores the last area computed by the AREA command.

ATTDIA, integer, DXF code 70.
Attribute entry dialogs.
- 1 = on, dialog box used when inserting blocks with attributes
- 0 = off, dialog box not used

ATTMODE, integer, DXF code 70.
Controls attribute visibility:

- 0 = none,
- 1 = normal
- 2 = all

ATTREQ, integer, DXF code 70.
Controls attribute prompting during INSERT.
- 1 = on
- 0 = off

AUNITS, integer, DXF code 70.
Angle units format:
- 0 = Decimal degrees
- 1 = Degrees/minutes/seconds
- 2 = Gradians
- 3 = Radians
- 4 = Surveyor's units

AUPREC, integer, DXF code 70.
"UNITS" precision for angles, how many decimal places printed for angles.

BACKZ, real.
The distance to the back clipping plane, see Chapter 10, section 10.4.

BLIPMODE, integer, DXF code 70.
Blip mode on if nonzero, so little crosses will be drawn at the points where entities are selected or edited or moved. A redraw will get rid of these "blips".

CDATE, real, read-only.
Stores calender date and time. The format is a little strange, it is a real number coded as follows:

```
YYYYMMDD.HHMMSS
19891225.160345 // 1989, 12th month, 25th day, 4:03 pm
```

You should use the C function sprintf() to put this real number into a string and then extract the actual date and time. As an alternative C programmers (as opposed to AutoLISP programmers) should consider using the ANSI functions time() and strftime() which will format the date and time any way you want. See for example Chapter 13, section 13.4.1.

CECOLOR, DXF code 62.
Current entity color number:
- 0 = BYBLOCK
- 1..255 standard AutoCAD colors.
- 256 = BYLAYER

CELTSCALE, real, DXF code 40.

Current global entity linetype scale.

CELTYPE, string, DXF code 6.
Entity linetype name, or "BYBLOCK" or "BYLAYER".

CHAMFERA, CHAMFERB, real DXF code 40.
First and second chamfer distances.

CHAMFERC, real, DXF code 40.
Chamfer length.

CHAMFERD, real, DXF code 40.
Chamfer angle.

CHAMMODE, integer.
The input method by which AutoCAD creates chamfers.
* 0 Two chamfer distances required.
* 1 One chamfer length and an angle required.

CIRCLERAD, real.
The default circle radius. 0 means no default.

CLAYER, string, DXF code 8.
Current layer name.

CMDACTIVE, integer, read-only.
A bit-code that indicates what soprt of command is currently active. It is a bit-sum fo the following codes:
* 1 Ordinary command is active.
* 2 Two commands are active, an ordinary one and a transparent one (such as 'ZOOM) .
* 4 A script is active.
* 8 A dialog box is active.

CMDDIA, integer.
Codes if dialog boxes are enabled for other than PLOT and external database commands.
* 0 Disables dialog boxes.
* 1 Enables dialog boxes.

CMLJUST, integer DXF code 70.
Current multiline justification.
* 0=Top
* 1=Middle
* 2=Bottom

CMLSCALE, real, DXF code 40.
Current multiline scale.

CMLSTYLE, string, DXF code 7.
Current multiline style name.

COORDS, integer, DXF code 70.
If and how coordinates are displayed, see Chapter 5.
- 0 = static coordinate display
- 1 = continuous update
- 2 = "distance < angle" format

DELOBJ, integer, DXF code 70.
Controls object deletion when (for example) you revolve a polyline to produce a solid three-dimensional object. The original polyline will be deleted or retained after the revolution accprding to the setting of this variable.
- 0=deleted
- 1=retained

DIMALT, integer, DXF code 70.
Alternate unit dimensioning. Alternate units are used to make conversion from imperial (feet, inches and so on) to metric (meters, centimeters etc) and vice versa.
- 0 = No alternate unit dimensioning
- 1 = Alternate unit dimensioing active

DIMALTD, DXF code 70.
Number of dimensioning alternate unit decimal places.

DIMALTF, DXF code 40.
Alternate unit scale factor. The scale factor for converting between imperial and metric.

DIMALTTD, integer, DXF code 70.
Number of decimal places for tolerance values of an alternate units dimension.

DIMALTTZ, integer, DXF code 70.
Toggles suppression of zeros for alternate tolerance values.
- 0=zeros not suppressed
- 1=zeros suppressed

DIMALTU, integer, DXF code 70.
Units format for alternate units of dimension style family members other than angular units.

- 1=Scientific
- 2=Decimal
- 3=Engineering
- 4=Architectural

DIMALTZ, integer, DXF code 70.
Toggles suppression of zeros for alternate unit dimension values.
- 0=zeros not suppressed,
- 1=zeros suppressed

DIMAPOST, string, DXF code 1.
Alternate dimensioning suffix, for example "mm".

DIMASO, DXF code 70
Associative dimensioning
- 1 = create associative dimensioning
- 0 = draw individual entities, associative dimensioning not active

DIMASZ, real, DXF code 40.
Dimensioning dimension line and leader line arrow size.

DIMAUNIT, integer, DXF code 70.
Angle format for angular dimensions.
- 0=Decimal degrees
- 1=Degrees/minutes/seconds
- 2=Gradians
- 3=Radians
- 4=Surveyor's units

DIMBLK, string, DXF code 2.
Arrow block name if you do not want to use the standard arrow head.

DIMBLK1, DIMBLK2, string, DXF code 1.
First and second arrow block names if DIMSAH is on.

DIMCEN, real, DXF code 40.
Size of center/mark lines for the dimensioning DIMCENTER, DIMDIAMETER, and DIMRADIUS:
- 0 No center marks or lines are drawn.
- <0 Center lines are drawn.
- >0 Center marks are drawn.
The absolute value specifies the size of the mark portion of the center line.

DIMCLRD, integer, DXF code 70.
Dimension line color,

- 0 = BYBLOCK
- 1..255 normal AutoCAD colors
- 256 = BYLAYER

DIMCLRE, integer, DXF code 70.
Dimension extension line color, see DIMCLRD for color range.

DIMCLRT, integer, DXF code 70.
Dimension text color, see DIMCLRD for color range.

DIMDEC, integer, DXF code 70.
Number of decimal places for the tolerance values of a primary (not alternate) units dimension.

DIMDLE, real, DXF code 40.
Dimension line extension.

DIMDLI, real, DXF code 40.
Dimension line increment, used to offset parallel dimension lines so that they do not overwrite each other.

DIMEXE, real, DXF code 40.
Extension line extension, how far the line extends beyond the dimension line.

DIMEXO, real, DXF code 40.
Extension line offset from "origin" of the dimension, usually the object being dimensioned.

DIMFIT, integer DXF code 70.
Controls the automatic placement of text and arrowheads. See your AutoCAD manual.

DIMGAP, real, DXF code 40.
Dimension line gap. Serves several purpose, one of which is the distance from the end of the dimension line broken to insert (dimensioning) text to the text itself. See also DIMTAD.

DIMJUST, integer, DXF code 70.
Horizontal dimension text position coded as follows:
- 0 = above dimension line, center-justified between extension lines,
- 1 = above dimension line , next to first extension line,
- 2 = above dimension line , next to second extension line,
- 3 = above, center-justified to first extension line,
- 4 = above, center-justified to second extension line

DIMLFAC, real, DXF code 40.
Linear measurements scale factor

DIMLIM, integer, DXF code 70.
Dimension limits (e.g +/- 0.001) generated if nonzero.

DIMPOST, string, DXF code 1.
General dimensioning suffix applied to dimension text.

DIMRND, real, DXF code 40.
Rounding value for dimension distance text. Setting this value to 0.5 will round
dimension text 3.3 to 3.0 and 3.7 to 4.0.

DIMSAH, integer, DXF code 70.
Controls which blocks used as arrow heads in dimensioning:
- 0 Use DIMBLK if defined, else normal arrowheads
- 1 DIMBLK1 and DIMBLK2 arrow blocks used

DIMSCALE, real, DXF code 40.
Overall dimensioning scale factor.

DIMSD1, DIMSD2, DIMSE1, DIMSE2 integer, DXF code 70.
Codes if first (or second) dimension (or extension) line is suppressed.
- 0 = not suppressed
- 1 = suppressed

DIMSHO, integer, DXF code 70.
Dynamic dimensioing for associtaive dimensions while dragging:
- 1 = Recompute dimensions while dragging
- 0 = Drag original image

DIMSOXD, integer DXF code 70.
Controls drawing of extension lines outside dimension lines:
- 0 = Do not suppress dimension lines outside dimension lines
- 1 = Suppress dimension lines outside extension lines

DIMSTYLE, string, DXF code 2.
Current dimension style name.

DIMTAD, integer, DXF code 70.
Sets the vertical position of text in relation to the dimension line.
- 0 = Center the dimension text between the extension lines.
- 1 = Places the dimension text above the dimension line unless the dimension
  line is not horizontal and text inside the extension lines is forced horizontal

(DIMTIH = 1). The distance from the dimension line to the baseline of the lowest line of text is the current DIMGAP value.
- 2 = Place the dimension text on the side of the dimension line farthest away from defining points.
- 3 = Place the dimension text to conform to a JIS (Japanese Industrial Standards).

DIMTDEC, integer, DXF code 70.
Number of decimal places used to display tolerance values.

DIMTFAC, real, DXF code 40.
Dimension tolerance display scale factor, the height of tolerance text compared with the height of dimension text.

DIMTIH, integer, DXF code 70.
Text inside horizontal dimensions if nonzero

DIMTIX, integer, DXF code 70.
Forces dimension text to be inside extensions if 1.

DIMTM, real, DXF code 40.
Minus tolerance, see also DIMTP.

DIMTOFL, integer, DXF code 70.
If non-zero and even if text outside extensions, force line between extensions.

DIMTOH, integer, DXF code 70.
Aligment of text which is outside dimension lines:
- 0 = align text with dimension line
- 1 = draw text horizontally

DIMTOL, integer, DXF code 70.
Dimension tolerances generated if nonzero. Setting this variable resets DIMLIM.

DIMTOLJ, integer, DXF code 70.
Vertical justification for tolerance values relative to normal dimension text:
- 0 = Top
- 1 = Middle
- 2 = Bottom

DIMTP, real, DXF code 40.
Plus tolerance, see also DIMTM.

DIMTSZ, real, DXF code 40.
The size of ticks (oblique strokes used instead of arrows) size. 0 means no ticks.

DIMTVP, real, DXF code 40.
Dimension text vertical position, when DIMTAD is off.

DIMTXSTY, string, DXF code 9.
Dimension text style name.

DIMTXT, real, DXF code 40.
Dimensioning text height.

DIMTZIN, integer, DXF code 70.
Controls the suppression of zeros for tolerances.
- 0 Suppresses zero feet and precisely zero inches.
- 1 Includes zero feet and precisely zero inches.
- 2 Includes zero feet and suppresses zero inches.
- 3 Includes zero inches and suppresses zero feet.
Adding 4 suppresses leading zeros in all decimal dimensions. Adding 8 suppresses trailing decimal zeroes. Adding 12 suppresses both leading and trailing decimal zeroes.

DIMUNIT, integer, DXF code 70.
Controls the units format for all dimension style family members other than angular:
- 1 = Scientific
- 2 = Decimal
- 3 = Engineering
- 4 = Architectural

DIMUPT, DXF code 70.
Sets cursor functionality for text positioned by the user:
- 0 = User sets only the dimension line location
- 1 = User sets the text position as well as the dimension line location

DIMZIN, integer, DXF code 70.
Controls zero suppression for *feet* and *inches* dimensions, see DIMTZIN for the codes.

DISPSILH, integer, DXF code 70.
Controls the display of silhouette curves of body objects in wire-frame mode, Release 13.
- 0 = No silhouette
- 1 = Silhouette present
Often wireframe representations objects seem particularly empty; this variable allows you to show not only the wireframe but also the "silhouette" of the object,

thus filling it out a bit. You will have to do a REGEN after changing this variable to see the difference. See also ISOLINES in this appendix.

DISTANCE, real.
Similar to the AREA variable and contains the last distance calculated by the DIST command.

DONUTID, DONUTOD real.
The default inside and outside diameters for a doughnut (DONUT command).

DRAGMODE, integer, DXF code 70
Controls the dragging of objects when moving, scaling, rotating and so on:
* 0 = Off
* 1 = On
* 2 = Auto
The normal value is 2, since computers these days have no problems with dragging even large entities in AutoCAD.

DWGCODEPAGE, string, DXF code 3.
Drawing code page, same as the variable SYSCODEPAGE.

DWGNAME, string, read-only.
What the user entered as the name of the drawing, including the path if she specified it. Unamed drawings will have DWGNAME="UNNAMED" in English speaking countries. This variable will also be changed by the SAVEAS command. See also the variable DWGTITLED.

DWGPREFIX, string, read-only
Stores the path name of the drawing without the drawing name itself. Ends in a backslash "\".

DWGTITLED, integer, read-only.
Set to 1 if the user has titled the drawing, 0 otherwise.

DWGWRITE, integer.
Records the setting of the last open dialog box read-only flag:
* 0 = The drawing was opened in read-only mode
* 1 = The drawing was opened in read-write mode.

EDGEMODE, integer
Set how the commands TRIM and EXTEND determine cutting and boundary edges (lines, circles, ellipses etc.):
* 0 Use the selected edge without an extension (e.g. an arc is an arc).
* 1 Extends the selected edge to its natural boundary (e.g. an arc becomes a circle).

ELEVATION, real, DXF code 40.
Current elevation set by ELEV command, allows you to draw two-dimensional objects "floating" above the current UCS.

ERRNO, integer.
Stores the number of the last error caused by an application. See Appendix E and the standard AutoCAD include file OL_ERRNO.H and the C file ADS_PERR.C which comes with your AutoCAD CD-ROM or distribution disks.

EXPERT, integer.
Sets the amount of warning messages to the user. 0 does not supress any messages, whereas 5 supresses a lot of messages. See your AutoCAD User Manual. I have never found any need to change this variable.

EXPLMODE, integer.
Sets whether or not the EXPLODE command works with non-uniformly scaled blocks:
• 0 Does not explode NUS blocks.
• 1 Explodes NUS blocks.
An NUS block is a block inserted with differing X and Y scale factors. Old versions of AutoCAD could not explode non uniformly scaled blocks.

EXTMAX, real, DXF codes 10, 20, 30.
The X, Y, and Z drawing extents, top right corner in the world coordinate system.

EXTMIN, real , DXF code 10, 20, 30
The X, Y, and Z drawing extents, bottom left corner in world coordinate system.

FACETRES, real.
Allows control of the smoothness of shaded, rendered, and hidden line-removed objects. The values can be 0.01 to 10.0; I would recommend numbers between 0.5 and 2 as a good compromise between looks, speed and memory consumption.

FFLIMIT, integer.
Sets a limits to the number of PostScript and TrueType fonts you can have in memory. 0 means no limit, other valid values can be from 1 to 100.

FILEDIA, integer.
Allows the supression of (most) dialog boxes::
• 0 = disable dialog boxes.
• 1 = allow dialog boxes.

Even if dialog boxes *are* suppressed you can temporariy activate them by responding with "~" in response to the prompt.

If a script or AutoLISP or ADS function is active the prompt appears whatever the setting of FILEDIA. This obviously helps programming the `ads_command()` function.

FILLETRAD, real, DXF code 40.
The current fillet radius.

FILLMODE, integer, DXF code 70.
Fill of SOLIDs on if nonzero. SOLIDs not viewed in plan fill will *never* be filled, FILLMODE is ignored.

FONTALT, string.
The name of the alternate font to be used if a specified font file cannot be located.

FONTMAP, string.
Name of a file containing several lines, each line being pairs of fonts. The first font of the pair is the original font, the second font of the pair is the font to be used if the first cannot be found. The first and second fonts are separated by a semicolon ";".

FRONTZ, real.
The distance to the front clipping plane, see Chapter 10, section 10.4.

GRIDMODE, integer.
Set the grid of the current viewport:
- 0 = No grid
- 1 = Grid displayed

GRIDUNIT, real.
The X and Y spacing of the grid.

GRIPBLOCK, integer.
Sets how grips are displayed within blocks:
- 0 = Show grip at insertion point of block only.
- 1 = Show grips on objects within the block.

GRIPCOLOR, integer.
Sets the color of the grips, valid colors are from 1 to 255.

GRIPHOT, integer.
Selected grips are shown as filled blocks. This variable sets the color of these filled blocks, from 1 to 255.

GRIPS, integer.
Enables and disables grips:
- 0 = Grips off
- 1 = Grips on

GRIPSIZE, integer.
Sets the size of the grip box, in pixels, valid from 1 to 255

HANDLES, integer, read-only.
Shows if HANDLES are enabled. They are always enabled in Release 13, so this variable is always 1, and this is one of the reasons that Release 13 drawings are bigger than Release 12 drawings. HANDLES are a way to keep track of objects even after a drawing has been saved and then re-read. The entity name of an entity can change with time, but a HANDLE never changes. Entity names are only valid for the drawing session in which they have been obtained. See ads_handent() in Appendix B.

HIGHLIGHT, integer.
Sets object highlighting (dotted lines) when a user select an object
- 0 highlighting off
- 1 highlighting off

HPANG, real.
The hatch pattern angle

HPBOUND, integer.
Selects what sort of object is created by the commands BHATCH and BOUNDARY:
- 0 = Create a polyline
- 1 = Create a region

HPDOUBLE, integer.
Controls hatch pattern doubling (i.e. create a second set of lines at 90 degrees to the normal set) when user-defined hatching models are used:
- 0 Disable doubling
- 1 Enable doubling

HPNAME, string.
Sets the default hatch pattern name, with a maximum of 34 characters, spaces not allowed.

HPSCALE, real.
The hatch pattern scale factor, must obviously be non-zero.

HPSPACE, real.
The spacing between lines of user-defined hatch patterns.

INSBASE, real, DXF codes 10, 20, 30.
Insertion base set by BASE command (in WCS). If the drawing is going to be inserted into another drawing as a block or external reference INSBASE tells you where the origin of the block (i.e. the current drawing) will be.

INSNAME, string.
Sets the default name for the commands DDINSERT or INSERT.

ISAVEBAK, integer.
Controls the creation of a backup file for incremental saves:
• 0 = no backup file created
• 1= backup file created.

ISOLINES, integer.
Like the variable DISPSILH, this variable helps in the visualisation of wire-frame objects. Increasing the value draws more lines which follow the surface of the object. Valid values are from 0 to 2047, though sensible values are probably from 4 to 32. As with DISPSILH you should do a regen after having changed this value to see the effect.

LASTANGLE, real, read-only.
The angle of the last arc entered.

LASTPOINT, real.
The value for the last point entered by the user (mouse or keyboard), even if it was not selecting an object.

LENSLENGTH, real.
The current lens length in millimeters, used only in perspective view for the current viewport. This is a way of specifying ZOOM in perspective. The bigger this number   the more the view is zoomed. Changed with the DVIEW command; see Chapter 10.

LIMCHECK, integer, DXF code 70.
Controls the creation of objects outside the limits of the drawing:
• 0 = Objects can be created outside limits
• 1 = Objects cannot be created outside limits.
I usually keep LIMCHECK off so that the application can draw anywhere it wants to.

LIMMAX, LIMMIN, real, DXF codes 10, 20.

XYdrawing limits top right corner and bottom left corner in the world coordinate system.

LOCALE, string, read-only.
The ISO code for the language AutoCAD is using.

LOGINNAME, string, read-only
The login name of the user who installed AutoCAD.

LONGFNAME, integer, read-only.
Tells you if long file names are supported or not. On the INTEL platforms long filenames are supported with Windows-95 and Windows NT, but not with Extended DOS or Windows 3.1:
- 0 = long file names *not* supported
- 1 = long file names supported

On some platforms this variable may be called LONGFILENAME.

LTSCALE, real DXF code 40.
Global linetype scale.

LUNITS, integer, DXF code 70.
Units format for coordinates and distances, the values are:
- 1 Scientific
- 2 Decimal
- 3 Engineering
- 4 Architectural
- 5 Fractional

L stands for "Linear".

LUPREC, integer, DXF code 70.
Decimal places for coordinates and distances.

MAXACTVP, integer, DXF code 70.
Maximum Active Viewports, sets maximum number of viewports to be regenerated at one time.

MAXSORT, integer.
Sets when to stop sorting lists in dialog boxes (for example lists of filenames in the open dialog box). If this variable is 0 then no files are sorted. AutoCAD 13 for Windows seems to ignore this variable (the lists are always sorted), whereas Release 13 for DOS honors it.

MENU, string, DXF code 1.
Name of menu file. Appears in the DXF file. For the equivalent variable see MENUNAME.

MENUCTL, integer.
Set the page switching of the screen menu:
* 0 = Screen menu does not switch sub menu when there is keyboard entry
* 1 = Screen menu switches pages when there is keyboard entry
It is usually set to 1, but occasionally set to 0 for older custom menus.

MENUECHO, integer.
Can be used to suppress the echoing of commands and responses from screen menus:
* 1 Suppress echo of menu items
* 2 Suppresses display of system prompts during menu.
* 4 Disable control-P menu echo toggle (DOS)
* 8 Displays input/output strings; this is optional debugging aid for DIESEL macros.
Menu echoing can be turned on and off by hitting control-P (DOS).

MENUNAME, string, read-only.
This string stores the current menu name, and it can save your application from re-loading a (custom) menu which is already present.

MIRRTEXT, DXF code 70.
Controls how the MIRROR command effects text:
* 0 = Do not mirror text
* 1 = Mirror text

MODEMACRO, string.
This variable is used to display text on the status line. In DOS versions the status line is at the top of the screen (if enabled), and the MODEMACRO string covers the LAYER string. In Windows the status line is at the bottom, and the MODEMACRO text is displayed in a box at the extreme left. You can use this variable to show your user what "mode" your application is in, for example "deleting tubing..." or "calculating energy consumption..." and so on, See Chapter 4, section 4.8.

MTEXT, string.
Contains the name for the editor to be used for MTEXT (Multiple line text) objects.

OFFSETDIST, real.
Controls the offset distance (used in the OFFSET command which creates concentric circles, parallel lines and so on):
* <0 "Through a point" mode
* >0 Default offset distance

ORTHOMODE, integer , DXF code 70.
Orthogonal mode:
- 0 = Off
- 1 = On

OSMODE, integer DXF code 70.
Object snap modes, a bit-sum of the following:
- 0 NONe
- 1 ENDpoint
- 2 MIDpoint
- 4 CENter
- 8 NODe
- 16 QUAdrant
- 32 INTersection
- 64 INSertion
- 128 PERpendicular
- 256 TANgent
- 512 NEArest
- 1024 QUIck
- 2048 APPint

PDMODE, integer, DXF code 70.
Controls how points are displayed. The interior shaper of the point is selected with one of the following:
- 0 = a dot
- 1 = nothing
- 2 = a plus
- 3 = an x
- 4 = a tick

The point symbol can be surrounded by a circle by adding 32 one of the above, by a square by adding 64, and a circle and square combined by adding 96. Unfortunately this variable applies to *all* points in the drawing.

PDSIZE, real, DXF code 40.
Point display size:
- < 0 = A percentage of the viewport size, -3 means -3% of the viewport size
- > 0 = An absolute size, +3 means 3 feet (or meters or whatever)

It is applied to all points in the viewport.

PELLIPSE, integer.
If nonzero the ELLIPSE command will draw true ellipses, else ELLIPSE will draw a polyline representation.

PERIMETER, real.

Records the last perimeter value calculated by AREA, LIST or DBLIST commands.

PFACEVMAX, integer, read-only.
Sets the maximum number of vertices for each sub-face in a PFACE. To see the sub-faces explode the PFACE, they become 3DFACEs.

PICKADD, integer.
Controls the selection of entities:
• 0 = Add the just selected entities to the selection set, remove the previous ones. Override this by holding the shift key down.
• 1 = Add all the entities selected. Remove entities by holding down the shift key.
This could be a useful variable when you want some initial control as to how the user is allowed to select entities; see Chapter 6.

PICKAUTO, integer.
If non-zero allows the user to draw a selection window straight away without having to type "w" or "c" to get a window or crossing selection.

PICKBOX, integer.
Sets the size of the object selection box in pixels.

PICKDRAG, integer
Selects whether two mouse clicks are required to draw a window (0) or one mouse pick and a drag (1).

PICKFIRST, integer.
If 1 you *can* pick the object and then issue the command. If 0 you *have to* issue the command and then pick the object. The former is more "Windows-like".

PICKSTYLE, integer, DXF code 70.
Controls how groups (named collections of objects, new in Release 13) and associative hatches are selected:
• 0 No group or associative hatch selection
• 1 Group selection only
• 2 Associative hatch selection only
• 3 Both group and associative hatch selection

PLATFORM, string, read-only.
Tells you on what platform you are running. It is a text description of the machine and operating system. Release 13 under Windows 3.1 gives the following value for PLATFORM:
"Microsoft Windows Version 3.10 (x86)"

Do not rely on this string being exactly the same on the same platforms, the manual says that it *may* give one of the following:
"Microsoft Windows", "Sun4/SPARCstation", "386 DOS Extender", "DECstation",
"Apple Macintosh", or "Silicon Graphics Iris Indigo". As you can see the one I got was none of the above!

PLINEGEN, integer, DXF code 70.
Sets the generation of linetype patterns around vertices of a 2D polyline as follows:
- 1 = Linetype generated in a continuous pattern around vertices.
- 0 = Each segment of the polyline starts and ends with a dash, so vertices clearly visible.

PLINEWID, real, DXF code 40.
Default polyline width.

PLOTID, string.
Used to change the default plotter using a string.

PLOTROTMODE, integer.
Change the orientation of the plotter.

PLOTTER, integer.
Used to change a plotter by integer.

POLYSIDES, integer.
Sets the default number of sides for a POLYGON command.

POPUPS, integer, read-only.
Is 0 if the current driver does not support pop up menus. Any decent driver *will* support pop-up menus, and Windows always does.

PROJMODE, integer.
Sets the projection mode for EXTEND and TRIM commands:
- 0 = No projection, true 3D mode
- 1 = Project to the XY plane of current UCS
- 2 = Project to the current viewing plane

PSLTSCALE, integer, DXF code 70
Sets special paper space linetype scaling:
- 0 = No special linetype scaling
- 1 = Viewport scaling controls linetype scaling

PSPROLOG, string.

Used for customization of encapsulated postscript (EPS) files created with the PSOUT command

PSQUALITY, integer.
Determines the quality of a postscript file input using the PSIN command. It can have a dramatic effect on the post script block which you get:
- 0 PostScript image generation diabled
- <0 Sets the number of pixels per drawing unit for the PostScript resolution
- >0 Sets the number of pixels per drawing unit, but uses the absolute value.AutoCAD will show the PostScript paths as outlines and will not fill them

QAFLAGS, integer.
This is an undocumented system variable. It probably stands for Quality Assurance FLAGS, perhaps used for testing. The only thing I know about it for sure is that if it is set to 2 you will not be promted when listings screenfulls of data (using for example the LIST command). The default setting is 0. It is more than likely that each of the 16 bits in the integer switch on or off some feature of AutoCAD. (This information came from the Internet AutoCAD user group comp.cad.autocad by the way.)

QTEXTMODE, integer, DXF code 70 .
Quick text mode:
- 0 Qtext off
- 1 Qtext on
QTEXT replaces text with bounding boxes, and is used to reduce regeneration time when you are not actully interested in reading the text.

RASTERPREVIEW, integer.
Sets if and how preview images are saved in the drawing file:
0 Only BMP (bitmap)
1 Both BMP and WMF (Windows Meta File)
2 Only WMF.
3 No preview image.

REGENMODE, integer, DXF code 70.
REGENAUTO on mode on if non-zero.

REINIT, integer.
Setting this variable initialises IO devices. You can sum the following values to initialise more than one device at a time:
- 1 Digitizer port reinitialisation
- 2 Plotter port reinitialisation
- 4 Digitizer reinitialisation
- 8 Regen, display reinitialisation

- 16 Reload PGP file

RIASPECT, real.
Raster image input aspect ratio (ratio of width to height of an image). This is used by the PCXIN, GIFIN, and TIFFIN to stretch and squash the images to the desired aspect ratio.

RIBACKG, integer.
Sets the raster image background color. If you wanted to import a TIFF map where most of the image was white (color number 7 for example) with coloured roads rivers and so on, then you would set RIBACKG to 7. This would make AutoCAD ignore white pixels (95% of our hypothetical image) thus saving 95% file and memory space.

RIEDGE, integer.
Setting this to a non-zero value means that edge detection will be performed with the PCXIN, GIFIN and TIFFIN commands. The resulting block will show only the *edges* present in the image.

What is an *edge* ? It is where there is a difference between the value of a pixel and the value of its surrounding pixels. Obviously this can have any number of values, and RIEDGE gives you the ability to select only edges above a certain magnitude. The lower the value of RIEDGE (down to 1), the more edges will be detected.

Applications of edge detection can be found in image processing, especially medical image analysis.

RIGAMUT, integer.
Sets the number of colors that an imported raster image is converted to. Although this can be useful for graphics drivers with limited color range it is more useful to reduce the size of the resulting block. The range is from 8 to 256.

RIGREY, integer,
Imported color raster images are converted to the few grey scales that AutoCAD has available. If you are not interested in the colors in the image this can save space in the drawing:
- 0 = Do not convert to grey image
- 1 = Convert to grey image.

RITHRESH, integer.
Raster image importing commands ignore any pixel values below this threshold. You can use this threshold to tidy up "dirty" images (scanned paper drawings with faded coffee cup stains and faint ink smudges for example).

SAVEFILE, string.
Tells you what the name of the autosave file is.

SAVEIMAGES, integer.
When applications create their own object types in a drawing, it can be impossible to see them if the application is not present when the drawing is loaded. Without the application you cannot edit the objects, but you may be able to see them; see Chapter 14. The values are:
- 0 = The application decides whether or not to save images
- 1 = Always saves images, drawing file size gets larger
- 2 = Never saves images

SAVENAME, string, read-only.
The file name you save to.

SAVETIME, integer.
The time period, in minutes, between automatic saves.

SCREENBOXES, integer.
The number of text boxes along the righthand side of the screen, normally at least 20 in AutoCAD under DOS, and often disabled in AutoCAD under Windows. You can write strings to these boxes with `ads_grtext()`; see Appendix B.

SCREENMODE, integer.
This tells you which screen is visible. It is the bit-sum of the following:
- 0 Text screen is displayed
- 1 Graphics screen is displayed
- 2 System configured as dual screen
  Under Windows this variable always seems to be 3, and both the text and graphics "screens" are visible.

SCREENSIZE, point, read-only.
Current viewport size in pixels.

SHADEDGE, SHADEDIF, integers, DXF code 70.
See Chapter 10 for a full explanation.

SHPNAME, string.
Default shape name.

SKETCHINC, real, DXF code 40
Sketch record increment for the SKETCH command.

SKPOLY, integer, DXF code 70
How to SKETCH:
- 0 = sketch lines

- 1 = sketch polylines

SNAPANG, real.
Sets the angle of SNAP (and GRID).

SNAPBASE, real.
Sets the X-Y origin of SNAP (and GRID).

SNAPISOPAIR, integer.
Current isometric plane for the viewport. Used when simumlating three-dimensional drawings with two-dimensional drawings:
- 0 = left
- 1 = top
- 2 = right

SNAPMODE, integer.
Controls if SNAP is ON. You should disable SNAP if you use `ads_command()` because some snapping may occur when you do not want it!
- 0 = Snap off
- 1 = Snap on

SNAPSTYLE, integer.
Sets normal (0) or isomentric(1) snapping.

SNAPUNIT, real.
X Y snap spacing for current viewport

SORTENTS, integer.
Controls the display of object sorting. Used when snapping: if several objects are overlapping the SORTENTS value decides which one to select.

SPLFRAME, integer, DXF code 70.
Spline control polygon display:
- 0 = Off, spline control polygons invisible
- 1 = On, you will see the spline control polygons, and you can edit them

SPLINESEGS, integer, DXF code 70.
Contains the number of line segments per spline patch

SPLINETYPE, integer, DXF code 70.
Spline curve type for PEDIT Spline:
- 5 = Quadratic B-spline
- 6 = Cubic B-spline

SURFTAB1, integer, DXF code 70.

Mesh density in the first (M) direction (REVSURF and EDGESURF), and the number of tabulations generated by RULESURF and TABSURF.

SURFTAB2, integer, DXF code 70.
Mesh density in second (N) direction.

SURFTYPE, integer, DXF code 70.
Surface type for PEDIT Smooth:
- 5 Quadratic B-spline surface
- 6 Cubic B-spline surface
- 8 Bezier surface

SURFU, integer, DXF code 70.
Surface density (for PEDIT Smooth) in M direction.

SURFV, integer, DXF code 70.
Surface density (for PEDIT Smooth) in N direction

SYSCODEPAGE, string, readonly.
Tells you which codepage is specified in ACAD.XMF. Codepages are tables which set the particular character set for a particular language. See your DOS or Windows manual for more information.

TDCREATE, reale, DXF code 40.
Date and time of this drawing creation.

TDINDWG, real, DXF code 40.
Total editing time for this drawing

TDUPDATE, real, DXF code 40.
Date and time of last drawing update.

TDUSRTIMER, real, DXF code 40.
User elapsed timer.

TEMPPREFIX, string, read-only.
Stores the path name of AutoCAD's temporary file directory. You may like to use the same directory for any temporary files that your application creates. Temporary files exist only while AutoCAD (or your application) is running.

TEXTEVAL, integer.
Sets if strings are evaluated as AutoLISP expressions or not. If this variable is non-zero then strings starting with (or ! are taken as AutoLISP expressions.

TEXTFILL, integer.

When non-zero Bitstream TrueType and Adobe Type 1 fonts are filled, otherwise text is displayed as outlines.

TEXTQLT, real.
The quality of the representation of Bitstream TrueType and Adobe Type 1 fonts. 100 is top quality, 0 is low quality.

TEXTSIZE, real, DXF code 40.
Current default text height

TEXTSTYLE string, DXF code 7.
Current text style name

THICKNESS, real, DXF code 40.
Current thickness set by ELEV command

TILEMODE, integer, DXF code 70.
Sets whether how viewports can be arranged:
- 1 = Viewports have to be tiled, i.e. they cover the whole graphics area and do not overlap.
- 2 = Viewports in paperspace can be separate and/or overlap each other.
See your AutoCAD manual for a description of "Paper Space".

TOOLTIPS, integer, Windows only.
If 1 then tips are shown when the mouse cursor goes over tool icons.

TRACEWID, integer, DXF code 40.
Default trace width. Do not use TRACE, which is a very old entity type, use PLINE.

TREEDEPTH, TREEMAX integers, DXF code 70.
Variables to allow user control over how AutoCAD arranges its three-dimensional data base.

TRIMMODE, integer.
Trims of selected edges:
- 0 = Leave selected edges intact.
- 1 = Trim selected edeges to endpoints fillet arcs and chamfer lines.

UCSNAME string, DXF code 2.
Name of current UCS, if it has one.

UCSORG, real DXF codes 10, 20, 30.
Origin of current UCS in the world coordinate system, see Chapter 9.

UCSXDIR, real, DXF codes 10, 20, 30.
Direction of current UCS X axis in the world coordinate system, see Chapter 9.

UCSYDIR, real, DXF codes 10, 20, 30
Direction of current UCS Y axis in the world coordinate system, see Chapter 9.

UCSFOLLOW, integer.
If 1 then every time you change the UCS the view changes to draw it flat in the viewport. The UCS is "stuck" to the screen, and the rest of the drawing moves.

UCSICON, integer.
If 1 then the UCSICON is visible; see Chapter 9, Table 9.1 and Figure 9.2.

UNDOCTL, integer, read-only.
Shows how UNDO is set:
• 0 = UNDO disabled
• 1 = UNDO enabled
• 2 = Only one command can be undone
• 4 = Auto-group mode is enabled
• 8 = A group is currently active

UNDOMARKS, integer, read-only.
Stores how many marks have been placed using the UNDO MARK command.

UNDOONDISK, integer, DXF code ?
Sets where UNDO data is kept:
• 0 = In RAM
• 1 = On disk

UNITMODE, integer, DXF code 70.
Sets the UNITS display format:
• 0 = display fractions, feet-and-inches, and surveyor's angles as previously set
• 1 = display fractions, feet-and-inches, and surveyor's angles in input format

USERI1 to USER I5, integer, DXF code 70.
Five integer variables for use by third-party developers. Useful only when applications do not have to store a lot of data and in situations where only one application will ever have access to the drawing.

USERR1 to USERR5, real, DXF code 40
Five real variables intended for by third-party developers, see USERI1 above.

USERS1 to USERS5, string.
Five user string variables, *not* saved to the drawing file.

USRTIMER, DXF code 70
Sets the user timer:
- 0 = Timer off
- 1 = Timer on

VIEWCTR real, DXF codes 10, 20.
XY center of current view on screen.

VIEWDIR, real, DXF codes 10, 20, 30
Viewing direction, from target to camera; see Chapter 10, section 10.4.

VIEWMODE, integer, DXF code ?
The mode of the current viewport; see Chapter 10, section 10.4.

VIEWSIZE, real DXF code 40
Height of view.

VIEWTWIST, real, DXF code ?
Stores the twist of the current view. Move your head so that the (normally) horizontal line from your left eye to your right eye is off the horizontal. How much it is off corresponds to the twist angle. Changed with the DVIEW command, TWist option.

VISRETAIN, integer, DXF code 70.
Controls visibility in external references:
- 0 = Do not retain xref-dependent visibility settings
- 1 = Retain xref-dependent visibility settings

VSMAX,VSMIN, real, read-only.
The virtual screen X Y Z limits, what you zoom to when you type ZOOM with the Vmax option. Zooming out of these limits will force a regen

WORLDUCS, integer.
Is 1 if the current UCS corresponds to the WCS, 0 otherwise.

WORLDVIEW, DXF code 70.
See Chapter 9, section 9.3.3. Sets if we want to change coordinate system to WCS during certain commands:
- 1 = Set UCS to WCS during DVIEW/VPOINT
- 0 = Do not change UCS

Appendix D
DXF codes

D.1 Introduction

This appendix contains the meanings of DXF codes used in DXF files and in the result buffers of ADS database access functions. See Chapter 18 for a general introduction to the DXF file format.

D.2 Negative group codes

The following negative group codes do not appear in DXF files, but are used in programming:

- -5 Persistent reactor chain.
- -4 Conditional operator; see Chapter 6, section 6.3.5
- -3 Extended data (XDATA) sentinel
- -2 Entity name reference
- -1 Entity name, which changes each time a drawing is opened.

D.3 Positive group codes

The following codes are used in both DXF files and in programming:

- 0 String, the entity type
- 1 Primary text value for an entity
- 2 Name, attribute tag, etc
- 3, 4 Textual or name value

- 5 Entity handle, a string of up to 16 hexadecimal digits
- 6 Line type name
- 7 Text style name
- 8 Layer name
- 9 Variable name (followed by $VARNAME, and the another group giving the variables value). See also Chapter 18, section 18.4.1
- 10 "1st" point (list of three reals), start of line, center of circle, 1st corner of a 3DFACE, etc. An application will only see the 10, (codes 20 and 30 are implied). 10 20 and 30 are all present in a DXF file
- 11-18 Other points, again a program will *not* see 30-38, they are implied. DXF files *do* contain the 30-38 codes. 11 12 and 13 are the second third and fourth corners of a 3DFACE for example
- 39 The entity's thickness (if non-zero)
- 40-48 ads_real values (text height, scale factors, etc.)
- 49 More ads_real values
- 50-58 Angles
- 62 Color number
- 66 "Entities follow" flag, for example, attributes in a block
- 67 Which space the entity is in. If not present or has value 0 in model space, or else in paper space.
- 70-78 Integer values such as flag bits, modes, counts etc.
- 90-99 32-bit integer values
- 100 Subclass data marker (with derived class name as a string)
- 102 Control string followed by "{arbitrary name" or "}"
- 105 DIMVAR symbol table entry object handle
- 210 Extrusion direction. With DXF there is also the 220 and 230 codes (Y and Z). An application sees only the 210 code, with all three coordinates in the ads_point result buffer
- 280-289 8-bit integer values
- 300-309 Strings
- 310-319 Binary chunks
- 320-329 Object handles
- 330-339 Soft pointer handle (specifies pointer to other objects in drawing)
- 340-349 Hard pointer handle (specifies pointer to other objects in drawing)
- 350-359 Soft owner handle (specifies ownership to other objects in drawing)
- 360-369 Hard owner handle (specifies ownership to other objects in drawing)
- 999 Comments
- 1000 A string (up to 255 bytes long) of XDATA
- 1001 Registered application name (string up to 31 bytes long) for XDATA
- 1002 XDATA control string ("{" or "}")
- 1003 XDATA layer name
- 1004 Chunk of bytes (up to 127 bytes long) in XDATA
- 1005 Entity handle in XDATA, string of up to 16 hexadecimal digits
- 1010A point in XDATA
- 1011A 3D WCS position in XDATA

- 1012A 3D WCS displacement in XDATA
- 1013A 3D WCS direction in XDATA.
- 1040 ads_real value in XDATA
- 1041Distance ads_real value in XDATA
- 1042 Scale factor in XDATA
- 1070 16-bit integer in XDATA
- 1071 32-bit signed long integer in XDATA.

D.4 Group codes related to graphical entities

This section lists the group codes that apply to graphical entities.

D.4.1 Common group codes

The following group code apply to almost all graphical entities:
- -1 Entity name
- 0 Entity type
- 8 Layer name
- 5 Handle
- 6 Linetype name (only present if not BYLAYER)
- 48 Linetype scale, default 1.0
- 62 Color number (only present if not BYLAYER). 256 indicates BYLAYER. A negative value indicates that the layer is off
- 67Absent or 0 indicates that the entity is in model space. 1 indicates that the entity is in paper space
- 90ADE lock

D.4.2 Group codes of specific graphic entities

In the following tables when a default value is specified it means that the group is optional, and if it is not present then the default value is used.

3DFACE group codes	
10	First corner
11	Second conder
12	Third corner
13	Fourth corner, equal to third corner if 3DFACE has only three corners
70	Invisible edges flags, a bit-sum, default 0: • 1 = First edge invisible

- 2 = Second edge invisible
- 4 = Third edge invisible
- 8 = Fourth edge invisible

	3DSOLID group codes	
1	First line of file structure
1	Further lines of file structure
3	First line of file structure (if previous group 1 was more than 255 chars)
3	Additional lines (if previous group 1 was more than 255 chars)
1	Last line of file structure

	ARC group codes	
10	Center
39	Thickness (0 if not present)
40	Radius
50	Start angle
51	End angle
210	Extrusion direction. Present only if the extrusion is not parallel to the World Z-axis, default (0,0,1)

	ATTDEF group codes	
1	Default value (string)
2	Tag string
3	Prompt string
7	Text style name, default: STANDARD
10	Text start point
11	Alignment point, present only if 72 or 74 group is present and not 0
39	Thickness, default 0
40	Text height
41	Relative Xscale factor for Fit-type text, default 1
50	Text rotation, default: 0
51	Oblique angle, default: 0
70	Attribute flags, Attribute is (bit-sum the following):

	1 Invisible
	2 Constant
	4 Verified on input
	8 Preset
71	Text-generation flags, default 0 (see also TEXT)
72	Horizontal text justification type, default 0 (see also TEXT)
73	Field length, default 0
74	Vertical text justification type, default 0 (see also TEXT)
210	Extrusion direction. See ARC group code 210 above

ATTRIB	
1	Value (string)
2	Attribute tag (string)
7	Text style name (optional; default: STANDARD)
10	Text start point
11	Alignment point, present only if 72 or 74 group is present and non-zero)
39	Thickness, default 0
40	Text height
41	Relative Xscale factor for Fit-type text, default 1
50	Text rotation , default 0
51	Oblique angle , default 0
70	Attribute flags:
	1 Attribute is invisible (does not appear)
	2 This is a constant attribute
	4 Verification is required on input of this attribute
	8 Attribute is preset (no prompt during insertion)
71	Text-generation flags, default 0 (see also TEXT)
72	Horizontal text justification type , default 0, see TEXT
73	Field length, default 0
74	Vertical text justification type, default 0, see TEXT
210	Extrusion direction. See ARC group code 210 above.

BODY, see 3DSOLID

CIRCLE	
10	Center point
39	Thickness, default 0
40	Radius
210	Extrusion direction. See ARC group code 210 above

DIMENSION	
-3	Application ID "ACAD". This begins the section of xdata that describes any dimension overrides that have been applied to this entity
1	Dimension text entered by the user (optional; default: the measurement)
2	Name of block that contains entities that make up the dimension picture
3	Dimension style name
10	Definition point
11	Middle point of dimension text
12	Insertion point for clones of a dimension (Baseline and Continue)
13	Definition point for linear and angular dimensions
14	Definition point for linear and angular dimensions
15	Definition point for diameter, radius, and angular dimensions
16	Point defining dimension arc for angular dimensions
40	Leader length for radius and diameter dimensions
50	Angle of rotated, horizontal, or vertical linear dimensions
51	Horizontal direction (optional)
52	Extension line angle for oblique linear dimensions (optional)
53	Rotation angle of dimension text (optional)
70	Dimension type: 1 Aligned 2 Angular 3 Diameter 4 Radius 5 Angular 3 point 6 Y-type ordinate 70 X-type ordinate

	128 Added to other codes if text is not at the default location
210	Extrusion direction. See ARC group code 210 above

ELLIPSE	
10	Center
11	Endpoint of major axis (relative to center)
40	Length of minor axis (percentage of major axis length)
41	Start parameter
42	End parameter

INSERT	
66	Variable attributes-follow flag, default 0
2	Block name
10	Insertion point
41	Xscale factor, default 1
42	Yscale factor, default 1
43	Zscale factor, default 1
50	Rotation angle, default 0
70	Column count, default 1
71	Row count, default 1
44	Column spacing, default 0
45	Row spacing, default 0
-3	Application ID "ACAD". This begins the section of xdata that contains the hatch properties.

LEADER	
2	Dimension style name
72	Leader path type 0 Straight line segments 1 Spline
73	The number of vertices in the path
10	Vertex coordinates (multiple entries)
11	X axis direction vector (WCS)

12	Z axis direction vector (WCS)
340	Hard reference to associated text entity
-3	Application ID "ACAD". This begins the section of xdata that describes any dimension overrides that have been applied to this entity.

LINE	
10	Start point
11	End point
39	Thickness, default 0
210	Extrusion direction. See ARC group code 210 above

MLINE	
7	Style name (string, max 32 chars. The name of the style used for this mline. An entry for this style must exist in the ACAD_MLINESTYLE dictionary)
41	Scale factor (real)
73	Number of vertices (integer)
10	Vertex coordinates (multiple entries, one entry for each vertex). Each segment vertex is followed by mline segment parameterisation data.

MTEXT	
1	Text string. If text string is less than 255 characters, all characters appear in group 1.If text string is greater than 255 characters, the string is divided into 255 character chunks, which appear in one or more group 3 codes. If group 3 codes are used, the remainder of the string is placed in the group 1 code.
3	Additional text (always in 255 character chunks, optional)
7	Text style name (STANDARD if not provided)
10	Insertion point
11	X axis direction vector (WCS)
12	Z axis direction vector (WCS)
41	Reference rectangle width
71	Attachment point: 1 TopLeft 6 MiddleRight 2 TopCenter 7 BottomLeft

	3 TopRight
	8 BottomCenter
	4 MiddleLeft
	9 BottomRight
	5 MiddleCenter
72	Drawing Direction:
	1 Left to Right
	2 Right to Left
	3 Top to Bottom
	4 Bottom to Top

POINT	
10	Point
50	Angle of Xaxis for the UCS in effect when the point was drawn, default 0. Used when PDMODE is non-zero.
39	Thickness, default 0
210	Extrusion direction. See ARC group code 210 above

POLYLINE	
66	Vertices-follow flag (always 1 for a polyline)
10	A "dummy" point. The X and Y coordinates are always 0, and the Z coordinate specifies the polyline's elevation.
70	Polyline flag (bit-coded, so may be combined) , default 0:
	1 This is a closed polyline (or a polygon mesh closed in the Mdirection).
	2 Curve-fit vertices have been added
	4 Spline-fit vertices have been added
	8 This is a 3D polyline
	16 This is a 3D polygon mesh
	32 The polygon mesh is closed in the Ndirection
	64 This polyline is a polyface mesh
	128 The linetype pattern is generated continuously around the vertices of this polyline
40	Default starting width, default 0
41	Default ending width, default 0

71	Polygon mesh Mvertex count, default 0
72	Polygon mesh Nvertex count, default 0
73	Smooth surface Mdensity, default 0
74	Smooth surface Ndensity, default 0
75	Curves and smooth surface type, default 0, these are integer codes, *not* bit-coded: 0 No smooth surface fitted 5 Quadratic B-spline surface 6 Cubic B-spline surface 8 Bezier surface
39	Thickness, default 0
210	Extrusion direction. See ARC group code 210 above

RAY, new in Release 13	
10	Base point
11	Direction vector

REGION, see 3DSOLID

SEQEND	
-2	Name of entity that began the sequence

SHAPE	
10	Insertion point
40	Size
2	Shape name
50	Rotation angle, default 0
41	Relative X-scale factor, default 1
51	Oblique angle, default 0
210	Extrusion direction. See ARC group code 210 above
39	Thickness, default 0

SOLID

10	First corner
11	Second corner
12	Third corner
13	Fourth corner. (If only three corners entered, this equals the third corner)
39	Thickness, default 0
210	Extrusion direction. See ARC group code 210 above

SPLINE	
70	Degree of the spline curve
71	Spline flag (bit values): 1 Closed spline 2 Periodic spline 4 Rational spline 8 Planar 16 Linear (Planar bit is also set)
72	Number of knots
73	Number of control points
74	Number of fit points (if any)
42	Fit tolerance
43	Control point tolerance
44	Fit tolerance (if a fit spline)
12	Start tangent (optional)
13	End tangent (optional)
40	Knot value(s). (Multiple group 40 entries can exist)
10	Control point(s). (Multiple group 10 entries can exist)
11	Fit point(s). (Multiple group 11 entries can exist)

TEXT	
10	Insertion point
40	Height
1	Text value (the string itself)
50	Rotation angle, default 0
41	Relative X-scale factor. For Fit-type text (optional; default: 1.0)
51	Oblique angle, default 0
7	Text style name (optional; default: STANDARD)
71	Text generation flags, default 0:2 Text is backward (mirrored in X) 4 Text is upside down (mirrored in Y)

72	Horizontal alignment, default 0, these are integer codes, *not* bit-coded:
	0 Left
	1 Center
	2 Right
	3 Aligned (if vertical alignment = 0)
	4 Middle (if vertical alignment = 0)
	5 Fit (if vertical alignment = 0)
73	Vertical alignment, default 0, these are integer codes, *not* bit-coded:
	0 Baseline
	1 Bottom
	2 Middle
	3 Top
11	Alignment point (optional; present only if 72 or 73 group is present and non-zero)
39	Thickness, default 0
210	Extrusion direction. See ARC group code 210 above

TOLERANCE	
10	Insertion point
11	X axis direction vector (WCS)
12	Z axis direction vector (WCS)
1	Primary text value
3	Dimension style name
-3	Application ID "ACAD". This begins the section of xdata that describes any dimension overrides that have been applied to this entity.

TRACE, this entity type is ancient, do *not* use it.	
10	First corner
11	Second corner
12	Third corner
13	Fourth corner
39	Thickness, default 0
210	Extrusion direction. See ARC group code 210 above

VERTEX, part of a polyline group	
10	Location
40	Starting width, default 0
41	Ending width, default 0
42	Bulge, default 0
70	Vertex flags, default 0:
	1 Extra vertex created by curve-fitting
	2 Curve-fit tangent defined for this vertex. A curve-fit tangent direction of 0 may be omitted from the DXF output but is significant if this bit is set
	8 Spline vertex created by spline-fitting
	16 Spline frame control point
	32 3D polyline vertex
	64 3D polygon mesh vertex
	128 Polyface mesh vertex
50	Curve fit tangent direction (optional)

VIEWPORT	
10	Center point
40	Width in paper space units
41	Height in paper space units
69	Viewport ID. (Changes each time a drawing is opened, never saved. Except for the paper space viewport, which is always 1)
68	Viewport status field
-3	Application ID "ACAD". This begins the section of xdata that describes the viewport.

XLINE	
10	Base point
11	Direction vector

D.5 Group codes which apply to all non-graphical entities

- -1 Entity name. Changes each time a drawing is opened.
- 0 Entity type
- 5 Handle
- 70 Bit-coded flag values:
    - 16   Table entry is externally dependent on an xref
    - 32   The externally dependent xref has been successfully resolved
    - 64   The table entry was referenced by at least one entity in the DWG.
- 90 ADE lock.

D.6 Group codes for non-graphical entities by entity

DICTIONARY	
90	Maximum number of entries to appear in this object record
300	Entry name (repeats for each entry)
360	Handle of entry object (repeats for each entry)

ACAD_GROUP	
2	Group name
3	Group description
70	Selectability flag
240	Index count of entities in group
5	Handles of entities in group (multiple entries; one for each entity in group)

ACAD_MLINESTYLE	
3	Style description (string, less than 256 characters)
51	Start angle (real, radians, default: 90 degrees)
52	End angle (real, radians, default: 90 degrees)
70	flags (bit-coded) 1= fill on 2 = display miters
62	Fill color

71	Start cap attributes (bit-coded) 1 = draw line 2 = draw inner arcs 4 = draw outer arc
72	End cap attributes (bit-coded) 1 = draw line 2 = draw inner arcs 4 = draw outer arc
73	Number of elements in this style (integer)
49	Element offset (real, no default). Multiple entries can exist, one entry for each element
62	Element color (int, default: 0). Multiple entries can exist, one entry for each element
6	Element linetype (string, default: CONTINUOUS). Multiple entries can exist, one entry for each element

APPID	
2	User-registered application name (for XDATA)
70	Standard flag values

BLOCK (Block descriptions also contains the entity groups common to graphical entities)	
2	Block name
70	Type flag (bit coded values, may be combined): 1 This is an anonymous block (generated by hatching, associative dimensioning, other internal operations, or an application) 2 Variable attributes follow 4 This block is an external reference (Xref) 16 This block is externally dependent 32 This is a resolved external reference, or a dependent of an external reference 64 This definition is referenced
10	Base point
1	Xref pathname (optional; present only if the block is an xref)

DIMSTYLE	
2	Dimension style name

70	Standard flag values
170	DIMALT
171	DIMALTD
143	DIMALTF
274	DIMALTTD
286	DIMALTTZ
273	DIMALTU
285	DIMALTZ
4	DIMAPOST
41	DIMASZ
275	DIMAUNIT
5	DIMBLK
6	DIMBLK1
7	DIMBLK2
141	DIMCEN
176	DIMCLRD
177	DIMCLRE
178	DIMCLRT
271	DIMDEC
46	DIMDLE
43	DIMDLI
44	DIMEXE
42	DIMEXO
287	DIMFIT
147	DIMGAP
280	DIMJUST
144	DIMLFAC
72	DIMLIM
3	DIMPOST
45	DIMRND
173	DIMSAH
40	DIMSCALE

281	DIMSD1
282	DIMSD2
75	DIMSE1
76	DIMSE2
175	DIMSOXD
77	DIMTAD
272	DIMTDEC
146	DIMTFAC
73	DIMTIH
174	DIMTIX
48	DIMTM
172	DIMTOFL
74	DIMTOH
71	DIMTOL
283	DIMTOLJ
47	DIMTP
142	DIMTSZ
145	DIMTVP
340	DIMTXSTY
140	DIMTXT
284	DIMTZIN
270	DIMUNIT
288	DIMUPT
78	DIMZIN

ENDBLK, No groups, end block definition (appears only in BLOCKS table)

LAYER	
2	Layer name
70	Layer bit-flags:
	1 If set, layer is frozen, otherwise layer is thawed
	2 If set, layer is frozen by default in new viewports

	4 If set, layer is locked
62	Color number (if negative, layer is Off)
6	Linetype

LTYPE	
2	Linetype name
70	Standard flag values
3	Descriptive text for linetype
72	Alignment code
73	Number of dash length items
40	Total pattern length
49	Dash length (optional; can be repeated)

STYLE	
2	Style name
70	Standard flag values
40	Fixed text height
41	Width factor
50	Oblique angle
71	Text-generation flags (bit-coded values, may be combined): 2 Text is backward (mirrored in X) 4 Text is upside down (mirrored in Y)
42	Last height used
3	Primary font filename
4	Big font file name (empty string if none)

UCS	
2	UCS name
70	Standard flag values
10	Origin (in WCS)
11	X axis direction (in WCS)
12	Y axis direction (in WCS)

VIEW	
2	View name
70	View flag:1 If set, this view is a paper space view
40	Height
41	Width
10	Center point (a 2D point) (in DCS)
11	View direction from target, in WCS
12	Target point, in WCS
42	Lens length
43	Front clipping plane
44	Back clipping plane
50	Twist angle
71	View mode, same values as the VIEWMODE system variable

VPORT	
2	Vport name (Might not be unique. All vports in the current configuration are named *ACTIVE, and the first *ACTIVE vport in the table is the one currently displayed)
70	Standard flag values
10	Lower-left corner (a 2D point)
11	Upper-right corner (a 2D point)
12	Center (a 2D point)
13	Snap base point (a 2D point)
14	Snap spacing (XandY)
15	Grid spacing (XandY)
16	Direction from target point
17	Target point
40	Height
41	Aspect ratio
42	Lens length
43	Front clipping plane
44	Back clipping plane
50	Snap rotation angle

51	Twist angle
68	Status field
69	ID
71	View mode, same values as the VIEWMODE system variable
72	Circle zoom percent
73	Fast zoom setting
74	UCSICON setting
75	Snap on/off
76	Grid on/off
77	Snap style
78	Snap isopair

Appendix E Error codes

E.1. Introduction

This appendix list error numbers and meanings. For the returns codes of `ads_command()`, some of which report errors, see; Table 4.2 in Chapter 4.

E.2. ADS error codes

See also OL_ERRNO.H and ADS_PERR.C an C-include and a C-source file helpful for error messages. Use the latest versions you can find as they are updated with every release of AutoCAD.

1	Bad symbol table name
2	Bad entity or selection set name
3	Exceeded maximum number of selection sets
4	Bad selection set
5	Incorrect use of block definition
6	Incorrect use of xref
7	Pick failed
8	End of entity file
9	End of block definition file
10	Failed to find last entity
11	Illegal attempt to delete viewport object
12	Operation not allowed during PLINE
13	Bad handle
14	Handles not enabled (before Release 13)
15	Bad arguments in coordinate transform request
16	Bad space in coordinate transform request
17	Bad use of deleted entity
18	Bad table name

19	Bad table function argument
20	Trying to set a read-only variable
21	Zero value not valid here
22	Value exceeds valid range
23	Complicated REGEN in progress
24	Trying to change entity type
25	Invalid layer name, the layer probably does not exist
26	Invalid linetype name, the linetype probably does not exist
27	Invalid color name
28	Invalid text style name, the style probably does not exist
29	Invalid shape name
30	Invalid field for entity type
31	Trying to modify deleted entity
32	Trying to modify seqend subentity
33	Trying to change handle
34	Trying to modify viewport visibility
35	The entity is on a locked layer
36	Invalid entity type
37	Invalid polyline entity
38	Complex entity in block in not complete
39	Bad block name field
40	Duplicate block flag fields
41	Duplicate block name fields
42	Invalid normal vector
43	Block name missing
44	Block flags missing
45	Bad anonymous block
46	Bad block definition
47	A mandatory field is missing
48	Bad extended data (XDATA) type
49	Incorrect nesting of list in XDATA
50	Incorrect location of APPID field
51	Maximum XDATA size exceeded
52	Null response to entity selection
53	Duplicated APPID
54	Trying to make or modify viewport entity
55	Trying to make or modify an xref, xdef, or xdep
56	ssget filter: unexpected end of list
57	ssget filter: missing test operand
58	ssget filter: bad opcode (-4) string
59	ssget filter: incorrect nesting or empty conditional clause
60	ssget filter: mismatched begin and end of conditional clause
61	ssget filter: wrong number of arguments in NOT or XOR clause
62	ssget filter: beyond maximum nesting limit
63	ssget filter: bad group code

64   ssget filter: bad string test
65   ssget filter: bad vector test
66   ssget filter: bad real test
67   ssget filter: bad integer test
68   Digitizer is not a tablet
69   Tablet is not calibrated
70   Bad arguments
71   ADS error: Cannot allocate new result buffer
72   ADS error: Null pointer detected
73   Cannot open program file
74   Application is already loaded
75   Maximum number of applications loaded
76   Cannot execute application
77   Incompatible version number
78   Cannot unload nested application
79   Application rejected unload
80   Application is not currently loaded
81   Not enough RAM to load application
82   ADS error: bad transformation matrix
83   ADS error: bad symbol name
84   ADS error: bad symbol value
85   AutoLISP/ADS operation while a dialog box was displayed not allowed
86-91 Reserved for future use
92   Not allowed when a command is in progress
93   Invalid value type
94   Bad viewport ID
95   Invalid view definition
96   Unexpected group code
97   Duplicate group code specified
98   Invalid ssget mode string
99   Arguments are not in agreement
100   Cannot call setvar recursively

E.3 ARX error codes, differences between ERRNO and ARX error values

The error codes listed in the following table can be returned from an ARX application or function call. The 1000+ error codes are valid values for the ERRNO variable available in Lisp and ADS. 1000+ just marks them as ARX error codes. You need to subtract 1000, then you get the error codes defined in `acdb.h`. ARX always return the codes defined in `acdb.h`. The error status enumerator definition starts as follows:

```
struct Acad {
    enum ErrorStatus { eOk                    =  0,
                       eNotImplementedYet      =  1,
...
```

The ERRNO equivalents are:

1001 eNotImplemented
1002 eNotApplicable
1003 eInvalidInput
1004 eAmbiguousInput
1005 eAmbiguousOutput
1006 eOutOfMemory
1007 eBufferTooSmall
1010 eHandleExists
1011 eNullHandle
1012 eBrokenHandle
1013 eUnknownHandle
1014 eHandleInUse
1015 eNullObjectPointer
1016 eNullObjectId
1017 eNullBlockName
1020 eNullEntityPointer
1021 eIllegalEntityType
1022 eKeyNotFound
1023 eDuplicateKey
1024 eInvalidIndex
1025 eDuplicateIndex
1026 eAlreadyInDb
1027 eOutOfDisk
1028 eDeletedEntry
1029 eNegativeValueNotAllowed
1030 eInvalidExtents
1031 eInvalidAdsName
1032 eInvalidSymbolTableName
1033 eInvalidKey
1024 eWrongObjectType
1035 eWrongDatabase
1036 eObjectToBeDeleted
1037 eInvalidDwgVersion
1038 eAnonymousEntry
1039 eIllegalReplacement
1040 eEndOfObject
1041 eEndOfFile
1042 eIsReading

1043 eIsWriting
1044 eNotOpenForRead
1045 eNotOpenForWrite
1046 eNotThatKindOfClass
1050 eInvalidDxfCode
1051 eInvalidResBuf
1052 eBadDxfSequence
1053 eFilerError
1054 eVertexAfterFace
1055 eInvalidFaceVertexIndex
1056 eInvalidMeshVertexIndex
1057 eOtherObjectsBusy
1058 eMustFirstAddBlockToDb
1059 eCannotNestBlockDefs
1060 eDwgRecoveredOK
1061 eDwgNotRecoverable
1062 eDxfPartiallyRead
1063 eDxfReadAborted
1064 eDxbPartiallyRead
1065 eDwgCRCDoesNotMatch
1066 eDwgSentinelDoesNotMatch
1067 eDwgObjectImproperlyRead
1068 eNoInputFiler
1070 eDxbReadAborted
1071 eFileLockedByACAD
1072 eFileAccessErr
1073 eFileSystemErr
1074 eFileInternalErr
1080 eWasErased
1081 ePermanentlyErased
1082 eWasOpenForRead
1083 eWasOpenForWrite
1084 eWasOpenForUndo
1085 eWasNotifying
1086 eWasOpenForNotify
1087 eOnLockedLayer
1088 eMustOpenThruOwner
1089 eSubentitiesStillOpen
1090 eAtMaxReaders
1091 eIsWriteProtected
1092 eIsXRefObject
1093 eNotAnEntity
1094 eMultipleReaders
1095 eDuplicateRecordName
1096 eXRefDependent

1100 eWasNotOpenForWrite
1101 eCloseWasNotifying
1102 eCloseModifyAborted1102
1103 eClosePartialFailure1103
1104 eCloseFailObjectDamaged1104
1105 eCannotBeErasedByCaller1105
1110 eInsertAfter
1120 eFixedAllErrors
1122 eLeftErrorsUnfixed
1123 eUnrecoverableErrors
1124 eNoDatabase
1125 eXdataSizeExceeded
1126 eRegappIdNotFound
1127 eRepeatEntity
1128 eRecordNotInTable
1129 eIteratorDone
1130 eNullIterator
1131 eNotInBlock
1132 eOwnerNotInDatabase
1133 eOwnerNotOpenForRead
1134 eOwnerNotOpenForWrite
1150 eGeneralModelingFailure
1151 eOutOfRange
1152 eNonCoplanarGeometry
1153 eDegenerateGeometry
1154 eInvalidAxis
1155 ePointNotOnEntity
1156 eSingularPoint
1160 eStringTooLong
1161 eInvalidSymTableFlag
1162 eUndefinedLineType
1163 eInvalidTextStyle
1164 eTooFewLineTypeElements
1165 eTooManyLineTypeElements
1166 eExcessiveItemCount
1167 eIgnoredLinetypeRedef
1168 eBadUCS
1169 eBadPaperspaceView
1170 eSomeInputDataLeftUnread
1171 eNoInternalSpace
1180 eUserBreak

Appendix F Further sources of information

F.1 Introduction

This appendix is about where to find out more information which will be helpful to you when you program AutoCAD in C and C++. The addresses of companies mentioned in the book are also given.

F.2 Books

F.2.1 C programming

The C Programming Language, 2nd Edition, Kerningham and Ritchie, Prentice Hall.

No serious C (or C++ for that matter) programmer should be without this book. It is a good introduction to the language with a (short) reference manual as an appendix. Make sure you get the second edition which covers the ANSI C standard.

F.2.2 C++ programming

The C++ Programming Language, Bjarne Stroustrup.

This is the C++ equivalent of the Kerningham and Ritchie book mentioned above. The size of the book reflects the difference between C and C++, the edition I have (published by Watcom) has 668 pages, nearly 2.5 times as long as the C book! Still, it is a good general introduction to the language. Get the latest edition you can, as the language has not yet stopped evolving.

Learning C++, Neil Graham, McGraw Hill.
This is a decent introductory text to C++ programming.

C++ Pointers and Dynamic Memory Management, Michael Daconta, John Wiley-QED.
   A good explanation of the use of pointers and references in C++ for programmers who understand the basics of C++ programming. Correct usage of pointers and references is an important but not trivial C++ subject.

F.2.3 Graphics progamming

Graphics Gems III, David Kirk, Academic Press.
   The third book of a series that (currently) goes up to Graphics Gems V (which I have not yet seen). The format is a book and a disk full of routines (mostly in C) for graphics programmers. It is really only for experienced programmers who need special routines. A sample of the table of contents will give you an idea of the sort of subjects covered:
- "Compact Isocontours from Sampled Data"
- "Cross Products in Four Dimensions and Beyond"
- "Fast Random Rotation Matrices"

Graphics Gems III contains a disk with all the routines from the first, second and of course the third volume of the series.

Visual Cues, Practical Data Visualization, P Keller and M. Keller, IEEE Computer Scociety Press.
   This book has hundreds of pictorial examples of how to visualise complex data, and gives advice on such things as which colors to use, how to visualise multidimensional data and so on. The applications covered are GIS, medical, volume rendering, physics, weather, engineering and so on. There are no programs or code fragments in this book, its purpose is to advise on the look of your programs output.

F.2.4 AutoCAD

It cannot be taken for granted that an AutoCAD programmer is also an expert in using AutoCAD; there is just too much to know, and while the AutoCAD *user* may spend hours every day in practical use of the program, the programmer is busy creating applications. Still, AutoCAD programmers should be at least *decently* skilled users of the program. For this reason you should get hold of at least one general book covering the AutoCAD version you are using.

Strangely enough books on AutoLISP can help the AutoCAD C/C++ programmer with tips and shortcuts to often required operations in AutoCAD. The AutoLISP book I have often used is:

1000 AutoCAD Tips and Tricks, G.Head and J Head. Ventana Press.

You should get hold of the edition which covers the release of AutoCAD you are using.

F.3 Magazines

AutoCAD magazines tend to carry very detailed and very general information at the same time. For example a general overview of new features in the latest release of AutoCAD and bit-twiddling AutoLISP routines. Both are useful to the AutoCAD programmer.

Cadence
A general AutoCAD magazine published in the USA but available (by post) all over the world. Source code (usually AutoLISP) is available electronically via Internet and CompuServe. Published by Miller Freeman Inc., 600 Harrison St., San Francisco, CA 94107, USA. Fax (303) 661-1994.

AutoCAD Tech Journal
Contains up to date technical information for programmers of AutoCAD. Published by the same company which produces *Cadence*, see above.

CADUser
A UK publication (with "local" versions in Australia and New Zealand, Germany, Norway, Benelux and France). Lighter than Cadence, aimed more at the user than for the programmer. Published by Compudraft Ltd., 24 High St. Beckenham, Kent, BR3 1AY, UK.

CAD++ Newsletter
This is more of a general view of CAD software in general, not specifically for AutoCAD. It sometimes has technical programming articles.
XYZ Publishing,
34486 Donlyn Ave.
Abbotsford, BC
V2S 4W7,
Canada

Many countries have their own AutoCAD magazines, generally "independent" of Autodesk. You should get hold of at least one copy of your local AutoCAD magazine to see if it would help you in your programming work.

F.4. World Wide Web addresses and Internet user groups

Both the World Wide Web and Internet user groups can be used to obtain information about AutoCAD. You should use the Internet user groups to ask other users and programmers about problems, and the World Wide Web pages will give you more general information, and lots of time-consuming pretty pictures. Nuggets can be gleaned from both sources.

`comp.cad.autocad` is an active user group, with both users and Autodesk themselves contributing. Another group is `alt.cad.autocad`. In both of these user groups you will find email and WWW addresses of companies and individuals working with AutoCAD. About 5% of the content is about programming, but if you post a message about a specific AutoCAD programming problem you will probably get at least few replies.

The Autodesk WWW site is `http://www.autodesk.com`.

The Autodesk ftp site is `ftp.autodesk.com`, and is where you will find patches and other files useful for AutoCAD users and developers.

David Whynot's page is a good starting point for searching for data on AutoCAD shareware and other information. The address is:

`http://www.buildingweb.com`

A list of many other popular CAD sites can be found at:

`http://www.cadonline.com/topten.htm`

Information about, and images produced by, the program I wrote for Martini S.p.a. (see Chapter 19) can be found at the web site:

`http://www.pianeta.it/martini/moonlite.htm`.

F.5. Company and society addresses

Autodesk Inc.
111 McInnis Parkway
San Rafael, CA 94903
U.S.A.

Autodesk Development B.V.
Rue du Puits-Godet 6
2005 Neuchatel
Switzerland

AutoCAD Developers Group Europe (ADGE)
Gerbergasse 1, CH-4001, Switzerland
Fax +41 61 601 7241

Martini SpA. (creators of the MOONLITE lighting simulation, Chapter 19)
Via Provinciale, 24, 41033, Concordia, (MO), Italy.
Tel: +39 535 48111 Fax: +39 535 48220

BASIC d.o.o. (creators of LISP2C, see Chapter 19)
61000 Ljubljana, Jesenkova 5, Slovenia,
Tel: +386 61 314 069, Fax: + 386 61 318 211
Compuserv: 70541,1765

BASIS Software Inc. (creators of Vital LISP, see Chapter 19)
770 East Market St. Suite 185, West Chester, PA 19380
Tel: +1 610 429 9294, Fax: +1 610 4299034

Kovac Software (DWG file reader and writer libraries, Chapter 18)
30 St. Marys Road, Little Hayword, Staffordshire, ST18 0NJ, U.K.

Index